2 $\underline{^{00}}$
10/03

D0393965

Close to Home

A DAILY DEVOTIONAL
FOR WOMEN BY WOMEN

ROSE OTIS, EDITOR

REVIEW AND HERALD® PUBLISHING ASSOCIATION
HAGERSTOWN, MD 21740

Copyright © 1996 by
Review and Herald® Publishing Association

The authors assume full responsibility for the accuracy of all facts
and quotations as cited in this book.

Manuscript edited by Jeannette R. Johnson
Designed by Patricia S. Wegh
Cover photos by Phil Banko (roses) and Mel Curtis (garden path)
Typeset: 10.5/11.5 Berkeley Book

PRINTED IN U.S.A.

00 99 98 97 96   5 4 3 2 1

R&H Cataloging Service
Otis, Rose, ed.
    Close to home.

    1. Devotional calendars—SDA.   2. Devotional
calendars—women.   3. Women—religious life.
4. Devotional literature—SDA.   I. Title.

                242.643

ISBN 0-8280-1109-5

Bible texts credited to Amplified are from *The Amplified Bible.* Copyright © 1965 by Zondervan Publishing House. Used by permission.

Scripture quotations credited to CEV are from the Contemporary English Version. Copyright © American Bible Society 1991, 1995. Used by permission.

Texts credited to Clear Word are from *The Clear Word,* copyright © 1994 by Jack J. Blanco.

Scripture quotations credited to EB are from *The Everyday Bible, New Century Version,* copyright © 1987, 1988 by Word Publishing, Dallas, Texas 75039. Used by permission.

Bible texts credited to Jerusalem are from *The Jerusalem Bible,* copyright © 1966 by Darton, Longman & Todd, Ltd., and Doubleday & Company, Inc. Used by permission of the publisher.

Texts credited to Message are from *The Message.* Copyright © 1993. Used by permission of NavPress Publishing Group.

Scripture quotations marked NASB are from the *New American Standard Bible,* © The Lockman Foundation 1960, 1962, 1963, 1968, 1971, 1972, 1973, 1975, 1977.

Texts credited to NEB are from *The New English Bible.* © The Delegates of the Oxford University Press and the Syndics of the Cambridge University Press 1961, 1970. Reprinted by permission.

Texts credited to NIV are from the *Holy Bible, New International Version.* Copyright © 1973, 1978, 1984, International Bible Society. Used by permission of Zondervan Bible Publishers.

Texts credited to NKJV are from The New King James Version. Copyright © 1979, 1980, 1982, Thomas Nelson, Inc., Publishers.

Bible texts credited to NRSV are from the New Revised Standard Version of the Bible, copyright © 1989 by the Division of Christian Education of the National.Council of the Churches of Christ in the U.S.A. Used by permission.

Texts credited by RBV are from the Revised Berkeley Version. Copyright © 1959, Hendrickson Publishers, Inc.

Bible texts credited to RSV are from the Revised Standard Version of the Bible, copyright © 1946, 1952, 1971, by the Division of Christian Education of the National Council of the Churches of Christ in the U.S.A. Used by permission.

Bible texts credited to TEV are from the *Good News Bible*—Old Testament: Copyright © American Bible Society 1976; New Testament: Copyright © American Bible Society 1966, 1971, 1976.

Verses marked TLB are taken from *The Living Bible,* copyright © 1971 by Tyndale House Publishers, Wheaton, Ill. Used by permission.

Biographical Sketches

Betty Adams is a retired schoolteacher and mother of three adult children. She is the communication secretary and coeditor of the newsletter at her church in California. Betty enjoys camping, traveling, reading, sewing, and grandchildren. Her articles have been published in *Guide*. MAR. 12, MAY 10, SEPT. 4, DEC. 7.

Juliana Agboka writes from the Ivory Coast, where she is a homemaker and wife of the Adventist Chaplaincy Ministries director of the Africa-Indian Ocean Division of Seventh-day Adventists. She enjoys reading and writing. MAY 24.

Deborah Aho lives and works with her husband and three children at Riverside Farm Institute in Kafue, Zambia. The institute is a 3,000-acre agricultural training program that selects spiritually minded students and apprentices them as lay workers for Christ. She manages the business office there and is actively involved in administration, the Volunteer Missionary program, and as editor of the institute's newsletter. JUNE 15, OCT. 1.

Larita J. Alford, a native of Bermuda, moved to the United States to complete her college studies, which have taken her to several countries in South America and Mexico. Currently she is the dean of arts and sciences at a community college in Tennessee, where she lives with her husband, George, a dentist. Her hobbies include singing, studying foreign languages, reading, traveling, and stamp collecting. She has visited South Korea and several countries in Europe. SEPT. 25.

Maxine Williams Allen is a computer systems analyst living in West Virginia. She is a "hobbyist" writer and seminar presenter, currently developing the Follow the Leader seminar series. Maxine is active in her local church in the areas of family life, women's ministry, and ministering to missing members. She enjoys reading, writing, traveling, computer technology, and meeting people. She and her husband are the happy parents of a new son. JULY 4, AUG. 9, NOV. 11, DEC. 31.

Zeola Germany Allston recently retired from teaching after 40 years in education. She coedited *A Star Gives Light,* an Adventist Black history resource guide. She enjoys public speaking, writing and performing dramatics, calligraphy, knitting, crocheting, sewing, and traveling. She and her husband, Thomas, have four adult children and four grandchildren. AUG. 11.

Marlene Anderson has written for several women's devotional projects. She sent this year's entry while living in Mississippi. She fell asleep in the Lord in the autumn of 1995. MAY 25.

Thelma Lewis Anderson, an instructor for a federal government agency, resides in Laurel, Maryland. She has been active in the personal ministries department of her church for many years. Her greatest joy is introducing others to God through Bible studies. OCT. 27.

Caroline Andrew, a mother of two, lives in Australia. She has worked for an independent publishing ministry and has had articles and some of her artwork published. She enjoys graphic arts and uses this whenever possible for her church. Caroline also enjoys helping people, cooking, and sharing her experience and recipes with those unfamiliar with vegetarian food. APR. 30, OCT. 14.

Nell Rice Anthony is a retired educational administrator, consultant, professor of education, and classroom teacher from Huntsville, Alabama. She holds a doctorate in education from Teachers College, Columbia University, and has taught on all levels. Nell has done consulting work at several colleges and universities around the country, including Alabama State University, Alabama Agricultural and Mechanical University, and Oakwood College. She and her husband have one son, Harold, Jr. AUG. 16.

Indrani J. Ariyaratnam taught school before marrying her minister husband. Being a pastor's wife has been the joy of her life, for it has led to meeting many interesting people and experiencing exciting adventures. Originally from Sri Lanka, then from India, Indrani is now the women's ministries director of the Pakistan Union of Seventh-day Adventists, where the Ariyaratnams have lived for the past 10 years. AUG. 17.

Alma Atcheson lives in Coff's Harbour, New South Wales, Australia, where she is a housewife, communication secretary, and assistant welfare leader. She has three grown children and enjoys gardening, writing, and volunteer visiting at convalescent homes. AUG. 21, SEPT. 30.

Rosemary Baker, a freelance writer living in Iowa, is the author of the children's book *What Am I?* She enjoys working with children, and her ideas have appeared in *Shining Star* and *Kids' Stuff* magazines.

She is a member of the Iowa Poetry Association and is active in church and volunteer work. Her hobbies are arts, crafts, music, poetry, and painting. **MAR. 6.**

Audrey Balderstone is the mother of two sons, and she and her husband operate a garden landscaping company in England. A recent graduate of an honors degree program at the University of London, she conducts a bimonthly home fellowship group meeting while maintaining her interest in community activities and flower arranging. **FEB. 8, DEC. 27.**

Marie Balla is a widow and an L.P.N. currently working at the Florida Hospital in Orlando. She is the secretary for the board of directors and the librarian at her church. **FEB. 24.**

Rosa Taylor Banks is the associate secretary and director of the Office of Human Relations in the North American Division of the General Conference of Seventh-day Adventists in Silver Spring, Maryland. **MAY 11.**

Mary Barrett is a pastor's wife, mother of two young daughters, and a homemaker living in England. When possible, she preaches, gives Bible studies, and works on various church programs with her husband. Her hobbies include being with friends, reading, walking, and craft work. Mary also writes for Christian magazines. **JAN. 17, FEB. 18, JULY 7, AUG. 13, AUG. 18.**

Moira Barthle is a wife and mother/home school teacher of two active boys. She likes walking, reading, studying, and entertaining and has served as the women's ministries coordinator and on the executive planning committee of her church for two years. **DEC. 24.**

Pam Baumgartner, a missionary wife and mother of four children, is national coordinator for child evangelism in the Nicaragua Mission of Seventh-day Adventists. She enjoys writing and counseling troubled young people. **JAN. 10.**

Dawna Beausoleil, a former teacher, lives in Thunder Bay, Ontario, where her husband pastors a very large geographic district. She is a published writer, an amateur oil painter, and loves camping, crafts, and jigsaw puzzles. **JAN. 1.**

Judi Wild-Becker lives in the Napa Valley in California. Her interests include performing in local churches as a vocalist with the Lorna Lawrence Women's Ensemble, varied literary pursuits, and extensive travel. **SEPT. 6.**

Annie B. Best writes from Washington, D.C., where she is a retired public school teacher with two grown children. She enjoys reading, listening to music, and shopping for her two grandchildren. Annie has worked in the cradle roll and kindergarten departments of her church. **OCT. 17.**

Karen Birkett is originally from Barbados, but has lived most of her life in Toronto, Ontario. She has been involved in the children's and youth departments of her church. Her hobbies include reading, knitting, embroidery, writing, and camping. **JUNE 4.**

Ann Blandford works as an assistant to her pastor husband. She is a freelance writer whose interests range from music to gems and minerals, bird watching, and cooking. She spent six years in mission service, establishing the first women's ministries department in Hong Kong and Taiwan. **MAY 6.**

Marieda Blehm is a retired church school teacher who worked for four years in eastern Asia. Her various church offices include women's ministries coordinator and Vacation Bible School teacher. Her hobbies include baby-sitting her little great-nieces and travel. She has been in all 50 states. **SEPT. 24.**

Rhonda Huffaker Bolton is a homemaker and mother of one young adult daughter and a teenage son. She and her husband, Bob, who live in Washington State, recently celebrated their twenty-fifth wedding anniversary. She loves to read. **OCT. 10.**

Joan Bova is a public speaker, head elder, and women's ministries coordinator in her local church. She is involved in disability ministries and is the assistant director of an independent living center. She and her husband live in Florida and are foster parents, caring for abused children. **MAY 27, SEPT. 7.**

Carol Brackett, a nurse and mother of two grown sons, made a midlife career change, graduating in December 1995 with a bachelor's degree in nursing. She is now pursuing a master's in nursing, with an emphasis on family practice. She enjoys reading, scuba diving, traveling, shopping, meeting new people, and learning. **JAN. 18, JUNE 29.**

Jeanette Bryson teaches high school English in Massachusetts and, using E-mail, is working on her doctorate at Andrews University in Michigan. She is the mother of three, grandmother of three, and a published author of one book and several articles and mission stories. A native Californian, Jeanette is attempting to make the cold New England winter her friend by learning cross-country skiing. **JAN. 22.**

Betty R. Burnett, from "Charlevoix the Beautiful," Michigan, works for the Department of Agriculture. Married for 38 years, she is the mother of five and the grandmother of nine. She assists her church family as an elder, adult Bible class teacher, and friend. Her favorite pastimes are reading, music, and walking in the fields and woods with her special "little people." JULY 28.

Andrea A. Bussue was born on the island of Nevis. She holds a master's degree in education and works at a special education facility in Washington, D.C., with children who are developmentally delayed. She has been a superintendent at her local church in Maryland, and loves children, reading, traveling, sewing, cooking, and meeting people. APR. 1, AUG. 20, OCT. 15, OCT. 29, NOV. 26.

Maria A. Butler is a proofreader and Bible school instructor at Christian Record Services. Her articles and poems have been published in a number of magazines and in three poetry anthologies. She lives in Lincoln, Nebraska, with one cat. SEPT. 15.

Luan Cadogan, a secretary, wife, and mother of two children, writes from Toronto, Ontario. As the children's program coordinator for her church, she enjoys planning creative programs for them. Other hobbies are gardening, writing, reading, and music. OCT. 18.

Sheryl Calhoun writes from Maryland, where she is a homemaker, wife, and mother of three. She is also a registered nurse who works occasional shifts in the emergency room. Her interests include cooking, sewing, and music. SEPT. 21.

Margaret Campbell has worked as an accountant, teacher, and registrar. She and her retired minister husband have two daughters and two granddaughters. Her hobbies are gathering poems and other material for scrapbooks and keeping in touch with her granddaughters. MAR. 19.

LaKetia W. Carrell has received her master's degree in counseling and is working as a counselor-in-training in the field of general counseling. She and her husband, Lee, co-lead family life ministries at their church. They have a 7-year-old daughter named Holly. OCT. 9.

Emilie K. Winston Cartwright is a graduate of Andrews University currently working as a freelance writer and homemaker. She lives in Chicago with her husband, George, and their daughter, Zoe. JUNE 16.

Janice M. Carver is a final inspector for SCI Systems in Colorado Springs, where she has lived almost 30 years. She also works as a substitute teacher for the Candyland Daycare Center. Janice has had several poems published and in her spare time enjoys writing, sewing, quilting, and crafts. APR. 19, SEPT. 12.

Virginia Cason and her doctor husband, who live in California, have reared four children. Virginia is a homemaker, public speaker, and writer of children's Bible lessons and a songbook. She teaches voice and is a radio DJ, a ham radio operator, and a private pilot. She is the daughter of H.M.S. Richards, Sr. MAY 26.

Ann Castellino is a elementary school teacher and mother of two teenage children. She is actively involved in her church and enjoys music, country walks, nature, travel, and young children. SEPT. 11.

Donna Yeoman Cathell has a B.A. degree from Loma Linda University and is working on her M.A. in rehabilitation counseling at California State University. She is also caring for her mother in Loma Linda and enjoying a fulfilling church life. Donna has two special redheads for daughters. APR. 18.

Joy Norman Cavins works as a librarian at Oakwood Academy in Alabama. She enjoys reading, sewing, crafts, and collecting quotations. She has taught for many years in the children's departments at church. She and her husband have three teenagers. SEPT. 1.

Fonda Cordis Chaffee, a certified home economist and registered dietitian, writes from the University of Eastern Africa in Kenya, where she has worked for the past six years. She is a widow, mother of two children, and a grandmother. When she is not traveling around the world, she enjoys gardening and crocheting. DEC. 1.

Birol C. Christo lives with her husband in India. She is a retired teacher, the mother of five grown children, and the Shepherdess International coordinator for the Southern Asia Division of Seventh-day Adventists. Birol spends all her spare time sewing and making craft items to sell as fund-raisers to help orphans. FEB. 19.

Ginger Mostert Church, the mother of two grown sons, is a marketing representative for the Review and Herald® Publishing Association. She teaches seminars on outreach, and she has had articles published in several magazines and local newspapers. She and her husband, Dennis, live in Maryland. She enjoys cross-stitching, reading, writing, sharing ideas in seminars, and flowers of all kinds. FEB. 1.

Alberta Bennett Ciccarelli writes from Glendora, California. MAR. 30.

Doreen Kitto Clark worked for 40 years as a business and English teacher and as an executive secretary. Her last teaching position was at Maui Community College on Molokai Island. She enjoys traveling, writing, and caring for her small great-grandson. She and her husband publish the church's monthly newsletter. SEPT. 16.

Susan Clark lives in California with her husband and two active college students. She is a member of the local women's ministries council and enjoys leading a weekly women's Bible study. Other interests include quilting, gardening, and supporting the activities of her family. SEPT. 17.

Carel Clay lives in Napa, California, with her husband and daughter. She has two grown stepchildren. She teaches nursing at Napa Valley College and is currently completing her master's degree in nursing. She has taught cradle roll, youth, and adult Bible classes. Carel enjoys quilting, sewing, writing, public speaking, cats, and being a mom. APR. 8.

Dolores Clegg writes from Parkersburg, West Virginia, where she is a mother of four and grandmother of five. She likes sewing, gardening, and growing flowers to share. DEC. 22.

Celia Cleveland, who lives in Huntsville, Alabama, is a retired Bible instructor, responsible for bringing more than 3,000 souls to the Lord. She enjoys Bible reading, music, spending time with her grandsons, and traveling with her husband. SEPT. 3.

Joy Colburn is a pseudonym for a mother who is learning much from God and her children about patience, acceptance, and intercessory prayer. She continues to pray for her children and many others who need to understand how much God loves them. NOV. 2.

Clareen Colclesser is a retired nurse and recent widow. She is blessed with two grown children, six grandchildren, and two great-grandchildren. She enjoys staying active in her church, poring through her stacks of interior decorating books, and writing letters and short stories. MAY 30.

Arlene E. Compton is a retired teacher and nursing administrator. Remarried eight years ago, she is the mother of one daughter, a stepson, and a stepdaughter, and the grandmother of four grandsons. Her writings have appeared in *Outlook* and *Forum*. JAN 16, JULY 26.

Daphnie M. Corrodus hosts a weekly religious television program in Jamaica. A mother of three grown children, she also enjoys gardening, dressmaking, writing, and architecture. She is involved in family life ministries in her church. JAN. 28.

Eva Alice Covey, mother of six and grandmother of 15, was a schoolteacher before her marriage and is now a widow living in Canada. She enjoys sewing, crocheting, playing the piano, raising flowers, and writing. She has had one book and several magazine stories published and is currently working on another children's book. MAY 7.

Lena Cressotti has retired but still keeps very active in her church in Connecticut. She and her husband of nearly 40 years spend six months in Connecticut and six months in Florida. They have five grown children and five grandchildren, ranging in age from 3 to 16. Lena has started writing her life story. Her other interests include swimming, reading, playing the organ, doing crafts, and oil painting. AUG. 14.

Celia Mejia Cruz is the administrative secretary in the Department of Women's Ministries at the General Conference of Seventh-day Adventists. A pastor's wife, local church elder, and mother of four adult children and one teenager, she enjoys people, her family, teaching the preteen Bible class at her church, presenting seminars, and preaching. Some of her interests are needlework, reading, writing, dogs, and ceramics. MAR. 8, JULY 17, AUG. 1, DEC. 12.

Christina Curtis is a reading specialist with a master's degree in education who, at one time, also studied to become a Benedictine nun. When she has the time, she enjoys writing, organic gardening, and camping all over the United States. SEPT. 13.

Sherolin Daley is a registered nurse and nursing supervisor living in New York with her pastor husband. She is the president of the Northeastern Conference Shepherdess Association. OCT. 11.

Laura Pascual Dancek lives in Port Charlotte, Florida, with her husband, Ed. She is a speech/language pathologist. JUNE 1, JULY 12, OCT. 23.

Jayne Doswell Darby, retired after 37 years of teaching and secretarial work, has returned to work as an administrative secretary at an academy in Pennsylvania. A local church elder, she enjoys reading, crocheting, knitting, and playing the piano. Her articles have appeared in the *Adventist Review, Guide,* and *Message,* as well her local newspaper. JUNE 28.

Joella Brown Davis and her husband, Bob, have three children, ages 12 to 18. She is busy home-schooling the youngest two and looks forward to attending college herself when they go to traditional school. She enjoys reading, writing, boating, and her all-too-infrequent horseback rides. JULY 1.

Lynn Marie Davis is a sign language interpreter in the Georgia school system and coordinates interpreting services at her church as well. She has lived in Asia and Europe, and she has traveled across America as a singer with Heritage and Harvest Celebration singers. Lynn's favorite pastime is facilitating and participating in personal growth workshops. A good brisk walk is her sport of choice. MAY 29.

Ruth F. Davis lives in Huntsville, Alabama, with her husband. She is the mother of three graduates of Oakwood College. She chairs the family and consumer sciences department at Oakwood College and is an ordained elder of the college church. Ruth is active in other church and civic activities. SEPT. 22.

Dinalva Pessoa de Carvalho lives in Niteroi, Argentina, with her pastor husband. They have two daughters and a son, who is also a pastor. Her favorite activities are missionary work, reading, and walking. NOV. 30.

Nelma Drake and her husband, Harold, own and manage retirement centers in Idaho. Her present interest and emphasis is family life, but she also enjoys reading, painting, knitting, and needlepoint. She has been blessed with one son, one daughter, and five grandchildren. MAR. 2.

April Dunnett is working for the National Trust's property, Mottisfont Abbey, in England as an assistant gardener, mainly with the Old and Ancestral Rose Collection. She has taught literature, fine arts, and communications in Nigeria and Kenya. Her interests range from arts and crafts to folk guitar and her own handbell choir, Forest Bells. NOV. 19.

Sylvia Ellis is a teacher and minister's wife who, along with her husband, has worked in the United States, as well as at Pakistan Adventist Seminary, teaching English. For the past 12 years she has taught in one-room church schools. She is the mother of four sons and enjoys writing and gardening. SEPT. 18.

Christina Ennis is a medical technologist at Denver Veterans Affairs Medical Center in Colorado. She teaches in the junior and earliteen division of her church, and her favorite pastime is devouring a good book. JUNE 10.

Sally Ettari writes from New York, where she is a wife and mother of three. Sally is a composer with a master's degree in music. SEPT. 28.

Jocelyn Fay writes from Hagerstown, Maryland, where she is copy editor at the Review and Herald® Publishing Association. She collects Cat's Meow Village pieces and antique blue-and-white china, and is researching her New York and New England family history. MAR. 17.

Nadia Farah, a Jordanian, is secretary to the director of Adventist Development and Relief Agency in Jordan. She is active in her local church in Amman, particularly in the children's Sabbath school department. Her hobbies include cooking, walking, and listening to music. MAR. 1.

Mercy M. Ferrer works with her husband in the Middle East Union of Seventh-day Adventists in Cyprus. They have two teenage children. She is a registered nurse and assists her local church in its health outreach programs. Mercy enjoys nature, working with young people, reading, cooking, and word games. NOV. 24.

Karen Flowers and her husband, Ron, are codirectors of family ministries at the General Conference of Seventh-day Adventists. They live in Maryland and have two adult sons. Karen reads, knits, and practices her long-neglected flute for fun. Her treasures are counted in friends and family. JAN. 20, FEB. 14.

Heide Ford is the assistant editor of *Women of Spirit*, the Adventist women's magazine. She is a registered nurse and holds a master's degree in counseling. Her interests include reading, writing, studying different cultures, and motorcycling. MAR. 13, JUNE 20.

Edna Maye Gallington lives in Riverside, California, and works in communications. She is a graduate of La Sierra University and has taken public relations studies at the University of California at Riverside. She enjoys playing the piano, creative writing, hiking, and working in her church. JULY 16, DEC. 23.

Eve Gilkeson is a teacher who lives in California with her husband and two daughters. She is working on a master's degree. JULY 30.

Carol Gillham is a pastor's wife, homemaker, and mother of four. She likes to write, sew, work on her computer, and train horses. Carol's church involvement includes being communication secretary, newsletter editor, and team worker with her husband. She is also the editor of *Rocky Mountain Shepherdess*, a newsletter for pastors' wives. JUNE 22.

Evelyn Glass is a wife, mother, grandmother, and farmer. She heads the Women's Ministries Department for the Mid-American Union Conference of Seventh-day Adventists and serves as an elder and clerk at her church. Her interests include folk painting, refinishing furniture, public speaking, and writing for local and state newspapers and Christian publications. MAR. 31, APR. 21.

Hazel Marie Gordon is the women's ministries adviser for the Southern Union Conference of Seventh-day Adventists, where her husband serves as president. Hazel is known for her musical abilities in both voice and piano, and in public speaking. She has two grown daughters, three grandchildren, and many friends. JAN. 7, MAR. 16, DEC. 10.

Kathryn Gordon is a social worker who served as a student missionary to Japan and Korea during college. She enjoys racquetball and windsurfing, and once had a close encounter with a moose while canoeing in Canada. OCT. 12.

Carrol Grady lives with her minister husband in the beautiful Northwest, where she has started an AIDS ministry. She is a secretary, editor of several newsletters, and a church elder. The love of her life is Jesus, and the loves of her life are her husband, children, and grandchildren, quilting, writing, and playing the piano. SEPT. 26.

Ellie Green is the president of Frederick Nursing Consultants in Frederick, Maryland. She's a prolific writer and full-time lecturer who enjoys speaking at Christian women's retreats. Her hobbies are oil and watercolor painting, chalk painting, crocheting, and knitting. She has a son who is an attorney, a daughter who is a nurse, and a husband who is a rocket scientist for NASA. MAY 3.

Glenda-mae Greene is the assistant vice president for student services at Andrews University, Berrien Springs, Michigan. This third-generation educator has taught at all levels, from kindergarten to college, and has spoken to various church groups on women's and singles' issues. Glenda-mae loves photography, tapestry-making, and long walks along shorelines. A devoted Scrabble player, she enjoys words, but most important, the Word. FEB. 26, JUNE 18, DEC. 13.

Meibel Mello Guedes writes from Brazil, where she is the director of women's ministries for the Central Brazil Union Conference of Seventh-day Adventists. She has two children, Simei and Rosa; her husband, Arlindo, is a pastor-evangelist. AUG. 7.

Donna J. Habenicht teaches child psychology at Andrews University, Berrien Springs, Michigan. She coordinates the younger Bible school divisions for the campus church and frequently conducts workshops and seminars for parents and teachers. She loves to read, play the piano and organ, travel, and play with her grandchildren. A writer for religious magazines, Donna is also the author of *How to Help Your Child Really Love Jesus*. FEB. 7, APR. 13.

Alberta Hack is a wife, mother, piano teacher, music committee member, church pianist, school board member, and editor of her church's publication for women. Her interests are flowers, music, and home decorating. She worked in the primary Sabbath school division for 21 years. APR. 14, JUNE 6.

Barbara Hales is a wife, mother, and family life educator living in Indiana. She enjoys putting Scripture to music, singing, and writing. Barbara is a presenter at Family Life International and teaches at Ivy Tech State College. FEB. 6, OCT. 7.

Dessa Weisz Hardin is a wife and mother of three adult children. She enjoys traveling as a historian and visiting her two daughters in Europe. She spends time volunteering with schoolchildren. OCT. 8.

Lea Hardy, a former English and religion teacher, now finds her greatest satisfaction serving as a local church elder, speaking, and conducting spiritual gifts seminars. She is a published author who enjoys reading and spending time with her family. MAR. 15, DEC. 11.

Beatrice Harris is a retired Bible instructor and church school teacher. She is a local church elder, associate personal ministries leader, and published author of religious articles. She has two grown children. MAR. 4.

Peggy Harris is a church elder, musician, writer, Kiwanis Club member, and WASH (Women and Men Against Sexual Harassment and Other Abuses) board chair. She has her own insurance business and presents biblical hospitality seminars. SEPT. 8.

Susan Harvey lives in Hagerstown, Maryland, with her husband, Rhea. She is the director of promotion and women's resources at the Review and Herald® Publishing Association. She previously worked as a professional interior designer and design teacher. She has two grown sons and enjoys reading, walking, and traveling. SEPT. 29.

Suzanne Hayford, of Syracuse, New York, is a teacher and volunteer tutor of English as a second language. She enjoys reading, writing, gardening, and amateur radio. She is communication secretary and is active in children's ministries at her church. **Aug. 27.**

Heartsong is a pseudonym. **Apr. 17, Dec. 17.**

Alice Heath is a clinical nurse specialist in obstetrics living in northern California with her husband and three children. She is working toward a postgraduate degree in ethics/theology. She considers having ten minutes all to herself a great gift. **Mar. 24.**

Ursula M. Hedges is a secondary school teacher/administrator. Born of missionary parents in India, she and her Australian principal husband have given 10 years in mission service in the Pacific, as well as many more in Australia and New Zealand. Ursula has published books, stories, and articles. Other hobbies include interior design, producing dramas, and cooking. Her family brings her great pleasure. **Aug. 15, Sept. 14., Sept. 20.**

Edna Ferris-Heise was born of missionary parents on Lord Howe Island in the Tasman Sea. She writes for religious journals and the local city newspaper. She was also the ghost writer for *In Letters of Gold*. Edna has been the guest speaker for Christian seminars and a presenter for family life workshops. Other hobbies include knitting rugs for refugees, reading, and gardening. She and her husband have three grown children. **Feb. 20, Nov. 8.**

Lorabel Hersch is on the pastoral staff of the Southern College church in Tennessee. A former librarian and English teacher, she writes for religious magazines and has authored a number of Bible lesson quarterlies for youth. She and her husband have six children and seven grandchildren, and they both enjoy foreign and domestic travel. Lorabel treasures friends of all ages and backgrounds. **Oct. 24.**

Charlotte Fermum Hessa is the wife of the editor-in-chief of the Brazil Publishing House in São Paulo. She has translated some articles for the *Adventist Review* and has written the 1995 junior devotional, *Queremos Ver Jesus (We Wish to See Jesus).* **June 23.**

Eleanor Hewes and her husband spent 15 years as missionaries in Zimbabwe and Kenya. She is a retired church school teacher with two married daughters. Her hobbies are soul winning, entertaining, spending time with her grandchildren, and teaching the children in her home church. **Dec. 15.**

Karen Holford writes from England, where she is a pastor's wife and mother of three young children. She works part-time as an occupational therapist in a head injury rehabilitation clinic. Karen is the author of *The Loneliest Grief* and *Danger at Deerwood Grove.* **May 18, May 23, Nov. 5, Dec. 4.**

Tami Horst is the women's ministries director for the Pennsylvania Conference of Seventh-day Adventists. She also serves in her local church as head deaconess and women's ministries leader. She enjoys speaking, writing, bicycling, walking, and spending time with her friends and family. She and her husband have two sons. **Apr. 27, June 12, July 13.**

Lorraine Hudgins is retired with her minister husband, Franklin, in Glendora, California. Her poems, articles, and plays have appeared in various religious publications. She has written two books of poems: *Almost Home* and *Going Home Together.* **Feb. 9, Apr. 4, Apr. 9, Apr. 20, May 12, Dec. 25.**

Barbara Huff writes from Mound, Minnesota. She is the wife of a church administrator, mother of two adult children, and a grandmother. She is a freelance writer, as well as the communication and women's ministries director for the Minnesota Conference of Seventh-day Adventists. **Apr. 28, Aug. 28.**

Charlotte Ishkanian is the editor of a denominational magazine and lives in the Washington, D.C., metropolitan area. She is mother of three young adult girls and is involved in children's ministries at her home church. **Aug. 22.**

Anita Wakem Jacobs is the editorial assistant for *Listen,* a positive lifestyle magazine for teens. She has taught Bible classes for all ages and is currently working with juniors. A few years ago she won a ribbon at the Pennsylvania State Fair for one of her cross-stitch pictures. She enjoys quilts, dolls, playing in the bell choir, and singing in the church choir with her husband. They have three grown children and two grandchildren. **Sept. 9.**

Anna Johansen fortunately likes to travel and meet people, for the Lord's work has taken her and her husband from Iceland to West Africa, from Scandinavia to the Middle East. Other interests include music, crossword puzzles, and cross-stitch. Her three grown children live in Denmark. She writes from Cyprus. **Mar. 27, July 19.**

Madeline S. Johnston, writing from Berrien Springs, Michigan, where she and her husband live, is a freelance writer and mother of four grown children. A former missionary, she has written several books and numerous articles. Knitting, genealogy, Scrabble, photography, traveling, and bird-watching are among her special interests. SEPT. 27.

Edna Lee Jones is a mother of three and grandmother of seven. Her most enjoyable hobby is her grandchildren, but she also likes painting in oils, doing all types of crafts, and gardening. She works part-time and stays active in her church. AUG. 6.

Sophie Kaiser is currently the Sabbath school general superintendent at her church in California. Her hobbies include gardening, cooking, baking, traveling, and crafts. AUG. 2.

Beate Karbstein is a secretary, women's ministry coordinator, and professional masseuse who lives in Australia. She is active in her church as a deaconess and junior-earliteen teacher. Her achievements include being a mother for 12 years and developing a love for Jesus in her son, writing an article about grief, writing several skits that have been performed, and selling some of her paintings. FEB. 3, APR. 15.

Marilyn King is a retired registered nurse. She and her husband live in Oregon, where she is active in the church, school, and community. Marilyn enjoys family, nature, teaching Bible classes, and health evangelism. MAY 28.

Ruth Kloosterhuis, living in Burtonsville, Maryland, is a minister's wife, homemaker, mother of two sons, and grandmother of five. She and her husband have spent 19 years in mission service in the Caribbean and Africa. Ruth is involved in local church activities and enjoys entertaining, decorating, walking, playing the piano and organ, and baby-sitting her grandchildren. APR. 16.

Hepzibah G. Kore is a minister's wife in Bangalore, India. She is the coordinator of women's ministries and Shepherdess International, as well as the director of the children's ministries and family life departments of the South India Union of Seventh-day Adventists. She has one son and a daughter. Hepzibah enjoys reading and working with women. JULY 20.

RosaLynda "Gini" Kosini lives in San Antonio, near Texas hill country. She has served her church as communication secretary. Gini is a business correspondence specialist and a novice lyricist. JAN. 25, JULY 5.

Betty Kossick and her husband live in Cadillac, Michigan. As a newspaper journalist she enjoys the popular column, Faces in the Crowd. Betty cofounded the Dayton, Ohio, Christian Scribes in 1979, served as the group's first president, and continues to be a long-distance member. She is active in her church and in Toastmasters International. MAR. 21, DEC. 28.

Andrea Kristensen, a single parent of a teenage son, is the editor of junior and earliteen Bible lesson quarterlies and *Junior/Earliteen Program Helps*. She lives in Maryland and enjoys biking, rafting, reading, writing, cooking, and attending concerts and living-history events. APR. 3.

Lorna Langley lives in Canada with her husband and home-schools their two children. She is involved in the children's department at her church and enjoys writing, sewing, reading, and knitting. APR. 6, JULY 29.

Eileen E. Lantry is from northern Idaho. She is a librarian, teacher, homemaker, minister's wife, and Bible instructor. She spent 14 years as a missionary in eastern Asia and has authored 13 books. Eileen loves nature, gardening, hiking, and cross-country skiing. JUNE 30.

Lorna Lawrence holds a doctorate in clinical pastoral counseling. She is presently enrolled in a chaplaincy program in California. In her spare time she continues to conduct the Lorna Lawrence Women's Ensemble and is the program therapist for Brainworks Unlimited at a hospital health center. She coauthored her first book, *Thresholds to Thriving,* with Arlene Taylor. JAN. 27, JULY 18, NOV. 12, DEC. 5.

Gina Lee is a freelance writer who teaches a writing class for the city of Burbank, California. She shares her home with four cats. APR. 11.

Irma Lee is a freelance writer living in Washington, D.C. The mother of one grown son, she enjoys photography, poetry, violin music, and listening to the sea. JULY 31.

Hilda Limongan, originally from Indonesia, has lived in California for the past 13 years. A clinical nurse educator at Riverside Community Hospital, she has worked as a registered nurse in hospitals, home care, and high schools. Hilda loves reading, listening to music, crafts, and step aerobics. SEPT. 5.

Karen Lindensmith is a pastor's wife and a mother of two young children, John and Emily, both "made in Japan." She and her husband worked in that country for six years, teaching in language schools before pastoring Japanese churches. The family lives in North Dakota. JAN. 24, FEB. 15, JUNE 27.

Merri Long has done a lot of the preliminary work for this devotional. She is a pastor's wife and stay-at-home mother of preschool-age girls. She loves to collect recipes, make scrapbooks, play her digital piano, and study sign language. She dreams of the day when she can spend an uninterrupted afternoon curled up on the sofa with a book other than *The Poky Little Puppy*. JAN. 2, JULY 15, OCT. 13, DEC. 19.

June Loor, a retired nurse, has been blessed with 40 years of serving by the side of her minister husband. They have two children and five grandchildren and live in the woods on a mountain ridge in North Carolina. June's favorite things are grandchildren, mountains, the ocean, traveling, and remodeling/building houses. FEB. 11, SEPT. 23.

Betty-Anne Lowe, from Bermuda, is the mother/stepmother of three grown children and one teenager. She works as an administrative assistant. Betty-Anne's hobbies include walking, swimming, and reading. She is active in her church as a primary teacher, deaconess, and communication worker. FEB. 10.

Evangeline Lundstrom is an elder and secretary at her church in Ohio. She enjoys traveling, canoeing, bird-watching, and music. Her twin sons, first-year college students, have left an empty nest, felt also by her husband, a doctor of internal medicine. MAY 20, AUG. 23.

Julie M. Lyles is a homemaker and mother of three children, ages 11, 8, and 3, two of whom she home-schools. She also leads out in the cradle roll division and sings in the choir of her church. She writes from her home in Hedgesville, West Virginia. OCT. 6.

Pat Madsen does extensive traveling, but calls California her home. She is the Bible school superintendent at her church and is involved in a Bible study group. A former editor-in-chief of her high school paper, Pat is a published writer of poems, stories, and songs. APR. 10, APR. 24, DEC. 8.

Sherry Manison taught school for seven years in Ohio and West Virginia before returning to college to receive her degree in personal ministries. She was a Bible instructor in New Orleans for three years and is now taking classes toward an M.A. degree in pastoral ministry. APR. 26.

Philippa Marshall writes from England, where she is trained in general nursing, relaxation, and massage therapy. Other interests include art and writing. The three greatest blessings of her life are being the mother of three, the grandmother of six, and a church member for more than 35 years. MAR. 18, APR. 23, JULY 11.

Peggy Mason, living in Wales with her husband and one of her two adult sons, is an English teacher and writer. Her hobbies include dried flower growing and arranging, cooking, sewing, and gardening. She is a pianist/composer and enjoys working for her church and community. MAR. 20, MAR. 23, JUNE 19, NOV. 20, DEC. 29.

Ellen Mayr is the women's and children's ministries director in the Sahel Union of Seventh-day Adventists. She and her pastor husband have been missionaries in Africa for 10 years and are the parents of two grown boys. Pastimes include reading, playing the piano, and writing. Ellen has prepared six series of sermons for children's evangelistic campaigns. MAY 21.

Linda McCabe is a pastor's wife and mother of two boys. She leads out in two women's fellowship and study groups, edits a newsletter for abuse victims, and speaks at retreats. She also writes, arranges, and produces music in her home studio for Thy Word Creations, a company that publishes children's scripture music materials. She and her husband are working on their second tape. FEB. 23, OCT. 25, NOV. 4.

Wilma McClarty is an English and speech professor at Southern College of Seventh-day Adventists, a wife, and the mother of two. She is a public speaker and writer who has received many honors and awards, one of the most recent being the Sears, Roebuck Teaching Excellence and Campus Leadership Award for 1991. JAN. 19. FEB. 22, MAY 15, JUNE 8, OCT. 5.

Maria G. McClean, originally from Barbados, lives in Canada with her husband, Wayne, and daughter, Kamila. She is a registered nurse and an ordained elder who is very active in her church. She enjoys singing, playing the guitar, working with youth, exercising, lecturing, and spending time with her family. OCT. 20, NOV. 3.

Idamae Melendy was an editorial secretary at the Review and Herald Publishing Association before retiring about 20 years ago. Many of her poems and articles have appeared in devotional magazines, as well as in *Ideals, Grit,* and others. Her hobbies are memorizing scripture, reading devotional literature, and conducting Bible classes. MAR. 28.

Retta Michaelis is a medical technologist working part-time at the Loma Linda University Medical Center Blood Bank. She is active with the women's ministries and the children at her church. Other interests include reading, writing, Bible study, and her family. She and her health-educator husband have two daughters, ages 10 and 12. **Jan. 15, Mar. 11, Apr. 5, Aug. 5, Aug. 19, Nov. 22.**

Regina Selma Marinho Miranda writes from Mantena, Minas Gerais, Brazil, where she is a clinical biologist and the wife of a minister. Her favorite activities are reading, research, and writing. Regina has been published in *Decisao, Life and Health,* and *RA.* **Mar. 5.**

Esperanza Aquino Mopera, a registered nurse, works for a home-care service company. Her four children have now completed their college educations. Her daughter is married and has given Esperanza three grandchildren to enjoy. **July 23.**

Ofelia Wichert Moroz lives in Porto Alegre, Brazil, where she works as the education supervisor for the Rio Grande do Sul Conference of Seventh-day Adventists. Her husband, David, is president of that conference. She is the author of four books, loves nature, and has a passion for evangelism, having helped with several conference and educational lectures. **May 13.**

Barbara Smith Morris is executive director of a nonprofit retirement center and a former Tennessee delegate representing housing and services needs of the low-income elderly. Active in both her church and her community, she is a presenter of seminars on elder-life issues. Barbara is the mother of four grown children and grandmother of six grandsons. She writes a daily devotional for the retirement center and loves to be surrounded by people of all ages. **May 16, Nov. 28.**

Muriel L. Moultrie enjoys starting her day with a reading from the women's devotional book. She writes from New Zealand, and is a first-time contributor. **Feb. 27, June 17.**

Bonnie Moyers likes to write, walk, curl up with a good book, and cook nutritious meals. She works as a certified nursing assistant, musician, and freelance writer. Bonnie and her husband live in Virginia, where she is active in church work. They have two grown children. **July 24.**

Lillian Musgrave and her husband have made their home in northern California for more than 30 years. They have three children and three grandchildren. Lillian enjoys reading, writing, music, church work, cooking, needlework, and family activities. **Dec. 6.**

Joan Minchin Neall was born in Australia, lived in England, and now makes her home in Tennessee, where she is a registered nurse. She and her pastor husband have four grown children. She is the women's ministries leader at her church and enjoys nature, sewing, journalism, and her grandchildren. **Jan. 6, Nov. 25.**

Joyce Neergaard lives on the Mediterranean island of Cyprus. She works with her husband in the Adventist Development and Relief Agency (ADRA) for the Middle East Region. As a nurse, Joyce enjoys assisting her church community outreach programs by teaching a variety of health promotion classes. She also likes to sing, write, sew, and listen to the sea. **Oct. 28.**

Anne Elaine Nelson is the mother of four grown children and helps her husband with his two companies in Michigan. She is a retired teacher, but she still tutors and is active in her church as the Bible school superintendent and teen worker. Special interests are travel, grandchildren, and "creative memories." Her book *Puzzled Parents* is designed to help parents get their child ready for school. **Aug. 24.**

Mabel Rollins Norman, wife, mother, and grandmother, resides in Avon Park, Florida. She is a published writer and helps with in-prison Bible studies and seminars. She enjoys sewing, crocheting, knitting, oil painting, reading, and sending encouraging cards. **Feb. 12, Feb. 21, Mar. 22, Aug. 30, Oct. 22.**

Connie Wells Nowlan has been an English teacher, an academy girls' dean, a preschool teacher and director, a wife, a biological mother, an adoptive mother—and always a writer. Her devotionals are the results of her experiences in her varying professions. **July 14, Dec. 18.**

Martha Montgomery Odom, a published author, is a retired teacher and secretary living in Chattanooga, Tennessee. She served with her missionary husband, Robert, in Spain, Panama, and the Philippines. **Jan. 14, Apr. 22.**

Erika Olfert was born in Yugoslavia and migrated to Canada as a teenager. She and her minister husband have been missionaries in India, but now live in Washington State. She is a nurse, working as a consultant and teacher. She is the youth and women's ministries leader at her church and the mother of two grown boys. When time permits, she enjoys oil painting, sewing, knitting, swimming, bicycling, singing, and housecleaning. **Jan. 8, Jan. 23.**

Edna May Olsen has lived in England nearly seven years since her husband retired from the United States Army. Her three daughters and granddaughters live in California. She is involved in her small church and is a published writer. Her hobbies include reading, writing, and hiking with the local Ramblers. **Mar. 7, June 14, Dec. 21.**

Myra Omeler, on "sabbatical" from her nursing profession, home-schools her children. She enjoys hiking and reading. Myra lives with her pastor husband in Massachusetts, where she volunteers for the Boston Van Ministry, a health-screening community outreach program. **June 5.**

Rose Otis is the director of women's ministries for the General Conference of Seventh-day Adventists. Since the office was established in 1990, she has helped to develop programs that benefit women around the world. Her work includes training leaders and speaking to women's groups. She enjoys her grandchildren, writing, and being home. **MAR. 29, OCT. 31, DEC. 16.**

Ofelia A. Pangan and her pastor husband were sent to work in Laos and Thailand for 21 years, then to Ontario, Canada, for nearly 10 years. They now work in central California, where her husband pastors two churches. Ofelia loves gardening, reading, traveling, and crocheting. She is the mother of three grown children and has three granddaughters and one grandson. **JUNE 7.**

Revel Papaioannou has had three elderly relatives take the place of four adult sons in her home in Greece. Church work, English lessons, fell walking, and gardening keep her more than occupied. Collections of stamps, coins, and telephone calls wait for less busy times. **DEC. 14.**

Julia L. Pearce, a wife, community worker, and nurse, chairs the Nursing Department at Pacific Union College. She enjoys reading, sewing, writing, and traveling, but she has interests in church and health education as well. Julia is a consultant for women's health and gives presentations on women's history and health. **OCT. 2, NOV. 18.**

Kathleen Stearman Pflugrad and her husband, David, live in Grayling, Michigan. They enjoy camping, hiking, and wilderness canoe trips. She has served in a variety of local church offices and has written for religious magazines. **JUNE 26.**

Betty Phillips is a bookkeeper living in Washington State. She has also worked as a secretary and teacher's aide. Her interests include reading, knitting, church work, and enjoying time with her family. Betty and her husband, a retired elementary school teacher, have two adult children. **JUNE 3.**

Felicia Phillips is the wife of an Adventist Development and Relief Agency director and the mother of three college-student sons. Felicia has an M.A. degree in theology and is a chaplain at Manila Sanitarium and Hospital in the Philippines. She serves as an elder in her church and enjoys preaching, teaching, giving Bible studies, and homemaking. **MAY 1.**

Birdie Poddar is from northeastern India. She is the wife of a retired division communication director, mother of three grown children, and grandmother of three grandsons. She worked as an elementary teacher, cashier, cashier accountant, and statistician before retiring in 1991. Sewing, gardening, and composing poems are some of her hobbies. **JULY 22.**

Myrtle A. Pohle spent seven years in mission service with her husband in Guatemala and Mexico before settling in Tempe, Arizona, where they established a hospital and helped build a church. She has three children and many foster children and has served as a chaplain's assistant and Bible instructor for 20 years. An author of numerous articles and poems, as well as a book entitled *The Truth Seekers*, she received a citation from the city of Tempe for being one of the outstanding women of the year. She also was honored by Loma Linda University as Woman of the Year. **MAR. 10.**

Vivian Prewitt is a teacher, wife, and mother of two sons. She enjoys being active in local church affairs, occasionally giving the sermon. Adventurous activities, such as hiking, skiing, sailing, and snorkeling, are her favorites. Vivian does wildlife photography and has had two books and several magazine articles published. **OCT. 30.**

Barbara Horst Reinholtz is the published author of a number of children's stories and poems. Until her recent retirement, she served her denomination in various capacities, including immigration officer, advising supervisor, and secretary. She is a church deaconess and the wife of a university professor. They have three married children and two grandchildren. Hobbies include collecting cookbooks and meaningful quotations, crocheting, music, and people. **AUG. 8, OCT. 16.**

Julie Reynolds, a registered nurse, is a full-time homemaker and the mother of two young girls. She is the women's ministries coordinator for her area in North Carolina. Her favorite activities include gardening, hiking in the mountains, walking on the seashore, and playing with her children. **FEB. 25, JUNE 13.**

Jill Hines Richards enjoys cross-stitch, bird-watching, reading, crafts, skiing, and interior design. She lives in Montana with her husband, a teacher at Mount Ellis Academy. Jill is currently working on her doctorate in curriculum instruction. **MAY 14.**

Lynda Mae Richardson is the single mother of an autistic child. She has been involved in the music and women's ministries departments at her church and writes, produces, and directs church programs. A published writer, Lynda also enjoys singing, computers, writing, hiking, friends, and nature. OCT. 26, DEC. 2.

Daise Lucidi Franca Rios and her husband live in Brazil, where she is studying to be an educator. Teaching is one of her favorite activities; another is reading. She has also written children's textbooks. She is active in her church as a pianist, an assistant, and a counselor. She has lectured to women and young people. Daise's personal pleasure is to be surrounded by her family. MAY 8.

Jeanette Ritz is a retired registered nurse who lives in Washington with her husband, a retired physical therapist. They feel fortunate to have both of their children, who are also registered nurses, and four grandchildren living near them. Jeanette enjoys sewing, cooking, and sharing with others the wonderful message of God's love and His soon coming. MAY 22.

Kay D. Rizzo is a freelance writer living in central California. She is the author of 13 books. JAN. 3, JUNE 21, AUG. 25.

Emilie Robertson, a minister's wife for more than 30 years, is a photojournalist who enjoys writing, exploring, sewing, drawing, and painting. She has held numerous church offices, including communication secretary, for more than 25 years. Emilie is currently the activities director, head cook, and assistant manager of the retirement village at Eden Valley Institute in Colorado. SEPT. 10.

Mindy Rodenburg is a nursing student who has lived in Indiana, Washington, Virginia, Maryland, British Columbia, and Alberta. Her hobbies include writing, sewing, cross-stitch, swimming, water-skiing, and traveling. Her dorm room is like a magnet, drawing friends in for foot, back, neck, and shoulder massages, haircuts, or just a good chat. JAN. 5.

Jean Reiffenstein Rothgeb and her husband work for an orthopedic surgeon in the mountains of Utah. Their hiking days are over, but they can drive to the most remote areas, where quiet meditation is welcome. They have two daughters, four grandchildren, and one great-granddaughter. Jean's regret is that she does not have enough time to spend sewing and doing cross-stitch, but the rewards of being a grandmother more than make up for it! JAN. 4.

Terrie Ruff is an assistant professor in the behavioral science department at Southern College of Seventh-day Adventists. She loves working with people, singing for the Lord, and public speaking and has taught Bible class at her church. She also volunteers in the community with agencies such as Senior Neighbors and is proud to be a big sister with the Big Brothers/Big Sisters of Chattanooga. NOV. 9.

Deborah Sanders shares from her journal *Dimensions of Love* and goes by the pen name Sonny's Mommy. She lives in northern Alberta, Canada, with her husband of more than 25 years. They have two children. She is active in her church and community and works full-time in construction with her husband. AUG. 31.

Shiela Birkenstock Sanders is a widow living in California's Napa Valley, where she is a counselor for mentally challenged adults. She enjoys people, photography, music, being out in nature, and working as the Bible school superintendent at her church. Shiela is the mother of two daughters and has three grandchildren. She also has a stepson, a stepdaughter, and five stepgrandchildren. JULY 21.

Jeannie Schmidt lives in central New York with her husband, Len. They own a successful manufacturing business. She enjoys songwriting and singing, reading, cooking, skiing, and spending time with her family. MAR. 26.

Cheri Schroeder is a wife, home-schooling mother of four, women's ministries director for the Northern New England Conference of Seventh-day Adventists, comanager of an apartment building, and Bible school teacher. Her Native American upbringing directly influences her choice of hobbies—gardening, knitting, spinning, and painting (when she has the time). DEC. 26.

Susan Scoggins moved to Russia at the end of 1995 with her husband, the publishing director for the Euro-Asia Division. She is a wife and mother who has spent more than 20 years supporting her husband in church work in the United States, Lebanon, and Rwanda. NOV. 15.

Marie H. Seard is a retired administrative assistant for student services in the Washington, D.C., public school system. She enjoys reading, writing, photography, and shopping. MAY 2.

Donna Lee Sharp is a retired social director and administrator of retirement facilities. She enjoys the piano and organ, photography, hiking, traveling, bird-watching, and gardening. Donna has four sons, one daughter, one stepdaughter, and five grandchildren. JULY 6.

Carrol Johnson Shewmake is a retired academy librarian living with her retired minister husband in southern California. They have four children and seven grandchildren. Her hobbies include nature, sewing, and people. Over the years Carrol has written numerous stories and articles for religious publications and other periodicals. A frequent speaker on prayer, she is the author of four books on this topic, plus one on witnessing coauthored with Daniel O'Ffill. **MAR. 25, JUNE 9, JULY 3, OCT. 4, NOV. 6.**

Judy Musgrave Shewmake is a wife and mother of three children, whom she home-schools. She is the editor of *The Adventist Home Educator,* a monthly newsletter for Adventist home schoolers. Her favorite hobby is writing, and she has had several articles published in home school periodicals. In any rare extra time, she enjoys reading, cross-stitching, and genealogy. **APR. 7, AUG. 10.**

Marion Seitz Simmons, a widow who has given 50 years of educational/pastoral service in denominational work, makes her home in North Carolina. In her ninetieth year, she still enjoys public speaking, vegetable gardening, writing, and volunteering at a local rest home. **JAN. 29.**

Elva E. Springer is a retired medical assistant and X-ray technician whose hobbies are camping, boating, flying, writing, and church activities. She has three children, eight grandchildren, and six great-grandchildren. She and her husband of 53 years still take their annual 5,000-mile motorcycle trip. **NOV. 7.**

Ivy J. Starks, a recent Oakwood College graduate, is the host of *Precious Moments,* a Friday/Saturday sunset program aired on Oakwood College Radio (WOCG) in Huntsville, Alabama. As the single parent of two daughters, Megan and Melissa, she enjoys singing, public speaking, and working with people. Ivy is president of the Oakwood College Secretarial Association. **MAR. 3.**

Kathleen Staubach, a native of California, graduated from Loma Linda University and has taught junior high math and Bible for the past seven years. She lives in California with her husband and three sons. Kathy is known for the stories she regularly uses to illustrate her points. **MAY 17, OCT. 21, DEC. 30.**

Ardis Dick Stenbakken is the associate director for women's ministries for the General Conference of Seventh-day Adventists. She was an Army chaplain's wife for 23 years until her husband "retired" to work at the General Conference of Seventh-day Adventists. They have one adult son and daughter. Ardis is concerned about women's issues and enjoys church work, crafts, reading, travel, and public speaking. **MAY 9, NOV. 13.**

Rita Stevens is a church administrator's wife in Anchorage, Alaska. She enjoys flying with her husband to many of the beautiful places in Alaska, meeting and entertaining people, walking, and doing crafts. The mother of two adult sons, Rita has worked as a medical technologist. **JAN. 26.**

Helen Stiles was a missionary to India from 1960 to 1975. For the past nine years she has been the editorial secretary of *Signs of the Times* magazine at the Pacific Press Publishing Association in Idaho. She enjoys globe-trotting. **MAY 31.**

Iris L. Stovall is a freelance writer. She serves as personal ministries leader and audio-visual technician at her church in Hyattsville, Maryland. She works as a part-time "floater" (temporary secretary) at the General Conference of Seventh-day Adventists. **FEB. 2, FEB. 16, NOV. 16.**

Grace E. Streifling is a quilting addict and retired registered nurse living in "Sweet Onion Country"—southeastern Washington State. She has also been a secondary level teacher, a missionary, and an author for *Our Little Friend* and *Primary Treasure.* Her four children have grown and flown. **APR. 12, MAY 5.**

Arlene Taylor is risk manager at St. Helena Hospital in northern California, as well as founder and president of her own nonprofit educational foundation. An internationally known speaker and brain function consultant, she is the creator of, and presenter for, Brainworks Unlimited, a four-day live-in program at the Health Center at St. Helena Hospital. **FEB. 17, JULY 9, SEPT. 19.**

Lucille Taylor, a retired librarian and new quilting enthusiast, is active in adult Bible class and women's and senior ministries at her church in Riverside, California. She has three sons, an adopted daughter, and five grandsons. **FEB. 5.**

Monica Stocker Taylor is a homemaker from Iowa who enjoys cooking, baking, sewing, writing, animals, and meeting people. She is the personal ministries director and superintendent in her church. **APR. 2.**

Marguerite Thygeson, a native of Washington, D.C., lives in Maryland and works as an analyst-programmer for the General Conference Information Systems Services. During the school year she spends two evenings a week tutoring for the Prepare Our Youth program. Her hobbies include vocal and instrumental music, knitting, brainteasers, and being near the ocean and mountains whenever possible. **JAN. 13.**

Peggy Tompkins is a retired church administrator's wife, mother of two grown children, and grandmother of four little boys. For the past decade she has compiled the magazine *The Heart of the Home* for the encouragement of mothers who choose to work at home. She enjoys working on many types of crafts. Nov. 10.

Kathleen Tonn-Oliver lives in California, where she is a creative and commercial writer and seminar presenter who has written 11 books and numerous articles. Kathleen is a recovering victim of child abuse who has done some writing on the subject. July 25.

Lilly Tryon writes from Pennsylvania, where she is a registered nurse, pastor's wife, and home-schooling mother of two boys. Her interests include being with her family, flower gardening, reading, writing, playing the piano, and singing. July 10, Aug. 12, Oct. 3.

Rita Van Horn is an assistant professor of nursing at Pacific Union College. She is working toward a Ph.D. in leadership from Andrews University in Michigan. She is involved in women's ministries in her church. Rita enjoys reading, cooking, and visiting with friends. She is the vice president of her local Toastmasters International club. Mar. 9, Apr. 25.

Nancy Van Pelt, a certified family life educator and family and consumer science professional, is an author and internationally known speaker. She has written 19 books, including *Creative Hospitality,* and her 20th is under way. Her hobbies are getting organized, entertaining, having fun, and quilting. Nancy and her husband live in California and are the parents of three grown children. May 19, June 2.

Janis Vance is a registered nurse and licensed counselor with a master's degree in educational psychology. She and her husband, Norman, are the parents of three grown children. She is also director of a home health agency and founder of Take Heart retreats, a spiritual ministry devoted to helping adults who were sexually abused as children. Jan. 11, Aug. 3.

Junell Vance has been the director of the Women's Ministries Department of the Atlantic Union Conference of Seventh-day Adventists for the past 10 years. She is a musician and a "retired" nurse who now spends her time nursing souls. She has two children, one foster son, and 10 grandchildren. Junell enjoys people, singing, and talking to birds. July 8.

Nancy Cachero Vasquez is an administrative secretary in the North American Division of the General Conference of Seventh-day Adventists. She is the wife of a vice president of the NAD and mother of three young adult children. Nancy's special interests are reading, writing, crafts, shopping, and baking. Jan. 21, June 25.

Tammy B. Vice writes from Alabama, where she is a wife and the mother of two energetic girls. She leads the children's choir at her church and enjoys writing children's stories and songs in her "spare" time. Sept. 2.

Nancy Jean Vyhmeister is the editor of *Andrews University Seminary Studies.* She also teaches research methods at the Theological Seminary at Andrews University and writes regularly for church periodicals. Nancy enjoys homemaking, traveling, and her family, which includes two married children and two grandsons. Mar. 14, June 11.

Celeste perrino Walker is a freelance writer living in Rutland, Vermont, with her husband, Rob, and 2-year-old son, Joshua. She has authored hundreds of articles and stories, a quarterly, and several books. In her spare time she enjoys hanging out on the CompuServe Adventist forum, trying to play the violin, painting in watercolor, backpacking, and cross-training. July 2.

Mae E. Wallenkampf has a master's degree in music and is now a retired music teacher living in Virginia. She enjoys reading, baking bread, and traveling. Mae has three children and five grandchildren. Aug. 26, Nov. 1.

Helen Lillian Walls is a single woman living in Pennsylvania. She loves witnessing for Jesus and visits church members in the hospital on her birthday and her baptismal anniversary, thanking God for preserving her life another year. Nov. 23.

Gwendolyn M. Ward, a retired schoolteacher, is the wife of Eric, retired senior pastor of the Oakwood College church in Alabama, a position he held for 21 years. Gwendolyn served on the music committee of that church and was secretary to the pastor. Other interests are piano playing, cooking, and gardening. Jan. 12.

Barbara J. Warren is a minister's wife, the mother of three adult children, and an associate college professor. She enjoys tennis, aerobic walking, and her two small granddaughters. Barbara stays active in both church and community work and conducts parenting workshops. Nov. 14.

Anna May Radke Waters is retired in Washington State, where she enjoys doing cross-stitch, playing Scrabble, writing, and working in her yard. She and her husband have five children and seven grandchildren. JUNE 24.

Ruth Watson is an office manager and diet consultant for two physicians, including her husband. She has also worked as an elementary church school teacher and a bookkeeper. The mother of three grown children, Ruth enjoys flower gardening and exercising. She has had several items published, including a children's songbook in Thai when she lived as a missionary in Thailand for 13 years. JULY 27, AUG. 4, AUG. 29, NOV. 29.

Dorothy Eaton Watts is a freelance writer, editor, speaker, and conference president's wife in Canada. She was a missionary in India for 16 years, founded an orphanage, taught elementary school, and has written 12 books, including the 1996 devotional for juniors, *Friends for Keeps.* Her hobbies include bird-watching, gardening, and hiking. JAN. 9, MAY 4.

Veyrl Dawn Were writes from South Australia, where she is a homemaker and the mother of one grown son. A nurse by profession, she served as a missionary in Kenya for eight years. She has written for various religious and professional publications. Hobbies include gardening, bird-watching, cooking, and knitting. Currently sharing leadership with her husband in ADCARE (Adventist Community Care), Veyrl conducts vegetarian cooking demonstrations. JAN. 31.

Penny Estes Wheeler, editor of *Women of Spirit,* writes from Hagerstown, Maryland. She has written eight books, her latest being *The Appearing.* Penny's kids provide many opportunities for her to travel. She loves saying hello, but hasn't yet mastered a tearless goodbye. JAN. 30.

Verna White worked in the Book Department of the Review and Herald® Publishing Association for 30 years before working in the Treasury Department of the General Conference of Seventh-day Adventists for 10 years. After retiring, Verna taught conversational English for International Teachers Service in Chongqing University in Chongqing, China. NOV. 17.

Carlene Will teaches seminars on home organization and personal devotions. She is the women's ministries leader for her local church and facilitates a weekly Bible study for women in her neighborhood. She is the mother of four boys and enjoys quilting and country life in Battle Ground, Washington. DEC. 3.

Debby Gray Wilmot is a musician, author, illustrator, and registered nurse living in California with her minister/chaplain husband and two teenage sons. She has taught piano and enjoys composing music, hiking, bodybuilding, playing on a softball team, and acrylic painting. Debby has been commissioned on several occasions to write theme songs for women's groups. She has been associated with a variety of musical groups and has cut a record with Maranatha Singers. OCT. 19, NOV. 27.

Patricia Wilson is a secretary in a juvenile home for boys in Flint, Michigan. Her hobbies are music, painting, writing, and reading. She has two daughters and one grandson. FEB. 4.

Earlene Wohlers, mother of three, manages her husband's dental practice. She is active in her church as an adult Bible teacher, youth leader, and women's ministries coordinator. Her hobbies include reading, walking, and camping, but her passion is golf. Earlene is studying at Washington State University. FEB. 13, APR. 29.

Lynda Wysong is the director of the Career Center at Union College in Lincoln, Nebraska. She is the mother of two teenagers who keep her active. Her hobbies include jogging, snorkeling, and working on a doctorate. FEB. 28.

Kathy Jo Yergen spent 16 years in Washington State and 17 years in Alaska. She currently resides in Beltsville, Maryland, where she and her husband work together in team ministry. Her interests include watercolor, drama, music, and poetry. NOV. 21.

Frances Young and her husband have two sons, ages 6 and 7. She is a senior student at the University of Central Florida, majoring in elementary education. She enjoys teaching, camping, rose gardening, computers, and writing. Frances has had stories published in *Our Little Friend* and *Primary Treasure.* DEC. 20.

Wilma Zalabak is a Seventh-day Adventist pastor in Calhoun, Georgia. Her "family" consists of a sheltie named Kari, and lots of books. She likes to read, be outdoors, and keep in phone contact with her thought and support network. DEC. 9.

New Beginnings

Then He who sat on the throne said, Behold, I make all things new. Rev. 21:5, NKJV.

*S*cripture tells us that God had no beginning and has no end. I shudder when I really consider what that means—never a chance for a new start. But then God doesn't need new beginnings like we do. How awful we'd feel if every time we made a mistake it was final—no new chances. And every time we finished something, that was it—no new opportunities to share it again. No, God in His mercy saw our need for new beginnings and granted to us an un-limited supply.

Let's reflect for a moment on some new beginnings:

A new day . . .
A new week . . .
A new year . . .
An anniversary . . .
A new grade at school . . .
A new season . . .
A new friendship . . .
Baptism . . .
Communion . . .
Forgiveness . . .
Spring's first blossoms . . .
A newborn baby . . .
A new journal or daybook . . .

Truly God has blessed us with new opportunities too numerous to count. His blessings are forever pouring over us afresh.

Perhaps you too have had a special and meaningful new start re-cently. But do we take advantage of each new beginning? Are we willing to risk leaving our comfortable rut to enjoy something new that God has planned for us? Are we willing to leave behind the mis-takes of the past and strive ever higher toward our goals in life?

I well remember my little students on the first day of school. It was always a delight to watch them. They'd carefully organize all their supplies in their clean desks. Their notebooks were fresh and new, with no mistakes. Clothes, brand-new or freshly ironed, and lockers as tidy as a pin. It was a new start, and they always made the best of it. By May it was a different story, but by

September we were all ready again for a new start.

May God grant that we make the very best of every new beginning He shares to bless us.   DAWNA BEAUSOLEIL

JANUARY 2

A Blank Page

He will again have compassion on us, and will subdue our iniquities. You will cast all our sins into the depths of the sea. Micah 7:19, NKJV.

I'm sitting at my desk staring at last year's New Year's resolutions. A few successes. Many failures. I had planned to accomplish so many things. I wanted to learn to play one new song each month on my piano. I now know a few lines of "Waltz in A Minor," by Chopin, and a half-dozen children's Bible songs. "Read one book a month" was discarded in March. I had planned to try a new recipe every week so that I could add 52 recipes to my cooking repertoire. I have added five. My goal to do 30 sit-ups each day, increasing by increments of ten each month, peaked at 60 sit-ups. And my number one goal for the year, eat chocolate only once a week, didn't make it past Thursday of the first week of the new year.

Am I discouraged? Hardly! I'm sitting at my desk now with a blank piece of paper in front of me, carefully calculating the goals I can realistically accomplish this year. The old year's resolutions have been crumpled up and tossed aside. They are forgotten. It's time to start looking ahead. That's why I love the new year so much. Nothing has been accomplished yet, but nothing has been a failure either. I can make it whatever I want. It's a new year, and I'm starting with a clean slate.

We don't have to wait for a special occasion such as Christmas, New Year's, Easter, or any other time of the year to begin a new life with God. We can begin one right now. Each day is a blank piece of paper on which we can start over again. Past failures are crumpled up and tossed aside. Sins are forgotten. It's a new day, and we're starting with a clean slate.

Of all the New Year's resolutions you will make—and break—this year, promise yourself to keep just one: that you will always begin each day with Christ as the center of your life. And even if you break that resolution, know that you can always start over again with a blank piece of paper. MERRI LONG

The Family Photo Album

I thank my God every time I remember you. . . . I always pray with joy, . . . being confident of this, that he who began a good work in you will carry it on to completion until the day of Christ Jesus. Phil. 1:3-6, NIV.

*I*t's January. The holidays are over. I've packed away Christmas for another year, and I'm ready to settle into the ho-hum routine of a central California winter, i.e., fog and drizzle. I wander through the empty house, picking up the remnants of the holiday—a stray shepherd behind the sofa, evergreen needles along the baseboards in the living room, wax from the overzealous and oversized candles.

The house is quiet—too quiet. The girls and their husbands have returned to their own homes. They flit into my life for a few slender days, and then they're gone again. And our communication is reduced to humorous greeting cards, phone calls, and E-mail letters. I forget how empty the nest can be until it has been filled for a few brief days, then emptied again.

My husband is back teaching his classes. All excuses I might have for not getting back to my daily writing routine have been removed. Well, almost. I still haven't taken the time to add the latest pack of family snapshots to our photo albums.

So I put on a Sandi Patty CD and crank up the volume. I get comfortable on the sofa and open the most recent family album. Once more I go through the stack of current shots: Richard decorating the tree, Rhonda opening a gift, Kelli sneaking cookies from the cookie jar, and Mark and Tracy playing Pit. I toss out a particularly unflattering close-up shot taken of me and my "turkey neck." I chuckle at the "five-second" grins clustered around the holiday table. Richard dashed into the frame before the flash fired but didn't have time to get his grin fixed. We take the same pose every year.

The music fades as I slip the last photograph between the celluloid pages. Memories. I sigh. Only memories now.

As I reach for my Bible, I invite the Holy Spirit to fill me. I turn to Philippians and read, "I thank my God every time I remember you. . . . I always pray with joy, . . . being confident of this, that he who began a good work in you will carry it on to completion until the day of Christ Jesus." And suddenly I am caught up in the excitement and in the possibilities of tomorrow, next week, next month, and verse by verse, I eagerly begin to unwrap the most valuable gift of the season—my God-given *gift of time*.

Thrilling. Mysterious. Exhilarating. Challenging. Frightening. Promising. And mine to experience.

I no longer want to tend timidly the grave of 1996. I no longer wish for the *good old days* that were. Instead, I turn to my heavenly Father and with eager expectations ask, "What's next, Papa?" (Rom. 8:15, Message).   KAY D. RIZZO

JANUARY 4

A Quiet Resting Place

The Sovereign Lord has given me an instructed tongue, to know the word that sustains the weary. He wakens me morning by morning, wakens my ear to listen like one being taught. Isa. 50:4, NIV.

We have a little room in our home called "that room." It seems to collect things that have no specific place in the rest of the house. Things such as a large picture frame picked up at a yard sale that I will use some day for framing the beautiful counted cross-stitch that I will make. The ironing board with the iron sitting idly on it. A couple of sofa pillows that are worn, but that we may want to take camping when we retire. You know the kind of "plan-to-do" things that collect. There are bookshelves lining the walls that hold the reading material of a lifetime, both old and new books that have inspired and entertained, and even books that our children and grandchildren still love to read.

My favorite piece of furniture in "that room" is an old French provincial chair—it is not a recliner, it only rocks and swivels. A footstool sits in front of it, and on the footstool resides my Bible, my lesson quarterly, and my devotional book. On the side table are all of the things I hope to get time to read, and whatever special book I am currently reading.

God comes very close to me there, and when I read the special texts in either the Bible or the devotional book, they are so meaningful—written just for me. When my Friend awakens me in the early-morning hours, I can hardly wait to see what wonderful thing He has for me that new day. Usually it is a special promise that I need for accomplishing the tasks of the day. Sometimes He tells me what I need to do to solve a problem that has kept me from sleeping well. Or perhaps He just assures me of His undying, eternal love, and I thank Him for this. He and I speak of private things, and He tells again of His endless offer of forgiveness. He tells me that He shed His blood for me and my family, and because of that we will meet in the mansions He has prepared for us.

My quiet resting place has become the most important part of my house, and the time I spend there is the most relaxing of my entire day.

I recommend to you a quiet place of your own—maybe a "that room," maybe a spot under a favorite tree, maybe just a little space beside your bed where each morning you can meet with this wonderful Friend. For He will be your friend too, if you ask Him to be. He will even awaken you early enough so you can have time to speak to Him and listen as He offers answers to your needs and pledges His love to you. He waits to hear your voice lifted in praise and thanksgiving. What joy awaits us in His presence!

JEAN REIFFENSTEIN ROTHGEB

JANUARY 5

Do You Refuse Life?

You diligently study the Scriptures because you think that by them you possess eternal life. These are the Scriptures that testify about me, yet you refuse to come to me to have life. John 5:39, 40, NIV.

*J*ane was deathly ill. She sat at home having a heart attack, reading a medical journal that presented new research on the treatment of cardiac arrest. Just a phone call away was her personal physician and 911, yet she read on. Jane died.

The above scenario seems rather far-fetched, but that was the type of situation Jesus addressed. He told the Jews that the life they were looking for in the Scriptures could be found only in Him. Did Jesus say the Scriptures were worthless? No. Worthless to give life? Yes. Jesus asserted that the value of the Scriptures was to point to Jesus as the Messiah.

What new light does that shed on our devotional lives? Maybe we should spend more time with God, rather than just reading about Him. The Bible is used to its fullest potential when it points us to Christ, the source of our life. Scripture tells us about God. The Bible gives us numerous word pictures of God's character, but it does not give us life.

Think of someone you have always wanted to know personally. Perhaps it's Mother Teresa or Queen Elizabeth, Sandra Day O'Connor, or even the person down the street. Imagine you were given nearly 70 accounts about that person, written by a variety of people who knew him or her. After reading those documents, you probably would have a fairly balanced view. But would you feel that you really knew him or her? Reading about people would not compare to talking with them, telling each other about yourselves.

That is the way it is with God. The Bible points us to Him, but it is vital to our spiritual health to spend time with God. Alone. Not just reading about Him. God—not the Scriptures—is the source of life.

MINDY RODENBURG

JANUARY 6

A Prayer for Today

This is the day the Lord has made; let us rejoice and be glad in it. Ps. 118:24, NIV.

*L*ord, today is Your day. Cause my heart to be attuned to Thee this day. Crowd out earthly thoughts, concerns, and worries. Lift me into that divine atmosphere of faith, trust, and hope. May Your peace surround me and fill my thoughts.

May the concerns of last week, yesterday, and tomorrow lie dormant as today I choose to take a day apart with You. As I follow a stream, sit on a moss-covered log in the meadow, or contemplate Your greatness from a jagged mountain bluff, may You be near. May the great outdoor cathedral of Your design speak to me, calm me.

As I seek to impart Your rejuvenation of my soul to a sick or discouraged one, encompass this one with Your love.

Thank You, Lord, for this day.   JOAN MINCHIN NEALL

"I Like You!"

And as we live with Christ, our love grows more perfect and complete. 1 John 4:17, TLB.

That Christmas the whole family gathered to enjoy a few hours together during the holidays in old New England. From the moment he arrived, our son-in-law Kurt hugged, tossed, tickled, and played with his nephew, Kurtis. Of course, all of us played, talked, and read to little Kurtis, but it was his big, jolly German uncle who was the most fun. Together they raced cars, put puzzles together, and played horse.

All too soon the fun visit came to an end. As Uncle Kurt and his wife, Auntie Marilee, stood in the kitchen saying their goodbyes, a solemn little boy looked on. Gazing up at his six-foot-three-inch idol, he said, "I like you!"

There is so much written in song, verse, and numberless books about love—but what about *like?* We can be perfectly acceptable Christians if we love our families and friends and neighbors. This is a love based on a principle Jesus taught and demonstrated over and over again—and this kind of love is most important. But what about *liking* people? That's a bit harder sometimes, isn't it?

I suppose the first place we should start is with ourselves—to like ourselves. I've noticed something over the years. When people are very unlikable, generally they are not very happy with themselves. To feel accepted and secure, self-worth through Jesus Christ is vitally important. We are then free to become a lovable and likable person in Jesus Christ.

Edward A. Gloeggler stated this truth beautifully: "Hearts that open to the love that is God feel loved in loving and served in serving."

Isn't that beautiful? When we make a determined effort to reach out to others, to laugh with them, cry with them, and serve with them, we will "like," and be liked.

John Wesley's well-known quote puts it this way: "Do all the good you can, by all the means you can, in all the ways you can, in all the places you can, at all the times you can, to all the people you can, as long as ever you can."

As we all travel toward the kingdom may others be able to say about us, as little Kurtis said that long-ago Christmas, "I like you!"

HAZEL MARIE GORDON

JANUARY 8

From My Heart to Yours

Ask and it will be given to you; seek and you will find; knock and the door will be opened to you. For everyone who asks receives; he who seeks finds; and to him who knocks, the door will be opened. Matt. 7:7, 8, NIV.

*T*he hustle and bustle of Christmas is over, and the new year is a week old. Let's reflect on the past seven days. Have you kept your New Year's resolutions? Is this year any different thus far, or is life back on the old track? I invite you to join me today in making God your daily partner through the remaining days of this year. He is able, faithful, and willing.

Ask the Lord to awaken you for the special time to talk and share with Him. Tell Him your plans, heartaches, concerns, and joys, and invite Him to have control of your heart for the day. He always has time to listen. Time spent with the Lord every day is rewarding throughout the day: There is more time available, problems become more solvable, priorities fall into line, and happiness is greater. The heart will be joyous and the mind lighter as we all grow to know Him as the true and faithful God who cares, comforts, and loves us.

"Love the Lord your God with all your heart and with all your soul and with all your mind" (Matt. 22:37). Taste and see that the Lord is good. Invite Him into your life as your daily partner. Let God make your heart new again every day. ERIKA OLFERT

JANUARY 9

Winter Birds

Come to me, all you who are weary and burdened, and I will give you rest. Matt. 11:28, NIV.

*M*y husband had left for work an hour before, but still I sat at the kitchen table, staring out at the frozen garden. Juncos and house finches scratched in the snow, looking for sunflower seeds. A flicker helped himself at the suet feeder, while chick-adees flitted in the bare branches awaiting their turn.

The cold, gray day fit my melancholy mood. My head ached, and I was worried about what my latest mammogram would show. Every pain or sniffle recently had reminded me of my mortality. I needed to write, but I had no energy. Fear froze my heart and creativity.

Sighing, I picked up my pen and recorded my feelings in my journal, sharing them in a prayer with One I knew would understand.

"Lord, like juncos flocking to the feeder, I come to You bent on survival, looking for a morsel of hope to keep me going, in spite of leaden skies. I scratch at the coldness, looking for but a seed of strength, for life amidst the feel of death.

"A friend is dead. I, too, shall die, early or late, only You know the answer. But until then, is life only a frustrated scratching for life among the snows of our existence?

"I long for roses and pansies, tulips and lilacs, the end of grayness. I want so much to glimpse the sun and feel its warmth, energy, and joy. Lord, help me see beyond the grayness of winter to the brightness of spring."

I looked again at my frozen garden. I pictured myself standing in the cold, shivering. And it seemed I could hear a faint whisper from beyond the grayness, "Dorothy, spring will come by and by. Just wait."

And my trembling soul whispered back, "Lord, I don't want to wait. I can't survive until spring!"

Then I imagined Jesus smiling as He beckoned me at an open door. "Then come on inside. It's warm in here!"

"Yes, Lord," I responded. Clutching the rags of my faith, I stumbled toward the open door. He drew me inside, and suddenly the winter didn't matter because I was in the warmth of His presence.

DOROTHY EATON WATTS

To Give Is More Blessed

Jesus himself said: "It is more blessed to give than to receive."
Acts 20:35, NIV.

*T*he small package I found in the mailbox held a sample product I had no use for. "It might be useful to someone else though, Lord," I commented. "Who needs it?" Immediately I thought of Joyce, a young theology student's wife. Chuck had gone back to school after his conversion. They already had a little girl, so money probably could get tight sometimes.

Joyce's personality is just what her name implies. She always smiled, never complained, never seemed to discuss burdens or worries. Perhaps because of that I'd not really thought of them as "needy," and felt a bit awkward as I began rounding up a few things to accompany the sample.

"Lord," I invited, "point out to me the things they can use."

As I ambled through the house, soap, pens, and toilet paper went into the sack, along with other things. When I got to the desk my eyes fell on a watch no one used. Feeling foolish, but obedient, I dropped it in among the other items. "Do You really mean for me to give this, too?" I asked my Companion. "Watches don't wear out on a frequent basis, You know."

Some things I'd even forgotten we had, but it seemed God directed me right to them. Other items I'd just purchased with specific plans for using them myself, but I could almost hear a whisper in my mind, "You'll never miss it." So into the bag went item after item.

At Joyce's I dropped off the things without staying long. I felt uncomfortable, as though I might be insulting my friend with this charity.

My fears turned to thrills when Joyce called me later. "We didn't get two checks we expected this month. We're more than $200 short. Our student's budget can't easily handle that deficit. Almost everything in the parcel you left was something we have already run out of, or soon will. God must have told you what to put in.

"And know what? I just got a job caring for a terminally ill gentleman but haven't known what I'd do because I had no watch with a second hand to use in taking his pulse. Thank you so much!"

Goose bumps rose on my arms as I listened. God really had guided me. Me! He heard my prayer. He led me through the house as I packed the bag. In fact, He started it all by getting the sample into my hands and suggesting I share it instead of tossing it in the trash. He used me to bless someone else.

And I suddenly realized *I* was the one He'd blessed most. I could almost see God chuckling as I discovered again His trademark—by getting me to show my love to someone else, He got to show His love to me.   PAMELA BAUMGARTNER

Be Strong and Take Heart

Wait for the Lord; be strong and take heart and wait for the Lord. Ps. 27:14, NIV.

One night my sleep was somewhat restless. I was away from home, presenting a seminar for hurting women. Even though the ministry was dealing with a delicate and sensitive issue and could be emotionally draining, I always looked forward to the weekends because of the spiritual focus and the peace we all experienced there.

As the needs for more seminars grew, I was feeling pressured to expand and commit to more speaking, writing, and training. Sometimes I felt overwhelmed, and like Gideon, I wanted to say to God, "We need more warriors." Yet it seemed that God kept cutting our potential staff members.

I woke up around 4:00 a.m. and couldn't go back to sleep. As I wrestled in my mind with God, I kept thinking that if God would just give me some answers and help, I could have peace of mind and get the needed rest to strengthen me for the next three days.

As I often do when I can't sleep, I take my Bible, open it, and start reading. My eyes fell on these words: "Wait for the Lord; be strong and take heart and wait for the Lord." As my heart raced and I became wide awake, I realized that I had never read this verse in the New International Version before.

What was God telling me—or preparing me for? The next night I again awoke at 4:00 a.m. with the most severe case of intestinal virus that had ever attacked my body. I had no control over my bodily functions and felt completely exhausted. How could I ever present a seminar for the next two days? When my copresenter came to my door at 7:30, I told her of my problem and that she would have to go on without me. She immediately rallied the troops, and suddenly I was the one being nurtured. One person went to town for medicine, several others handled organizational issues, and all of the prayer intercessors prayed for me. Several came to my room for special intercessory prayer, asking for God's will in all of this.

Well, my agenda for God was either for Him to heal me so I could go on with the weekend, or for me to stay sick and rest, and let the staff go on without me. As often happens, God, in His all-knowing way, had His own agenda for me. And as is always true, He knew the desires of my heart. He and I had been struggling with an issue that was based on my level of trust in Him. I, like Paul, often didn't meet my expectations of being the kind of Christian I wanted to be, and I was afraid that if really difficult trials came to me I might be overwhelmed and let God down. Perhaps part of this fear was still from early childhood when I felt God had abandoned me. I really thought I had worked all of this through, but God was going to show me in a powerful way that He would care and provide for me, even through the illness.

By 10:00 that morning I felt strong enough to go on with the seminar, but was unable to eat any food for two days. Even so, I experienced more strength and vitality and peace than I have ever experienced before. By the time the weekend was over, God had made clear to me the direction He wanted this ministry to continue in. In the days that followed, I discovered He was already providing in ways I hadn't even considered.

God has not promised to take me out of every difficult circumstance, but He has promised to give me the strength to go through those difficult circumstances. Oh, how I love Him! JANIS VANCE

JANUARY 12

The Still Small Voice

And after the earthquake a fire, but the Lord was not in the fire; and after the fire a still small voice. 1 Kings 19:12, NKJV.

*O*ne morning I was preparing to go to the grocery store to get something to cook for dinner. My husband was away for 90 days, conducting evangelistic meetings in Miami, Florida, and I had the total responsibility of caring for my children, alone, atop Missionary Ridge.

This particular Friday morning I was greatly impressed *not* to take the children with me—but I never have liked leaving them alone. As I approached my car that was parked on the side of the mountain, my heart was touched by the pitiful looks on the faces of my four children peering at me through the living room window. I could hear them pleading softly, "Mommy, why can't we go with you? Please, please, Mommy!" I assured them that I would be back within an hour. However, if they had asked just one more time to come with me, I probably would have relented.

Hastily I went to my parked car, got in, and started the engine. But the car wouldn't budge. I had forgotten to move the concrete block that was placed in front of the front wheel on the passenger's side. Leaving the engine running, I got out to move the block, something that I should *never* have done. After much pulling and yanking, I finally succeeded in removing the concrete block, only to see my car slowly begin to move down the hill.

I quickly grabbed the rear bumper and tried with all of my strength to hold the car back, but it began picking up speed and was soon pulling me down the hill with it. Just a few seconds after I decided to let go, I heard the car go over the edge of my yard and drop 50 feet to the bottom of the cliff. I was speechless and horrified!

When I went to the bottom of the cliff I could see that my car had landed on its nose. It was a total wreck. The rear seat had shifted to the dashboard. The front seat was under the steering wheel. Even my eyeglasses, which had been on the front seat, were in many bits and pieces. I was so happy I had listened to the still small voice I had heard so clearly in our morning's devotions. Thank God, my precious little children were safe in the house. Their lives had been spared, even though my car was a total loss.

Let's make it our practice every day to listen to that still small voice. The results could be lifesaving.   GWENDOLYN M. WARD

JANUARY 13

Prayers and Answers

Hear my prayer, O Lord, and let my cry come to You. . . . I lie awake, and am like a sparrow alone on the housetop. . . . For the Lord shall build up Zion; He shall appear in His glory. He shall regard the prayer of the destitute, and shall not despise their prayer. Ps. 102:1-17, NKJV.

The week had been a rough one. Work was not a gratifying experience, my husband was away on travel, I wasn't sleeping well. In other words, I was not a happy person. I had petitioned God but still was feeling pretty sorry for myself and overwhelmed. Then I remembered how I would sometimes sing to myself to improve my emotional state. So while waiting for the elevator in my apartment building, I began singing "His Eye Is on the Sparrow." By the time I got to the chorus—"I sing because I'm happy"—I felt like a real fraud. But I continued to sing anyway.

When I got to my car and climbed in, I looked through the windshield. There, sitting on the windshield wiper, was a bird! No, it was not a sparrow. In fact, I had never seen a bird like this one. I began to talk to the bird to try to shoo it away from the windshield wiper. I had to get to work; I didn't have time for this! But it stayed right there on its perch, singing to me. Finally I laughed and said, "OK, Lord, I got Your message." I turned around to back out of the parking space, and when I faced front again, the bird was gone. But my joy wasn't. I believe God sent that little bird to let me know that all was not as dark as I thought it was, and to give me evidence that He did hear me. He sent a sign of His love just for me!

How often do we try to "shoo" away God's blessings? Many times we are in too much of a hurry and miss the opportunity for joy and praise. We are so busy we fail to hear God's answers to our prayers or His gentle voice whispering "I love you." Sometimes He has to shout to get our attention.

Today, promise yourself to take the time to hear God whisper, "I love you."

"The Lord has appeared of old to me, saying: 'Yes, I have loved you with an everlasting love; therefore with lovingkindness I have drawn you'" (Jer. 31:3, NKJV).   MARGUERITE THYGESON

Coals of Fire

If thine enemy hunger, feed him; if he thirst, give him drink: for in so doing thou shalt heap coals of fire on his head. Rom. 12:20.

Our furlough was nearly due, so I returned to the United States with the children a few months early so our older son, Bob, could finish his eighth grade with other children. Having lived in the mission field all his life, Bob had never had the privilege of attending a real church school. I had always taught him at home.

We arrived in December, so Bob entered school in January when the school year was half over. It was a hard experience for him to be the new boy. The other children seemed to resent his coming in so late. One boy in particular seemed to have it in for Bob. Dick was a bully. He would pick fights with Bob whenever he could. He begged me for permission to fight back, feeling sure he could win a fight with Dick.

I had taught our boys not to fight. "No, let's try the Bible way first," I suggested. I read Romans 12:18-21 to him and told him to invite Dick to our apartment for supper. Bob was certain he wouldn't come, but asked him the next day anyway.

Dick was greatly surprised. "Who? Me?"

Bob assured him that we would have a pleasant evening.

I prepared a lovely meal, and we waited, wondering if Dick would come. About 6:00 we heard him arrive on his bicycle. He seemed rather embarrassed at first, but we welcomed him warmly. We had a good supper and then played games. The results were amazing. Dick never mistreated Bob again. Nor did any of the other boys in school. It was a wonderful experience for 12-year-old Bob, proving that the Lord's way is always best.

MARTHA MONTGOMERY ODOM

What Is My Message?

By this shall all men know that ye are my disciples, if ye have love one to another. John 13:35.

I stood waiting for the crossing guard to motion that it was OK for me to cross. I had come to school to help out in my daughter's third grade class, something I always enjoyed. As was usual on such occasions, I was loaded down with props and was anxious to cross quickly.

The seconds ticked by. Even though the man wearing the bright-orange vest held up his sign, cars kept driving past. He began to yell out to them to stop, but the drivers ignored him. It didn't take me long to understand the situation. Although the man was holding his sign up high, it was the wrong sign. He had the side that said "SLOW" pointed in the direction of the oncoming cars, rather than the one that read "STOP." Once the error was corrected, the cars came to a stop, and I was able to cross. The poor man had gotten so angry at the drivers, yet they were only acting on the message he was giving them.

That incident has caused me to ponder the message I may be giving as a Christian. Which side of my sign is showing? Does it clearly state "DISCIPLE OF JESUS," or has that message been muddled? Does my love for others tell clearly that I belong to God? I wonder. Is my Christianity genuine? Does it give people cause for pause, or do they simply continue on their way, scarcely impacted by my message?

What about my Lord, standing on the sidelines observing? I wonder if He has ever wanted to tell me that I'm holding up the wrong sign. Maybe He has, but I've been so busy trying to be heard that I've failed to look in His direction.   RETTA MICHAELIS

Am I a Witness?

Be thou an example of the believers, in word, in conversation, in charity, in spirit, in faith, in purity. 1 Tim. 4:12.

It was my last week to work. I was retiring! Oh, joy! At last! Thirty-five years had been enough! Even though I loved my work as chief nursing officer, health-care provision was becoming more and more difficult, and the budget was always getting sliced. Now we could barely cover the needed staffing requirements.

I had hoped I could just quietly slip away, but it was not to be. All week there had been luncheons and other special events, and finally a hospital-wide reception. One of my colleagues who was hosting the reception greeted me warmly with a lovely corsage. It was one of the most beautiful I had ever seen—roses and gardenias. The fragrance was wonderful. As she pinned it on my dress, she whispered in my ear, "This is from someone who would like to remain anonymous, but I think you, at least, should know. I'll tell you later."

Later my nurse friend told me the story of the corsage. One of the maintenance employees approached her when he learned she was organizing my reception, requesting that he be allowed to purchase a corsage for the event. He said that he just wanted to do something, and flowers seemed appropriate. I did not know this employee very well at all. We had exchanged the usual casual greetings when we would meet in the halls. I was puzzled about why I had received recognition from this quiet, shy person.

I sought him out and expressed my appreciation for the flowers. As we visited, he reminded me about the heart surgery he'd had the previous year. I had forgotten that I had sent a card wishing him well and mentioning "prayers for your recovery." That card, together with observations he'd made over the years, led him to conclude that I must be a Christian. "I truly admire that in a leader," he said.

Looking back over the years, I wondered how I had really influenced him. Or others. What more could I have done or said? The responsibility of witnessing is a heavy one. Do we consciously plan and approach this wisely? Do we realize how often opportunities present themselves, and yet we miss them? I must confess that I have missed many. I pray daily that the Lord will give me new opportunities and guide me to do and say just the right things.

So often during our day we encounter people who are thirsty for encouraging words—words of caring, hope, and spiritual direction. Let us continue to share Jesus with everyone we meet—by word, by prayer, and by witnessing. ARLENE COMPTON

JANUARY 17

The Day the Bread Didn't Rise

I have fought the good fight, I have finished the race, I have kept the faith. 2 Tim. 4:7, NIV.

*M*y husband adores home-baked bread, and so whenever I can, I make it. However, I do not like breadmaking. In fact, I hate the laborious kneading of the dough. Still, Jonathan appreciates the bread so much that I knead on!

Some time ago my husband spent a night away from home. Eager to welcome him back, I decided to make him not one but *three* loaves of bread. I had *really* missed him! Even so, I was not looking forward to the usual pounding of the sticky bread mixture. I thought I would take a shortcut and use a recipe that guaranteed perfect bread without kneading.

I was a little suspicious of the recipe as I poured the sloshy mixture into three bread pans to rise. And I was even more concerned when, after several hours, the mixture had risen no higher than the height of my fingernail. I assumed some "miracle" would take place after I put it in the oven to bake.

I had timed the baking of the bread to coincide with Jonathan's soon return, and he was certainly welcomed by the delicious smell of freshly baked bread. But instead of three rounded loaves of bread sitting on the kitchen counter, he saw three slabs of heavy dough, topped with several lumpy peaks. My shortcut had failed—miserably!

We live in a society that urges us to "find the easy way," to "take a shortcut" to achieve what we want. Sometimes we get away with it. Other times we don't. Sadly, this attitude trickles over into our relationship with God. A quick glance at the Bible lesson one evening, five minutes of Scripture reading while gobbling down breakfast, a few expressions of praise while jogging in the park, or a quick pleading with God to solve our problems while loading the washing machine.

God deserves more than the shortcuts we offer in our relationship with Him. God didn't take the easy way in offering Jesus as our substitute for sin's penalty, so let's make sure we don't take the easy way in our commitment to Him.   MARY BARRETT

JANUARY 18

Baskets

Cast your cares on the Lord and he will sustain you; he will never let the righteous fall. Ps. 55:22, NIV.

All my life I've been a basket lover. Whenever I find baskets I dig through them, looking for those with an unusual shape or design. I like to use baskets for anything and everything—flowers, magazines, cosmetics, towels . . . The list could go on and on! The more unique the handiwork, the more I'm attracted to it. Handmade baskets are the most prized of all my baskets; prized because I know someone spent many hours working with the reeds or vines to create a beautiful work of art.

During my devotional time one day I came up with an unusual metaphor for taking my cares to the Lord. In my mind's eye, I visualized myself struggling with a huge basket that was filled with all my worries, heartaches, prayer requests, disappointments, and longings. As I dragged it along (for it was too heavy to be carried), I saw myself coming to the feet of my Saviour. I tipped the huge basket over at the feet of Jesus, and all the problems rolled out before Him. With tears in my eyes, I looked up at Him and whispered, "Please, take them all; I can't carry them any longer."

Jesus has told us to cast our cares upon Him for He cares for us. I am so thankful that with the whole universe to supervise, our Lord and Saviour still has time to care for me. I come away from my prayer time with my burdened heart lightened, knowing that He will take care of my basketful of needs. And He'll do the same for you!

                                                                CAROL BRACKETT

Woe to Him!

If one falls down, his friend can help him up. But pity the man who falls and has no one to help him up! Eccl. 4:10, NIV.

*T*rue or false: The important thing to remember when getting married is to find the right mate."

I have always been glad I missed that question on my psychology exam. I marked "true" and got it wrong. The statement is false because the most important thing to remember when getting married is to *be* the right mate!

How many of us are the right mate? The right friend? A recent newspaper article reported that about 25 percent of those interviewed admitted they had many acquaintances but not even one close friend. Tragic. How many close friends do you have? But more significantly, how many people consider you to be a close friend?

Recently my husband and I were eating in a quaint little restaurant in the Smoky Mountain foothills. After the owner himself prepared our order, he came out and sat by us to talk. Soon into the conversation, he mentioned casually that after work he had to go and put flowers on his wife's grave, his mother's grave, and his son's grave. We listened attentively as his private tragedy unfolded.

"My wife's been dead 10 years. . . . My second marriage was a terrible mistake. . . . My mother died last July—the same month my son was killed in a car accident."

Too much grief for one to bear alone; too much unmitigated sorrow for one to endure by himself. Solomon was so very right when he wrote: "But pity the man who falls and has no one to help him up!"

We talked with him a few minutes longer, paid our bill, and left. But I couldn't easily forget the cook with the troubled life. Did he have even *one* true friend? Was he so desperate for someone to talk to that he risked exposing his loneliness to casual restaurant customers?

The apostle Paul encourages us to use the gift of Jesus, "who comforts us in all our troubles, so that we can comfort those in any trouble with the comfort we ourselves have received from God" (2 Cor. 1:4, NIV). If you are among the 25 percent who say they have not one close friend, then maybe no one considers you a best friend either. Take Paul's suggestion and use the comfort we get from Jesus as a base for befriending others.

"True or false: The most important thing to consider when selecting friends is to *be* a close friend."

True! Follow that advice, and maybe when you fall there will be someone nearby to pick you up.   WILMA McCLARTY

JANUARY 20

Warmth Always Wins

A cheerful look brings joy to the heart, and good news gives health to the bones. Prov. 15:30, NIV.

*T*here is an old fable about a contest between the seasons. Winter, Summer, Fall, and Spring were talking together. Spying a traveler walking along the road, Summer suggested a contest to the others. "Behold yon traveler with her cloak upon her. Let us see which of us can persuade her to take it off." Each season accepted the challenge, sure of victory.

Autumn tried first. "I shall blow and blow until her coat flaps in my wind and becomes a nuisance."

The traveler felt her cloak billow around her and nearly lost it a time or two, but the harder the wind gusted, the tighter she gathered her coat around her, clinging to it as though for dear life.

Winter went next. "I will freeze the coat and make it so stiff that it will be unbearable."

But even as the traveler's neck chafed beneath her collar, hardened by snow and sleet, the traveler thought, *Difficult as it is, I must hang on to my coat, for at least it protects me from the elements.*

Spring responded by saying, "I will soak the coat. Then it will become so soggy and heavy, surely the traveler will discard it."

The coat's weight did slow the traveler's pace to a near standstill, but still she continued to wear it. She reasoned that even if she removed the coat she would have to carry it anyway in such unpredictable weather.

Finally it came Summer's turn. Summer had little to say; the sun simply shone abroad on the earth until the warmth of its rays penetrated the cloak and lured the traveler out from under her wraps into the pleasant sunshine. And as the story goes, the traveler smiled, slung her old coat over her shoulder, and enjoyed the sunshine.

The moral? Warmth always wins!

It's a fable, to be sure. But as with most fables, it conveys more than a little truth. KAREN FLOWERS

Makeovers

The king's daughter is all glorious within: her clothing is of wrought gold. Ps. 45:13.

've always been fascinated with before and after pictures. It doesn't matter whether it's the remodeling of a room, the face-lift of an entire house, or, even more interesting, the before and after photos of people who were transformed from a "plain Jane" to the equivalent of a beauty queen through the talent of a great makeover artist. What wonders a new hairdo, makeup, and a smile can accomplish! I could sit and be awed for hours by the photos of these "miracles." And many businesses thrive on making such dreams come true.

I must admit that at times I've secretly wondered if anyone would be able to work such a transformation on me. Would people look at my before and after pictures and say, "Wow! I can't believe that's the same person!" But even if such a transformation were accomplished, at night when all of the makeup was washed off and the hairdo brushed out, the facade would be gone, and I'd look in the mirror only to see the "real me" again.

When I was a student in college our women's dean would often point us to a paraphrase of a Bible text inscribed on the wall of our dorm lobby, one we passed by several times a day. It said, "The king's daughters . . . all glorious within."

"Remember," our dean would say, "you are all daughters of a king—the King of the universe. And He wants you to be all glorious within."

People may not be able to see any physical beauty in me now, but God is working on me from the inside out. The exterior will have to wait until later. He is working to make me all glorious "within." And that will take a lot more than makeup. But I'm not discouraged, because His specialty is "makeovers." Remember the before and after "pictures" of Mary Magdalene, Rahab, the woman caught in adultery, and the woman at the well? He has one terrific portfolio!

I'm looking forward to seeing my after "picture" in the book of life and listening to the awed inhabitants of the universe say, "I can't believe that's the same person!" It will be a truly transforming miracle, made possible through the spilled blood of Jesus. And it will be a makeover that will last throughout eternity. The only thing that will wash away will be my sin.

But in the meantime, when there are times that it seems I still strongly resemble my before picture, please have patience with me, because God is not finished with me yet.   NANCY CACHERO VASQUEZ

JANUARY 22

Plague Spot

Serve one another in love. Gal. 5:13, NIV.

A young ruler came to Jesus and asked, "What shall I do that I may inherit eternal life?" Actually, he didn't just come up to Jesus. We are told he ran after Him and, kneeling at Jesus' feet, asked with sincerity and earnestness the question that had been pressing him.

Jesus asked this eager young man to look beyond the fact that he was keeping all the commandments and see the necessity of heart devotion. Jesus wanted him to give of himself. He needed the love of God to replace the love of self. Jesus called upon him to choose between the heavenly treasure and worldly greatness. Christ's words were really the same invitation that we read in today's verse.

Jesus had shown him the plague spot in his character. He wanted the heavenly treasure, but he also wanted the advantages his earthly riches would bring him. He loved the gifts of God more than he loved the Giver.

To give is an attribute of God. The greatest gift of all was given by God when He gave all He had. He gave the gift of His Son. The young ruler's wealth was a gift from God. Jesus was asking him to use it by sharing it with those in need.

God has entrusted each of us with gifts to share. Our gift may be talents, opportunities, or wealth. Often our gift may be nothing more than an ability to share of ourselves. What He is asking us to do in return for these gifts is to surrender ourselves to Him—to allow Him to show us our plague spot.

May we use the heavenly eyesalve to discern our plague spot. May we ask for the Spirit of God to lead us to yield to the invitation

to give of ourselves. This is a lifelong learning process. As we participate in this experience, may we think of the invitation and give of
ourselves on a regular basis throughout the year—to give of our talents, our opportunities to reach out to others, as well as giving of our
material wealth. We are being asked today to take part in this attribute of God. Let us answer this call and give wholly of ourselves.

JEANETTE BRYSON

JANUARY 23

Does God Really Care? Stop and Listen!

And all things, whatsoever ye shall ask in prayer, believing, ye
shall receive. Matt. 21:22.

*E*arly on a cold January morning we heard a knock on our
front door. Our neighbor's daughter stood there holding
Fluffy, our 14-year-old eight-pound white poodle. Our neighbor
had found Fluffy wandering around about a block up the street.
Because of a cardiac problem, in the past year Fluffy had become
partially deaf, blind, unsteady on her feet, and gradually more disoriented. I began to fear that someday she would become lost, so
when I was at home I monitored her frequently when she went out
through her pet door.

When I returned home late that same evening I went upstairs to
our bedroom to check on Fluffy. Her bed was empty, and she was
nowhere to be found. I called out to my husband, who was working on the computer, to help me look for Fluffy.

We took off in our car to search the streets while our neighbors,
on foot, helped search the immediate neighborhood. In addition to
being a dark, moonless evening, our task was made even more difficult because we do not have streetlights in our subdivision. And
the weather forecast was calling for freezing temperatures throughout the weekend.

I was hysterically crying and begging the Lord, who takes care
of the birds and knows the number of hairs on our heads, to please
let me find my Fluffy before she would freeze, starve, or be otherwise injured and die out in the cold.

By the time we began our second trip around the division, I was
so anxious I could not think clearly. When I finally stopped for a few
minutes to gather my composure a thought came to my mind: *"Stop*

and *listen* to the Lord." A calm feeling flooded my soul. I thanked the Lord and asked Him to direct me where to go next. The thought came to my mind to go once more over the route that Fluffy had taken that morning. I turned the car around and calmly informed my husband that I would take one more drive in that direction.

We'd gone just a short distance down our street when I saw Fluffy, limping slowly across the road. "Thank You, Lord, for caring, loving, and hearing me!" I prayed joyfully.

"Stop and listen." A women's retreat speaker I once heard suggested that just as the Lord is willing to listen to us we too need to be willing to stop and listen to Him. By reading the Scriptures we reinforce our mind with His Word and begin to understand His great love for us. Thus, we begin to mature and tune into His leading, and when in trouble we are then able to lean with trust and assurance on Him.

Does God care? Oh, yes, He really cares. The Scriptures are full of promises of His care if we would only *stop* and *listen*.

ERIKA OLFERT

JANUARY 24

When It's Too Late to Pray

When the Lord saw her, his heart went out to her and he said, "Don't cry." Luke 7:13, NIV.

First, her husband. Now her son. The widow sat down at the kitchen table. For days she had cared for her son, hoping the fever would break. "You're going to make it." She would squeeze his hand and cheer him on. But always, always the fever returned with greater intensity. Now she rested at the table, but only for a moment. She had to make funeral arrangements.

As the widow trudged through town with the funeral procession she felt that Someone was watching. She looked up into the face of a Man.

"He said, 'Don't cry.' Then he went up and touched the coffin, and those carrying it stood still. He said, 'Young man, I say to you, get up!' The dead man sat up and began to talk, and Jesus gave him back to his mother" (Luke 7:13-15).

The people in the procession were amazed and said, "God has come to help his people" (verse 16). God has come to help His people. What an insight! It sounds so simple, but in the rush of our daily lives we often forget that God *has* come to help His people. God has come to help you. God has come to help me. Here. Now. But how?

Can you think of any problem in your life that is too big for God to handle? The widow's son was dead! What could be more irreversible than that? It was time to quit praying and start mourning. But Jesus saw the hopeless situation and did something about it. It is never too late to pray. A Christian author states it beautifully:

"Prayer is the answer to every problem in life. It puts us in tune with divine wisdom, which knows how to adjust everything perfectly. So often we do not pray in certain situations, because, from our standpoint, the outlook is hopeless. But nothing is impossible with God. Nothing is so entangled that it cannot be made right by the loving Spirit of God. No mistake is so serious that it cannot be remedied. No human relation is too strained for God to bring about reconciliation and understanding. No habit is so deep rooted that it cannot be overcome. . . . Whatever we need or desire, if we trust God, He will supply it" (*Review and Herald,* Oct. 7, 1965).

No, God is not in the business of changing every unpleasant situation in our lives. Sometimes He only changes us. When we pray persistently, He gives us the insight to know how to deal with whatever problems life throws at us. He gives us the strength to endure them, and that in itself changes circumstances. Come to think of it, changing us may be a bigger miracle than resurrecting a loved one!

It is never too late to pray. God has come to help His people.

KAREN LINDENSMITH

JANUARY 25

Where Was I?

For I know the plans I have for you . . . plans to prosper you and not to harm you, plans to give you hope and a future. Jer. 29:11, NIV.

*W*hen things go wrong, plans fail, or tragedy strikes, we are compelled to ask, "Where was God when—?" For many Christians the answer is in faith alone. For me, I've recognized His presence in comfort, and where it fit His will, in intervention. In some circumstances, though, to wait for an answer was the answer—perhaps as it unfolds here, or will be later revealed in the earth made new. Either way, the Lord has promised that I have a place and purpose in all His moves.

To help me hold on while I must wait, I ask a different kind of question:

Where was I . . .

. . . when God the Father, His Son, and the Holy Spirit created the foundations of the world?

On Their minds as They surveyed how I would fit into Their scheme. So They designed me in detail to contribute to the world around me.

. . . when in Eden came the Fall?

On the Father's heart when it broke for all humanity, when He began planning a way so I wouldn't be eternally separated from Him.

. . . when David's psalms proved him the victor over the stings of life?

In the triune's inspiration that moved Their messenger to write those words to uplift and strengthen me.

. . . when Jesus' warm voice bade the children to sit at His feet?

Among the soiled but eager ones, who would always be accepted and embraced.

. . . when in Gethsemane, the Saviour pleaded on raw knees?

Between palms folded in prayer. It was for my sin, when in agony He moved His thirsty lips.

. . . when Christ carried the world's burden, the sin, the cross?

My weight bore down on His shoulders. Mine was the splinter that caught on His torn robe . . . that pricked at His hands . . . that drew first blood.

. . . when the stone rolled out to give way to the Bright and Morning Star?

The thought of me was His purpose, His motivation to come forth from darkness to light. The thought of me . . . And He did it anyway.

. . . when He designed a home in heaven and promised to return to take me there?

In His every plan, so that where He is, I may be also.

And where I was, you were too.   ROSALYNDA "GINI" KOSINI

Does Jesus Care?

Casting all your care upon Him, for He cares for you. 1 Peter 5:7, NKJV.

Arriving at the spiritual retreat in Nome during the winter of 1995, I felt the excitement in the air. Several women asked me, "Have you heard about the 14-year-old boy who unexpectedly got here from Selawick?"

It seems that a special teacher in his school offered to pay his way to this winter's retreat. In 1993 he had become a Christian and had given his life to Jesus. Little did I know that today's text would be illustrated in the life of this young Eskimo boy. At meeting time I noticed this adventuresome young man, Lory Larkin, had made a new friend and was sitting on the front row in eager anticipation of the opening meeting. That's where he would sit at every meeting.

Caris Lauda, a caring, enthusiastic retired pastor, was the evening speaker. He told us of a previous trip to Selawick, Alaska, in 1969 or 1970, during which he had recorded a 100-year-old grandma singing a song. The tape recorder was turned on, and we were amazed to hear Lory's great-grandma Larkin singing, "'Does Jesus care when my way is dark with a nameless dread and fear? As the daylight fades into deep night shades . . .'"

The words of this old hymn, written at the turn of the century, were taken from our text today. I am sure to Grandma Larkin the words had a deeper meaning than they would to most people. Selawick is a small village located above the Arctic Circle where the sun shines only a few minutes a day during the winter. There the word "dark" takes on an added dimension.

The next evening many of us were waiting in the Nome airport, grounded for six hours on account of weather problems. During that time I had the opportunity to become better acquainted with Lory. He was looking forward to telling his dad about hearing his great-grandmother sing. A village so isolated from the rest of the world had given us a message that Jesus cares.

Does Jesus care? Yes, He does! More than 25 years had passed since Pastor Lauda had recorded that song. More than 10 years before Lory was born, a message had been left for him. I'm sure he will never forget that Saturday evening when we heard a frail voice sing, "Does Jesus Care?" As the chorus says: "O yes, He cares—I know He cares! . . . When the days are weary, the long nights dreary, I know my Saviour cares."

How loud that message resounded! May each of us always remember: He cares! — RITA STEVENS

Repaired Anew

Like clay in the hand of the potter, so are you in my hand. Jer. 18:6, NIV.

*M*y home contains many keepsakes from my travels around the globe. I look at the silk screens and see the town in which I had lived in Japan. Each memento triggers many memories of people, places, and events. The ivory reminds me of Hong Kong; the lacquerware of Vietnam.

One day I took a last look around as I closed and locked the front door. I would be away for six weeks on a trip through Central America. Although I would miss my home, I was looking forward to my trip.

The time passed rapidly, and all too soon I found myself pulling into my driveway. I could hardly wait to unpack and arrange my new mementos. I opened the front door and discovered, to my horror, that my home had been robbed and vandalized during my absence. I felt outraged that a stranger had violated my little sanctuary on earth.

Quickly I took inventory and, to my great dismay, found that some of my most treasured mementos were among the most damaged. Some of them, including the Oriental fans and lamps (collector's items), were absolutely irreplaceable. I could not bring myself to part with these special treasures. I would simply have to find a way to fix them. Out came the soldering iron, wire, mending tape, glue, and other items that I used in a meticulous marathon to repair each treasure.

Usually I do not keep broken or damaged items, but these mended pieces have become even more valuable to me. As I view and touch them now, I know each scar, each reinforced tear, each mended crack. They are mine. Bought and labored over with love to restore them as close to perfection as possible.

During this process I discovered another dimension of God's

love. Our Lord purchased us when we were broken and damaged in some way. Fortunately, we were counted too valuable to discard. All heaven cooperated, spending hours on repairs, reinforcement, and reinstatement. Our cracks are mended, our tears repaired, our brokenness healed through spiritual surgery.

Treasuring and cherishing us, God loves human beings unconditionally. We can know that even though damaged, we are counted as valuable. LORNA L. LAWRENCE

JANUARY 28

A Morning Prayer

It is a good thing to give thanks unto the Lord, and to sing praises unto thy name, O most High. Ps. 92:1.

This day is mine to use, dear Lord:
Each moment is sublime.
I thank You for this precious gift,
This sacred part of time.

I thank You for awaking me
To see this brand-new day,
And for the privilege I have
To use it as I may.

I thank You for Your promise, Lord,
To ever be with me;
And as I face today I seek
A closer walk with Thee.

I thank You for the strength You'll give
For me to work and play,
And for Your power to overcome
The evil one today.

I thank You for the good I'll do
Because You guide me, Lord;
And for the peace of mind I'll have
By trusting in Your Word.

I thank You for the friends I'll meet
And for the love I'll share.
I thank You for the chance to show
Some sinner that You care.

Again, I thank You for this gift
In sacred trust to me,
And may each precious hour be used
To praise and honor Thee.

DAPHNIE M. CORRODUS

JANUARY 29

She Pleased God

By faith Enoch was translated that he should not see death; and was not found because God had translated him: for before his translation he had this testimony, that he pleased God. Heb. 11:5.

For many years I have read the faith chapter, which has also been called the Bible's Hall of Fame. Until recently all I saw about Enoch was that by faith he was translated and did not see death. Studying it in depth recently my eyes caught these three words: *he pleased God.* Then I thought, *Wouldn't it be nice if at my memorial service (should I sleep before the return of Jesus) it could be said of me, "She pleased God"?*

Some women of the Bible had the same problems many women face today. They met them, and pleased God.

Does anyone reading this have a mother-in-law problem? Ruth, a widow of Moab, might have. She loved her husband's mother, even leaving her homeland to go with Naomi. Even though Ruth was a good woman, she took counsel from Naomi and followed her advice. Not only were these two kindred spirits, but Ruth accepted her mother-in-law's God, the true God of Israel. Ruth pleased God.

Is anyone married to a hard-hearted, tightfisted husband? Think of Abigail, married to Nabal, a drunkard, and an arrogant man who refused to furnish David's men provisions for when their food supply was low. When Abigail heard of it from one of Nabal's workmen, she immediately prepared baskets of food, loaded them on the asses, and delivered the provisions in person to David. Not until the next morning, when Nabal was sober, did she tell him what she had done. Her intervention prevented David's men from coming and killing her husband. Abigail pleased God by her wise and understanding ways.

Priscilla, with her husband, Aquila, was a tentmaker. They were both climbing the success ladder together and earning an honest living. They worked hand-in-hand, and while making tents preached the story of Jesus Christ to Jews and Gentiles. Their Christianity was evident in the workplace, in the synagogue, and in their home.

Is any reader a widow, a single parent, or in a divided home? Timothy's mother, Eunice, will always be remembered as one who believed in the Old Testament scripture "Train up a child in the way he should go" (Prov. 22:6). She and her mother, Lois, believed in the importance of early childhood training. They gave to the known world in their day a young man dedicated to God and devoted to the apostle Paul, with whom he labored so faithfully. Truly, Eunice pleased God in the rearing of her son.

Living to please God is my aim. What's yours?

Marion Seitz Simmons

January 30

A Lesson in Love

Share with God's people who are in need. Practice hospitality. Rom. 12:13, NIV.

Daylight was fading when we arrived in Sucava, Bukovina, a city in northeastern Romania. We were travel-weary, for we'd spent all day sightseeing through the beautiful Carpathian Mountains. I was excited by everything. Not only did I treasure visiting with my daughter Robyn—a teacher in a Romanian Adventist high school—but my grandmother had been born in Bukovina. I'd never imagined I would actually visit the land of her birth.

Arriving in Sucava, we discovered that the empty apartment we'd planned to use for three days had been rented, so Lari, our escort and guide, went to plan B. Lari also worked at the high school and knew students in town. After a phone call he told us we'd be staying with one of them.

It seemed such an imposition. Three people—including a total stranger—barging in unannounced. It just wasn't done! I whispered my feelings to Robyn. The typical Romanian apartment has one bedroom, and I cringed at the thought of our hosts being polite while figuring out what in the world to do with us.

Danny welcomed us in. His mother was still at work, he said. His father was away. We piled luggage and backpacks in their entry, and I sat down on the couch while Robyn and Lari made themselves at home. They knew Danny. They'd been there before.

Then Lari sat down beside me and, speaking softly, said, "I know this isn't what we'd planned." (Obviously Robyn had *told!*) "And if you are not happy, we can go to a guesthouse. But they do not mind our staying."

I nodded, unconvinced.

Mrs. Rastoaca arrived moments later. Lari introduced me—interpreting both English and Romanian. She kissed me on both cheeks in welcome, then bustled about to make sure we had supper. At bedtime she went to a cot in the kitchen. Robyn and I slept in her bed.

We spent the next day, Friday, sightseeing from one attractive village to another, returning a little before sundown. We were hot and dusty, and remembered that the apartment complex temporarily had no hot water. Mrs. Rastoaca greeted us with a smile, a hug, and lilting Romanian. A huge pot of water simmered on her stove so we could wash up.

The next day we had dinner with another family, and spent the afternoon discussing our world church. I ached to know Romanian so a translator wouldn't be necessary. Mrs. Rastoaca was a pediatric nurse in an orphanage and asked if we'd like to visit it. We spent a wonderful hour playing with the babies.

The telephone was ringing when we returned to Danny's apartment. It was another family, the Boiculeses. They'd been expecting us for supper. Oops! So out we went again. More good food—bread, tangy soft cheese, stuffed peppers, and plums for desert. A bag of leftovers was urged on us as we said goodbye.

"I'll eat with you on your last morning here," Mrs. Rastoaca said shyly as we sat down to breakfast the next day. Afterward, she too filled a bag with food for us to enjoy on our return trip.

It's humbling to be so totally and splendidly wrong!

But what a lesson in New Testament hospitality.

PENNY ESTES WHEELER

The Birth of a New Day

In the morning, O Lord, you hear my voice; in the morning I lay
my requests before you and wait in expectation. Ps. 5:3, NIV.

*O*ne of the joys of my life has been the early-morning hours,
watching a new day dawn as darkness turns to light. My
mind floods with happy memories of childhood life on the farm—
the faithful horses waiting at the gate to be fed; rounding up the
milking cows; paddocks, white with frost; the feel of frozen grass
crackling underfoot, while fingers and toes were numb with cold;
and each breath bringing condensation like smoke around my face.
Sitting on a small stool, bucket between my knees, head buried in
the cow's warm flank, I'd listen to the rhythmic song of milk streaming into the bucket.

With spring, the countryside turned green, trees and gardens
blazed with color, and birdsongs filled the early morning air as both
birds and animals rejoiced with me in the new day. During summer
months the early morning raids on the orchard or vineyard brought
their own rewards. Running into the wind on a balmy autumn morning—how I thrilled to the wind in my face. What a joy to be alive!

With the years came change. Student nursing days. Mornings
filled with caring for the sick, and an inner joy with each smile of
appreciation as patients were made comfortable and ready to face a
new day. Then a different scene. Walking the tree-lined road from
house to mission hospital in Kenya. The countryside, dotted with
the thatch-roofed homes of the local families. Happy and contented
children wending their way toward a water tap, containers balanced
on their heads. The gentle land breeze drifting toward beautiful
Lake Victoria . . . Each new day a joy to be alive!

Today I walk the streets of suburbia. Each new day still has its
own beauty and character. Some days dawn with a clear sky, and
the beautiful morning star attracts my attention as I look upward.
These mornings remind me of the times in my life when "all is well
with my soul." Then come the clouds, without a break to let the
light shine through. How like those many times in my life when all
is darkness, and light seems far away. Sometimes the rain falls. What
happiness it brings, especially after a long, dry summer, as I watch
the earth respond with new life. We all need "showers of blessing"
to wash away cares and despondency.

Some mornings when the sky is alive with color—colors that no human artist could paint—I walk with my head lifted up, lest I miss any of the beauty. I thank the Lord for each new day, for the joy of being able to see such beauty, and I invite Him to bring beauty and compassion into my life that others may get to know my Creator, Sustainer, and Redeemer. The laugh of the kookaburra and the warble of the magpie in the stillness of the morning bring music to my ears.

Let us recognize each new day as a special gift, as a time to draw near and commune with our Lord, and give thanks for His continued blessings that are "new every morning."   VEYRL DAWN WERE

FEBRUARY 1

Reacting With Love

If someone says, "I love God," and hates his brother, he is a liar; for he who does not love his brother whom he has seen, how can he love God whom he has not seen? 1 John 4:20, NKJV.

*W*e enter into some form of dialogue often during the day. Friends meeting friends. Exchanging news and information. Yet sometimes this simple act of sharing can wound the innocent and guilty alike.

"Have you heard the latest?"

"Yes, I just don't understand."

"Nor I! How could she have done it?"

"And that's not all. I heard that . . . Can you believe it?"

Snippets of news. Gossip. Conversations. As I listened, my mind traveled to another place and time. Jesus sits quietly, teaching the people. Suddenly the picture changes. A sneering group of scribes and Pharisees pushes a frightened woman into the midst of the gathering. The leader shouts triumphantly, "She's been caught in the act of adultery. Surely she deserves to die!"

How would you answer?

In exaggerated tones the man continues, "Now Moses, in the law, commanded us that she should be stoned. But what do You say?"

Jesus' immense compassion shines through. He stoops down and writes on the ground with His finger, as though He does not hear.

"So when they continued asking Him, He raised Himself up and said to them, 'He who is without sin among you, let him throw a stone at her first'" (John 8:7, NKJV).

Are you amazed that Jesus didn't write out the woman's sins? Instead, He began listing those sins of the scribes and Pharisees, beginning with the oldest down to the youngest man present. What a God! Silently each man vanished as he saw his sins written in the dust. Jesus gave each man a bold yet gentle reminder that we are to love and understand—not condemn and destroy.

Lord, as Your daughter, how can I say that I love You, that I am becoming more like You, and then hurt another? How can I pass on stories that doom a sister or brother to be despised, discouraged, or cast out if I am truly filled with Your love? Empower me to protect and guide those around me. Help me reach out with Your divine, compassionate love. Let me speak the language of heaven. Where once I stood as judge and jury, let me kneel at Your feet in prayer and supplication. You say it so clearly: "As the Father loved Me, I also have loved you: abide in My love" (John 15:9, NKJV). Lord, let me demonstrate this kind of love to others.

GINGER MOSTERT CHURCH

FEBRUARY 2

Dog Lovers, Beware!

Woe unto them that are wise in their own eyes, and prudent in their own sight! Isa. 5:21.

Our family was visiting my brother in Georgia for the first time. We would be attending my husband's family reunion in the same city.

My brother had a large black dog chained in the backyard. The dog's name was Bear, and indeed he did look like a bear! He looked kind of friendly, but my brother warned us that he was the terror of the neighborhood whenever he got out of the yard.

My entire family loves dogs, but especially my husband, Joe, who grew up with lots of dogs and cats. Without telling anyone, Joe decided to befriend Bear. Walking to the dog's fence, he extended his hand. Bear tucked his tail and backed up. Joe stepped forward and extended his hand farther. The dog backed up again and barked.

Not the least bit discouraged by the dog's lack of sociability, Joe pressed on. Petting this dog would be a challenge. Again Joe reached out to pet Bear. The dog growled and suddenly lunged forward, giving Joe's right hand a nasty bite.

We couldn't understand why, after three warnings from the dog, Joe would pursue this friendship. No explanation made any sense. He just wanted to pet him. His hand was swollen and terribly painful for the remainder of our vacation. This, of course, meant curtailed activities, doctor's visits, antibiotics, pain medicine, X-rays, consultations, and eventually surgery and physical therapy that restored 95 percent use of his right hand again. Fortunately, he is left-handed, so he was able to function fairly comfortably after two weeks of great discomfort.

Isn't our relationship with the devil like this? We reach out, foolishly, knowing danger is imminent. Still we reach out, hoping for the slightest indication that this "bear" will become friendly, even against all odds. If we'd only realize the danger before it's too late! When the devil sinks his teeth into our tender skin, the wounds go deep. The scars usually last forever.

Thanks be to God, our attending physician, for being able to bring physical and spiritual healing to our wounds and make us whole again. IRIS L. STOVALL

My Weakness = The Lord's Strength

Have mercy upon me, O Lord; for I am weak: O Lord, heal me; for my bones are vexed. Ps. 6:2.

It was a Sabbath morning in spring. We had organized a special spring festival Sabbath in our little church in Germany, and I was involved in organizing several special items. The children, whose leader I was at the time, were performing, and I was to sing a song. All this would not have been so terrifying if I had not had a terrible cold that seemed rooted in my vocal cords. The cold made me very weak, my head was spinning, and my voice was scratchy.

My solo was the last number. I had the children all organized for their pieces, and everything went well. During that time, however, I felt a war raging inside me. One voice suggested that I not perform—the congregation would understand. They could see, and would certainly hear, that I was not feeling well. The other voice suggested that I go ahead and trust in the strength of the Lord.

"I have no trouble trusting in You, Lord, but this is different," I argued. I didn't want to make a fool of myself. I didn't want to ruin the lovely program. I didn't want to sound like a crow trying to sing like a nightingale. "Lord, I want to glorify *You* this morning. I want to sing for *You* and not for myself. I want these people to hear *You* through me. I leave it all up to You."

My turn came. I stood before the congregation, weak, spinning head, and crow-voiced. I quickly sent another emergency prayer to heaven. And then I sang—like I had never sung before. My voice was sweet and sure, my head stopped spinning, and I felt strong. In fact, I felt as if someone were standing behind me and holding me up, giving me strength. As soon as I finished, my weakness, spinning head, and croaky voice returned.

This experience is special to me, and I marvel every time I think about it.   Beate Karbstein

February 4

What First?

But seek ye first the kingdom of God, and his righteousness; and all these things shall be added unto you. Matt. 6:33.

Lord, I'm so busy, as busy as can be.
Surely You have noticed me working diligently.
I've laundry to do and a house to clean,
And You must see that garden I've got to glean.

I'm sure that You've seen me going off to work.
I must earn a living—this duty I can't shirk.
Why, I've shopping to do and bills to pay.
It just keeps me hopping all through the day.

Time is so valuable, and I don't want to waste it.
So I work hard to savor life, to really "taste" it.
I've meetings to go to and meetings to chair.
I've got to bathe the children and comb their hair.

The clock keeps moving, and I must keep up.
I have three kittens and a cute little pup.
I must take them to the vet today and give them
    baths, too.
And I just don't know if I'll have any time for You.

I don't mean to be disrespectful or leave You out.
I'm just trying to figure out what life's all about.
I've been meaning to give You more time in my life.
I suppose if I did I'd have so much less strife.

But really, God, I just don't know how to fit You in.
Could You teach me how to be like a child once again?
To take time to listen, and learn how to grow,
And how to really live and be happy, and let others
    know?

My priorities aren't right, and that sure is true!
I want to learn to be busy getting to know You.
That's where true quality time is, and where I want to be.
Please, God, teach me to let go of this selfish me.

I want to put You first in all that I do,
To put "things of earth" last and be true to You.
I know that if I put You first on my list,
All else will fall into place, and I will be blessed.

Lord, teach me, change me, and make me today
All that You want me to be, here and always.
Please fill me with Your sweet Spirit, and let me be
Always, forever, busy with Thee.

PATRICIA WILSON

FEBRUARY 5

God's Quilt

But he knoweth the way that I take: when he hath tried me, I shall come forth as gold. Job 23:10.

*A*s a new quilter, I have been amazed by the correlation between quilting and living a Christian life. In our first class introduction, I found it mind-boggling that the hundreds of designs came from the five basic geometric figures—circle, oval, rectangle, square, and triangle.

Aren't we all different personalities, yet each one of us has the same basic functions?

Next I had to choose the design, quilt size, fabric, and colors. This is a very personal, and often excruciating, decision that only I could make.

God, too, gives each of us the power of choice.

After the fabric was washed and ironed to prevent shrinking, I was ready to make my templates. The directions gave explicit measurements that must be strictly adhered to if I didn't want to end up with a big mess. Through trials, errors, and some successes, I sewed my pieces together, referring often to the directions and example. Fortunately, our teacher was always there—helping, patient, kind, and enjoying my successes as much as I did.

God has given explicit guidelines to enable each of us to live a life that is pleasing to Him. He knows how beautiful colors can be when sewn together in love. As our teacher, God too is loving, long-suffering, and so patient and forgiving as we choose and prepare the fabrics of our lives, rearranging and redoing our life pieces over and over again to form a correct and beautiful design.

It gives me confidence knowing that through all the trials, setbacks, and mistakes I may make, God does know the way I am taking, and I too can become someone very beautiful and very precious to Him.

LUCILLE A. TAYLOR

FEBRUARY 6

Making the Impossible Possible

This may seem impossible to you, but not with God, because with Him nothing is impossible. Mark 10:27, Clear Word.

It had been months since I last saw her. She said she'd been ill, her husband was out of work, and all their utilities had been shut off. They needed $50 for the water bill, $75 for the electric bill, and $125 for the gas bill. She was going to a local agency that morning to see if they would help. We talked for a few minutes, and I offered several suggestions and told her I'd pray for them. I left as soon as possible.

As I drove away from their home, a battle began to rage within me. That family needed *my* help. But what could I do? Then I remembered a small savings account that I seldom used. I thought it had about $40 in it. Not much, but I could give them what I had.

I asked the bank teller for the balance in my account. To my surprise, the balance was more than enough to pay the gas bill. Receipt in hand, I returned to her house later that afternoon. She met me with a smile. The agency had paid the electric bill, and a stranger had bought the old car parked in their driveway for $50—just enough to pay the water bill. Her only worry now was how to pay the gas bill.

We embraced, and I pressed a greeting card into her hand containing the receipt for the gas bill. With tears streaming down my cheeks, I left in haste, marveling that my God had done the impossible. All their utility bills had been paid in one day.

I wonder how often we limit God by concentrating on what we don't have, rather than saying "I'll give what I have." Do we forget that "our little becomes much when we place it in the hands of God"?

God can use us to make the impossible possible.

BARBARA J. HALES

FEBRUARY 7

Blessings for Me—Today

Now when he saw the crowds, he went up on a mountainside and sat down. His disciples came to him, and he began to teach them, saying . . . Matthew 5:1, 2, NIV.

lessed are the poor in spirit, for theirs is the kingdom of heaven" (verse 3, NIV). When I am spiritually needy, God will fill that need with His righteousness.

"Blessed are those who mourn, for they will be comforted" (verse 4, NIV). When I repent of my sins and feel guilty and discouraged over my lack of progress in the Christian way, God will forgive me and comfort me with the assurance of His constant acceptance and love.

"Blessed are the meek, for they will inherit the earth" (verse 5, NIV). If I am willing to be led by God instead of trying to control my own life, He will give me every good thing (for me) on this earth. He will lead me so that I will indeed have the deep desires of my heart in this life.

"Blessed are those who hunger and thirst for righteousness, for they will be filled" (verse 6, NIV). If I eagerly and earnestly seek God's way through daily time with Him and an all-day prayer attitude, if this is the top priority in my life, He will, indeed, fill all the loneliness and insecurity with His love so that I will be satisfied.

"Blessed are the merciful, for they will be shown mercy" (verse 7, NIV). If I am forgiving and tolerant of others, always thinking the best of everyone, believing that they, too, are growing in Christ, God will be merciful and forgiving toward me. And that same attitude will be reflected back to me from other people.

"Blessed are the pure in heart, for they will see God" (verse 8, NIV). If I always do the right thing because it is right, even though it may be unpopular, and live a life of integrity before God, one day I will see Him face-to-face. Because I have nothing to hide, I will also see His ways now more clearly.

"Blessed are the peacemakers, for they will be called sons of God" (verse 9, NIV). If I show God's spirit of peace and help others get along peaceably, God will call me His daughter and claim me as a real member of the heavenly family.

I will, in the end, be filled with happiness and a deep, abiding joy, for I will be walking hand in hand with Christ through every day, no matter what it brings.   DONNA J. HABENICHT

FEBRUARY 8

Making Your Own Shadow

I can do everything through him who gives me strength. Phil. 4:13, NIV.

My sister was pretty, while I was plain. She was fun and vivacious, while I was quiet, studious, and conscientious to the extreme. Everyone loved her. People would even stop on the street to admire and talk to her. They didn't seem to notice me.

At school, however, things were different. Margaret was not academically inclined, and loved mischief more than math. She was popular with everyone in the school, and although she did enough work to get by, she was made to feel inferior to her big sister. "Why can't you be more like Audrey?" was a phrase that often rang in her ears at school.

The damage had been done. Margaret grew up in my shadow, believing that I could do everything better than she could. A loving husband, two beautiful children, and lots of friends did nothing to dispel that early misconception. Even when she became a Christian and realized how much she was valued by God, Margaret still labored under the mistaken idea that somehow she was not quite good enough.

Then God decided to show her that her attributes are as valuable in His sight as any academic achievement. He sent her Lavine, a baby with so many disabilities that all she can do is hear. When Lavine's parents couldn't look after her, she was fostered by Margaret's friend, Mary, with Margaret helping her. After a time Margaret and Norman assumed full care of Lavine. They learned to change a tracheotomy tube, to carry a suction unit with them at all times, to deal with epilepsy, cerebral palsy, paralysis, and blindness, while at the same time stimulating Lavine through the only senses left to her, touch and hearing. They learned to deal with doctors, consultants, social workers, and attorneys.

Through all this, Margaret was learning that she was valuable. My sister no longer lives in my shadow. Her own shadow grows longer every day, and she is living proof that "I can do everything through him who gives me strength."

All of us are equal in God's sight. The lowliest worker is of as much worth to God as the highest executive in the land. We each need to realize that God has work for us to do. If you are housebound, God can use you. No matter what your abilities are, He can use you. Just give Him your heart and your life and you will never again feel inferior to another, for He will assure you that you are the daughter of the King.

AUDREY BALDERSTONE

FEBRUARY 9

Beet Juice

Blessed is he whose transgressions are forgiven, whose sins are covered. Ps. 32:1, NIV.

As a college student more than a half century ago, I traveled with my parents to visit my aunt Nell and uncle Joe in South Lancaster, Massachusetts. I especially wanted to be on my best behavior for two reasons: my favorite aunt and my fiancé would be there.

Aunt Nell was preparing dinner, so I wandered into the kitchen to help. There on the stove was something I had never seen before. It was a fat kettle, with a heavy lid securely fastened on it. A little cap dangled atop the lid. My aunt said it was a pressure cooker.

I had heard about this marvelous invention but had never seen one in operation. I was fascinated by it. As I watched, the cap on the lid began to wobble back and forth ever so slightly. The wobbling increased. Now each time it wobbled, a shot of steam was rhythmically released. Something wasn't right. Perhaps if I steadied it the problem would be corrected. Carefully I raised my finger and gently touched the side of the cap.

To my utter horror, the cap blew off with such force it startled me. A column of steam shot upward, and there on the ceiling appeared a brilliant spot of red beet juice—two feet wide! Embarrassment cannot describe my feeling. With no place to hide, no possible way to remove the spot, and too proud to cry, I stood there, panic-stricken, silently asking God to make it disappear somehow. I knew my aunt Nell had every right to be angry with me. And all I could say was "I'm so sorry!"

From the corner of my eye I saw her approaching, and in a moment I felt her comforting arm around me. "Don't feel bad," she whispered. "Tomorrow the painters are coming to redecorate the whole house, and that spot will disappear."

Disappear! God had already answered my prayer! The spot *would* be removed! Oh, how grateful I was.

Through these more than 50 years this experience, so devastating to me then, has been a blessing I will not forget. Like the stain of beet juice on that pure white ceiling, our hearts can become stained with sin, seemingly too great to be forgiven. We're ready to give up, for we see no way out of our dilemma. Then our Saviour, with a heart full of love, embraces us and whispers forgiveness. Yes, and He promises to make the stain disappear.

Oh, what a loving Friend we have, whose arms are extended wide to comfort, to cleanse, and to bring healing to our hearts!

LORRAINE HUDGINS

The Riddle

In the midst of the street of it, and on either side of the river, was there the tree of life . . . and yielded her fruit every month. Rev. 22:2.

The other day my 13-year-old son came to me with a riddle he had made up. "If the Lord revealed to you that you were going to die in two hours, what food would you like to eat?" he asked.

Without hesitation I told him that I would lose my appetite. Food would be of no interest to me.

The next person he asked gave him her list of favorites—macaroni and cheese, chicken, gingerbread with an extra heaping of whipped cream—and she went on and on. I could not understand how she would be hungry, knowing she was going to die in two hours.

Self-examination is hard work, but once I had time to think about my answer to my son's question I had to admit that my spiritual life needed some assistance. Whenever I am upset or anxious or under heavy stress, food is the furtherest thing from my mind. Quite honestly, I lose my appetite. Why should death and the reward promised to us as Christians reduce me to a state of loss of appetite? If I am assured that my spiritual condition is all that God expects it to be and all that it can be by my diligence, then I will not feel anxious, upset, or stressed, and certainly I will be able to think of something to eat.

Christ offers the bread of life in His Word to all of us, and if eaten daily it will take care all life's upsets and anxious moments and will alleviate stress. With the strength and confidence we are to have in God and His Word, I can now give the correct answer to my son's riddle: I would ask to eat of the tree of life.

May we eat and be nourished on God's Word today and every day, beginning now, so that we can have the assurance God offers and indeed eat of the tree of life. BETTY-ANNE LOWE

A Cry in the Night

Praise the Lord, you his angels, you mighty ones who do his bidding, who obey his word. Ps. 103:20, NIV.

As the rain beat down heavily on the tin roof of the old farmhouse and the lightning flashed, I gathered my two little ones about me, reading to them the familiar Bible stories from their favorite Bible storybook. The thunder was especially loud during this storm, and at times it was even difficult to continue the reading, but our bedtime story hour came to an end and our two little ones were tucked into their beds at the end of the hall. I got ready for bed and comforted myself with further spiritual reading.

The storm continued. At times it was frightening to live several miles out of town in the upstairs of an old farmhouse. Finally I heard the sound of a car coming up the long gravel driveway. My pastor husband had arrived home from his evening's church work. Soon he appeared in the bedroom and began to prepare for bed. During our conversation regarding his activities of the evening, the loudest clap of thunder of all banged over our heads. I thought I heard the children cry and asked my husband to go to their room and check on them.

As he opened our door we were shocked to find the hall filled with smoke. Lightning had struck the house! He ran to the top of the stairs only to find flames of red reflecting on the landing at the bottom. Immediately we made our way down the stairs. We were able to pass by the flames and run to the kitchen, where we began a bucket brigade. Soon, with the help of unseen angels, we managed to put out the fire. Had we been unable to reach the kitchen, the old house would have been completely destroyed. The volunteer fire department could never have reached our home in time. I quickly ran back up the stairs to check on the children and found that they were sound asleep. I knew then that it must have been an angel sent by the Lord to make a cry in the night to save us.

As the years go by and life gets tough, I often remember how God protected us with a cry in the night. Have you heard your cry in the night? JUNE LOOR

Trust

When I am afraid, I will trust in you. Ps. 56:3, NIV.

*B*linking back the tears, I grabbed the corner of the seat beside me to keep from falling in the aisle of the overcrowded bus. With one hand on the steering wheel, the bus driver gestured wildly with the other as he carried on an animated conversation with the passenger seated directly behind him.

The bus, top-heavy with produce, was headed for market. Every seat was filled, so I had to stand. Through the window, valley scenes of houses, gardens, and trees flashed by. Strange thoughts flooded my mind. *What if the bus crashes? Will the insurance back home take care of that? Will we get off this mountain alive? I should have stayed home and not come with my daughter and her husband to Jamaica!*

Lord, help me not to be scared, I prayed. I stole a glance around at the other passengers. *How can they sit so calmly?* I thought. *Am I the only person who is afraid?*

Across the aisle from where I stood sat a woman, arms folded across her ample bosom, a sleeping baby sprawled on her lap. Other passengers sat quietly, as if in deep thought. A few talked softly. I seemed to be the only troubled person.

Soon the bus rounded Horseshoe Curve, the last bend before the foot of the mountain. I gripped the handle more tightly and stiffened my legs to steady myself. The bus screeched to a halt.

My son-in-law helped me out of the bus. "How was it, Mom?" he asked.

"I was frightened out of my wits!" I replied.

"Oh, the man is a skillful driver and knows how to stay on the mountain," he attempted to assure me.

I thought of the woman with the sleeping baby sprawled on her lap. She sat calmly, and so did the other passengers, because they were accustomed to riding the bus. They knew the driver and trusted him.

When we know and trust Jesus we need not have any fear, either. When He is in control of our lives, we can be as calm and assured of our safety as were those passengers on that crazy bus ride.

MABEL ROLLINS NORMAN

Best Friends

Two are better than one, because they have a good return for their work: If one falls down, his friend can help him up. But pity the man who falls and has no one to help him up! Eccl. 4:9, 10, NIV.

*H*alf listening to the morning news, I scrounged up lunch money, found a briefcase, and scrambled the eggs. While retrieving the nearly burned toast from the defective toaster, I heard the phrase "best friends." I am blessed with a best friend, so my attention shifted from the morning frenzy to the news.

Two women, best friends for 20 years, were sitting in a hospital room. One, the donor, and the other, the recipient, in a kidney transplant. They had been close friends—soul mates—since high school. Then one of them developed a kidney disease and required dialysis. Life had become rather grim, and she would die if she did not receive a kidney transplant. Her devoted friend suffered with her. The pain of love was dreadful. The friend offered to donate one of her kidneys; after all, she had two. When the physical and psychological testing was completed, it was determined that they were a perfect match.

"I'm not asking you to go through this," whispered the sick friend.

"I know you're not asking. I am volunteering" was the reply.

After the surgery the press arrived with cameras and questions. "Was it painful?" a reporter asked.

"Yes, extremely painful," replied the donor, "but I would do it a hundred times over to save my friend."

They were committed to each other, each feeling what the other felt, hurting when the other hurt. The bond went deep, so deep that it seemed only right for one to share the body of the other.

The unselfishness, love, caring, and tenderness all spoke to my heart. Do I love my friend enough to risk dying so she could live?

Jesus demonstrated His unspeakable love for me. He volunteered to be the donor for my heart transplant. "My heart is here if you want it. I'm volunteering." Jesus knew I might reject His sacrifice, but He made it anyway. He is committed to me, feels what I feel, hurts when I hurt. It seemed only right for Him to share His body with me. Christ, my Friend, went through excruciating pain so I could have abundant life. He would do it a hundred times over, if needed. I didn't ask Him to go through it. He volunteered.

Jesus said, "As I have done, you should do. There is no greater love than this, that a man [or woman] should lay down his [her] life for a friend" (see John 15:13). Would I endure certain pain to give my husband, child, or best friend a chance at a healthier life? A great and noble act like that would definitely make a difference in their life.

But how about decisions that would not make the 5:00 news? Am I willing to give up cherished things in my life for family or friends? Perhaps my "kidney donation" is feeding the hungry, rendering financial aid, lending a listening ear, or taking time to laugh with someone who is lonely. What sacrifices do I make to give a part of myself to someone? Jesus is my donor. He offers me life and with unconditional love says, "Do unto others as I have done unto you."

EARLENE WOHLERS

FEBRUARY 14

The Moment of Dawn

A new commandment I write to you. . . . He who says he is in the light, and hates his brother, is in darkness until now. He who loves his brother abides in the light. 1 John 2:8-10, NKJV.

A rabbi once asked his students, "How can we determine the hour of dawn, when the night ends and the day begins?"

One student asked, "Is it when you can distinguish between a dog and a sheep in the distance?"

"No," the rabbi answered.

"Is it when you can distinguish between a fig tree and a grapevine?" asked a second student.

"No," said the rabbi.

"Please, tell us the answer then," urged the students.

Said the wise teacher, "It is when you have enough light to look human beings in the face and recognize them as your brothers and sisters. Until then the darkness is still with us."

Jesus gave spiritual significance to human relationships, placing them in the same realm as our relationship to God (Matt. 22:37-40). True religion holds on to these two—love for God and love for human beings—at the same time. When one is emphasized to the exclusion of the other, religion becomes warped, with mysticism marking one extreme and a purely social gospel the other.

It is interesting that those parts of the New Testament that are addressed specifically to Jewish Christians place heavy emphasis on the importance of human relationships. Paul, in such a milieu, makes this startling statement: "The entire law is summed up in a single command: 'Love your neighbor as yourself'" (Gal. 5:14, NIV).

Why such an emphasis? I believe there are at least three reasons:

1. Human beings need a human experience in unconditional love to comprehend God's love. It is true that the only love human beings can, by nature, extend to one another is conditional love. But as Christ dwells within us, His love can be made our own. By grace, we can flesh out in real life the warmth, comfort, security, and love intended by the biblical imagery of God as father, mother, husband, and friend. In Christ, we can offer one another experiences that give substance to "agape."

2. By our love for one another, our love for God is manifested. Jesus painted a picture of the end time when saints will be surprised to find themselves counted among the righteous. And when they ask why, He will respond, "Inasmuch as you did it [showed love] to one of the least of these . . . you did it to Me" (Matt. 25:40, NKJV). The surest proof of our acceptance of Christ's atoning righteousness will be evidenced in our everyday relationships.

3. Relationships carry spiritual weight because it is through our love for one another that the world will be discipled for Jesus Christ (see John 13:34, 35). Great teachers have come and gone for centuries, but none have changed history like Jesus of Nazareth. Millions still await word of Him. Countless thousands look on with a question for those of us who claim to be His followers: "Who do you say that He is?" The way we do relationships may well constitute the most significant part of our response. — KAREN FLOWERS

FEBRUARY 15

Accept No Substitutes

The kingdom of heaven is like a merchant looking for fine pearls. When he found one of great value, he went away and sold everything he had and bought it. Matt. 13:45, 46, NIV.

*C*ubic zirconium. They say it looks like real diamonds. A young man working in a jewelry store believed it. When he repaired jewelry, he replaced all the diamonds with cubic zirconium. He then sold the diamonds for cash and had accumulated quite a sum of money before the inevitable happened. Can you imagine how the owners of those diamonds felt? Something just wasn't the same about their jewel. They had been robbed! It wasn't hard to guess who the culprit was.

Satan is in the business of replacing God's diamonds with this world's cubic zirconium: power, pleasure, possessions. Jesus Christ and all that He represents are the only true diamonds.

When my husband and I lived in Japan we visited Pearl Island. It was here that Kokichi Mikimoto irked his first oyster by inserting a small mother-of-pearl bead under its shell to produce the first cultured pearl—a pearl created entirely of the oyster's secretions.

Before Mikimoto, the French invented the first imitation pearl back in the seventeenth century. They found that by dipping an alabaster bead in a pearl solution of fish scale essence and lacquer, they could produce something that looked like a pearl.

But before the cultured pearl and before the imitation pearl was the natural pearl—the pearl Jesus spoke of. The merchant had to *seek* this fine pearl. Imitation pearls are manufactured—no need to seek them. The farmers insert a core into the oysters and confine them to netted areas for about three years. After that, the farmers harvest the pearls. Not so with natural pearls. Divers must collect many oysters, but only a few will have pearls. And even fewer of them will be perfect spheres large and lustrous enough to command a great price.

When the merchant found the priceless jewel, what did he do? He sold everything he had to get it. If that had been a cultured pearl, or worse yet, an imitation pearl, or (perish the thought) a plastic bead, the man would have been a fool. But he was a pearl expert. He knew value when he saw it, so he sold everything he had to get it.

Power, pleasure, possession—plastic pearls. Ultimately these things are worthless, but Jesus is the genuine article. No amount of seeking and no amount of sacrifice can equal the value of knowing Christ. The apostle Paul knew value when he saw it. He said, "I consider everything a loss compared to the surpassing greatness of knowing Christ Jesus my Lord, for whose sake I have lost all things. I consider them rubbish, that I may gain Christ" (Phil. 3:8, NIV). He was no fool. And neither are we when we follow his example.

KAREN LINDENSMITH

In a Ditch

For the Lord watches over all the plans and paths of godly men, but the paths of the godless lead to doom. Ps. 1:6, TLB.

*O*n a chilly February morning I was driving down an icy country road. Worse, I had a great fear of the very deep ditches that hugged both sides of the narrow road. I had never driven in this area before, so I had one eye on the map and one eye on the road. Occasionally, I glanced over at my cat, Trixie, in the carrier on the passenger seat next to me. She was meowing loudly, quite unhappy about being stuck in the carrier. I talked to her softly as I carefully navigated.

After a while, out of habit, I rested my right hand on the passenger seat. *Ye-ow!* Trixie's claws viciously dug into my hand. I wriggled my hand, frantically attempting to free it. Just as I neared an intersection where I was to turn left, I got my hand back. I tried to execute a quick, one-handed turn. A skid. *Bumpety-bumpety-bump.* And half the car was swallowed up in the muddy expanse by the side of the road. I was in a ditch! Shaken, scared, but safe.

Numerous motorists stopped immediately to offer assistance. A city worker drove to fetch a tow truck for me after commenting that it was the only way I'd get out of the ditch. The tow truck pulled my car backward to get it out. Fifteen minutes later and $32 poorer, I was driving again, the only obvious damage being to my ego and my pocketbook.

Isn't our trip to heaven much like this? Traveling along, guided by our road map. Negotiating life's unfamiliar paths while enjoying God's goodness toward us. Looking forward to completing the trip safely. Oops! Slick or icy streets. Bumps. Sharp curves. Hidden entrances. Narrow roads. Ditches, too.

How many ditches have you fallen into? May the Lord lift you out of them with His steady hand.   IRIS L. STOVALL

FEBRUARY 17

Serendipity

And we know that in all things God works for the good of those who love him. Rom. 8:28, NIV.

We were moving to a new house. Because it was only 15 miles away, we moved piecemeal, a carload here and a carload there. Midway through the process we identified several pieces of furniture that would not be needed in our new location. Among them were three twin beds, a sofa bed, two lamps, a small table with four chairs, and a microwave oven. My husband suggested that he call the thrift shop and arrange to donate the furniture.

A week went by and he hadn't called, so I reminded him. Several more days went by. No progress. I was getting slightly irritated. After a few more days, I offered to call the thrift shop myself.

"No," he said, "I'll take care of it."

The next evening he told me that a thrift shop volunteer would pick up the items at 10:00 the following morning. I was so relieved. "It can't get out of here too soon," I told him. "We have only a few more days, and we'll be out of here too!"

At work the next morning I overheard a conversation between two employees. They were collecting furniture for a displaced father and four children, ages 7 to 13. "They have just rented a house," one woman said. "So far I've got a chest of drawers and a twin bed. Wouldn't it be wonderful if we could find three more beds?"

I groaned inwardly and interrupted their conversation. "I had three twin beds that I would have been delighted to donate, but they were picked up this morning at 10:00."

"Are you absolutely certain?" they asked in unison.

I looked at my watch. It was 10:15. They might still be there.

My husband answered the phone and in response to my breathless query said, "The thrift shop truck couldn't come today because the volunteer was called unexpectedly to jury duty. I know you'll be disappointed," he continued, "but don't worry, we'll have the stuff out of here first thing Monday."

"Thank heaven the truck didn't come!" I shouted into the phone. "There is a homeless family who needs every piece of furniture we were going to send to the thrift shop!"

"How serendipitous," my husband laughed.

Serendipitous indeed! By the following Sunday afternoon the

furniture was being put to very good use, and I had learned another helpful lesson. In spite of my irritation and repeated attempts to unload that furniture, it was ready and available when it was truly needed. The delay reinforced my decision to try to take life as it happens instead of getting uptight when things don't occur according to my schedule. I am learning to watch on a daily basis and take note of how God works things out for our good.   ARLENE TAYLOR

FEBRUARY 18

Flowers for Eternity

Now to him who by the power at work within us is able to do far more abundantly than all that we ask or think. Eph. 3:20, RSV.

When my eldest daughter was young, I read a particular story to her. I have long since forgotten the name of the book and the author, but its message has left an imprint on my heart. I would like to share that story with you.

Once upon a time there lived a little boy who wanted to be like his father, who was a gardener. Their cottage was surrounded by the most beautiful flowers imaginable. The boy wanted to grow such glorious flowers too. Following his father's instructions, he dug up a small patch of earth, planted some tiny seeds, and waited for the flowers to emerge. So excited was he about the prospect of being a great gardener like his father that he visited his patch in the garden every day. Eagerly he looked for small green shoots to push through the brown soil.

Days passed. Weeks passed. Even months passed, but there was no sign of any growth. In frustration, the boy ran to his father crying, "My flowers are not growing!"

"How do you know?" asked the father gently.

"Every day I visit my garden, dig up the seeds, and look to see if they are growing. Then I put them back in the soil," the forlorn boy replied.

The father smiled and tenderly explained to the boy that it is only when seeds are left in the soil, watered regularly, and warmed by the bright, radiant sunshine that flowers grow in profusion.

God asks each one of us to be a part of His gardening enterprise, to plant seeds by sharing with others the positive impact Jesus has made in our lives. He then asks that we water the seeds through the power of prayer, enabling Him to send the Holy Spirit to shower the seeds with His influence.

He wants us to be like the sunshine and, through warming acts of kindness, hospitality, and friendship, encourage the seeds to blossom. We do not need to fret or worry about the seeds or examine them for growth if we have done all that God asks of us. Planting crops for Jesus is not easy. It is hard work. It takes time, love, and commitment. And it can be discouraging. Farmers have always spent more time planting and nurturing their crops than reaping them. But planting seeds for Jesus is exciting, too. In so doing, people have the opportunity to commit their lives to Jesus Christ and to blossom throughout eternity. Now, isn't that worth the effort?

MARY BARRETT

FEBRUARY 19

The Test

Behold, to obey is better than sacrifice, and to hearken than the fat of rams. 1 Sam. 15:22.

I was walking home from the office one beautiful, sunny afternoon. As I opened the gate to our yard, I noticed my 9-year-old son, John, playing marbles on the path with his friend. So engrossed was he in the game that he didn't even seem to notice as I passed by.

"John," I called, "come home." Would he come? Or would he pretend that he hadn't heard me?

Before I had time even to reach the back veranda, I heard him say, "Yes, Mommy. I am here." Upon hearing my command, he had instantly picked up his marbles and, wishing his friend goodbye, said, "I am going home. My mama wants me." He had obeyed immediately and instinctively.

I was very happy, of course, but I felt a little guilty. I put my arms around him and hugged him. "I called you just to see if you would obey me immediately. You have passed the obedience test with flying colors!" I kissed him and told him to go out and play again.

Even though John has forgotten it, I remember this incident clearly. I often wonder why my son obeyed me without question. Was it love, or trust, that prompted obedience? Or was it both?

God is delighted when we obey Him willingly and instinctively.

True obedience is principle, resulting from trust. My relationship with God is real, for I have tasted of His love. Through the varied experiences of life I have learned to trust Him, and obeying Him is a delight. Blessed are those who have learned to obey the Father instinctively and immediately.   BIROL C. CHRISTO

Like Her—Like Him

When he comes back he will take these dying bodies of ours and change them into glorious bodies like his own. Phil. 3:21, TLB.

I still remember receiving the telephone call that brought me the news that my favorite aunt had died. There was something so special about my relationship with this lady that made the bereavement much more than a news item to me. You see, I was named after this lovely relative. I can remember wiggling delightedly when she tousled my curls with her soft, white hands, smiling until the light danced in her warm, brown eyes as she called me her "little namesake."

I used to ask my mother why, since I was named for her, I could not be as beautiful as she. Being a wise woman, my mother would gently reply, "My darling child, suppose you try to be as sweet as she is. That is a far better ambition."

But even in this, I found that success was pitiably small.

Then my aunt married, and her marriage brought her a great degree of financial security. So my young mind jumped across the years again and arranged another hopeful likeness to my aunt. Maybe I would become as wealthy as she!

But now my sweet and gentle namesake aunt, my pattern of performance, has fallen asleep. If my own dear mother were still living, I think she would say, "My dear, I do hope that you have learned by now not to pattern your life on frail mortals, even mortals as lovely as your auntie Edna. For humans can fail you; humans can be lost in death."

And, strangely, it is in the heeding of that advice that contentment has returned to my soul. For you see, both my aunt and I are namesakes of Someone Else. We both took the name of Christ as ours and were proud to be called Christians. Now, no matter how Auntie Edna might have wished it, she could not provide for me one shred of help in attaining the ambitions she had unconsciously stirred in me. She could not give me beauty like hers, nor her loveliness of character. But my divine namesake, this Christ whose name I so joyfully carry, can and will provide me with every holy characteristic I crave.

Do I long to be like Him in patience? He says, "Take Mine; it is My gift to you. Claim it every time you need it."

Do I covet His courage? He says, "In My lifetime I carved out a courage that I offer to you to claim whenever you need it."

All my needs He has promised to supply, for He has riches untold.

There's one more promise that my dear aunt could not supply, but my Lord can: "Who shall change our vile body, that it may be fashioned like unto his glorious body" (Phil. 3:21).

I did so want to be like my aunt, but maturity has taught me that the pursuit of pride doesn't satisfy. So I now rest in the promise of the One whose name I bear when He assures me that I shall be like Him.

EDNA FERRIS-HEISE

FEBRUARY 21

Spiders Help Too

Let's celebrate! I've found the coin I lost. Luke 15:9, CEV.

Have you ever hidden something from yourself? It was right there a few moments or days earlier, but now it is nowhere to be found. Where is it? Hiding, like Jerry's overdue books and library card, or Mary's new hair bows.

Every Friday I wrote my plans for the following week in a monthly planner. Every night, before going to bed, I usually checked the progress of my activities for that day and made the necessary adjustments. Usually, my plan book was in plain sight on my study table. But on Monday morning it wasn't there.

I searched the bookshelves and looked under my desk and in other places where I thought the book could have accidentally fallen or been put. Sometimes I find it helpful to retrace my steps mentally when I need to find something. So I sat at my desk and tried to recall some of what I had written.

"Lord, please help me find that book," I groaned.

While sitting deep in thought, my eyes detected movement. Looking up, I saw a spider suspended by its web from the ceiling.

Slowly the web grew longer, and the spider came closer. I sat very still so as not to frighten it before I went into action. The spider finally landed on top of some magazines and papers stacked on the sewing basket that stands beside my study table. I grabbed a fly swatter, and while I was attempting to flatten the spider, the magazines and papers tumbled to the floor and scattered at my feet. And there, among the rubble, I saw my monthly planner.

"Thank You, Lord," I sighed.

I thought about the parable of the lost coin. My book, like the coin, did not know it was lost. The coin's owner searched diligently, sweeping every crack and crevice until the coin was found. Then she rejoiced and called her neighbors in to help celebrate her good fortune.

The book was as important to me as that single coin was to the poor woman. Searching yielded nothing. However, when I stopped looking and talked with God about it, He arranged for a spider to help me. I should never be reluctant to pray, even about small matters. These words from *Steps to Christ* came to mind:

"Nothing that in any way concerns our peace is too small for Him to notice. . . . No anxiety [can] harass the soul, . . . no sincere prayer [can] escape the lips, of which our heavenly Father is unobservant, or in which He takes no immediate interest" (p. 100).

With this assurance, I am confident that God saw my distress and arranged the solution in the best way possible at that moment.

MABEL ROLLINS NORMAN

FEBRUARY 22

Words and the Image of God

And God said, Let us make man in our image, after our likeness. Gen. 1:26.

*H*uman beings are made in the image of God. God has language; He talks. So do humans. But do animals? Do creatures have language? Linguists argue both positions, yes and no. Are animal sounds the same as human words?

Of course, anyone knows that animals make noises, even patterned noises with predictable consequences. A trip to any barnyard will supply convincing examples: a mother hen calling her chicks; a baby goat responding to its mother's bleats; the threatening snarl of a protective mother dog. Even more striking, wolves can spread the news from wolf pack to wolf pack, over distances covering several hundred miles, that the caribou are coming. And when the thundering herds rush north to their summer feeding grounds the lean wolves are ready, waiting at just the right spots for their "meals on hooves."

Animal *communication?* No doubt about it. Animal *language?* Not really.

Of all life that God created that week in Eden, only man "became a living soul" (Gen. 2:7). That description was not elaborated on, not defined, in the rest of Scripture, except by implication. But some linguists feel that language remains one of the most distinguishing differences between people and animals.

No one but human beings can share the past, comment about the present, and speculate about the future with words. Only humans can say words about words. No one but men and women can do these Godlike activities. No one but they were made in the image of God. Animals just don't qualify.

What about the few chimpanzees that have learned to say some words? One trainer claims that her chimp actually composed a few original simple sentences. Amazing? Absolutely. But think of any human baby born in any culture who uses any of the 5,000 languages humans can speak. If normal, this infant can master any language he or she grows up with, no matter how complicated the syntax or vocabulary.

By comparison, a smart chimp might learn six words in a few years, while a child knows thousands of words by first grade and as many as 70,000 in adulthood, a feat a jungleful of chimps could never duplicate. In fact, if linguists are correct, the average adult speaks enough words in a day to fill a small book. Animal noises and human words just are not the same.

But gifts sometimes bring accountability. If God's divine gift to humans was language, then their human gift to God should be the responsible use of words.

Words. Use them carefully, reverently. Without them, one's humanity is in jeopardy.   WILMA McCLARTY

A Mother's Prayer

He tends his flock like a shepherd: He gathers the lambs in his
arms and carries them close to his heart; he gently leads those
that have young. Isa. 40:11, NIV.

It's been a long day, and they are all tucked in. The last drink,
the last kiss. "Mama, hug me again!" a little voice calls out.
As you finish the dishes and pick up the toys, you think back
over the day . . .

Did I do the right things, did I spend enough time
Loving them, molding and shaping their minds?
Did I tell them what's right, but then do what's wrong?
Did my life cancel out what I say?

Please love my children, Lord, just as You love me—
I can always come to You unconditionally;
Because You never change, I can live without fear.
I know You love my children; please love them through
  me.

When I think how You came down to be one of us here,
In Your life, in Your work, You had burdens to bear.
Yet You weren't too busy to talk with a child—
And You're never too busy for me.

Can I tell them, "I've something important to do;
Don't bother me," knowing inside that it's true
That they'll learn who You are by looking at me?
What kind of God do they see?

Please be close to them, Lord, as You are close to me;
In big things and in small things, I want them to see
That You're always there and that You understand.
I know that You are close to them; please love them
  through me.

I trust in Your word that you'll hold me tight;
My grip is so frail when compared to Your might.

I've learned that it is not by my strength that I win,
But by believing Your promise to me.

Please hold my children, Lord, just as You hold me;
You don't ask for my promises, and so I believe
The good news You've given, the promise You've made
That You'll hold my children, Lord, just as You hold on
    to me.

LINDA McCABE

How God Used an Ant

Let us discern for ourselves what is right; let us learn together
what is good. Job 34:4, NIV.

Early one morning the aroma of freshly baked muffins filled the
air, tickling my nostrils and teasing my taste buds. The sun,
just peeking above the eastern horizon, pushed gray shadows of
night into shades of beautiful blue and lovely hues of pink. Basking
in the quiet moments, I began to give serious thought to some challenges in my life that I was facing, when an ant caught my eye.

This ant, on the inside of my screen, must have gained entry
through a tiny hole. It was frantically trying to find its way out and
hurried back and forth, up and down and across the screen. The
poor thing was running in circles. Sometimes it would get right up
to the edge of this hole—and even stuck its head through a couple
times—then quickly dart back and continue its search.

Watching this helpless little creature just running around in circles, but really getting nowhere, reminded me that all through life I
have choices. It doesn't matter what sort of situation I may find myself in, I still have a choice. Nothing requires me to stay put.

The ant had a choice: either to enter the hole, or walk away. It
chose to enter the hole. *Bad choice!* Even when it realized this wasn't
the best decision at the time, the ant still had a choice. It could have
chosen to stay and make the best of a bad situation, or free itself by
going back outside. But it was afraid. I suspect fear of the unknown
held the ant captive to its circumstances, so it stayed on its merry-
go-round.

We are not any different than that ant, really. We too have

choices. With the help of God, I made the necessary changes in my life, and the challenges I was facing took care of themselves. You can do that, too. You don't have to run around in circles like that poor little ant. Just ask God for His help. He is ready, willing, and able to give it.　　　　　　　　　　　　　　　　　　　MARIE BALLA

FEBRUARY 25

Be Yourself

Like a muddied spring or a polluted well is a righteous man who gives way to the wicked. Prov. 25:26, NIV.

When I was 3 I remember going visiting with my mother. While the grown-up women chatted, I wasted no time in making new friends with the other children.

Once, within a few, short minutes of entering one particular home, I succeeded in revving up two sedate boys (who could typically be found reading quietly in a corner of the house). As the boys and I zoomed past our mothers' skirts, Mrs. Lindforce looked up from her ironing and said to my mother, "Barbara, my boys really liven up when Julie comes to visit."

Indeed, I could influence the children with whom I played. And, in turn, other children influenced me. I would wind into higher gear when Mom would visit another family, whose children were frequently disobedient and wild. Even though I remember thinking that they acted despicably, somehow I could not keep myself entirely from similar behavior. Once back in the car and heading home, I became my sweet self again. Well, almost. Now, as the mother of two preschool girls, I can see this same phenomenon taking place in their little lives.

I wonder: Are children the only ones who are easily influenced by their peers? Even as an adult I find myself influencing and being influenced by those around me. My girlfriend, Beth, loves the words "fabulous" and "horrendous." Since our friendship has developed, I find myself using these two words more frequently. Debbie tends to giggle a little at the end of her sentences. I catch myself doing the same while chatting over the phone. It seems part of human nature for people to subconsciously mimic each other. Research has found that mirroring each other can actually be a positive means of increasing rapport and communication.

I want to be like Jesus. I want to be loving and redemptive with the people I meet. I want to represent my Saviour by upholding love and virtue. Have I shunned righteousness to gain the approval of others, or for fear of offending others or of being labeled Goody Two-shoes? One would think that these fears would disappear post-adolescence. Ironically, even within Christian circles negative labels attached to certain values still abound. Even though others may frown at me for choosing a different way than they have, I pray that I will walk joyfully in the wonderful path that my Lord has placed before me. I want to be true not only to my God but also to myself.

JULIE REYNOLDS

FEBRUARY 26

Help, Lord, I'm Having a Bad Day!

What you're after is truth from the inside out. Enter me, then; conceive a new, true life. Ps. 51:6, Message.

Years ago, in my rather radical administrative days, I made a presentation to a subcommittee of the board of the college where I worked. I wanted to push for a proposal that I was sure would improve student life. Mindful of the fact that the composition of that subcommittee was mostly male, I deliberately chose to highlight my feminine side. Instead of wearing the politically correct, tailored, dark suit, I chose a black-and-white dress. It was a particularly well-made crepe creation with a swirling skirt and flaring sleeves.

Knowing that I needed to keep the board members' attention riveted on the subject at hand, I did all the things required of a good communicator. I walked around the board room during my discourse, maintaining eye contact with each person and building up their interest, which I sensed had been piqued.

As I concluded, imagine my delight when two hands shot up— almost in unison. I acknowledged the man whose son I had taught two years earlier, and who, I was quite sure, supported my proposal.

"Excuse me, I don't mean to be out of line, but aren't you wearing your dress on the wrong side?"

I was mortified. He was right. The seams had been so carefully sewn that only close scrutiny could reveal that the dress was indeed inside out. I have no idea how I got out of that situation, though several people later assured me that I managed to do so with a modicum of finesse. I could not wait to get home to call my mother. Ruefully, I recounted the tale of my embarrassment. Peals of laughter swept over the phone lines. I expected that. Minutes later she managed to regain her composure, and I steeled myself for the maxim I knew was coming—"Pride goeth before a fall!"

Instead, she issued a powerful one-liner: "Now what?"

It took me a minute to process her question. Finally I realized that I needed to learn how to have a bad day successfully.

Than night I turned to Psalms. David surely had his share of disasters, and his repentant journaling in Psalm 51 helped me realize that my incident was rather insignificant. It was neither soul-shattering nor life-threatening. I would get over it. Adversity, while inevitable, is rarely terminal. I suspect that we can't help the way we feel initially, but we can learn how to deal with these emotions. We can hold them in, deny them, act them out, or turn them over to God. David poured out his feelings to God and asked for His cleansing. "Soak me in your laundry and I'll come out clean, scrub me and I'll have a snow-white life" (Ps. 51:71, Message).

Calamities are stressful, but the way we perceive them and deal with them is so much more significant. God, the true light, never gives us more than we can handle.

Heavenly Therapist, help me to recognize a bad day for what it is—a single day, not a month, or even a week. Work on my heart so that even if I wear it inside out, it will be just right!

GLENDA-MAE GREENE

FEBRUARY 27

A Small Part

Go home to your family and tell them how much the Lord has done for you, and how he has had mercy on you. Mark 5:19, NIV.

On a visit to my homeland in 1982, I stopped off in London to spend a weekend with a friend I hadn't seen for many years. As we talked, I was surprised to hear that her pastor was the same man who had pastored my mother's church in Scotland during my rebellious teenage years.

Thirty years later I was now a converted Christian and eager to meet our former pastor again. As we talked about the directions in which the Lord had led us, I related to him the circumstances concerning my conversion.

Back in New Zealand several months later, I came home from church one day feeling utterly dejected and inadequate after listening to a speaker telling of the thousands of conversions taking place in South American churches, and about certain individuals who had led hundreds of people to Christ. By the end of the day I was in tears and found myself asking God, "Where on earth do I fit in with spreading the gospel for You? I can't think of a single individual I have led to Christ." I didn't feel any real response from my prayer, and the weekend passed slowly.

Monday at work still found me feeling depressed, and I decided to come home for the lunch hour instead of staying at work, as I usually did. While I was there, the mail arrived with a letter from my friend in London. At the end she wrote, "The week after you left London, our pastor used the story of your conversion as the basis of his church sermon. At the end of it he invited anyone in the congregation who would like to give their life to Christ to come forward. I just wanted you to know that as a result of your story, a young man who was struggling with the same problem you had came forward and gave his life to Jesus."

Wow! My heart bubbled over with praise to God, who loved me so much He had the answer to my prayer on the way days before I even prayed it!

I saw my friend and our recently retired pastor again last year. I asked what had became of that young man.

"He is now studying for the ministry," the pastor said.

Lord, thank You for all the people who will be reached through that young man, and whom I will have the pleasure of meeting in Your kingdom. Thank You for making me a small part of Your grand plan to spread the gospel of our Lord Jesus Christ.

MURIEL L. MOULTRIE

FEBRUARY 28

Swimming With Sharks

For I am convinced that neither death nor life, neither angels nor demons, neither the present nor the future, nor any powers, neither height nor depth, nor anything else in all creation, will be able to separate us from the love of God that is in Christ Jesus our Lord. Rom. 8:38, 39, NIV.

This week I swam with a shark. (Not intentionally, let me assure you!) It was about five feet long, cruising over the coral just below me. Compared to the rough barracuda buddies it was swimming with, it looked sleek and professional. I turned to talk to my friend snorkeling nearby, and discovered he was already halfway back to our sailboat. Suddenly all those beautiful tropical fish weren't so appealing. The ocean looked endless, and the five-foot swells made me feel insignificant.

Then I remembered the text I had read just that morning: "Our fears for today, our worries about tomorrow, or where we are—high above the sky, or in the deepest ocean—nothing will ever be able to separate us from the love of God demonstrated by our Lord Jesus Christ when he died for us" (Rom. 8:38, 39, TLB).

We all have days that make us feel as if we are swimming with sharks. Sometimes as a single parent I feel that way when I am dealing with one of my teenagers on a touchy issue, or as I'm balancing the checkbook. It may be when I have to make a presentation to people who don't really relish the news I'm bringing. Or when, as a teacher, I'm working with colleagues who are critical of the position I've taken. When I was a pastor's wife there were times when the sharks were the saints in the church. Sharks can be anything we're afraid of or worried about. Sharks rob us of our peace of mind. They make us wary and jittery just knowing they're around. We aren't able to enjoy the beauty surrounding us when we see sharks.

Paul tells us that nothing can come between God's love and us—nothing! No sharks. No waves. No worries. That's reassuring! As I write this, bobbing off the coast of Florida in a 34-foot sailboat, the ocean seems vast. But God's love will go to any length and any depth to reach me!

What are the sharks in your life? Are they stealing your peace, your joy, and your appreciation of life's beauty? How many times have you worried yourself right out of His care? If you *truly* believe that nothing can separate you from His love, then do not worry or fret or agonize.

Lord, please help me today to know and practice Your love—even if I swim with a shark.

LYNDA WYSONG

I Go!

Then we shall see face to face. Now I know in part; then I shall know fully, even as I am fully known. 1 Cor. 13:12, NIV.

*I*t was only a month after deciding to join the church that I left it. Somehow I just couldn't stay firm to my convictions, and I stumbled out the back door of the church that I had so proudly entered by the front door such a short time before.

One day as I sat pondering my future, I felt the urge to open a drawer in my closet. There I found a book of meditations, which I opened at random. My eyes fell on the words "Fear not." After reading the whole paragraph, I discovered that Jesus had spoken these words to Peter when he started walking on the sea and was about to sink and drown. Jesus told him, "Fear not."

I felt that these words were directed to me, and I determined to return to God. Although I had left Him, He'd never forsaken me. What a wonderful God He is! Two months after my return to the church, I began to wonder about the verses in Deuteronomy 6:5: "Thou shalt love the Lord thy God with all thine heart, and with all thy soul, and with all thy might." I told the Lord that I wanted to love Him with all my heart, soul, and strength, but didn't know how. I could love my child, whom I could see and touch, but how could I love God when I couldn't see Him?

The answer came when I was returning from a trip with my husband and children. They started talking about the rainbow and its beautiful colors. I was amazed to hear of its beauty, because I had never actually seen one. The following day I looked through the living room window, and there it was—a clear, full rainbow with all its colors. I was so excited I called out to my husband and children to come see this spectacular sight.

Whenever I remember this experience, the tears flow. The rainbow, as mentioned in the Bible, means so much. Our God is so loving; He cares for all of us, no matter how sinful we are or how far away we have wandered. He is a living God, always at our side. How can we not love Him with all our heart, soul, and strength?

God still lives and intervenes in our lives. We can commune with Him directly and personally through daily Bible study and prayer. And although for a time He is out of our sight, He is busy preparing to receive us and will come in majesty and great glory to take us home to live with Him forever. Then I will no longer need to see Him in the rainbow; I will see Him face-to-face.

NADIA FARAH

MARCH 2

Easy Yokes and Light Burdens

He gives strength to the weary and increases the power of the weak. Isa. 40:29, NIV.

*T*his text calls to mind a particularly vivid scene, reminiscent of my years in Africa. We were almost due for the rainy season, and the shortage of water on the Solusi mission compound was rapidly approaching the crisis stage. There were about 700 of us dependent on a dam that was dry. In anticipation of the coming rainy season and the realization that the dam needed enlargement, we bought a yoke of oxen and an ancient tractor to do the job. I remember that old tractor wheezing about in the bottom of the dam and the oxen struggling up the side to deposit load after load of dirt from the bottom of the reservoir to the top of the dam wall.

Because wealth is not widespread in Africa, a matched team of oxen is not a particularly common sight. Some odd combinations often appear. Many times a big sturdy ox would be yoked to a smaller, younger, or older ox, and the great creature would often pull more than its share of the load. However, the weaker ox had to pull as much as it could. Two pulling together accomplished more than two working alone. It was hard work, and they had to hit the yoke together in order to pull the load up out of the mire. If one ox chose to stand while the other one pulled, they went around in a circle.

"Take my yoke upon you" means that we are to step into harness with the Lord, for He can outpull and outwork us in every situation. He can surpass anything that we might be trying to do alone. If I step into place beside Him and begin pulling to the best of my strength, I can know that the furrow we are plowing will be making a difference in the ministry to humanity. Sometimes He seems to move me along beyond the limits of my strength, but never beyond His limits, for He has no limits except when I refuse to take His yoke.

He never forces anyone. He doesn't seem to be concerned about mismatched capacity. In Him I am strong because He carries me along with Him by His great, gentle strength. He promises, "My yoke is easy and my burden is light." NELMA DRAKE

Plugged In but Not Turned On

Let this mind be in you, which was also in Christ Jesus. Phil. 2:5.

*R*ushing and last-minute to-do's seem to be the life of many single parents. As a member of this group I find myself constantly in many single-parent situations. Being absentminded is only one of many.

I wanted to put a load of clothes in the washer; get the children up, dressed, and fed; and iron my clothes. This was my morning routine. I had gotten up in plenty of time to complete this list of things, but had not factored in a telephone interruption. Instantly my schedule was thrown off. *No problem,* I thought; *I'll just make up the time by not washing the clothes.*

I plugged in the iron and proceeded to get the children up and dressed. Everything seemed to be moving along quite well. But there was something very wrong with the iron. It was not taking out the wrinkles. I gave it the wet finger test. It was not heating up. I checked the outlet to make sure it was plugged in securely, shook the iron to make sure there was water, and began to wonder what could possibly be the problem. Finally, upon checking the iron settings, I discovered the iron had never been turned on.

Many Christians walking this journey are plugged in but not turned on. We come to church each week, sit in the pew, but never get "turned on" or involved. Convinced we're ready for heavenly liftoff, we cease to get turned on by what the Holy Spirit is endeavoring to convey through the minister's message.

Being turned on by the Holy Spirit and plugged into the Word of God develops a well-pressed Christian experience. It alleviates the wrinkles of life—earthly cares, job pressures, home concerns—enabling us to receive all the blessings He is waiting to bestow.

IVY J. STARKS

Don't Worry

Look at the birds of the air; they do not sow or reap or store away in barns, and yet your heavenly Father feeds them. Are you not much more valuable than they? Matt. 6:26, NIV.

The flash of wings whir past as our two parakeets fly from the birdcage to the window perch. Their little feet run back and forth on the bar that runs the width of the window. They chatter and peck each other.

The turquoise of Pretty Boy's body is topped by the yellow crown of his head. By contrast, Pretty Girl is a sparkling white, with streaks of turquoise on her back and breast. Their beauty and animation provide entertainment as their carefree antics continue throughout daylight hours.

Except for the short flights to the window bar, they are caged. Are they unhappy because they are caged? In that cage is their nourishment, their protection, their home. Several times they have somehow gotten down on the floor and are unable to find their way back to the cage. As soon as we place the cage close to them on the floor, they go in happily.

The poet and writer Maya Angelou, in her book *I Know Why the Caged Bird Sings,* infers that the bird sings because it feels secure from outside dangers, secure in the care of its master and owner. Do we feel "caged" or "shut in" when we accept Christ and His lifestyle? In that very caging there is protection and shelter. "He that dwelleth in the secret place of the most High shall abide under the shadow of the Almighty" (Ps. 91:1).

Jesus used birds as an example of the futility of worrying. He said, "Do not worry about your life. Look at the birds of the air."

Pretty Boy and Pretty Girl are completely dependent on us, yet they show no sign of insecurity. We feed and care for them. How much more does our heavenly Father care for our needs? Why should we worry?

Let us remember to thank God for daily protection and care, assured that He will help us to trust His care completely.

BEATRICE HARRIS

The Greatest Contribution

Mary has chosen the good portion, which shall not be taken away from her. Luke 10:42, RSV.

*T*hroughout history many women have offered their parcel of contribution, making the world a sweeter and more pleasant place to live in. Annie Sullivan was able to love to the point that she gave meaning to Helen Keller's existence. Because of her teacher's dedication, this blind and deaf girl became a world-renowned writer. Mother Teresa of Calcutta, India, is so altruistic that she opted for the mission of loving those who mattered to no one: lepers and abandoned children in the slums of India.

And you? How do you feel when you think about the lives of these women? What mark have you left in the world?

Let us consider the lives of two other women. In Mary's home Jesus found nourishment, rest, and much friendship. Martha, a dedicated and solicitous woman, also lived there. She went to work to offer the Master the best that she had. Mary, however, valued staying close to the Master. She so deeply wished to enrich her spirit with Jesus' presence that she sat at His feet, an attentive and reverent listener.

And you? The days seem too short for everything that needs to be done. In the effort to offer the best to your loved ones, is there an affectionate gathering missing? Would Jesus find tranquillity in your home?

Whether you are married, a mother, single, or divorced, the only thing necessary to reach the ideal is simply making your life a ministry of love. A ministry capable of appeasing the heart of your husband. A ministry that remains patient even when the nearly ready meal burns, or when the children cry, fight, or become rebellious.

The greatest contribution we can give the world is to be women, women filling the place that God has reserved for us in the world. Single women cultivating the spirit and the intellect, not only transitory beauty and sensuality. Wives able to love continually. Mothers understanding that in each attitude, in each look transmitted to the children, is the character of God. Elderly women, like Naomi, an example for the younger women.

A Christian woman who understands that alone she cannot fulfill the place God reserved for her in the world, but decides to take time each day to sit at Christ's feet and receive strength, is exactly what God envisions for each of us. Put *your* name on the blank space: _____ chose the good part!

May God enable us to accomplish the noble mission of being a woman!   REGINA SELMA MARINHO MIRANDA

MARCH 6

God's Mysterious Ways

God is our refuge and strength, a very present help in trouble.
Ps. 46:1.

*W*hile on a much-needed vacation trip to Hayward, Wisconsin, my husband and I noticed a red light suddenly flashing on the instrument panel. We were miles from the nearest town and on a wilderness stretch of road. There was no phone or apparent help available. After prayer to God for guidance, we decided to proceed ahead, hoping we could reach assistance quickly.

Finally we came to a tiny town that boasted one small garage. The owner examined our car and determined the alternator was the problem. But he didn't have a replacement in stock. So he recharged our battery and warned us that the car could stop at any time. We prayed again and left.

A dense gray fog swirled around us, and a driving rain began to fall. Because of the battery's weakened condition, we could use the windshield wipers only sparingly. A difficult situation had become even more critical for us.

Two hours later, after several sessions of fervent prayer, we finally reached Hayward and drove immediately to the nearest garage. The rain was still with us, but we thanked God for His help. The garage mechanic agreed that a new alternator was needed for our car. But his garage didn't stock parts for a car as old as ours, and it would take several days to order an alternator. We were dismayed. In addition to this problem, my husband's health condition was beginning to need attention because of the stress of the situation. We prayed again for God's intervention.

Suddenly the parts manager decided to look in his unit again to see if he had anything he could use to help us. A few minutes later he returned with a smile on his face and a box in his hand.

"You have lucked out!" he exclaimed. "I found your part on a shelf back there. I know it wasn't there when we took a recent inventory, but here it is!"

We all marveled! God had not only supplied the needed part, but had it waiting for us to pick up when it was required. How wonderful is His love and care for us!   ROSEMARY BAKER

Hidden Treasure

But lay up for yourselves treasures in heaven, where neither moth nor rust destroys and where thieves do not break in and steal. For where your treasure is, there your heart will be also. Matt. 6:20, 21, NKJV.

*W*e pass the field frequently. In this place on a bright spring day in 1942, a Mildenhall, Suffolk, farmer was busy plowing. A flock of seagulls following behind his tractor circled eagerly, snatching at the worms that surfaced with every turn of the blade.

As the farmer guided the tractor down the even furrows, perhaps he wondered how many hundreds of years this field had been plowed. "And what were they like, all those other people who also called this place 'home'?"

Suddenly he was jolted out of his daydreaming when the plow jammed against something metallic and broke loose from the tractor. He climbed down and began tugging at whatever had caused the problem. Finding he couldn't move it, he went looking for a spade. He soon unearthed several large pieces of tableware, among which was a beautifully engraved bowl and an enormous plate. Pleased with his find, he took them home, cleaned them up, and put them on a shelf, where they remained for many months.

A visitor recognized them as solid silver—fourth-century silver, in fact—and worth a fortune! How they had come to be buried in the field for 16 centuries is anybody's guess. It is thought that possibly the owner had been a high-ranking Roman soldier on occupation duty in what is now England. Perhaps he feared being robbed by roving savages, or maybe he went home on temporary duty, expecting to return for his treasure later on. We'll never know, but the possibilities are exciting to contemplate.

And how many farmers had plowed that field, some possibly in dire financial straits, and never for a moment realized that under-neath their feet lay such a fortune.

Under English law, buried treasure belongs to the Crown, and therefore the Mildenhall treasure now resides in the British Museum in London for all to see and admire.

Jesus once told a story about buried treasure a man found in a field that unfortunately belonged to someone else. Perhaps he too was plowing. He was tremendously excited about his find, but in order to make it his, he had to buy the field. So he went and sold all that he had, bought the field, and thereby became owner of the trea-sure as well (Matt. 13:44).

The treasure of which Jesus is speaking is the gospel, or the good news, that He loves us, forgives our sins, and is one day coming to take us to live with Him forever. This treasure is priceless, but in order for it to be ours, we too must sell all that we have to obtain it.

EDNA MAY OLSEN

MARCH 8

Peeping Tom

So, if you think you are standing firm, be careful that you don't fall! 1 Cor. 10:12, NIV.

I was attending a small Christian college in Tennessee in 1964, when my sister, Blanche, called one day. She and her hus-band, Jerry, would be passing through on their way to visit his par-ents, who lived an hour's drive from the college. I accepted Blanche's invitation to join them for the weekend.

The drive up into the Tennessee mountains was beautiful, and the yard of our hosts' quaint white house spilled over with flowers. I was a bit shocked to discover that a hand pump brought water to the kitchen! And an outhouse and a bathhouse shed served as a bathroom. I had grown up in New York City and Miami, Florida, and thought everyone in America had running water and indoor plumbing. Well, I never did adjust to going outside to the "bath-room" in the dark with a flashlight!

Late Friday night, after everyone else was asleep, Blanche and I sat in the living room talking and fixing our nails. Suddenly I looked up and saw a man's face in the window. I screamed, "There's a man!"

Then Blanche screamed, and everyone came running to the living room. Jerry and his dad ran outside with flashlights to search. Blanche called the police. But in the darkness of the night the man was gone, vanished from sight into the woods surrounding the house. We stayed up late that night, talking about the incident. We were too shaken to sleep.

That incident reminds me that Satan is stalking us, hoping to catch us off guard so that he might trick us and grab us. The only way we can be prepared for his attacks is through daily Bible study and prayer. CELIA MEJIA CRUZ

Not of This World

My prayer is not that you take them out of the world but that you protect them from the evil one. They are not of the world, even as I am not of it. . . . As you sent me into the world, I have sent them into the world. John 17:15-18, NIV.

One of the favorite afternoon activities at the Maluti Adventist Hospital in Lesotho was a walk out in the country to see the waterfalls. Now, walking wasn't necessarily my favorite activity, but my students begged me to go with them one afternoon. We loaded the students and staff into a flatbed truck and drove to the trailhead of the waterfall, which was not too far from the hospital. The reason I didn't like these hikes was that the trails were often made by sheep and goats and were very narrow and over rocky terrain. It was hard for me to keep my balance as we walked single file. I was always at the tail end and afraid of falling.

We picked our way along the side of the creek, across a meadow, and down the jagged, rocky hill to the bottom of the falls, hugging the side of the cliff as the path wound its way behind the falls into a darkened niche. It had rained a lot that year, and the rivers and creeks were full of water. This stream ran across the plateau to the edge of the cliff and plunged over the side, spraying its mist everywhere. I found myself behind the falls looking through the mist over the green valley, watching the water tumble down the hillside to the valley floor below.

As we backed up to escape getting wet from the spray, I began to survey the surrounding area where our group was standing. The cliff, hollowed out by the wind and time, made this a refuge behind the waterfall—a protective haven for sheep and goats, as evidenced by a strong smell of manure. The shadows made this hollowed-out space dark. I looked around for other signs of life. Imagine my surprise to see a beautiful white lily popping its head up through the muddy floor in the corner of this dark refuge. I called it a "trumpet lily" because of its shape.

My teaching instincts took over as the students and staff gathered around me to examine this beautiful specimen of God's handiwork. We talked about how the cliff protected this exquisite flower from the wind and allowed the morning sun to shine in the dark area while the spray of the waterfall gave it water. The students commented that the lily was pure white in spite of its dark, muddy, deplorable environment. It seemed to lift its head high, reflecting the beauty of its Creator. I related this lily to the text for today, wanting my nursing students to see that in spite of their surroundings or where they lived, God would protect them and they could witness the beauty of Christ by helping humanity.

The walk was worth the effort. I learned a lesson. Whenever I see a lily like the one in Lesotho, I remember Jesus' prayer "Don't take them out of the world, but protect them from the evil one." We must pray to be a witness, pure and white like the lily, wherever the Lord leads us.   RITA VAN HORN

MARCH 10

Heavenly Promissory Notes

You are the God who performs miracles; you display your power among the peoples. Ps. 77:14, NIV.

*G*uatemala City, March 1925. Time for the rainy season. But it had not started. The atmosphere was laden with an unexpressed foreboding. The young missionary couple, oblivious of the weather, was absorbed with their tasks. Myrtle was learning the language, foods, and customs of a new world. Ernest, reared as a pioneer missionary's son in South America, was thrilled to be home again.

As they sat down to eat that afternoon, Ernest began enthusiastically telling his bride about the thrilling events of his morning. The story was never finished.

"Listen! What is that rumbling sound?" Myrtle stepped to the open window and gasped, "It's a tornado!" As the roar grew more ominous with each passing second, she exclaimed, "It's right upon us!"

The young couple dropped to their knees for a quick prayer.

"For he shall give his angels charge over thee, to keep thee in all thy ways." Myrtle cashed a check with heaven's Bank Teller. As she prayed, there was a crash. Then the roar of the tempest gradually subsided, and the house stopped shaking.

The couple got up and cautiously opened the door. The air was still filled with debris, and a sheet of metal roofing fell into their yard. In the garden they found two large silk oaks twisted off near the ground. The storm had then turned sharply to the right, destroying a liquor store across the street before dissipating itself in the canyon beyond.

Have you made a practice of cashing promissory notes with your heavenly Banker? He looks down with longing eyes upon each of us today, as though we are the only ones standing in line waiting for Him. Why not cash in one of His promises for yourself today?

MYRTLE A. POHLE

MARCH 11

Working Together

For it is God who works in you to will and to act according to his good purpose. Phil. 2:13, NIV.

I have often thought back on my days as a child, fondly remembering those times I spent with my dad. There were times when I sat next to him in his old 1957 pickup while he made the rounds to check on the irrigation of his crops; times when I rode behind him on his horse, my small arms barely able to reach around his waist; times when he would reach over and pat my blond head.

One time I remember vividly was the day he asked my sister and me if we would like to make something for our mother. The "something" turned out to be a cutting board made in the shape of an elephant. It was an ambitious project for two small girls, but our efforts paid off. Mom was very pleased, and our elephant saw many years of use.

The ironic truth was that my sister and I had done very little of the actual work on the project. Most of our "help" involved my dad's big hands guiding our smaller ones as the work progressed. He did the work—we took the credit.

This same division of labor is often true in the spiritual realm as well. Many of us become involved in ministry, working side by side with the Lord. And as with our cutting board project, our efforts involve simply placing our hands in God's while He does the work. When we are asked to speak, we discover that it is He who speaks through us. Fresh ideas that pop into our heads actually originate in His. We find we can do things that are beyond our own capabilities.

We might wonder why He needs our help at all. The truth is, He doesn't. He asks for our help because our happiness depends on it. There is no greater joy than working with our Father's big hands guiding ours.

RETTA MICHAELIS

MARCH 12

The Source

> I am the vine; you are the branches. If a man remains in me and I in him, he will bear much fruit; apart from me you can do nothing. John 15:5, NIV.

*T*here had been many interesting experiences on this mission trip to Mexico, including helping to build new schoolrooms and holding Vacation Bible School for the local children. Each day a group of young people would accompany a doctor and dentist to a different village to help its needy residents. And each day would find the makeshift clinic set up in a different place, but always under less-than-ideal circumstances. Often it would be held in some part of a small church building, usually with no electricity or running water.

Then came the day that we were to be in a village that boasted a government clinic. We were looking forward to working with real facilities at last. As we drove into the little town, the neat white building on the right side of the street was easy to locate. We began to unload our supplies and set up, eager to treat the people who were already beginning to gather. What a treat to have nice, clean sinks and electric lights to work with!

But then we noticed a strange thing. The sinks were not connected to any water pipes, and nothing happened when we turned on the light switches. The villagers told us that money had run out before the clinic could be completed. So while everything appeared to be in order, these facilities were useless because they were not hooked up to any source. We had to use our portable generator again and depend on buckets of water brought in by nearby residents.

On our way back to camp that afternoon we couldn't help thinking of the parallel to our own lives. We may be nicely dressed, have plenty of money, a pretty face, and other things the world equates with success, but unless we have a vital connection to the Source, we can't let our light shine or share the water of life. And we don't have to worry about a lack of money, because He gives the water of life freely.

Let us pray today that we will be connected to God—our source of life—so that we will bear much fruit.   BETTY ADAMS

MARCH 13

Focus of Delight

This is my Son, chosen and marked by my love, delight of my life. Matt. 3:17, Message.

*C*oncerts make me chuckle. The closing ritual—you know how it goes. The last song is played, and the performer bows. We applaud enthusiastically. She leaves the stage. We continue clapping. She returns and bows again. We applaud some more. She leaves again. We're still clapping. She returns to bow again. We keep applauding. Then, lo and behold, as if the thought just occurred to her, she plays an encore! One more bow, more applause, and she finally exits the stage.

What would happen if after washing the dishes, typing a letter, attending a patient, or grading papers you took a bow and received enthusiastic applause? What a difference that would make in our work! Affirmation! We just love it, but more than that, we really do need it, too. That's why I was so thrilled when I discovered that God the Father is not afraid to express affirmation.

As I was reading Matthew's Gospel I realized that though there are a lot of red letters indicating Jesus' words, I rarely read anything that God the Father spoke. Matthew 3:17 is an exception. Here the Father says, "This is my Son, whom I love; with him I am well pleased" (NIV). God not only expresses affirmation of Jesus at His baptism, but affection.

He uses similar words speaking about Jesus on the Mount of Transfiguration. Isn't it significant that the few times in the Bible that God the Father speaks, it is in a warm, affirming manner? That's a great trait of our heavenly Father's for us to emulate. Our spouses, kids, and coworkers would love it.

Peter, recounting the experience on the Mount of Transfiguration, quotes the Father's words: "This is my Son, marked by my love, focus of all my delight" (2 Peter 1:17, Message). Wow! Jesus is the focus of all His delight! The amazing thing is that God feels the same way about all His children (see John 17:23). I am the focus of all His delight. And you are the focus of all His delight. Tuck it into your heart and savor His delight.   HEIDE FORD

MARCH 14

A Sleeping Bunny

Be self-controlled and alert. Your enemy the devil prowls around like a roaring lion, looking for someone to devour. 1 Peter 5:8, NIV.

Delicately Lady Bunny hopped around our backyard, nibbling at tender bunny tidbits. Something so sweet and demure could only be a lady, I decided. Day after day she returned, becoming more and more comfortable with the squirrels and the birds at the feeder.

As I was setting the table for supper last night, I spied her resting comfortably by the fir tree. All of a sudden I noticed a dark form sneaking across the lawn, headed directly for Lady Bunny. It was the neighborhood stray cat, intent on supper! I banged loudly on the windowpane, hoping to avert disaster. The cat stopped in its tracks, glanced at the window, and decided that I posed no threat to her prowl. Lady Bunny, I now realized, was asleep, blissfully unaware of her predicament. Before I could get to the back door, it was all over. The cat had pounced on Lady Bunny's neck and was dragging her limp body into the woods.

If only Lady Bunny had not been sleeping! Her tummy full, comfortable in her now-familiar surroundings, she had given in to a natural urge. And death had come on swift, padded feet.

My mind turned at once to 1 Peter 5:8. The lion, the crafty old devil, catches those who are not alert. As I pondered the verse I realized that usually my adversary is more like the stealthy cat than a roaring lion. He comes quietly, swiftly, with deadly aim. Especially when I am asleep or distracted. My task is to keep alert, awake, and vigilant lest I become another Lady Bunny.

Not to fear! The verses that form an envelope for the roaring lion verse give me fortitude to face the foe. In verse 7 I am admonished to cast all my anxiety on the One who cares for me. In verse 9 I am encouraged to resist. In verse 10 I am assured that "the God of all grace, who has called you to his eternal glory in Christ, will himself restore, establish, and strengthen you" (RSV).

In His hand I am safe. NANCY JEAN VYHMEISTER

MARCH 15

I'm Too Busy!

How gracious he will be when you cry for help! As soon as he hears, he will answer you. Isa. 30:19, NIV.

God gave me a little girl to love and train. Since I wanted to be the perfect mother, I read everything I could find on the subject of child rearing. One article advised that rather than frustrate my toddler by saying no too often, I could, whenever appropriate, tell her that I couldn't do what she wanted immediately, but would as soon as possible. It sounded reasonable to me, a busy working mother. But I had no realization how often I had used that line until one day I called my 2-year-old to come to me.

"I can't wite now," she chirped. "I too busy."

Of course, I had to go stop her from whatever had originally prompted my call, but the rueful smile on my face told Cheryl that she had sidestepped Mommy's discipline *that* time! I also learned that I must be careful how I applied what I read.

How grateful we can be that God is never too busy to hear our earnest prayer! He may indeed tell us to wait awhile, but we need to remember that the wait is for our own best good, never because God is too busy.

Little ones know us and look to their moms and dads before they know and depend on God. They need to learn that parents, like God, are never too busy to hear their childish petitions. Even if they must sometimes "wait awhile," their parents too have their best interests at heart.

When these children become adults, they will remember that early training and will keep their eyes fixed on their heavenly Father as they call upon Him, knowing that His answer will come, and powerfully. May we remember this lesson in our lives too.

LEA HARDY

Where Is the Joy?

The joy of the Lord is your strength. Neh. 8:10, NKJV.

When I was growing up, one of my favorite little choruses was the familiar little song "I have the joy, joy, joy, joy, down in my heart." Its lilting melody and sweet words always gave me a lift. I am sorry to say, though, that through the years I haven't always demonstrated that joy as I should have. You see, there have been many times that it was so far down in my heart that it was pretty well hidden from me—and from everybody else.

I am making a new determination that with God's help I will first do my best to remove all stones and thorns from others' paths, and then spread for my family and the world a fragrant, flower-strewn pathway of deep, true, and boundless joyfulness.

All of us can look back at the great moments of joy in our lives: our marriage, the birth of our children, baptism, graduation. But even these happy and joyous occasions are often mingled with a touch of sadness. "If only so and so could have been here"; "If only it hadn't . . ." On and on we go, wishing for everything to be perfect. So you see, the most important thing we need to do is to decide to be joyful where we are, *with what we have,* no matter what happens to us. While we look vainly for more happiness and joy in this old world, it would be well to consider the truth that the meaning of an event depends on who experiences it and how.

G. K. Chesterton once said, "An adventure is only an inconvenience rightly considered. An inconvenience is only an adventure wrongly considered." If he meant that, he could have enjoyed a traffic jam, had he been in the right frame of mind.

Someone has suggested, "When choosing your attire for the day, be sure it includes a happy face," because "a smile is a curve that can set a lot of things straight" and "all people smile in the same language."

"I have the joy, joy, joy, joy, down in my heart!" How about singing that little chorus with me right now—and sing it with a smiling, happy, joyful, shining face! What a beautiful witness you will be to what *true joy* really is!

HAZEL MARIE GORDON

Chocolate Cupcakes

Be kind and compassionate to one another. Eph. 4:32, NIV.

*I*t was one of those "3-h" afternoons—hazy, hot, and *very* humid—and Mandy and I were out in it, coming home from her annual visit to the vet. I had just settled the cat, in her carrying case, into the car when a pickup truck pulled up behind us in the parking lot. Leaning out and pointing to my back wheel, the driver said, "Ma'am, you'd better fix that flat tire before you go anywhere."

I hadn't noticed the flat. We needed help.

The receptionist at the vet's office cheerfully offered me the phone to call the auto club. Then she added, "I'll go get you a cupcake. Chocolate always helps at times like this." She disappeared, returning a minute or two later with a white-frosted chocolate cupcake, probably left over from a lunchtime treat. Someone had decorated it with chocolate sprinkles and two tiny pawprints.

What a creative and appropriate touch, I thought, eating it gratefully as I sat down on a waiting-room bench.

Mandy huddled in the corner of her pet carrier, too frightened of the dogs in the waiting room even to utter a pitiful yowl, her usual carrying-case behavior. The auto club dispatcher had promised help in "45 minutes or less." Together the cat and I hunkered down for a long wait.

To my surprise, a tow truck pulled into the parking lot in about 10 minutes and singled out my car. In no time Mandy and I were headed home, spare tire firmly in place and flat tire in the trunk to be repaired later.

When things like this happen, I like to remember that it's not only in major cities that angels assist us; they're also with us through inconveniences such as this unplanned-for delay on a steamy Friday afternoon. I imagine that angels rather enjoy working through ordinary but willing human beings to get us safely on our way again with a warning, a helpful word, a thoughtful deed—or even a chocolate cupcake.   JOCELYN FAY

Spring

For, lo, the winter is past, the rain is over and gone. S. of Sol. 2:11.

As I gazed across the fields, thoughts raced through my
    mind.
Then, feelings of thankfulness that winter is behind.
The snowdrop gave me hope, the primrose gave me
    joy.
The daffodil gave me peace.
For a moment I became gold and regal, cream and
    white,
Tall stems of green, a daffodil in the light."

The very first snowdrop this year told me it won't be long—
spring is just around the corner. Then I saw some primroses clustered together under a shrub, hiding from the cruel wind, and I
really felt spring was near. These little flowers are such a blessing
and a promise to the human spirit. We often think of Easter and
new beginnings at this time. Maybe it can mean a new beginning for
you, too. Perhaps after a long winter you can emerge like a new
spring flower.

Have you ever closely examined a daffodil, which was beautifully created for our pleasure? Have you felt its soft petals in wondrous shades of yellows and golds? The bulbs have been lying
quietly in the dark earth, waiting patiently for the time of renewal.
Then suddenly they bloom in all their glory. Can you become a daffodil in your imagination? Feel its beauty and give God thanks for
this ability to use your mind with new eyes and a new heart. Spring
is not only a season. Spring is also an attitude of mind, leaving behind the long, cold winter and hearing new whispers of hope in the
days to come.

Getting out in the fresh spring air can be an absolute joy, as you
look around and see the beauty of the land. God has given us so
much for which to be thankful!

Even though the nights may be long and dreary, the days will
become longer and lighter. Leave your mistakes and troubles behind—let them go and come alive like the daffodils. The cool kiss
of spring will touch you, and a new dawn will appear before you.

It's a time of hope, joy, and renewal!   PHILIPPA MARSHALL

Come, Lord Jesus

Let not your heart be troubled: ye believe in God, believe also in me. In my Father's house are many mansions: if it were not so, I would have told you. I go to prepare a place for you. And if I go and prepare a place for you, I will come again, and receive you unto myself; that where I am, there ye may be also. John 14:1-3.

Train whistles . . . The long, plaintive cry of a train whistle gives me a lonely feeling. It brings back poignant memories of my childhood when my mother and two sisters and I lived on the Alberta prairie with our uncle. Hearing of fabulous gold mines up north, our father had left with the promise that he would return a rich man. So we waited, prayed, and hoped. But he did not return.

The three of us girls, young and naive, clung together many times as we listened to the whistle of the steam engine and saw the long passenger train speed through the valley to our little town. We prayed that our hardly remembered father would be on that train. We imagined him getting off the train, waiting for his baggage, then coming by car to our uncle's farm. Then we watched for the cars. One was coming our way . . . Would our father be in that car? No, it turned south. Another appeared. In anticipation we held our breath. But it too passed by.

Jesus has promised to come again. He left a message in John 14:1-3 that He will come again. And He has promised riches and heavenly mansions and eternal life. His promises are sure. He will not fail. Even now He is preparing those mansions for us. "I have gone to prepare a place for you."

As children we were not concerned about the gold or the riches our father promised to bring with him when he returned. All we prayed for, all we looked forward to, was to see him and be with him again.

As we look forward to Jesus' return we will not be looking for the houses and golden streets He has promised. The joy of seeing our Saviour and being with Him will be our ultimate reward. So we wait, pray, and hope. Come soon, Lord Jesus. We want to see You!

MARGARET CAMPBELL

MARCH 20

Springtime in Your Life

Therefore, if anyone is in Christ, he is a new creation; the old has gone, the new has come! 2 Cor. 5:17, NIV.

*W*hat a pleasure it gives a teacher to be able to write on a student's report "Shows promise." But appearing to be promising isn't everything.

When Enrico Caruso was a boy, his mother tried to stop him from singing. She said his voice sounded like the wind going through the shutters! She was not to know that he would become the greatest voice of his time.

How different things are with God. Take springtime, for example. Every year He shows just what He can do with unpromising material: wizened brown lumps burst into the yellow, white, and gold of daffodils, snowdrops, and crocuses. Stark black twigs uncurl powdery catkins and shake out fresh green leaves. Every springtime is a miracle!

And what about you and me? Whether or not anyone else sees promise in us, God does. So if your faith has gone a bit gray, if you don't seem to be getting anywhere, remember His plans to prosper you and give you hope and a future. Ask Him to count you in on the springtime experience, and He'll perform a miracle in your life just as He does in the fields and the forest. God not only sees promise in you; He'll develop and grow it, making something of your life far beyond your expectations.   PEGGY MASON

MARCH 21

To Be a Hyacinth

But thanks be to God, who always leads us in triumphal procession in Christ and through us spreads everywhere the fragrance of the knowledge of him. 2 Cor. 2:14, NIV.

*S*pringtime brings many new things. One of the most wonderful is the hyacinth. It's not a flashy flower, however; its presence is most obvious because of its full fragrance. It's a flower that cannot be hid, for even one flower gives off abundant perfume.

Oh, how I yearn for the presence of hyacinths in my life each day. A favorite poem honoring the flower speaks to my very soul:

> Hyacinths to Feed Thy Soul
> If of thy mortal goods thou art bereft
> And from thy slender store two loaves alone are left,
> Sell one and with the dole
> Buy hyacinths to feed thy soul.
> —Attributed to the Gulistan of Moslih Eddin Saadi

This humble flower reminds me of Jesus. And I wonder, as a Christian, am I like the lovely hyacinth, small in my blooming spot yet full of aroma for Jesus? I've lived many places. Was His fragrance left behind because I was there? Do people know about Him because I bloom where I am now? Is His sweet odor evident, like the hyacinth's?

Pondering these thoughts, I make a perfumed promise to be a hyacinth for Jesus, not only in springtime, but all year long, each year of my life, wherever I am. I want to live out 2 Corinthians 2:14 by being a fragrant friend of Jesus and all the others He allows me to meet, to know, and to love along the way.   BETTY KOSSICK

MARCH 22

Peace in the Storm

Acquaint now thyself with him, and be at peace. Job 22:21.

A huge pine tree towers above our house. One day while admiring the grandeur of the tree, I spied a nest. I scanned the tree with binoculars until my eyes found the nest, where a mother robin sat calmly, waiting for her eggs to hatch.

A few days later an unexpected storm toppled trees in the area, scattering limbs, twigs, and leaves in every direction. I remembered the robin and went to the backyard, expecting to see the nest and its contents spilled onto the ground. I didn't see anything, so I scanned with my binoculars until I once more found the nest. Sure enough, there sat mother robin, calm and undisturbed, as if there had been no storm.

Earlier that same day we had received an alert placing the area under a storm watch. An employee, radio blaring, ran into the room. The watch had now become a warning. A large group of employees hurried to the restrooms, while others of us went into a large classroom. We were advised to get down on the floor and, at a given signal, to place our heads between our knees.

Prayer was offered, and we scrambled to get under desks. A young woman said to me, "I'm going to stay close to you, if you don't mind." I told her that was all right. Suddenly a hand grabbed my leg and squeezed so tightly I was glad it wasn't my neck.

Sometimes the storms of life lash down with fury. In our distress we seek something or someone to hold on to. When problems of all kinds threaten our security, we become frightened and leave the security of our "nest" in search of help. Like the mother robin, it is possible to sit calmly, undisturbed and secure in the knowledge that God is in control. MABEL ROLLINS NORMAN

MARCH 23

That Weekend

That which was from the beginning, which we have heard, which we have seen with our eyes, which we have looked at and our hands have touched—this we proclaim concerning the Word of Life . . . which was with the Father and has appeared to us . . . to make our joy complete. 1 John 1:1-4, NIV.

On Friday, an actual, historical Friday, Jesus faced an ignominious and horrific death for you and me. The hill may have been far away, but God's own Son, the Creator of the universe, allowed it all to happen to Him to pay the price for our sins, yours and mine. This event was no cunningly devised fable, but reported by reliable eyewitnesses. His friends all had been at the back of the crowd. Not one of those who walked or saw or heard because of a miracle He had performed raised a voice in protest. God's own Son was treated as a criminal. And He went through it all for you and me.

On Saturday, an actual, historical Saturday, Jesus lay asleep in Joseph's tomb, apparently ending the hopes of all those who had looked to Him as their Redeemer, but misunderstood how it would come about. He died the death all men die, and a shabby death it was. God allowed it all to happen to Him for you and me.

On Sunday, an actual, historical Sunday, there happened a stupendous event, some say the most stupendous event of this world's history. Jesus defeated death. He rose. Not a spirit. Not a ghost. Not the figment of someone's imagination. But Himself, whole, real, flesh and blood. Not a cunningly devised fable, but recognized by those who saw Him, who heard Him, who touched Him. Reliable witnesses. Those who knew Him best. And the tomb was empty. What an incredible morning that must have been! Jesus, alive, forgiving. To those who had deserted Him, He was full of loving plans for their future, promising His presence with them always. And not only them, but all who would believe in Him and all the promises He made, and the life He offers in exchange for their sins. And He did all this for you and me.

Can we ever be the same again when we've taken all that in? Have we really taken it in?   PEGGY MASON

MARCH 24

Smiles

See how the lilies of the field grow. . . . Not even Solomon in all his splendor was dressed like one of these. Matt. 6:28, 29, NIV.

*E*ven beyond her natural flair for style, on that day my friend looked especially attractive. After talking with her for a few minutes, I commented that she looked very nice. Then with the finesse of a garden rake I added, "But I don't know why." Such tact! I was feeling so awkward over those last words, but she, ever gracious, remarked that perhaps it was the flowers. Yes, the flowers. The fabric of her dress was a profusion of rich and vibrant flowers.

Another day as I walked away from the farmers' market with my arms full of sunflowers, I noticed that when people looked at me, their faces broke out in smiles. And as I paused for a moment to watch other flower buyers, they too were smiling as they carried away their flowers.

Why is that? I wondered. When I give a gift of a flower I am rewarded with a smile (try it yourself and see). When I am given flowers, I can feel myself smile a huge wide grin. Maybe a smile is the human version of a flower . . . Or maybe a flower is nature's version of a smile.

Flowers are unique and varied, and each is beautiful. Shades and hues of color reflect the sunlight and accent their surroundings.

When a flower opens, it is as if nature is smiling up at us. And fragrance—roses and orange blossoms and honeysuckle, and lavender and lilacs fill our evenings with their perfume.

Flowers laugh up at us silly humans who are worried about so many things. Swaying in the breeze, responding to the sunlight, thriving right where they are planted, flowers grace our homes and our lives as they teach us to stand quietly and enjoy the gift of being. Just by existing, they produce pleasure and enjoyment, and sing of a Creator who is extravagant.

I wonder if God smiled when He created flowers. I wonder if He smiles when each one blooms. Do you think He finds pleasure as we take delight in this gift?

Perhaps whenever a flower opens, it is God smiling into our lives. Maybe that's why we can't help smiling back.   ALICE HEATH

MARCH 25

The Big Fat Woman in the Marketplace

Pray also for me, that whenever I open my mouth, words may be given me so that I will fearlessly make known the mystery of the gospel. . . . Pray that I may declare it fearlessly, as I should. Eph. 6:19, 20, NIV.

God spoke to me, using these very words during one special evening program planned and performed by five of my grandchildren. My two sons, their wives, my husband, and I were the delighted audience. Those five children had spent the preceding three days together for the first time in their lives, and they celebrated the joy of it by presenting this program to us. Guitar duets, vocal solos, duets, and choruses, all accompanied at the keyboard by our 11-year-old piano artist, delighted us. It was a once-in-a-lifetime experience.

The final number was a roof-raising rendition of the favorite song of our two 6-year-olds, "Hey, Mon." I smiled as the children began the song. It was when they began the second verse that I heard God speak to me—through singing child voices.

> "Well, the big, fat woman in the marketplace
> She yell so loud she get red in the face,
> She preach the gospel every day;
> If you listen, you can hear her say,

"'Hey, hey, mon, do you know my Lord?
  Hey, hey, mon, do you know my Lord?
  Tell the people from door to door,
  Hey, hey, mon, do you know my Lord?'"

You see, for the first time in my life I am fighting the battle of weight. Although you most likely wouldn't call me *fat,* my dress size has changed, and I am surprised when I catch a glimpse of myself in the mirror. I am no longer eager to speak or preach because I don't like how I look. But as I listened to the children sing, I suddenly longed to be like the woman in the marketplace. I wanted to be so on fire for the Lord that it didn't matter what I looked like. I wanted to boldly ask, "Do you know my Lord, my beautiful Lord?" I wanted to be that woman!

When the program concluded, I asked the children if they would mind if I added a testimony in response to their song. I told them I wanted to be like that woman in the song. I wanted to speak up for the Lord, no matter what I looked like, no matter where I was. My sons smiled and eyed me strangely. The children laughed, and we ended the evening by joining hands in a circle of prayer.

Large women; little, skinny ones; tall; short; young or old—whatever our physical makeup—may we be willing to shout out to whomever we meet, "Oh, say, do you know my Lord?"

CARROL JOHNSON SHEWMAKE

MARCH 26

I Will Tell of His Love

I will declare thy name unto my brethren: in the midst of the congregation will I praise thee. Ps. 22:22.

When I think of my Saviour at Calvary,
      How they scoffed and rejected Him there,
      And just one little word would have freed Him.
It was love, not the nails held Him there.

I will tell of His love, I will tell of His love.
I will tell how He died on the tree.
I will tell of His love for the sinner.
I will tell how He loves even me.

All the hairs of your head He has numbered,
And the fall of the sparrow He sees.
Not one thing in your life goes unnoticed
By the Saviour who loves you and me.

When He comes in the clouds in His glory,
And His dear face at last I shall see,
Then what joy it will be through the ages
Just to tell of His sweet love for me.

I will tell of His love, I will tell of His love.
I will tell how He died on the tree.
I will tell of His love for the sinner.
I will tell how He loves even me.

JEANNIE SCHMIDT

MARCH 27

Rejoice!

Rejoice in the Lord always. I will say it again: Rejoice! Phil.
4:4, NIV.

*I*t was getting close to Easter when the letter came informing
our little church that a special choir was being assembled to
perform an Easter cantata. We were being invited to participate. The
letter had been delayed, so rehearsals had already started some
weeks earlier. Another woman and I were two sopranos from our
church who could participate. When we asked the conductor,
Melissa, if she had any need of more sopranos, she answered, "I have
been praying, asking the Lord to send me two more sopranos!"

We went to the next rehearsal. Melissa, a young woman who
started each practice with prayer, reminded us that the reason for
our performing this concert was to praise the Lord, thanking Him
for the gift of His Son. The concert was a success, and it was a joy
to participate.

But what comes first to my mind as I think back on this experience is Melissa. She radiated such happiness, such assurance in the
knowledge of her salvation through Jesus Christ, that anyone who
saw and talked with her had to notice.

I wonder if people see me as such a happy Christian. I have

every reason to rejoice and be happy, to celebrate. I know that God loves me and is willing and able to save me. Do I show it?

We have no reason for long faces, for doubts, because we are assured of God's love and power to save us. He really cares. Isn't that reason enough to be happy and show everyone that we believe and rejoice always? Let's do it. ANNA JOHANSEN

MARCH 28

Faith Brought the Answer

O thou that hearest prayer, unto thee shall all flesh come. Ps. 65:2.

While I was employed in a hospital, it was my privilege to act as the public stenographer for patients. In this work I became acquainted with a number of refined, highly cultured individuals—teachers, city mayors, and business executives. In the 1920s patients were especially encouraged to remain in the hospital for several weeks, and sometimes for months or years, in order to learn a healthful lifestyle. Social events, especially those held in the evenings, were attended by employees as well as patients, and in this way employees had contact with patients they would not have otherwise met.

One female patient suffered severely from pernicious anemia. The giving of transfusions was far from perfect in those days, so not much could be done to alleviate the pain that accompanied this disease. This lady became well acquainted with Jesus during her long stay. When I had the opportunity I visited her, and we became friends. Then I changed employment and moved away to another city. Before leaving, I paid her one last visit. She was in great pain at the time, with one of her limbs cramping constantly. She asked that I offer prayer for her. I gladly agreed to do so. The nurses regularly offered prayer for their patients when they bid them good night. The physicians also prayed for and with their patients.

I knelt beside her bed, requesting that God, our Creator, who knew how much this lady could bear, would relieve her cramping, if it was His will. She was healed immediately and said I appeared like an angel to her. I later learned that this woman gave her heart to God before she left the sanitarium. I was especially blessed by this news, knowing that I, through my prayers on her behalf, had played a role in her conversion experience.

We never know just how or when our prayers for others will be answered, but we can be assured that our Lord hears our faithful petitions for these precious souls. IDAMAE MELENDY

Finding the Right Gift
Thanks be to God for his indescribable gift! 2 Cor. 9:15, NIV.

For more than 10 years now I have traveled extensively throughout the world. And this opportunity has given me a gift that is indescribable. I have found beautiful Christian sisters and brothers on every continent and on many islands of the earth. And it will be a joy to share heaven together.

Quite often before we say our goodbyes, these dear sisters whom I've come to work beside want to send me home with something that will remind me of them. And there's not enough space to begin to tell you of the variety of love gifts I've received. In Siberia I was gifted with two smoked fish, wrapped in brown paper and delivered with obvious sacrificial love. In Indonesia the ladies gave me a large, hand-woven "sack" with a loop that I am to place on top of my head, allowing the sack to hang down my back—to be filled with children and groceries, etc. I have never offered to let my grandchildren get into this sack, because I'm quite certain they'd take me up on the offer, and my head and neck are not accustomed to carrying such weights. In Riga, Latvia, my husband and I were given a large doll in native dress; in Africa, a beautiful handwoven basket in bright shades of raspberry and blue; and in Sacramento, California, a teapot with hand-painted roses.

Each gift is special—chosen with care, given with love, and many times out of sacrifice. There have been times I've resisted the urge to say "No, I can't accept this gift. You have needs of your own that must be met. Please, keep this gift and sell it. Feed your babies and yourself." But the words will never leave my mouth, try as I might to say them. Because there is such joy in giving a gift, I can't deny someone the gift of giving. And there is a second gift—because of the gift, the gift giver will not be forgotten.

After a week of leadership training in the Ukraine, our sisters wanted to give four of us a gift. Times were especially difficult. Food was scarce. And beyond this, it was almost impossible to find something special in the shops, even if you had money. So on the final day when we would say our goodbyes, one of the brothers was sent to town to purchase three gifts. Hurrying here and there, with the clock ticking away, he had almost given up hope when he paused to look through a cloudy window in a secondhand shop. There, on a shelf, stood four matching vases of the same size and style, but with different varieties of flowers painted on them. He rushed into the shop and asked the price of the four vases. He could hardly believe his ears when the lady behind the counter asked for the exact amount of money that he clenched in his fist buried deep in his pocket. Four women. Four vases. And the price was right! A gift of rare beauty had been found in a most unlikely place. There was no question that these four vases were meant for us. Even today my vase with the pink roses reminds me of God's leading every time I pass my china cabinet.

Our heavenly Father searched all of heaven for just the "right" Gift. A Gift that not only would bring joy, but was capable of giving life—eternal life! The Gift was extremely costly, but it was the only Gift that would do. And the Gift was none other than the Son of God. Jesus Christ, our Lord and Saviour! The wrapping was not gold foil, but a shroud. And the unwrapping was done by unseen, heavenly hands. One foggy morning the Gift walked free and disclosed to a woman with a scarlet past that He had paid the price for the sins of the world. Jesus Christ, the Son of God, disclosed this incomprehensible truth to a woman whose only hope was in staying close to the Gift. Her name was Mary—like His mother's.

Walk free, the Gift says over and over. I paid the price! The gift is Mine to give. And I choose to give it to *you!*   ROSE OTIS

MARCH 30

A Mother's Sacrifice

When they had twisted a crown of thorns, they put it on His head, and a reed in His right hand. And they bowed the knee before Him and mocked Him, saying, "Hail, King of the Jews!" Then they spat on Him, and took the reed and struck Him on the head. Matt. 27:29, 30, NKJV.

Stunned, I watched the angry mob push and shove the Saviour as the Roman soldiers placed Him under arrest. Anger seized me, and I felt pressed to go to His defense. Instinctively I wanted to protect Him from such nauseating cruelty—the feeling one gets when observing a bully mistreating an innocent victim.

Jesus turned to say goodbye to His mother, and it was this gesture that completely melted my heart. My eyes filled with tears, and I had no control over their warm cascade descending my face.

In 1990 my husband and I attended the magnificent Passion Play in Oberammergau, Germany. Since it is presented only once every 10 years, we felt it was an opportunity not to be missed. The scenes portrayed of our Lord's life made all of His suffering so intensely real that one could not help feeling quite moved emotionally and spiritually.

However, the particular scene that overwhelmed me was that of Jesus' farewell to His mother, Mary. Having raised a son of my own, my whole motherly being intensified with her experience. That moment of complete devastation made me aware of something I had never thought of before: the feelings of Mary, the mother of Christ. How did she feel as she witnessed her Son's crucifixion?

A Mother's Sacrifice

When I reflect on Calvary
And ponder how Christ died for me,
I also wonder how Mary felt
As near her Son's cruel cross she knelt.

The Messiah she had borne in strife
Was about to yield up His life.
It must have torn her quite apart;
His suffering must have wrenched her heart.

Did Mary stifle back her wails,
Or wince at the sound of the driven nails?
Could uncontrolled sobs be heard by all?
On the name of the Father did she call?

As she looked into His anguished face,
Did she wish that she could take His place?
While watching Him through tear-brimmed eyes,
Did she cover her mouth to muffle the cries?

While questioning why this had to be,
To the Father did she plea,
Reminding Him what He surely knew—
That Jesus was her dear Son, too?

ALBERTA BENNETT CICCARELLI

His Sheep

You are my sheep, the sheep of my pasture and I am your God, says the Lord God. Eze. 34:31, NRSV.

*T*here is a special feeling that fills us as we watch the young lambs romp and play in the pastures in the spring. They seem to be using pogo sticks as they stiffen their legs and bounce up and down. Covered with white wool, their nimble bodies twist and turn as they play, each one reveling in being alive.

Running to their mothers, the lambs nuzzle and find a delectable meal. Refreshed, with full tummies, they again rush off to play. The mothers seem to understand their lambs' need to exercise and have freedom to play. Back again, the little ones go to their mothers to nurse until they are full and contented. Then it's time to snuggle down for a nap, confident their mothers will watch over them.

Farmers too watch over their sheep. They have the ability to protect those entrusted to their care. A good farmer will maintain the pasture fences so they will be strong and enclose the sheep in a protected environment.

I too enjoy life. There are times I feel the need to play, to run through the grass and leave my cares behind. Later I need nourishment and rest. God understands my desires and needs, and allows me the privilege of indulging in play. He gives me rest and faithfully watches over me.

If I trust in Him and stay in the pastures He has provided, the fences He has built for me will envelop me in His protection. I have the blessed assurance that I am His sheep and He is my God.

EVELYN GLASS

The Sparrow's Lesson

Do not fear therefore, you are of more value than many sparrows. Matt. 10:31, NKJV.

*I*t's springtime! The trees are budding, the flowers are beginning to bloom, and the birds are warbling their songs. As I opened the door to allow the bright sunshine into the room, I noticed six sparrows on my front step pecking at some particles of food. Their drab color did not prevent them from enjoying their sparrow life.

My thoughts immediately turned to our text for today. Do I really believe that I am of more value than the sparrow? Why do I worry about my next meal, my month's rent, getting a job, or my brother's finding one as well? Does my attitude indicate that I am more valuable than the sparrow? Created in God's image, a child of the King, do I really believe that He can take care of my needs—spiritual, physical, emotional, and social? Do I wander about as though I have no heavenly Father who is interested in me? Do I get amnesia about the things that He has done for me in the past and increase my gray hair count by worrying unnecessarily?

Ann Landers, the syndicated columnist, once said, "Stop worrying. The bridges you cross before you come to them are almost always over rivers that aren't there."

I said a short prayer as I washed the dishes: "Lord, forgive me for doubting that You can provide for me. Thank You for the sparrows, insignificant and unattractive as they may seem when compared to the many more colorful birds, because they remind me of Your love for me. Like the sparrows, help me to trust You more. Amen!"

ANDREA A. BUSSUE

Chosen Ones

Ye have not chosen me, but I have chosen you, and ordained you, that ye should go and bring forth fruit, and that your fruit should remain: that whatsoever ye shall ask of the Father in my name, he may give it you. John 15:16.

She was just a tiny thing when we first brought her home. We chose her from a litter of 13 half-Dalmatian, half-"black dog" puppies. She was white, with a black mask on her face and a black saddle across her back, and had black velvet ears and the cutest white-tipped black tail. She would get more black spots later. We named her Shasta.

She was my companion and followed me everywhere. We "worked" together in the garden. While I pulled weeds she'd sit as close as she could to me, sometimes putting her head in my lap. When I arrived home after a three-week absence, she was there to greet me as soon as I opened the car door.

It had been an extremely hot day. We had been busy all day digging sweet potatoes. My husband decided to use the car to bring the potatoes up the hill to the house. Neither of us knew that Shasta had taken refuge from the heat under the car. It was an accident, but the unthinkable happened. Shasta lay dying; her eyes were fixed, and her head was seriously injured. However, at the sound of my voice she wagged her tail in one last display of love and trust. We buried her on the hill overlooking the garden.

Several days prior to Shasta's death I had been praying to know, to feel deeply, what an infinite sacrifice God our Father made in giving Jesus to come to this earth to live and die for our sins, to know some of the anguish He felt. When I look at Shasta's life and death I am reminded in a small way of Jesus' life and death. Just as I chose Shasta to be obedient and to serve me, so the Father chose to allow Jesus to come to this earth to live and die so we could be saved. Just as Shasta was killed by those she loved and served, so Jesus was killed by those He loved and came to save. As I watched Shasta dying, knowing there was nothing I could do to save her, so His heavenly Father watched Jesus die, knowing there was nothing He could do if we were to have the hope of eternal life.

Heavenly Father, I do better understand how You must have suffered when Jesus died on the cross, and how You must suffer when we suffer. Thank You, Father, for allowing me to be one of the chosen ones Jesus died to save.   MONICA STOCKER TAYLOR

APRIL 3

The Heavenly Guide

You're blessed when you stay on course, walking steadily on the road revealed by Yahweh. You're blessed when you follow his directions. . . . How can [I] live a clean life? By carefully reading the map of your Word. . . . Don't let me miss the road signs you've posted. . . . I'm a stranger in these parts; give me clear directions. . . . Barricade the road that goes Nowhere; grace me with your clear revelation. I choose the true road to Somewhere. Ps. 119:1-30, Message.

As a passenger in an automobile, I am not what one might call very alert about recognizing where I am. No matter how many times the driver may take the same route with me in tow, I go along, as we say, for the ride. My family and friends will attest that I am perfectly capable of suddenly "coming to," totally mystified, at any point in even a routine trip. "Where are we, anyway? How in the world did we get here?" I will quite likely demand to know.

"Where have *you* been?" someone will counter.

Who knows? Probably on a mental detour composing literature for the ages while simultaneously shooing the family pooch away from a freshly boiled-over puddle of applesauce.

Even when I am the driver, I am equally hapless and hopeless at following oral directions. I tend to get lost. Like most women, however, I am at least willing to pull into a service station to ask for help.

A biblical sense of onrushing doom seizes me and my eyes glaze over, however, when someone begins, "Well, you need to head out yonder. Proceed northeast on Broad Street for a few miles, then turn left onto Highway 30 somewhere beyond the I-80 overpass under construction. Go through that temporary one-way stuff and make a sharp right on alternate S.R. 134. Drive a couple miles and then hang a quick left in front of Harry's Bait Shop. If you see Sam's Laundromat on your right, you've gone too far. The place you want is down a ways on the left. You can't miss it."

Thus for understandable reasons I keep a whole fistful of maps and guidebooks stuffed into the glove compartment of my car. Sometimes even they come up short, but more often they serve as the critical link between me and my destination.

Fortunately for me, the Master Cartographer and Guide offers a heavenly guidebook to rectify the human defects in my sense of direction. "Yahweh, teach me lessons for living so I can stay the course. Give me insight so I can do what you tell me—my whole life one long, obedient response. Guide me down the road of your commandments; I love traveling this freeway!" (Ps. 119: 33-35, Message). With His divine travel assistance to direct my route from the asphalt jungle to the streets of gold, I really *can't* miss it.

ANDREA KRISTENSEN

APRIL 4

Seeking Jesus

When they did not find him, they went back to Jerusalem to look for him. Luke 2:45, NIV.

The hills are bright with songbirds and the flowers of
        early spring.
    Returning pilgrims from Passover lift their hearts
        to sing.
    A joyous Galilean couple mingle with their friends,
    And with them leave Jerusalem, as celebration ends.
    And everything seems well.

    All day the caravans traverse the steep and rocky road,
    Until at setting sun the weary travelers rest their load.
    With Joseph, Mary now prepares the simple meal
        at hand,
    Awaiting Jesus' cheerful help with duties they
        have planned.
    But Jesus is not here.

    Now puzzled, they begin to search among the
        pilgrim throng
    To find their Son, whose winsome voice is often heard
        in song.

But He is missing, and the pair is gripped with
    sudden fear.
They bitterly reproach themselves that Jesus is
    not here,
And night is drawing on.

With dark foreboding they recall how in His infancy
King Herod sought to kill their Child, and they were
    forced to flee.
Back toward Jerusalem they hasten, filled with
    wretched shame,
And pass two nights in anxious seeking, calling oft
    His name.
They cannot find their Son.

Once more with worshipers they mingle in the
    Temple there,
In desperate search to find their Boy, and on their lips
    a prayer.
They scrutinize each face; with grieving hearts
    they agonize,
Till suddenly, His captivating voice they recognize!
Their precious Child is found!

No other voice is quite like His—so filled with melody;
No other presence seems so blended with divinity.
"Son, why have You thus dealt with us?" His mother
    braves to ask,
But it is she who has neglected her important task,
And careless, lost her Son.

"Why were you searching?" Jesus gently questions,
    "Didn't you know
That I must be about My Father's business?" Now
    a glow
Of light from heaven is shining, and the parents realize
This Son whom they have reared is the Son of God in
    human guise,
Though only 12 years old.

Oh, have we too lost touch with Jesus? Do we slip away
Without His presence as we hurry through
    another day?
Do we attempt to shoulder burdens He would

gladly bear,
Then, like the travelers at dusk, find Jesus is not there
And face the dark alone?

Have we too sought Him weeping when our sorrows
    are too great
Because we have neglected Him and sadly made
    Him wait?
His lovely voice entreats us in our silent place
    of prayer.
If we but listen on our knees, we'll surely find
    Him there,
Just waiting at the door.

LORRAINE HUDGINS

APRIL 5

My Harbor

God is our refuge and strength, an ever-present help in trouble.
Therefore we will not fear. Ps. 46:1, 2, NIV.

*E*ven after 25 years the memory is fresh in my mind. Our
school was having a social function that evening, so my sister
and I hurried through supper and made our way back to the building to join our classmates. When we got there, parents and teachers
were pulling up in cars, and students were pairing off in twos and
threes and getting into the waiting cars. My sister had a boyfriend
and was soon seated in one of the cars with him and another couple.

All were soon on their way, leaving me standing alone on the
curb, trying to appear nonchalant. As soon as the cars were out of
sight I ran all the way home, tears blinding my eyes. All I wanted to
do was sneak quietly into my room and have a good cry. But as I
slipped down the hall, I heard my dad calling to me from the
kitchen, where he had been reading the paper. He had heard me
come in and knew that I was home before I should have been.

Pretending with Dad was useless. I sobbed out my story while
he listened quietly. The tears in his eyes assured me that although I
felt unwanted and all alone in the world, I was not. When I look
back on those unsteady teenage years, I realize that the one thing

that kept me going was knowing I had a harbor at home, a place where I was wanted and felt completely safe.

As a grown-up I can no longer run back home to find safety. But I do have a harbor. At times life can be an unsteady ocean of waves. Some problems seemingly have no solution. Hurts can capsize even the strongest of us. Thankfully, we can always turn to Jesus and find a safe harbor. A place of complete peace and safety in the midst of any storm!   RETTA MICHAELIS

APRIL 6

The Power of Love

In this was manifested the love of God toward us, because that God sent his only begotten Son into the world, that we might live through him. 1 John 4:9.

When my friend's son became gravely ill, she was told that an organ transplant could save his life. When she was tested and found compatible, it was agreed that she would become the donor.

One week before the operation, she was involved in an automobile accident that almost took her life. As everyone waited for her to recover, her son's condition deteriorated. Anxiously we sat by her bedside, waiting for her to regain consciousness. As soon as she woke up, she immediately expressed her concern for her son's condition.

"Please call the doctor," she whispered urgently. "I must find out how my son is."

When the doctor arrived, he explained the procedure again, and the possible side effects, even more dangerous now, since she was recovering from an automobile accident.

"Doctor, you don't understand," she pleaded. "You must make the necessary arrangements. I have to do everything possible so that my child might live."

After my visit was over, I sat in my car thinking about the strength of the love that would cause one to make provision to preserve the life of another, even at the cost of losing her own. Suddenly I got a clearer understanding of our heavenly Father's love and a deeper appreciation of the provisions that He made so that I might live—a sacrifice that caused great suffering in order to preserve my life.

I am thankful. I am humbled. I am in awe that the Creator of our universe cares so much about me that He was willing to make such a sacrifice. LORNA LANGLEY

Recharging Batteries

May the God of hope fill you with all joy and peace as you trust in him, so that you may overflow with hope by the power of the Holy Spirit. Rom. 15:13, NIV.

*D*uring Bible study the question was raised, "What does Sabbath mean to you?" Someone answered, "It's a time to recharge your spiritual batteries." Then the teacher explained that when you recharge a battery it is never as good as it was originally. I'm familiar with batteries, and I couldn't help thinking of the spiritual connotations here. Once a week may give your spiritual battery a boost, but it isn't the best way to charge your battery.

My family lives beyond the electrical lines. My computer, vacuum cleaner, refrigerator, stereo, and lights are operated by eight huge, deep-cycle batteries. In order to run our household, these batteries must be strong and charged. The batteries have no power of their own; they need strength from the solar panels that trickle-charge them all day long. This works very well, but once a week they need a deep charge from our generator to keep in tip-top condition. It would be impossible for our batteries to go all week long, waiting for that deep charge at the end of the week. They would give out within a few days, and we would have no power in our house. The trickle charge every day is the best way to keep them strong and usable.

Our spiritual batteries are very similar to my household batteries. We have no strength of our own. Yes, we need the special boost we receive from the Sabbath. The catch is that we can't survive on just one charge per week. We need the daily, and sometimes hourly, time with God to keep us charged. Psalm 105:4 tells us to "seek the Lord, and his strength: seek his face evermore." When the storms of life assail us and troubles cloud our skies, the daily, hourly charging of our spiritual batteries through communication with God is essential.

The Sabbath is a wonderful blessing, a time to reinforce our relationship with Jesus, recognize Him as the Creator, and strengthen our spiritual well-being. But remember, it is the daily relationship with Jesus that needs to be nurtured in order to have strong spiritual batteries. JUDY MUSGRAVE SHEWMAKE

APRIL 8

My Own Prodigal

But while he was still a long way off, his father saw him and was filled with compassion for him; he ran to his son, threw his arms around him and kissed him. Luke 15:20, NIV.

*T*wo months before the birth of our daughter, my 18-year-old stepdaughter came to my husband and me and demanded the money for her college education. "You can't love me now that you have a new daughter coming!" she proclaimed.

Her words hit me like ice water. For nine years I had loved her as if she were my own child. Having said her piece, she collected her money and walked out of our lives. Many friends reassured me that all would be righted after the birth of our baby. We all believed that once she saw her baby sister her heart would melt, and all of her concerns would disappear. But my stepdaughter has never seen her stepsister, so this happy scenario has not yet come to pass.

I often reflect on the similarities between my stepdaughter and the prodigal son (Luke 15:11-32): the demanding of an inheritance, the leaving without any thought of returning, and the older brother who stayed by the family. We are not told of the mother's reaction, how long the son remained estranged from his family, and whether or not his father had an anniversary reaction each year his son was away. What we are told is that his father saw him "while he was still a long way off." This father, so disrespected by his son, was waiting, watching, with his arms open for this child of his to come home. Never once did the father say, "Son, what have you done with your inheritance?" Instead he said, "Let's have a feast and celebrate. For this son of mine was dead and is alive again; he was lost and is found" (verses 23 and 24, NIV).

I too am like the father of the prodigal son, watching and waiting for my lost child to come home. I will greet her with open arms and give her the biggest hug I can, for in spite of our disagreements, I love her. I will not question what she did with her money or what happened in the time that we have been estranged. I too will "kill the fatted calf" (verse 23, NIV) and celebrate, for our family will be whole again.

This experience has taught me the true meaning of unconditional love and forgiveness. If I, with my selfish human nature, can so love and forgive, how much more genuine is the love of our heavenly Father? Our earthly minds cannot grasp the depth or breadth of love the Father has for His children. Our heavenly Father stands with His arms outstretched. He longs to hold us close and say those precious words, "For this son of mine was dead and is alive again; he was lost and is found."

Come home today! Your Father is waiting.   CAREL CLAY

APRIL 9

No Tears in Heaven?

And God shall wipe away all tears from their eyes. Rev. 21:4.

Have you laid to rest your precious child—
    A daughter or a son?
Are you grieving o'er a little one
    Whose life had just begun?
Have you lost your dear companion
    And you fear to be alone?
Do you feel they've taken with them
    All the joy you've ever known?

You've heard about that wondrous place
    Where there are no more tears;
Where everything that grieves or hurts
    Forever disappears.
You count the days, and know that it
    Won't be so very long
Before your Saviour comes to place
    Within your heart a song.

But no more tears in heaven? Oh, I beg to disagree!
    When you reach those heavenly portals,
And you lift your eyes and see
    Your darling one with arms outstretched
And crown a bit askew

With eager steps run toward you
On that golden avenue.

Oh, there'll be tears aplenty
    Pouring down your happy face!
And tears will turn to laughter
    As the two of you embrace.
With sadness all forgotten,
    There will be so much to say
You'll have no more tears of sorrow.
    God will wipe them all away!

LORRAINE HUDGINS

APRIL 10

An Eye-opening Space Trip

For the Lord himself shall descend from heaven with a shout, with the voice of the archangel, and with the trump of God: and the dead in Christ shall rise first: then we which are alive and remain shall be caught up together with them in the clouds, to meet the Lord in the air: and so shall we ever be with the Lord. 1 Thess. 4:16, 17.

One of these days (very soon, I hope) I'm planning to ride a "shuttle" into outer space. I plan to take a long vacation. It will be a trip that is far different from any trip this world has ever known. I won't have the least worry about the liftoff. We will be in secure hands. The Captain of the shuttle has never had an accident and has an absolutely perfect record for safety. In fact, I am sure I will find that it will be a remarkable experience feeling the freedom from walking and the thrilling sensation of space under my feet.

The countdown will be on schedule. I will have a very special Tour Guide on this once-in-a-lifetime journey. And I expect to meet a lot of friends along the way. Indeed, I hope to see people I have not seen for many years.

I am counting on seeing the universe from a different perspective than the limited view I now have. Maybe I'll get a close-up view of the Milky Way and see the planets clearly without the aid of a telescope. Imagine capturing the magnificent beauty of Saturn with its regal rings from a front-row seat.

I am getting so excited about this trip! Don't you want to accompany me? The price of the trip is right, and the accommodations are "out of this world." The food will be absolutely heavenly. In fact, I'm going to enjoy this trip so much that I plan to stay for eternity. Goodbye, cruel world!   PAT MADSEN

APRIL 11

My Dream Bed

Human desires are like the world of the dead—there is always room for more. Prov. 27:20, TEV.

*W*hen I was growing up, one of my dearest dreams (next to having a dog of my own) was to have a room of my own. It would be my own private place, done up in brown, and in that room I would have my very own daybed. A neighbor of mine had a daybed, and I loved it because it was a couch by day and a bed by night. I thought that was very clever. But, alas, I had to share a room with my sister, and my folks said no to both the daybed and the dog.

When I moved out I got my own room and my own dog, but I waited for more than 10 years for the daybed. There were so many other things to spend money on, and I had a perfectly good bed and couch that were donated to me by friends. Finally, though, after poring over ads for almost a year, I bought the daybed of my dreams.

A funny thing happened when the store delivered the bed. It came unassembled, and the deliverymen put it together for me. It turned out to be way too big for my tiny living room or my bedroom. It didn't look that big in the warehouse, but in my home it was a monstrosity. After crawling over it a few times to get to the other side of the room, I moved it into my spare room.

Once the beautiful new daybed was in that room, I realized I was badly in need of new curtains. After I got the new curtains, I saw how shabby the rest of the room looked, how much it needed redecorating.

Getting my dream bed didn't satisfy me—it only made me want even more new things. That one purchase intoxicated me and led to even more purchases. Finally, because of lack of funds, I had to put a halt to my redecorating frenzy. I've learned that instead of desiring more and more earthly possessions, I want a closer relationship with Jesus Christ, for only He can truly satisfy the longings of my heart.

GINA LEE

A New Point of View

And may God, the source of patience and encouragement, enable you to have the same point of view among yourselves by following the example of Christ Jesus. Rom. 15:5, TEV.

*M*y dream of mission service came true after I was married and had four children. Mission life was an education unsurpassed by any university for intensity and clarity. Our family of six sailed out through the Straits of Belle Isle into two and a half years of experience that changed all of us.

On arrival at the Nigerian Training College and Adventist Secondary School in eastern Nigeria, we were advised early on that the indigenous Ibo people were dishonest, lazy, and untrustworthy. That was a very discouraging and unnerving revelation. Then my housekeeper, an Ibo man in his 30s, who was well educated in caring for the needs of pale-faced, ignorant, weak-kneed missionaries, took me to the mammoth market, where I would be doing my trading, and introduced me to his "brothers"—the shopkeepers there who were his friends. A very heartwarming welcome!

Two experiences revealed to me the facts about the Ibo character. First, my husband lent a student the amount of money he needed for his entrance fee because his government stipend had not arrived on time.

"You might as well tell that money goodbye right now," we were told. But three weeks later the student came to the door and handed my husband the exact amount of the loan.

The second experience occurred some time later when I went to the market and purchased, among other things, some batteries. While standing out in front waiting for my ride home, someone tapped me on the shoulder. Turning around, I faced one of the shopkeepers.

"Please, madam, you paid too much for your batteries. My son was tending the shop because I was out for lunch, and he did not know the right price. Please, come back and I will give you your change."

During the rest of our tour, I shopped there many times and was always treated most graciously; never was I cheated. I came home loving those people.

There were, of course, other experiences that are now pleasant memories. As I said before, the tour was a course in living, unsurpassed for intensity and clarity, in the basic goodness of humanity, regardless of origin or color. — GRACE E. STREIFLING

APRIL 13

God's Voice in My Ear

Ears that hear and eyes that see—the Lord has made them both.
Prov. 20:12, NIV.

My fingers flew over the typewriter keys as I hurried to finish a writing deadline. It loomed over me like a dark worry cloud, blocking out everything else. Suddenly, in the midst of my concentration, a small voice whispered, "Go check on Nancy."

I don't have time to go outside now. I've got to finish this before noon! And my fingers kept on typing as I pushed the small voice aside.

Five or 10 minutes later the voice again intruded on my concentration. "Go check on Nancy."

I don't have time! I've got to finish this! I'm sure she's OK. And I continued typing.

Nancy loved to play outside. With her older brother at school, she often played alone all morning. Our large yard held endless possibilities for an inquisitive 5-year-old who loved bugs and animals and plants. Situated at the end of a private road near Bella Vista Hospital in Puerto Rico, it was the perfect place for a nature lover like Nancy.

Again the voice—more insistent now: "Go check on Nancy!"

This time the voice got my attention. *Three times! I'd better go check on her!*

As I stepped out the front door and looked around I spotted Nancy, sound asleep, lying on a retaining wall no more than eight inches wide. The drop on the other side of the wall was at least 12 feet. If she had moved during her sleep, she could easily have fallen and been seriously hurt. Quietly I glided toward her, gently touched her, and softly called her name. Her eyes opened to my smile, and we carefully moved off the wall.

Thank You, Lord! Thank You for guardian angels, and thank You for Your persistence! And please help me to pay attention to Your voice the first time You speak.

How grateful I am that God does not give up easily. He calls me gently, persistently. His voice reminds me of changes He wants to make in my life—changes that have been needed for many years, and yet He does not give up. I am confident He will never abandon me and His voice will lead me through every day. My job is to listen and respond, just for today.   DONNA J. HABENICHT

APRIL 14

Cross-examination

We don't have a priest who is out of touch with our reality. He's been through weakness and testing, experienced it all—all but the sin. So let's walk right up to him and get what he is so ready to give. Take the mercy, accept the help. Heb. 4:15, 16, Message.

When I kneel at the manger to adore a baby God I see beauty. His new, smooth, soft skin; the starlight and angel brightness; the grand heavenly music; and the wonder of a brand-new life all make the scene lovely. I gaze on His small, helpless body with feelings of warmth, tenderness, and love. I feel good about myself as I kneel before a tiny baby God. He could use my protection and care, and that makes me feel worthwhile and needed. Yet one of the main reasons for this first, lovely scene was so the final act could play out.

When I kneel before the cross to gape at a dying God I see ugliness. His bloody, torn flesh; the rough splinters; rusty nails; gloomy clouds; and the finality of a life being tortured to an end all make the scene hideous. There is no music, only sounds of thunder, and from the crowd, jeering, crude jokes, and oaths. From Jesus' dry, cracked lips come groans of loneliness, thirst, and concern. A naked body stretches out in grotesque display. My hands cover my eyes, but I force myself to peer through my fingers. What I see makes me feel revulsion, nausea, pain, horror. I'm also bothered that I can do nothing to help a middle-aged God-man hanging so far out of reach. In fact, I am part of the reason He suffers. His willing offering of His entire being for His enemies makes the way I love even my family and dear friends seem like a stingy pittance. I feel like a zero.

Why does Christ hanging on the cross make me feel so exposed? I don't know. All I do know is that when He looks at me with His omniscient eyes, where I should see hatred, disgust, and loathing I see instead compassion, forgiveness, understanding, and love.

ALBERTA HACK

APRIL 15

He Cares

Call upon Me in the day of trouble; I will deliver you, and you shall glorify Me. Ps. 50:15, NKJV.

In May 1988 we migrated from Germany to Australia. My husband's cousin took us in for the next four months until we bought a house. Both of us found work right away, and we were able to save a bit of money while living at the cousin's house.

Before our emigration, we had handed in our tax return. Any replies were to be sent to my parents, who would pass them on to us. Because we left Germany in the middle of the financial year, we were not sure what the outcome of the tax return would be. However, it appeared there would be a payment.

After about three months our goods arrived in Australia. We were glad to hear this good news. But with it also came bad news—news we had not counted on. When we had arranged for the transport of our goods in Germany we had arranged only for port-to-port delivery, since we didn't have a residential address at that time. It was our responsibility now to find transport from port to home, which we had completely forgotten about in the excitement of starting a new life in a new country. The cost for the transport amounted to $2,450. This was just about the amount we had been able to save while living in my cousin's house, and we had already allocated it for other urgent matters.

Very disappointed and discouraged, we paid this money for the transport of our goods. The other pressing matters would have to wait. Even though we felt discouraged, and even upset, we didn't pray about it. We just accepted it as "one of those things that happen." But the Lord wanted to show us that He cares.

We were still feeling very low the next day when we received a letter from my parents saying that our tax return resulted in a refund that they had paid into our Australian account. This news blew our gloomy moods away. When my husband went to the bank to check on the money transfer, the account stated the sum to be $2,400.

Coincidence? Maybe. Yet we prefer to think that God cares. Very humbly, even embarrassed and ashamed that we hadn't brought this concern before Him, we thanked the Lord. And if we had called upon the Lord, as the text for today suggests, I'm sure our attitude wouldn't have been so negative, and we would have had the experience of yet another answer to prayer.   BEATE KARBSTEIN

APRIL 16

Exemplary Love

A new commandment I give unto you, That ye love one another; as I have loved you, that ye also love one another. John 13:34.

*T*was one of 10 children. My parents became Christians about the time I, their ninth child, was born. With such a big family, their pastor advised them to move out of the city to a farm in the country, so they purchased an 80-acre farm in Michigan.

There was plenty of work for our big family—no time for mischief! In the summer we raised acres of onions. My big brothers would truck them to the market in Detroit. This made work for all of us. I too went out in the fields to weed onions, even when I was as young as 5. I recall my mother's words of praise when I would work rather than play.

My mother toiled from early morning until late at night. Little did I realize then her great responsibilities. If one of us would get sick, we saw her look of concern. The child in greatest need received her focused attention. Sometimes I saw her praying beside a big leather trunk in our storeroom upstairs. I sensed her intimate relationship with Jesus. I felt her deep, unconditional love. As a little girl I remember thinking, *I know what Jesus is like. He's just like Mama.*

Sometimes I wondered how my mother could be happy sacrificing so much for the family. She seldom bought anything for herself. She thought of our needs first. When I was learning to sew, I made my mother a new dress. It was just a cotton dress of pink floral print. It could not have been made very well. But I remember the delight and appreciation in my mother's eyes for that new dress. And I knew it was sincere.

When I quarreled with my younger sister, Alice, I noticed how grieved and hurt my mother looked. She would often say, "Dear children, I want you to love each other. Are you going to treat each other like that when you grow up? I want you always to love each other." We, as a family, haven't forgotten her words.

A few months ago Alice and I were visiting together in our childhood home and sorting through all the family heirlooms. There was the old leather trunk. Alice reminded me how our mother used to pray next to that trunk. Then she expressed her desire to preserve that old trunk with its beautiful memory of our praying, God-fearing mother.

Whenever I read of Jesus' commandment to His disciples to love one another, I am reminded of the words of my mother—remarkably similar to the words of Jesus. The greatest legacy my mother left me was her example of a selfless, self-sacrificing life.

RUTH KLOOSTERHUIS

APRIL 17

My Garden

He will satisfy your needs. . . . You will be like a well-watered garden. Isa. 58:11, NIV.

I've been bitten by the gardening bug again. It happens every spring. Not that I've ever had anything that remotely resembles a flourishing, healthy garden, but I still get caught up in an overwhelming desire to make something—anything—grow. This year I decided to do a little reading on the subject—more than what I got from the seed packages. I read an article about a master gardener from England. This talented horticulturist said that pruning and weeding are very important because a garden is a careful balance of those plants that must be allowed to grow and spread freely, and those that must be strictly controlled. H'mmm . . .

My personality reminds me of a garden. I've got weeds, I've got roses, and I've got a lot of thorns. There are rocks in the soil and old roots left over from the one who used to be the gardener here. But I've got a new Gardener working in me now, and I'm trusting in Him to turn this wasteland into a plantation.

Sometimes I get impatient, and I want to be perfect *now*—especially when someone I love reaches out to me for fruit and gets nothing but leaves. But the Master Gardener knows what He's doing. It takes time. He's taking out rocks here and there, digging up roots, softening the soil, planting more seeds, pulling out weeds, cutting off dead branches, fertilizing, and all the other things a good gardener knows how to do. And when I am patient and focus on how far I've come rather than on how far I have to go, I can see how, season after season, there are a few more roses and a lot fewer thorns.

I take comfort in the thought that my Master Gardener is much more patient than I am, and that He can see what I'm going to be when He's finished. He knows that underneath this rocky, weedy ground there is a heart just waiting to break forth in blossoms of love for Jesus. After all, I'm the one who asked Him to take over and do His work in me. And every day before He picks up His shovel and hoe, He makes sure that I am still ready to yield to His tilling. I ask Him to please weed and prune, even if it hurts. That's my part; He does all the rest. And then He shines on me with His love and rains on me with His Spirit.

The best part is that after He has done all the work, and I have yielded up the harvest that He Himself has cultivated, *He* will say to *me,* "Well done." I'm so looking forward to offering my crop to Him!

HEARTSONG

APRIL 18

New Light

You are the light of the world. . . . Let your light shine before men, that they may see your good deeds and praise your Father in heaven. Matt. 5:14-16, NIV.

I really don't remember which of us three children took the lid off, but the batch of unleashed fireflies transformed our motel room into a setting of enchantment. The mystery of these on-again, off-again little helicopters was clearly of interest to Mom and Dad. I saw my parents, honest in their own expressions of wonderment, as children with us. I basked in our unilateral oneness. I imagined a peaceful smile on each face as we drifted off to sleep.

Now, as a parent, I see the spectrum of scenarios that might have taken place that hot summer night. Our parents could have spent the whole night smashing lightning bugs. They could have exhausted themselves attempting to retrap them. They could have condemned us for having exposed ourselves to these strange new creatures.

But my parents were able to pull back and be with us as the incredulous light display unfolded. They acknowledged the mysterious energy that permeated our Motel 6 suite. We prayed, then lay in bed, collectively observing the private light show.

At age 5, I gleaned a few insights from that night: Light comes with an energy all its own. Light is hard to resist and is hard to keep confined. Jesus called us "the light of the world." When we keep our light shining as brightly as the little firefly's, others will be drawn to it with the same sense of awe and wonder. Our influence will not be able to be contained.   DONNA YEOMAN CATHELL

APRIL 19

The Shadow of His Wings

How excellent is thy lovingkindness, O God! therefore the children of men put their trust under the shadow of thy wings. Ps. 36:7.

I remember it had been a beautiful day. The sun was out and the birds were singing. I decided to call a friend I had not talked to in a while. When she answered her phone the noise was unbelievable. It sounded like she was inside a giant popcorn popper. She had to yell for me to hear her, and from her words I learned that a terrible hailstorm was in progress and was heading in my direction.

I hung up the phone and ran outside. Looking to the north, I could see a massive wall, like a great and terrible army advancing, destroying everything in its path. I went back into the house and got down on my knees and began to pray. "Father, You promised to keep me in the shadow of Your wings, and I claim that promise now. Without Your protection everything we own will be destroyed." Within minutes the storm hit, more terrible in reality than it had been from a distance. I continued to pray throughout the storm.

When at last the storm had passed I got up from my knees and walked outside. All around were signs of destruction, but within our gate nothing was harmed. Even the petunias along the walk had hail all around them, but not a petal was crushed.

I know from experience that God does not always spare us trials; they are needed for our growth. But whether we go through trials or are spared from them, our loving Father will always keep us under the shadow of His wings.   JANICE M. CARVER

Of Cakes and Christians

These are they which came out of great tribulation, and have washed their robes, and made them white. Rev. 7:14.

*I*t was a beautiful day at *The Voice of Prophecy* radiobroadcast office in Glendale, California. Employees were beginning to gather on the patio to celebrate the twenty-fifth wedding anniversary of my boss, speaker-director H.M.S. Richards, Jr., and his wife, Mary.

I had spent the previous day baking and decorating their special cake. My husband and I had brought it from our car early that morning, tier by tier, to the little kitchen to be assembled on the cart and wheeled to the patio at the right moment. I had finished touching up the drop-string decoration and turned to get the fresh floral piece that would crown the top. At that moment an exuberant employee burst through the kitchen door. In her excitement her arm grazed the top tier, sending it crashing to the floor.

Stunned silence was followed by panic. In an instant the employee was down on the floor ready to scoop it all up in her hands.

"Stop!" I screamed. "Don't touch it! Maybe we can save it."

Together we plotted how it should be done. Half the tier was still intact; the rest was a mound of crumbs and icing. Carefully we placed a cardboard underneath it and lifted it to the counter. Then I remembered the container of icing I had brought along "just in case."

We worked steadily for the next few minutes and soon, with the help of a spatula and decorator tubes, the outside of the tier emerged almost as good as new. We placed the floral arrangement on top of the cake and triumphantly wheeled it to the patio just before the honored couple made their appearance. I had to confess to them why the top of their cake was not for eating. Only the snow-white icing had made it presentable.

Like wedding cakes, Christians endeavor to "stand tall" most of the time. We try, by our caring and concern, to reflect Jesus to those about us. But when we least expect it, something happens to change the picture, and down we go in defeat. We lie helpless under our guilt, and at that moment the enemy of souls stands ready to scoop us up and claim us as his own. But then something lovely happens. Our Saviour is there, and we hear His beautiful voice saying, "Stop! This is My child." Tenderly He lifts us up with His own nail-pierced hands. Graciously He forgives and renews us, and promises to cover us with His own white robe of righteousness if we will let Him. Unlike the cake, He cleanses us on the inside, too!

Soon the Master Designer will crown us with His beautiful, never-dying emblem of salvation and present us to the Father, tall, stately, and perfect all the way through. He's only waiting for us to surrender ourselves to Him with our whole heart.

LORRAINE HUDGINS

APRIL 21

Paying My Debts

When you make a vow to God, do not delay to pay it; for He has no pleasure in fools. Pay what you have vowed. It is better not to vow than to vow and not pay. Eccl. 5:4, 5, NKJV.

I had spent an enjoyable three days attending a seminar for Christian speakers and writers. While there, I met several interesting people who shared their experiences and knowledge. It was a time of personal growth and a time to make new friends and enjoy visiting with people of varied professions.

Going through my briefcase two weeks later, I looked at the various business cards of people I had met. As I looked at one card, I could not remember the individual. I tried my best to remember why I had this particular card. Then turning it over, I saw the note, "Send $12." With chagrin I remembered that I had purchased a book from her and promised to send a check to pay for it as soon as I got home. Quickly I got the checkbook and wrote a check and a note apologizing for my neglect.

There are times that I treat my relationship with God in the same manner. I make promises (vows) I have every intention of keeping. As time progresses I get busy with the ordinary things of life and forget what I had so solemnly promised. Then an event occurs that jogs my memory, and I am humbled as I realize that once again I have failed in my good intentions.

Then I claim the promise that God will forgive, and I have another opportunity to try again to fulfill my promise. What a loving God I serve!

EVELYN GLASS

Surely He Shall Deliver Thee

Thou shalt not be afraid for the terror by night; nor for the arrow that flieth by day; nor for the pestilence that walketh in darkness; nor for the destruction that wasteth at noonday. Ps. 91:5, 6.

It was early in the terrible civil war in Spain. I lay in the large maternity ward of the city hospital. The sirens sounded, warning everybody of an imminent air raid. The women in the ward began to cry and wail in fear. And they had good reason. The military barracks, the prime target of an air raid, were right next to the hospital. Any bomb striking that building would also hit the hospital. Nevertheless, I remained calm.

"Why aren't you crying?" a woman asked. "Don't you know that if they come and drop bombs, we may all be killed?"

"I am not afraid," I replied. "The Lord can take care of us here and protect us, if it is His will."

I had noticed the woman in a bed across the room reading a New Testament. She told us that she had bought the book in the market some time before, but had not had time to read it until now. I asked her to read Psalm 91.

She began to read to herself, but it was so wonderful and fitted our situation so perfectly that she began reading it out loud, beginning with the first verse. All the women in the ward ceased their wailing to listen to the wonderful words of that psalm, probably for the first time in their lives.

"I will say of the Lord, He is my refuge and my fortress: my God; in him will I trust. Surely he shall deliver thee. . . . He shall cover thee with his feathers. . . . Thou shalt not be afraid. . . . He shall give his angels charge over thee" (verses 2-11).

The Lord's presence could be felt in that hospital ward that day, and He did keep His promises. The planes flew over without dropping a single deadly bomb. That wonderful psalm has been even more precious to me since that experience. And so has my God.

MARTHA MONTGOMERY ODOM

Flowers

The flowers appear in the country-side; the time is coming when
the birds will sing. S. of Sol. 2:12, NEB.

*H*ave you seen the expression on the face of a tiny child
clasping a few daisies or buttercups, picked especially for
Mom? I can remember my children bringing me a bunch of wildflowers after a walk.

Think of the pleasure of a single red rose or a beautiful orchid
presented on an anniversary. The knowledge that someone cares,
combined with the visual beauty of the flowers, is always an appealing and unique joy to us all.

There is no other gift that can be given on so many different occasions—celebration, sadness, birthdays, and weddings. No wonder the
garden centers do so well! They have one of the greatest commodities,
bringing joy and comfort to the individual and to the community.

I once attended a lecture on horticultural therapy for people
with stress problems or some form of disability. Unable to have their
own garden, they can still enjoy growing plants with a little help and
guidance. Just watering them and taking care of them can be quite
therapeutic and relaxing. I visit two elderly women in their 80s and
90s who still get great pleasure from their plants.

Sometimes when I look at a lovely rose I can't resist stopping to
smell its fragrant perfume and touch its soft petals. The range of colors and subtle variety of shades are quite remarkable.

Admiring and appreciating the beauty of nature God has created
for our pleasure is a great comfort to me. To be able to get out in the
sunshine for a little while and meet other people is far better than
watching TV or videos at home.

Plant life is busy all day, doing its best to offset the harmful effects of pollution, smoke, and industrial irritants by putting oxygen
back into the atmosphere, as well as giving pleasure to us all.

In His wisdom the Lord has created flowers that grow well in
different climates. Let us enjoy and appreciate these wonderful gifts
of God's love. We can leave our cares and sorrows behind and feel
a silent healing and a real sense of peace and gratitude.

PHILIPPA MARSHALL

A Modern-Day Parable

Love not the world, neither the things that are in the world. If any man love the world, the love of the Father is not in him. 1 John 2:15.

*O*nce there was a beautiful young woman engaged to be married to the most perfect man in the universe. She loved him very much—in fact, she promised to love him only, and no other man. Her fiancé left to go to another country to build her a nice home to live in when they got married. He promised her a mansion in a perfect land.

She really did love him, but she was lonesome, and it wouldn't really hurt, she reasoned, to have a few good friends. Her first new friend was a man named Self. She enjoyed his company so much she began to forget about her true love. Then along came a man called Idols, who had much with which to charm her. And then she met this very alluring man named World. These three men took up so much of her time that she almost forgot about the promise she had made and the new home that was being built for her.

Occasionally she would find a minute to talk to her first love, but after she told him she loved him, she would spend the rest of the time telling him all the things that she wanted. A great many of these things were really things that would make her more pleasing to World, who was taking up most of her time now.

Her fiancé wooed her unceasingly. He put up with her affections for others, even though she had promised that he would reign supreme in her life. He continued to build a mansion for her in this perfect land, and his only thought was for the time when she would be by his side forever in a perfect world.

With almost all of her time now spent on World, Self, and Idols, she forgot that she would need a wedding dress. Once in a great while she would think *I really must get busy and sew a wedding garment befitting this very special occasion.* Yet she continued to wear her same old clothes on her frivolous adventures with World, Self, and Idols.

In Matthew 22:1-14, Jesus tells a parable about the necessity of wearing the proper wedding attire to the wedding banquet. How will it be when we attend the wedding? Will we be wearing Christ's righteousness, our wedding garment, or the same old clothes we always do?

PAT MADSEN

We Are His Children

How great is the love the Father has lavished on us, that we should be called children of God! And that is what we are! 1 John 3:1, NIV.

Many times in the past few years I have heard the expression "God takes care of children and fools." Usually people are referring to the last word of the sentence—fools. The first part of the expression, "God takes care of children," stirs up an image in my mind of a parent holding a newborn child who is asleep in their arms. I am attracted to a scene like this, not only because the child is cute, but because I want to feel that warm, cared-for, peaceful feeling that the child's face is showing.

One year ago I was diagnosed with cancer. The doctor ordered an MRI (magnetic resonance imaging) to find out whether the cancer had spread to other areas of the body. For two hours I had to lie perfectly still in this tube-shaped machine while the technician took pictures. Being a nurse did not prepare me for this experience. It was not until they turned the machine on that I discovered how frightened I really was. It sounded like a jackhammer was drilling right next to me. The loud noise made the walls of the tube vibrate against my body. As a feeling of panic set in, my mind went to the expression "God takes care of His children." I closed my eyes and prayed, "Lord, put Your loving arms around me, like a parent holding a child. I need to feel the trust, warmth, and love." I envisioned God's arms being placed around me, and the feeling of terror went away.

In the months that followed my surgery and recovery, I would often go back to that image in my mind. What a comfort and peace there is in the arms of Jesus! The doctor gave me a 99 percent chance of not having cancer again, a miracle in itself. I know that whatever may come, I will feel God's arms around me when I need Him. God does take care of His children!   RITA VAN HORN

Stinging Nettle and Hot Peppers

From the lips of children and infants you have ordained praise.
Ps. 8:2, NIV.

Today I learned something I should have learned a long time ago. While I was walking with friends along a path next to the Potomac River, three of the children began to veer off the path and follow a narrow trail leading to the river. Of course, Aunt Sherry had to go along.

Nine-year-old Rachel spotted them first and warned Sarah, Zachery, and me: "Watch out for the stinging nettles!"

The kids, raised in the country, had learned respect for nature's ways. All responded with deference to the plant. I, on the other hand, disregarded the warning—except to repeat it to the kids. Kids always need reminding.

On the way back we ran into the nettle patch again. Again the children warned each other. I was glad they had remembered and watched as they picked their way through the nettle jungle. Being an adult, I *knew* I wouldn't brush against it, and I wasn't so careful as the children. My "rashness" resulted in several welts on my bare legs. The kids patiently prepared jewelweed stalks to apply to my afflicted areas.

Sarah said, "Well, Aunt Sherry, maybe it's a good thing this happened. Now that you have made your reacquaintance with stinging nettle, you have learned an appreciation for it!"

Today I experimented with making salsa. I've finally figured out that salsa is anyone's guess—throw in whatever you like, and it should come out fine. So I bought two very small jalapeño peppers (I'm a *mild* pepper person), cut off the ends, and removed the seeds. Having worked with hot peppers once many years ago, I remembered how my hands stung, my face stung, my arms stung, my neck stung . . .

But today I *knew* that wouldn't happen; I was going to be careful. I would not put my hands anywhere else on my body. I threw everything into the food processor and made my salsa (it was pretty good, too!) and was in the process of filling jars for canning when my thumb caught fire. Then both hands. The only way to stop the burning was to keep my hands in cool or lukewarm water. I was sure I had a first-degree burn. Even now, hours later, after I've cleaned the kitchen and taken a shower, my thumb still throbs. (I'll bet the kids would have worn gloves.)

I wonder if I *know* too much spiritually, also. I *know* better than to get caught in little sins—overeating, missing my personal time with God, reacting negatively to someone. So I'm not as alert, and get caught easily. I need to be like the children who appreciate the little things that can hurt them or others, like a little plant. Or like little sins.

Lord, strip me of *spiritual adultness* and make me like the children.

SHERRY MANISON

APRIL 27

A Treasure in His Sight

Since you were precious in My sight, you have been honored, and I have loved you. Isa. 43:4, NKJV.

For as long as I can remember, Zachary has loved horses. One morning I took him to a farm where my brother works that breeds and raises horses. Zachary would have stayed there all day.

At supper that evening Zac told his dad all about Harris, a huge, white, gentle horse that my brother let him ride. I mentioned that I knew the horses were expensive and valuable, but to me they just looked like ordinary horses. We live in Amish country, and there are horses everywhere. Zachary, who had been listening to our conversation, piped up and said, "They are treasures." He saw them through different eyes. He saw them through his love for them. They were special, precious.

And that is how God sees each one of us. We look at the world and see a bunch of people. We pass people every day and don't see them as special and unique. They're just people in this crowded, busy world of ours. Sometimes we can even walk through church and just see people, never noticing the specialness in each one. We don't see past the surface to the joys and struggles underneath, the cares and thoughts.

God looks down from His throne in heaven and sees treasures, something precious, more valuable than all the wealth of heaven. I pray that God will open my eyes and help me to see people through His eyes and His love as the precious treasures they are. When I see people as His treasures, maybe I'll work harder to bring them to Him.

Zachary would do anything to get to spend time with horses. How many of your friends do everything they can to spend time with you each day? Many of my friends are so busy that we go for long periods of time without seeing each other. Yet God, who is in charge of all the universe, is never too busy. He is in charge of everything, yet He takes time to listen to us each day, to speak to us, to call us to Him.

He's willing to clean out the stalls of my life in order to spend time with me. I'm a treasure in His sight. So are you. The clerk at the grocery store is precious in His sight. The driver who pulled out in front of you on your way home is His treasure.

Is He a treasure in my sight? in yours? Are we willing to do whatever it takes to spend time with Him? Willing to let other things go so that we can be with Him? willing to put things aside in order to pray and to listen to Him? What do you treasure?   TAMI HORST

APRIL 28

That's What a Friend Is For

There is a friend who sticks closer than a brother. Prov. 18:24, NIV.

There was a reverent tone in the voice of the spry, mustached conductor as he told us tourists about the majestic redwoods that surrounded the narrow-gauged tracks on which our train was traveling. His spiel was not like the fast-forward monotone of many tour guides. The fact that the man recited these facts several times a day did not diminish the awe in his voice as he pointed out the 1,000-year-old giant that had fallen by the track. The conductor always referred to these grand trees as "he." He talked a lot about Mother Nature, and as I watched him interact with the kids on the tour, I knew in my heart that he believed in God. After we traveled a few more minutes our guide showed us a sky-scraping tree that had blown over in a storm some 50 years earlier and had landed in a clump of other redwoods.

"He fell nearly to the ground," said the guide, "but then his friends caught him and held him up. That's what friends are for. They catch you when you fall and then keep on supporting you. This tree didn't die, as you can see. It sent out new roots and has been growing safely all these years in the arms of its friends."

Wow! I thought. *Have I ever been that kind of friend?*

Sometimes I fear that in our frantic world we become too busy to be a friend. How about you? Does someone need you today? Is there someone falling whom you could catch and hold until she has grown new roots?   BARBARA HUFF

Flashing Lights

For it is light that makes everything visible. This is why it is said: "Wake up, O sleeper, rise from the dead, and Christ will shine on you." Be very careful, then, how you live—not as unwise but as wise. Eph. 5:14, 15, NIV.

Twilight was stretching itself thin as we pulled the boat from the water and began the routine of unloading the sweaters and life jackets into the van and securing the boat to the trailer. As we left the launch area, darkness surrounded us like a warm blanket. We had enjoyed the Friday evening boat trip on the lake and reveled in the brilliant sunset as it illuminated the mountain ridge beyond the lake. We were thankful to be in the van beyond the reach of the persistent mosquitoes!

We were well on our way down the winding road that led to the main highway when my husband thought something was amiss and stopped to check the trailer lights. There were none! He jiggled and wiggled the wires at the trailer hitch while I stood behind the boat and called out the results of his labors.

"The lights are on. No, they went off again."

He bent, plugged, and unplugged. After endless minutes he went to the van controls and turned on the flasher lights. They worked! We headed through the darkness with the flasher lights indicating to all we met and all who came from behind that we were having trouble. The flashing lights weren't really an indication of our condition, but they were the only way we had to let others see us as we traveled along.

How about my Christian journey? Do I have a "short" in my wires so I can't be seen as I travel along? Do my life lights blink on for a short time, then go out again so I can't be seen in the dark? Do others think they see a light, but by the time they can say anything it has gone out again? Perhaps even more tragic, do I travel life with my hazard lights flashing the whole way? Am I representing to everyone I meet, or to everyone following me, that something is happening when it really isn't? Perhaps I just want to be noticed in the dark, and there is nothing going on in front, behind, or inside.

The scripture says, "Let your light shine among men" (Matt. 5:16, NIV). Am I being true with my representation of Jesus? Do I have my "hazards" flashing instead of a warm, steady glow of a constant relationship with Jesus? As I thought about our trailer wiring, I realized I needed to check my spiritual "wiring" now and then. I need to make sure the connections are without corrosion so others can see the true light as I travel along life's road.   EARLENE WOHLERS

APRIL 30

Covering Up

Bear ye one another's burdens, and so fulfil the law of Christ. Gal. 6:2.

In the community where I live there is an elderly Christian couple who have painted a picture for me of the long-suffering and tender love of Christ. They have two children, now adults with their own families. But tragedy hit these children while they were still very young. Their mother became ill with meningitis. Although she did recover, the meningitis has left its scar upon her mind in the form of loss of memory. And the situation has not changed in all the years since then.

She cannot remember anything that happens to her in a day. You could meet her five times, and she would not recall having seen you. She could visit your home time after time for months, and it would most likely remain unfamiliar. Yet she remembers things before her illness. And she remembers her husband.

Her husband remembers her, too, in the most thoughtful way. He never leaves her alone, but takes her with him everywhere. He never excludes her from a conversation, even though he is not sure if she understands what is being said or to whom it is said. He will say things such as "Isn't that right, dear?" or "Whom did we see yesterday? Oh, that's right, it was . . ." and will complete his own question. He covers for her so well and so consistently that hardly anyone knows that his wife has this problem.

In many ways this man's devotion to his wife reminds me of the love of Christ for His children. He put Himself on the line for us. He was willing to surrender His life to cover our sins. Praise God, because of Calvary He considers us, who are under the curse of sin, as though we had not sinned! It is no wonder that "love is the fulfilling of the law" (Rom. 13:10).   CAROLINE ANDREW

MAY 1

A Joyful Noise

Let your light so shine before men, that they may see your good works. Matt. 5:16, NKJV.

*P*erhaps I was feeling a bit self-righteous as I left home that afternoon to conduct a story hour for the children in a government housing project for the most depressed of Costa Rican society. My husband would have to tend to the kids and the company. I was doing the Lord's work.

First, I visited in the homes and invited children to come to the open clearing for the story hour. People were friendly, and the children began to trail me from house to house until the train was quite long and noisy. I thought I must have looked like the Pied Piper.

At story hour that afternoon there was an unfamiliar girl in the group. From the first she seemed to be a troublemaker. During song service she blared like a foghorn. I tried to speak to her kindly. I gave her a frown, hoping that would help. I shook my finger at her. Nothing seemed to make a difference. When I began the Bible story, she distracted the others. As I brought out the visual aids, she came close, but then backed away with a grunt. I never could seem to get her under control, and it made the whole group restless. When it was over, I was exhausted. I asked one of the older girls why the girl had been so unmanageable.

"Oh, don't you know, teacher? That's Sandra. She can't hear or speak."

I felt my conscience stab me like a sword. Her blaring had been her attempt to make a joyful noise to the Lord. I wished I could hug that child and tell her that Jesus loved her and one day soon He would make her whole. But words wouldn't get through to her, only loving acts—and I had frowned, scolded, and shaken my finger.

Too often we jump to conclusions. Too often we impute evil motives to others. I think Stephen Covey has the right idea when he says "The challenge is to be a light, not a judge, to be a model, not a critic." Enacting the gospel was the only thing that could have made a difference for Sandra that afternoon.

I'm glad that God sees my heart, and not just my outward, bumbling behavior. Let's pray, "Lord, make me a light."

FELICIA PHILLIPS

MAY 2

Our Ever-mindful Father

When I am afraid, I will trust in you. . . . What can mortal man do to me? Ps. 56:3, 4, NIV.

After visiting St. Peter's Cathedral and the Sistine Chapel, we were leisurely walking down a busy street in Rome. In a quick moment I learned a very important lesson on dependence. A city bus came to a stop, and then a man with a stroller and a woman carrying a baby got off the bus. Before anyone else could get off, the driver began to close the door, not realizing that another passenger was at the door. A youngster, about 10 years old, was caught in the door as other passengers called out to the driver in Italian. The boy did not appear to be frightened. I assumed the reason for his calmness was that the man who got off first was his father, and he knew his father would not let him get left behind, nor would he let him get hurt. The father was also calling to the driver to open the door. The son trusted his father and knew everything would work out fine.

I thought about how our heavenly Father cares for us and watches over us. I thought of how He stands ready to help us, and how He does not want us to get hurt. In spite of our eagerness to be a part of the in crowd, and no matter how strongly we may desire to take the broad road, Christ stands waiting for us with outstretched arms, telling us through the voice of the Holy Spirit that He is always there, and we need not fear. Whatever our need, He will supply, according to His will; wherever He leads, He will guide.

My prayer is "Lord, may I remember that I have no reason to fear, for You are always with me." MARIE H. SEARD

The Day Mama Killed the Rake

He who trusts in himself is a fool, but he who walks in wisdom is kept safe. Prov. 28:26, NIV.

It was a glorious Friday afternoon, a perfect day to work in the yard. My son, daughter, and husband were cheerfully mowing, weed whacking, and trimming. My job was to clean the patio. I moved the patio furniture and began to sweep. As I swept back into the far recesses, I pulled forward a huge brown snake. As my broom touched it, it instantly wrapped itself around the broom straws and lower handle.

"Snake!" I screamed, holding out the snake-laden broom and hopping around the patio.

My family came running. My husband grabbed a garden rake and swept the snake off the broom, pinning it beneath the rake tines. "Go get me an ax," he yelled.

As I ran to the garage for an ax, I thought, *I'll kill this snake myself. That will really impress my two adult children!* My two children have grown up building a repertoire of stories that begin, "Remember when Mama . . ." I decided I'd show them this time.

Returning to the scene where my three family members gathered around one rake pinning down a large snake, I yelled, sending the adrenaline flowing wildly through my veins, "I want to kill the snake!"

"You?" my husband laughed in astonishment.

"Oh, brother," our son said, "this ought to be good—the ax woman cometh; everybody stand back."

Such skepticism only spurred me on. "I *can* do it. I don't need any help." As I raised the ax high over my head, I noticed that my son and daughter had moved several feet away, laughing hysterically. I closed my eyes and swung that ax with the force of all mothers everywhere who know they must make a point with their families.

The ax sliced down with a satisfying thud.

"Congratulations," my husband said. "You just killed our rake."

Sure enough, when I opened my eyes there lay the splintered rake handle severed from its tines, and the snake was slithering swiftly toward the woods. Family laughter was loud and long, and to this day, whenever a snake is mentioned, one of my children will say, "Remember the day that Mama killed the rake?" That is the trigger phrase that causes them to recount that scene, laughing uproariously.

Sometimes in our spiritual lives we also try to "kill the snake" by ourselves. We think, *I can do it,* and swing the ax with our eyes shut without asking for help. As today's text says, "he who trusts in himself is a fool, but he who walks in wisdom is kept safe." Sometimes it is not until we shatter the support that is holding the enemy at bay that we cry out for help. Make no attempt to kill the snake by yourself. Ask the Lord for His help.
— ELLIE GREEN

MAY 4

No Ticket!

I am the way. John 14:6, NIV.

*W*e were speeding along the highway en route from Frankfurt, Germany, to Calais, France, where we would catch the ferry to Dover, England. Along with friends, Don and Phylis Stoyanowski, we were beginning a 10-day holiday before attending our world church conference in Utrecht, Netherlands.

"Ticket booths are just ahead," Phylis announced to her husband, who was driving the van.

"What will we do for money?" I asked, worried because we had not yet exchanged any dollars for francs.

"They'll take plastic," my husband, Ron, assured me.

"There are no attendants," Don said. "Not a one! The booths are all automatic."

Sure enough, above each cubicle was a sign: "Tickets. Automatic." Nobody was around. What could we do? With a sudden inspiration, Don drove off the highway near the booth on the far right and around all the barriers.

"No!" I yelled. "You can't do this!"

"We just did!" Ron laughed.

"The police will come after us!" I worried. "We'll get caught!"

But no sirens went off, and no police cars followed us. Many miles later we came to another set of tollbooths. This time there was no way around, but at least some of them had attendants. Ron was driving now and pulled up beside a booth.

"Ticket!" the woman inside said.

"I have no ticket," Ron began. "You see, we—"

"You *have* to have *ticket*."

"You don't understand," Ron tried again. "We have no French

money, so we couldn't get a ticket, and we—"

"You *have* to have *ticket!*" the woman repeated. "Where did you come from?"

Then Ron got a sudden inspiration and pulled out the receipt for the toll we had paid in Germany.

"I will use this," the woman said, frowning, "but after this you *have* to have *ticket!*"

We finally figured it out. We had not had to pay at the previous set of booths. We only had to drive forward and take a ticket, just as we would in a parking lot at home. We felt pretty foolish! How could we be so dense?

How like my journey in life. I mused, *When God doesn't pounce on me when I go my own way, I think I've escaped the consequences of disobedience. But the day of reckoning is coming. Sooner or later, I'll have to confess that my way wasn't the right way. God's way was the best way. I have to have* Jesus! DOROTHY EATON WATTS

MAY 5

"Lord, What Wilt Thou Have Me to Do?"

I have learned, in whatever state I am, to be content. Phil. 4:11, RSV.

Growing up in a Christian home and wishing to serve the Lord in some way, I often wondered exactly where I would fit into God's plan. It was my firm belief that there was a place with my name on it.

Jeremiah knew his place; God told him (Jer. 1:5). Paul knew what he would be doing after his interview with Jesus at the gate of Damascus (Acts 9:1-5). Most of us have found general directions in the Bible, but no fanfare or blinding lights.

God has come to my rescue and spared my life so many times that I am convinced He found me employable. When I was 2 years old, my grandfather responded to a very strong impression that he should stop at our house on his way to town to see about the baby— me. He found me hanging by my neck between the crib bars. It took all the CPR he and my grandmother knew to bring me around. A few years later I survived smallpox. And at 10 it was an undiagnosed abdominal abscess.

During my teen years I lost interest in spiritual things. When the devil was not permitted to kill me, he tried to run me off the narrow way, and was almost successful. Nursing school and college hours were totally filled. There did not seem to be time for serious spiritual thought. Marriage and four children kept me busier than ever before. And at 46 I was widowed with four young children. That's when I found time to take stock of my life. I found God still waiting for me. In seventh grade I had memorized a poem, the last four lines of which had stuck in my mind and came back to me to strengthen me:

> "He who from zone to zone
> Guides through the boundless sky thy certain flight,
> In the long way that I must tread alone
> Will lead my steps aright."
>
> —William Cullen Bryant

It was not from the Bible, but it kept me in touch with my heavenly Father, who cared about wild geese, sparrows, and frightened widows. He showed me that my children were my spot in His plan. That caring for them, teaching them how to live, and introducing them to Jesus as their friend would be my post of duty. Understanding this brought me to my knees to learn of Jesus myself before I could teach them. I learned that my home was the place where I should serve, while others could serve better on the gospel front line. GRACE E. STREIFLING

MAY 6

God's Thoughts of Me Are so Special

How precious and weighty also are Your thoughts to me, O God! How vast is the sum of them! If I could count them, they are more in number than the sand. Ps. 139:17, 18, Amplified.

*T*aking time alone with Jesus each morning in a 10-point study of each book, chapter, and verse found in God's Word has brought revelations of a magnitude to satisfy every longing of my soul.

Imagining what the mind of God can do staggers me. As a father loves and pities his children, so God loves and pities me. He cheers me and wants to delight me as He beautifies, dignifies, and crowns me with His tender mercies and loving-kindness. His graciousness pours from His lips as He speaks to me.

I was pondering these thoughts when my dearest friend, Beth, called from the hospital to tell me the results of her tests. They showed she had cancer of the pancreas, and she was given only two months to live. I was shocked and devastated. The news of Beth's illness felt as though a bolt of lightning had struck deep into my heart. Yet suddenly my heartstrings were being covered with a warm gentle hand to absorb the shock and pain. Having just read in the Psalms that God's thoughts of us are as many as the sand of the seashore, I shared this with Beth to try to lift her spirits.

Trusting God is what life is all about. Can a loving, caring God, whose thoughts of me are so vast, and who gave His only Son to die so I can live forever, not be trusted in every aspect of my life?

God allows the eyes of my faith to behold His beautiful, loving face when it seems pitch-black darkness has engulfed me. God gives me beauty to behold, even in a land in which everything fades and dies. He paints a glorious sunset or sunrise, and the stars that shine so brightly at night give me assurance that God is in control and keeps everything in its order. Through each tragedy God becomes more real to me. I experience His loving touch as He seems to open heaven's windows with special bouquets of a soothing balm.

After one month Beth fell asleep peacefully in Jesus. What glorious peace God gives to His precious possessions. His thoughts of us are so many—surely His love and goodness know no bounds.

ANN BLANDFORD

In the Shadow of Your Wings

Because You have been my help, therefore in the shadow of Your wings I will rejoice. Ps. 63:7, NKJV.

I will sing in the shadow of Your wings,
  My God,
    When the sun beats down from a brazen sky,
    Or the dark clouds gather in threatening strength,
    And a storm is drawing nigh.

I will sing in the shadow of Your wings,

My Lord,
When deep waters roll over my soul,
When torturous thoughts my heart assail,
I will trust in You to be whole.

I will sing in the shadow of Your wings,
El-Shaddai,
Though on me every back has been turned,
I will nestle beneath their sheltering shade,
Content, although I've been spurned.

I will sing in the shadow of Your wings,
Adonai,
And my voice with glad praise will ascend,
Whatever the trials, whatever the cost,
I will sing, for You are my friend.

EVA ALICE COVEY

MAY 8

Recognizing the Love of God

O Lord, our Lord, how majestic is thy name in all the earth!
Ps. 8:9, RSV.

*T*hings seemed to run smoothly for that family of workers in the interior of Paraná. One conference series was ending, and the harvest of souls appeared bountiful. There were many plans to accomplish in that favorite district. Then, unexpectedly, a call came to go somewhere else. The whole family said no.

There was no peace, because the anguish for having denied a call seemed to suffocate them. Why go if we want to stay? Why say farewell to a field of work after 45 evenings of preaching the Word, and why leave just now at the time of harvesting? But there can be no peace if we say no when the Father gives an order!

One afternoon when the family was together in the parents' bedroom, the oldest daughter got up quietly and went to her room. A few minutes later she returned with an expression of joy on her face and a Bible promise: "I chose you; go do the work!" (see John 15:16).

With an air of decision the father stood up, straightened his shoulders, drew his 18-year-old son to himself, and spoke solemnly. "The decision is made. We will accept the call, because I want to be obedient."

Days later the couple were having their medical exams done prior to starting their new work. Something, however, was not right with the wife, and she had an emergency surgery scheduled. In her hospital bed, she opened her Bible and read from Isaiah 58:8: "Then shall your light break forth like the dawn, and your healing shall spring up speedily" (RSV).

Surgery was done, and cancer was found. Later she went to an oncologist, who declared, "If you had waited just a little longer, I would not have been able to give you a 90 percent probability that the illness will not return."

Ten years have elapsed, and here I am telling you my experience because I would like you to feel the same gratitude toward this marvelous God. I am sure He has done wonderful things in your life, too.

Psalm 8:3, 4 says, "When I look at thy heavens . . . what is man that thou . . . dost care for him?" (RSV). Permit Him to show you His love today, and recognize with me what it says in verse 9: "O Lord, our Lord, how majestic is thy name in all the earth!"

DAISE LUCIDI FRANCA RIOS

MAY 9

People Watching

The day of the Lord is near for all nations. Obadiah 15, NIV.

*M*aybe you are a people watcher as I am; people are so fascinating. Since I travel quite often, airports and planes have provided lots of people-watching opportunities. I always wonder where they are going and why—is it a happy or sad occasion? Are they seasoned travelers or totally baffled by all the ins and outs of modern-day travel? I often worry about elderly people trying to find gates or making that next tight connection.

Recently, on a flight from Vienna, Austria, to New York I had a people-watching opportunity. A pleasant European family sat across the aisle from us. The teenage children seemed to be relaxed and to understand English. The father asked a lot of questions of the flight attendant in German. The mother never fully relaxed; she spent a large portion of the flight studying an English lesson book and looking through a tour book about New York. I decided they were tourists, and this was their first trip to America.

As we got closer to our destination, the lady seemed to become more excited. When the pilot announced we would begin our descent soon, she buttoned up her sweater (the pilot had said it was about 90 degrees in New York City), put her scarf around her neck, and her bag over her shoulder. Her foot drummed faster and faster against the floor. She was ready!

Now I started to change my mind about her reason for going to New York; she must be going to meet someone she had not seen for a long time—maybe her mother, or a sister.

I don't know the ending to my story, because I went through the U.S. citizens' line at immigration, and the woman and her family went through the noncitizens' line. I never saw them again, but it did start me thinking.

How excited do we really get about going to heaven and seeing Jesus? I know one cannot live in a constant state of excitement, but do we *ever* really get excited, even for a little while, about meeting God in worship or in person? I'm sure it would thrill God if we did.

Often we talk about how wonderful it will be to get to heaven, to walk on the streets of gold, to have no more sickness or crying or death. But think of the excitement of seeing a long-missed loved one—Jesus. The trip has been a long one, and the destination must be near. Can you feel the excitement mounting? Are you ready for the final ascent? ARDIS DICK STENBAKKEN

MAY 10

"Thou Shalt Not Covet"

Then he said to them, "Watch out! Be on your guard against all kinds of greed; a man's life does not consist in the abundance of his possessions." Luke 12:15, NIV.

It was during the days of the Depression in the early 1930s. Many people had lost their jobs, and my father was one of them. With a wife and two small children to support, he had to find some way to make a living. And so he became a peddler, going from house to house in the more affluent part of town, selling pies and cookies baked by my mother. He also sold honey and eggs that he bought in bulk, and cottage cheese made from skim milk that could be had very cheaply at the local dairy. My brother and I wore hand-me-down clothes given to Daddy by some of his customers, and our Christmas toys came from the same source.

We always had a roof over our heads and enough to eat, but our frugal lifestyle persisted even after Daddy had a regular job with more money coming in. We used powdered skim milk, which I detested, and it was such a treat when we visited friends who drank "real" milk from bottles. I couldn't help envying their daughter, who had this milk as daily fare. And she was so much prettier than plain-Jane me. My mother made most of my dresses, many from printed flour sacks, and while they were all right, I longed for a store-bought dress. When a package of outgrown, ready-made clothes came from an older cousin, I felt like a queen. *It must be nice to have a rich father who can buy things like that,* I thought.

The years went by, and I grew up, married, and had a family of my own. It wasn't until my children were grown that I renewed contact with the friend and the cousin I had envied in my younger days. Only then did I begin to realize the meaning of true values. Both of them had lost a parent while they were in their teens, while my parents had lived to enjoy their grandchildren. My friend was still pretty, but her face reflected the pain she had suffered from a failed marriage. In every letter I receive from my cousin she mentions how fortunate I am to have had such caring Christian parents and children who have made a success in life. I found that although she had what money could buy while growing up, she never knew a real father's love and always wished she'd had a father like mine.

May God help each of us realize that there are many things more important in life than what money can buy. BETTY ADAMS

MAY 11

A Mother's Constant Prayer

I have no greater joy than to hear that my children are walking in the truth. 3 John 4, NIV.

From the time she was born she was a vivacious, bubbly baby with great lungs and a voracious appetite. I could actually hear her cries amid the sounds of the others as the nurses rolled the carts filled with hungry babies to their eager mothers during feeding time in the maternity ward.

I had longed for a little girl after giving birth to two equally energetic and, might I add, handsome boys. Thoughts of dressing my girl in pretty little dresses, combing her curly hair, and putting bows on her beautiful long braids had been my dream since childhood. Even the possibility of her wedding down the road, the happiest day of a woman's life, sent wonderful thoughts through my head as I held this little bundle in my arms. Imagine that! A mother thinking of her little girl's wedding when the child was only 1 day old. Only another mother could understand the long-range dreams we have for our children even when they are still in the womb and in the cradle.

The older Karmala became, the more she began to look like me. Her large eyes and long fingers, even her teeth and her smile, were evidences that she was indeed my new creation. I thank God again and again for allowing me to participate with Him in giving my precious daughter life.

But more important than having her mother's physical features, she has some of my personality, too. And even more important than this is the fact that she has Christian qualities and character. She is a young woman who has a plan for her life that includes God.

As I reflect upon my own life as a female child growing up in the South, there weren't many options available for me then. But the sky is the limit for my daughter and for all our daughters who are growing up in this generation. No young woman has an excuse today for not making the best possible choices for her life. There are just too many resources available now to help keep our daughters on the right track. It is possible today for women to have a vision, a task, and a hope.

True, mothers love all their children, sons and daughters alike. However, most worry more about their daughters, that they might have a better future by making the best of the present opportunities, opportunities that were not available to us in the past. This mother's constant prayer is that the power of the Holy Spirit will fill and indwell her daughter's life, and that all our children will make the best choices to become all that it is possible to be, through Christ.

ROSA TAYLOR BANKS

Mother's Day

Her children arise up, and call her blessed. Prov. 31:28.

*M*other's Day, in the purest sense, can occur most any time. It begins the day that tiny bundle from heaven is dropped into your arms, and then keeps right on happening— sometimes at the most unexpected moments.

It was Mother's Day when my little girl took her first faltering step; when my small son lisped his first sentence; when they trotted off to school that very first time. It was a proud Mother's Day when they graduated, and a happy one the day they were married.

But Mother's Days are not always joyful. They may be spent sharing the anguish of a broken heart or hovering over a hospital bed. But always, from bumped heads to broken legs, from failed promises to important decisions, they are special days when the heart beats strong for those we cherish. Sometimes our precious children are drawn away from the values they are taught. During those heartrending experiences each day becomes a special Mother's Day, when early-morning hours are spent in earnest prayer.

I recall with a sort of whimsical pain little embarrassments my children suffered in the growing-up process—the let-down hems; trousers that became too short almost overnight; an old secondhand trombone; a forgotten speech; spilled grape juice . . . And my mind wanders back to their trivial mistakes that I sometimes treated with too much importance, confusing mountains with molehills, and wrongs with inexperience. But their childlike trust forgave my impatience.

Perhaps, after all, we try so hard to teach our children that sometimes we miss the lessons we could learn from them:

> The dignity of being genuine and sincere.
> Tolerance that holds no grudges.
> Honesty that loves people for what they are inside.
> Humility that seeks no applause.
> Trust that transcends fear.
> Courage that rises from defeat and tries again.

Had I the privilege of rolling back the years, I would give my five children the one thing each wanted most—a little more individual time together for just getting better acquainted. I would let them know more often that they occupy first place in my heart. I would relinquish seemingly important tasks in favor of sharing their concerns. I would show more appreciation for the priceless love gifts their little hands had made. And I would practice the beautiful lessons they have taught me.

I thank my heavenly Father that five strong and beautiful bands of love reach from their hearts to their father's and mine, and have become part of a never-ending seven-banded circle that binds us together as we travel toward heaven's threshold.

And so on this Mother's Day the hearts of my little flock of five will turn homeward. And my heart will respond, not because of honor bestowed, but because these daughters and sons entrusted to my care have given my life meaning and completeness. For without them, there would be no Mother's Day at all.   LORRAINE HUDGINS

MAY 13

The Value of a Smile

A glad heart makes a cheerful countenance. Prov. 15:13, RSV.

A smile costs nothing, but results in much. It enriches the receiver and beautifies the countenance of the giver. It lasts for just a second, but many times memory will keep it forever. None of us are so rich that we can move ahead without it, and none are so poor that they do not become richer with its benefits. It brings gladness to the home and increases well-being among friends. It gives rest to the fatigued, encouragement to the disheartened, and joy to the sad. It is the best natural antidote against indisposition. It is the biggest and best business card. It soothes the nerves and brings health to the body. And finally, it gives brilliance to the eyes and charm to the character.

Smiling is a simple act. When we smile, only 16 muscles move; when we frown, 73 muscles are activated. What a difference! Thinking only about this savings, we should smile more.

Smiling is the result of a happy heart. When we smile we are telling others that we are optimists and that we trust in God. "The Lord has done great things for us; we are glad," says the psalmist (Ps. 126:3).

So, smile!   OFELIA WICHERT MOROZ

Keys

God made peace through his Son's death on the cross and so brought back to himself all things, both on earth and in heaven. Col. 1:20, TEV.

*C*orsage, camera, purse, and jacket. We were off to a special awards banquet, a memorable night. Memorable it was, because we forgot one small detail—the keys. Nothing is more memorable than crawling into a high window with a suit on.

Nothing can frustrate your day like losing your keys. Such an unfortunate event may cause you to feel frantic, vulnerable, or given to despair. In this "super-security, double lock" society we live in, keys are symbols of our protection and our power.

For years I felt frustrated and vulnerable as I searched for one essential key—the key to my salvation. I had Scripture-based theological answers, but my experiential knowledge was lacking, the key to fit the lock of deep understanding. After living in a Christian home and attending fine Christian schools, I was still missing the key for unlocking a meaningful relationship with Christ.

But now I stand at the cross, having the key to unlock the answers to all my questions. The cross has become the center focus of my understanding of the gospel.

1. The cross shows me what I am. Realities of life come into focus when one watches a loved one lowered into the grave, or watches others suffer with disease or a disability. Yet how much sharper is our focus when we envision Christ on the cross and contemplate the reason He died by such a method. The cross uncovers me as the real sinner, whose attitudes, thoughts, and actions killed my Lord and Saviour.

2. The cross, my source of self-esteem. Living the comfortable life filled with "important things" does not always bring one to the foot of the cross. After a temporary leave from a rewarding career and ministry, the loss of our one "good" car, and a move that thoroughly depleted our savings account, I felt hopelessly empty. Where did my self-esteem lie? Christ on the cross is my real source of self-worth. He believes in me. His love can be the only true source of self-esteem in this world of reversed priorities.

3. The cross, the key to my salvation from sin. Temptations for most Christians come in the form of thoughts and attitudes.

Meditating on the cross, examining the love and forgiveness shown can be a real "mind conversion" practice, in which resentment doesn't stand a chance. In light of my sin that crushed my Saviour's life, how can I be proud or judge others? Since Christ died for all, how can I be prejudiced, impatient, or self-centered? In contemplation of this, sin has no chance to exist.

I have come to understand that the cross in its beauty is the life-changing gospel in which I have found forgiveness, a sense of who I am, an unshakable self-worth, and a mind-changing power. The cross unlocks a storehouse of spiritual blessings and insight. With Isaac Watts I can sing, "At the cross, at the cross, where I first saw the light."

JILL HINES RICHARDS

MAY 15

Words of Indecision

Then Agrippa said unto Paul, Almost thou persuadest me to be a Christian. Acts 26:28.

*W*hen you were a child, did you play tricky word games with your friends, hoping to trap them into quick and, hence, foolish responses?

Remember the one that goes like this: You run up to a friend and say, "Would you rather be almost drowned or almost saved?" And you emphasize the word *saved* in hopes that the first answer will be "That's a stupid question, silly. Anyone would rather be almost saved—whoops!"

"Ha, ha, ha!" you howl with delight. "I'd much rather be almost drowned." And then you trot off to find another joke victim.

Such foolish games, weren't they? Aren't you glad you don't play them anymore?

Another favorite was to ask, "Pete and Re-Pete went out in a boat. Pete fell in. Who was left?" And when your friend replied "Re-Pete," you started all over again at the beginning. "Pete and Re-Pete went out . . ."

Word games only, with outcomes of little significance, a few moments of cheap hilarity for a semantics joker. But Paul was playing no word games with Agrippa; he was asking no childish riddle. Paul was inviting him to play in the game of life. Agrippa, however, wanted a spectator sport, not a game requiring the dedication of a committed player. Words of indecision . . . How often regretted.

She sat in my office, telling her sad tale between broken sobs. On three separate occasions over a period of several weeks her boyfriend of two years had asked her to marry him. Always she told him to wait because she couldn't decide at the moment. Then just the previous night he had called to tell her that their relationship was completely through.

"I told him that I would marry him." She cried some more. "But he said it was just too late—just too late."

When the poet Whittier wrote that the saddest words were "It might have been," he was referring to a might-have-been love relationship. How infinitely more sad are these words when used in reference to a might-have-been relationship with God.

Whittier was correct; there are no sadder words.

Would you rather be almost saved or almost lost? Agrippa would rather have been almost saved. How about you? I know what Paul's answer would have been for himself *and* for what he would have wanted for you: "And Paul said [to Agrippa], I would to God, that not only thou, but also all that hear me this day, were both almost, and altogether such as I am, except these bonds" (verse 29).

WILMA McCLARTY

MAY 16

The Widow's Mite

Jesus said, "I tell you the truth, this poor widow has put more into the treasury than all the others. They all gave out of their wealth; but she, out of her poverty, put in everything—all she had to live on." Mark 12:43, 44, NIV.

*H*urricane Andrew and its devastation made an impact on the very souls of people. The hearts of millions were touched by the needs of those who suffered the losses of life and property. All over our nation, groups and individuals joined forces to gather food and supplies to send to those in need.

At Cumberland View Towers, a retirement center for low-income elderly, the residents asked me to help them organize a collection of supplies to send to hurricane victims. I made an announcement and set a time for donations to be brought down. However, I did not anticipate the response I would receive! A steady stream of widows and elderly couples with sacks and boxes of food and supplies came throughout the afternoon. Another day was spent packing and making ready their gifts of love for distribution. When an inventory was completed, I was amazed that the little group of seniors, with an average income of only $457 per month, had given 568 food items from their cupboards. In addition to the food, 23 large boxes of dry goods, 94 articles of clothing, 70 household items, and 126 cosmetic items had been collected. A little later in the day two of the women came to the office and gave me $395 that they had collected. It was their wish that we buy flashlights to be sent with their other donations.

My first thought was, *I just can't take all of this from them. I know their circumstances and their own needs and limited incomes. They must surely have brought all their food to give, and now they are even bringing the money they have left to purchase more. How are they going to manage until the end of the month?* Then I remembered the widow's mite and the way the Lord blessed her for doing what she could. And I knew that not only would He provide for each one, but they had truly experienced how much more blessed it is to give than to receive.

"Everyone helped his neighbor, and said to his brother, 'Be of good courage!'" Isa. 41:6, NKJV.   BARBARA SMITH MORRIS

MAY 17

King of Hearts

I will give you a new heart and put a new spirit in you; I will remove from you your heart of stone and give you a heart of flesh. Eze. 36:26, NIV.

*I*n the literary classic *Alice's Adventures in Wonderland,* by Lewis Carroll, the Queen of Hearts orders a red rose tree to be planted in the royal garden. By mistake, the knave assigned to the job plants a white rose tree. Not wanting to be relieved of his head, when the error is observed he and the other knaves set about the task of painting the roses red. Foolish knaves! The roses were white. And no matter how skillfully they were painted, the following spring the new buds would emerge pure white. Even after years of painting the roses red, the new buds would continue to come forth in their true color. The task of covering up the mistake would never be achieved.

Those of us who become Christians and then set about to change our behavior in order to be worthy of the gift God has given us are like the foolish knaves. We are what we are, and all the hard work in the world will not keep our true selves from emerging at some point. It's a rather discouraging reality. But the wonderful promise we are given is that the Holy Spirit will work from within to turn our new buds into a color pleasing to the King of Hearts.

KATHLEEN STAUBACH

MAY 18

A Moving Experience

Your heavenly Father knoweth that ye have need of all these things. Matt. 6:32.

*I*t was time to move again. The whole idea crashed through my mind and upended my world. It had been only two years since the last move, and since then we'd had our third child, who was currently going through his own "unpacking" stage of development. After eight moves in 10 years I just wanted to be still for a while.

A few days later I was praying for comfort and strength to face all those empty boxes in the attic. I opened my Bible, wondering where to find some encouragement. My eyes caught sight of John 14:1-3. Such a familiar passage; it is a promise about heaven. Suddenly I saw the text in a new light. The words flowed into my mind and filled it with peace. God already knew the best place for us to be; all the houses in the world were in His hands. He was going ahead of us to prepare a special home for us. When it was all ready, He could come and take us there, and show us it was right.

One day Bethany said to me, "Mommy, if you could choose your bestest house, what would it be like?"

"Well, if I could choose, it would be out in the country, but very close to a good school. It would have a lovely garden for you to play in, and a big kitchen with room enough to eat in. There would also be a bedroom for you, one for the boys, and one for us, a study for Daddy, and a workroom for me. But that's just a dream. A log fire would be cozy, and maybe we could even have a conservatory and fill it with all our plants!"

We looked and looked, but nothing seemed right, and we wondered whether God was telling us we shouldn't move after all. We were driving through a village where there was a good school, and suddenly we remembered a house we had seen before. We drove past. It was empty and still for sale, and much cheaper than when we first looked at it. What's more, it had the very specifications as the "dream" home I had shared with Bethany! By the end of the day it was ours. Not a mansion in earthly terms, but certainly one by our standards!

All that was less than a week ago. There's lots to do, what with packing and getting everything ready, but I know I have nothing to fear for the future because this new home is truly His gift of love to us. It's the best place we can be.   KAREN HOLFORD

MAY 19

Mole People

They will build houses and dwell in them; they will plant vineyards and eat their fruit. . . . They will not toil in vain or bear children doomed to misfortune. Isa. 65:21-23, NIV.

According to Jennifer Toth, a reporter who lived among the people for a year, a large community of homeless (some estimate 100,000) live in underground communities beneath New York City. In abandoned tunnels, disused subway stations and sewers, a city exists beneath the streets. Deep in these tunnels people struggle to survive. Rats run in dark waves toward, not away from, people, and roaches crunch underfoot. Sewage seeps through rock walls. People live in almost total darkness with only occasional streams of light filtering through an overhead grate. They eat, sleep, and defecate there. The stench is so overpowering it sears the eyes, and at times it is barely possible to breathe.

The tunnels are old and resemble catacombs. Some reportedly go as deep as 10 stories down. The farther into the tunnels the people retreat, the more out of touch with reality they become. Through strange noises and sounds similar to those of trains, they say they are communicating with each other. Police rarely venture into such areas, so the people rule their own communities.

Because of the darkness in the tunnels many don't know each other's names. Most are wary as a result of past experiences. There is little trust down there. You can't trust others unless you can look into their eyes, and in the tunnels darkness prevails. It's dangerous to look too closely.

Most of the people are on drugs. Many of the women are prostitutes, and a woman usually stays with a man only because she thinks he can protect her. There's no future down there, and the people know it. They only exist. Neither is there any productivity, and they know that, too. Mole people get so isolated from society that it gets harder and harder for them to fit back in at any level.

Isn't it amazing that people can live like that when a simple solution could save their lives, offer hope, acceptance, peace, and joy? They live in abject poverty of soul and spirit, going through their daily routines blindly in their self-made exile, shackled by their own doing, barely aware they are feasting on rats.

We, like mole people, are free to do what we want and to make choices that will lead 10 stories underground. God sets us free to make such choices. But our God, in addition to being a God of choice and freedom, also says, "I have something so much better for you. Follow Me. Wait on Me. Deny yourselves just a small portion of temporary pleasure today, and I will give you permanent joy, peace, and a lifetime of companionship with Me."

Many of us can't wait to experience what God has to offer. Like mole people, we have sunk so low that we no longer have hope for the future. If we can't see or experience the benefits now, we reject His plan. The loss to us and our families now and throughout eternity is incalculable.

Let's lift our sights above the degradation of what the world has to offer so we can enjoy heavenly pleasures forever. Jesus is waiting, knocking at the door, with all the help we need. — NANCY VAN PELT

MAY 20

Collecting Bows

Whenever the rainbow appears in the clouds, I will see it and remember the everlasting covenant between God and all living creatures of every kind on the earth. Gen. 9:16, NIV.

I have never had a collection of hair bows. However, that special union of sun and shower that forms a rainbow, often with storm clouds around, has provided me with several particular memories.

My boyfriend (later to become my husband) and I were driving down a narrow country road in Maryland when a rain shower exploded overhead. We pulled to the side of the road and, as the rain subsided, discovered that behind us was a perfectly full rainbow. How great to share that moment with a special friend! Years later our family was on the upper level of the Canadian National Communications Tower in Toronto, Canada. A summer storm coming through surprised us with a circular rainbow that was right below us as we looked down. Another time our regular connecting flight home had been canceled, and we were rerouted onto a small commuter plane. Everyone was disgruntled by the delay and the necessary adjustment of arrival plans when the pilot announced that if we would look to our right, we would see a lovely rainbow. What beautiful sights these all were, but there was one other time that is very special to me.

My pregnancy had been eagerly awaited and for several years anticipated. Now I found myself in a private hospital room on the maternity floor, feeling dejected and numb. The final call had come from the nearby Children's Medical Center where our tiny premature daughter had been taken. It was the conclusion of previous calls that had reported that she was not doing well. It had happened so fast—I hadn't gotten a chance to hold her or to know her. I could just remember her little fists and wiggling toes. We had prayed for her. I had such hope and faith. But then she was gone.

This was January in Ohio, usually a cold and snowy time of the year. But this time there was a rather strange weather pattern, and it had brought unseasonable warmth. That afternoon as I looked up from my reading and out my fourth-floor window, tears once again came to my eyes. But this time it was because there before me, perfectly framed by my window, was the most beautiful rainbow. God had not forgotten me. I was convinced that that *bow* was placed there especially for me. What a lovely reminder of mercy, justice, care, and the promise of His love for me. How it lightened my heart that day. Even today I remember that moment of God's closeness. How He tended to my very personal needs. That rainbow was a special hug from God in radiant color.

You can collect them too.   EVANGELINE LUNDSTROM

MAY 21

Mycorrhiza Fungi

Hatred stirs up dissension, but love covers all wrongs. Prov. 10:12, NIV.

A couple years ago I read something very interesting that I would like to share with you.

Trees have made an alliance with an amazing microscopic symbiont, mycorrhiza fungi. Beneath the typical tree, roots generally reach half as deep and twice as wide as the tree we see above ground. When the roots of two trees touch, a battle for dominance usually ensues—unless the mycorrhiza fungi are on the scene. Forest scientist David Perry of Oregon State University has found that these fungi not only reduce competition between the trees, but also link together roots from trees of the same, or even different, species. In one experiment Perry grew seedlings and watched their roots join through the mycorrhiza. Then the scientist cast shade over one of the seedlings. The shaded tree began to draw nutrients from the sunlit tree through the fungal linkage between them.

"Thanks to these fungi," says Perry, "it could be that a whole forest is linked together like a community. If one tree has access to water, another to nutrients, and a third to sunlight, the trees apparently can share with one another" (Lowell Pointe, "What Good Is a Tree?" *Reader's Digest,* March 1990, pp. 36, 37).

While I was reading this lesson from nature, I began to think of it as a parable we can apply to our daily life. We can compare the trees to human beings. When we are the only ones and nobody can compete with us, everything works fine. But as soon as we realize that somebody else is also important, agreeable, and can do even nicer things than we can, we feel threatened.

What is the mycorrhiza fungus? We can compare it to love, the only thing that can help to make the relationship between human beings agreeable. We know that the origin of love is God. If love is present among us, even if we do not have all the advantages that others may have, we can be nourished and grow spiritually, just as do the trees that are linked together through the mycorrhiza fungi. We share the nutritious "sap" that we have, and can also receive it from others. When we help each other, our spiritual life becomes strong.

There is another kind of fungi that works contrary to the mycorrhiza fungus. It is the jealousy fungus. Instead of linking the trees together, it separates them. We can see this fungus working among the members of families, between friends, and among members in our churches. And its effectiveness is 100 percent. When we allow jealousy in our hearts, we are fighting against ourselves, because our happiness will go away, and much time and suffering will be expended trying to fight against the other one of whom we are jealous.

We know very well the experience of Saul and David. Had Saul used his energy in leading God's people instead of persecuting David, how differently his story would read.

"Envy is the offspring of pride, and if it is entertained in the heart, it will lead to hatred, and eventually to revenge and murder" (Ellen G. White, *Patriarchs and Prophets*, p. 651).   ELLEN MAYR

MAY 22

My Personal Angel

For he shall give his angels charge over thee, to keep thee in all thy ways. They shall bear thee up in their hands, lest thou dash thy foot against a stone. Ps. 91:11, 12.

*M*y husband and I and our two small children were going to Green Bay, Wisconsin, to visit my husband's twin brother. We arrived at the train terminal just as the train was preparing to leave. My husband and 6-year-old son ran on ahead. I followed as quickly as I could, holding on to my 2-year-old daughter with one hand and my suitcase with the other. As we passed the train engine, a sudden gust of steam frightened my daughter, and she began to cry. Of course, this caused a delay as I tried to comfort her, and moved her to the other side of me. By the time we reached the platform, we were the only two there. I cried out, "O God, help us."

Suddenly a tall young man grabbed my daughter and suitcase and said, "Follow me." I almost had to run to keep up with him. As we reached the last train coach, he placed my little girl on the steps and announced, "This is your coach."

I turned to thank him, but there was no one there. My questions at that moment were Who was he? How did he know where we were going? How did he know which coach was going to Green Bay, Wisconsin?

I know God saw our dilemma and sent my angel to help in our time of need. Thank You, God, for Your loving care!   JEANETTE RITZ

The Quilted Life

He who began a good work in you will carry it on to completion until the day of Christ Jesus. Phil. 1:6, NIV.

*F*ive years ago I fell in love with a beautiful quilt kit. Not having the patience to appliqué lots of pieces by hand, and being a beginner quilter, I found a kit containing ready-printed fabric. The design was beautiful: soft pinks, blues, and greens against a creamy background, in traditional appliqué patterns. Wreaths of roses, little hearts, and houses combined in various ways across the quilt squares.

Two babies and a couple house moves later, I actually found time to stitch the quilt top pieces together, stack them with batting and backing fabric, and baste the whole lot together with stitches fanning out across the quilt, then up and down, and side to side. The basting stitches looked big and clumsy. When my husband saw the quilt all basted together, he thought I'd ruined the whole thing. I explained the need to spend a lot of time carefully preparing before beginning to do the fine hand quilting.

Then I set up my quilting frame, and the fun began! I like to hand-quilt; it's soothing, faster than I imagined it would be, and more accurate than my machine quilting on such intricate designs. But it is still time-consuming. The frame is stashed away behind the sofa and brought out for odd moments of relaxation, but those come rarely with three children and a pastor husband! Every time I glimpse the quilt, I long for it to be finished, and I long to have a few minutes to sit with it (or even just a few minutes to sit down would be nice!).

But it is slowly being completed. One month may pass without any stitching, then I may have a burst of creativity and stitch a bit each day. I long to see it completed and its edges bound in the gently faded blue hues. I know it will be beautiful. I want to hang it on the stairwell wall, which looks empty without it.

Maybe God looks at me in a similar way. I may look messy at the moment—scrawled over with inelegant basting stitches—and the work is certainly slow and uncertain, and may come in fits and bursts. Sometimes I am just sitting behind the sofa, not doing a lot. Sometimes the work goes quickly, and it is easy to see the progress being made. Mostly the work is slow and laborious. Sometimes the quilting frame feels cumbersome, or the pain of a needle prick brings back memories of broken hands. But He knows just how I will look when I'm finished—and that makes all the painstaking effort worthwhile. And He can hardly wait till I'm finished, and He can put me in His home forever! KAREN HOLFORD

MAY 24

Saved From Untimely Death

Yea, though I walk through the valley of the shadow of death, I will fear no evil; for You are with me. Ps. 23:4, NKJV.

*W*e had been married for two weeks when my husband was sent to the United Bible Societies' office in Ghana. Early one morning I joined him on a trip. He was to travel from the northern town of Tamale to the northwestern town of Wa, a distance of about 350 miles. We were to stop at each of the mission stations along the way and hold discussions with missionaries and nationals who were translating the Holy Scriptures into Ghanaian languages. About 100 miles short of our final destination something happened. Taking a sharp curve, we suddenly noticed that heaps of laterite had been deposited on each side of the road in an attempt to regravel it. My husband swerved to the right to avoid the first set of heaps, then noticing other heaps just ahead of him, he swerved to the left. In the process, our car hit one of the laterite heaps. He lost control, and the car went off the road into the savannah-like grassland.

My husband was no longer in charge of the vehicle. And I, unlike my usual self, ceased to play my traditional role as codriver and instructor. The circumstances were beyond our control, but we had given our predicament to the Lord. My husband was completely relaxed behind the wheel—no brakes, no steering. The car rolled off the road and finally, on its own, came to a stop. Without saying a word to each other, we opened our doors and got out.

Then we realized what had happened. When we became helpless, the Master Driver took over the controls. We never saw anything ahead of us, but the car stopped just one foot short of a big tree. We could have crashed into it, but the Lord Himself was in control of the situation.

The very spot the car stopped was the next miracle—it was a smooth area from which we could drive back onto the road. We were full of praises for the Lord's deliverance. Despite a carburetor problem, we returned home slowly but safely.

"Yea, though I walk through the valley of the shadow of death, I will fear no evil: for thou art with me; thy rod and thy staff they comfort me" (Ps. 23:4).   JULIANA AGBOKA

MAY 25

No Trespassing

Blessed is he that readeth, and they that keep those things which are written therein: for the time is at hand. Rev. 1:3.

I looked over my shoulder and saw a huge red bull charging after us. "Hurry!" I yelled in Carl's ear, hoping he would hear me above the roar of the bike.

It was a beautiful afternoon, warm and sunny, a perfect day for a ride around the countryside. The afternoon passed quickly, and soon the sun would drop behind the mountain. We weren't dressed for the cool night air, so Carl decided we should take a shortcut back home, which necessitated cutting through a farmer's field. We shoved the bike under the fence and crawled after it. Hopping back on the bike, we rode until we came to a very steep decline covered with leaves. Once the bike hit the leaves, it slid out from under us, all the way to the bottom. We quickly followed. There we encountered another fence with "Keep Out" and "No Trespassing" signs tacked to fence posts. I didn't want to violate the warnings, but it was impossible to drag the bike back up that slippery, steep hill, and we could see the paved road just beyond another fence with a gate. So we threw the bike under the fence and crawled through. Just as we hopped back on, we spotted a very angry bull running up behind us.

Wasting no time, we gunned for the gate and the safety of the road beyond. Once again, we threw the bike under and crawled after it, a little faster than before, encouraged by the bull's nearness. The bull stood on his side of the gate, head lowered, pawing the dirt with his front hoof, bellowing as we sped away.

The Ten Commandments are similar to the fence posts with the "Keep Out" and "No Trespassing" signs. They aren't placed there so we can't have any fun, but rather for our own protection and safety. When we choose to ignore the signs, Satan will surely charge after us, just as that angry bull did. But when we heed the warnings, we will save ourselves much heartache and stress.

MARLENE ANDERSON

MAY 26

Bugs and Broccoli

So, do not let sin control you in your life here on earth. . . . But offer yourselves to God. Rom. 6:12, 13, EB.

*J*had to laugh the other day when I read that the Food and Drug Administration permits 269 aphids in a pound of frozen broccoli. I was incredulous! Imagine counting all of them! I wonder why the broccoli doesn't get a little pressure wash before it's packed. Permitted contamination, that's what it is!

Then there are those dreadful insects that descend upon me in clouds the moment I go outside. The wonderful rains we had last winter have made this summer hectic for me, as far as mosquitoes are concerned. Even at sunrise they are on duty to make me miserable. Unless there is a good breeze, day or night, these pests rule my life. Spraying doesn't seem to help; however, I've learned what does—Avon's Skin-So-Soft bath oil. Sure, I'm greasy all the time, but I have the softest skin you can imagine. Still, I'd just as soon not be greasy. Controlled contamination, I guess you'd call it.

But the worst are the ants! My kitchen has been overrun lately with the smallest, most aggressive ants I've ever been up against. They run around like crazy. And talk about persistent! That's their middle name. The ant traps I put out are totally ignored. Those determined little things raced around, over, under, and in every other direction but into the traps. They swarmed in the trash compactor, even though bits of stuff that might be a problem were safely encased in plastic bags. They were in the dishwasher, too, although the dishes had been rinsed in soapy water. Even though my kitchen was spotless (really!)—sink, floor, stove, everything—I could not get rid of those hysterical ants. I became almost as unhinged as they were. They were definitely in control of my life, and I hated it. Then help came.

Coffee grounds. Fresh coffee grounds. My friend insisted it would work, but I was skeptical. Yes, the stuff smelled strong. Yes, it looked terrible sprinkled on the kitchen tile. Yes, it was hard to endure, but now I'll take the coffee grounds any day! Three days with the coffee grounds was a lot better than another day with those wild ants controlling my life and calling the shots! No doubt they'll be back sometime, but for now they're gone, eliminated. And I like it that way.

In case you hadn't noticed, contaminating influences are all around us these days. Everywhere. It's easy to permit the lesser ones to pass by in life's wild ride, but the more we do allow, the harder they are to get rid of. We may try to control other contaminants, but they are still there, controlling us. The best solution is to get rid of them, eliminate them from our lives, and not allow them to take up residence where they will breed and multiply.

The best eliminator gives the quickest service. His name is Wonderful, Counselor, the Mighty God, the Everlasting Father, the Prince of Peace. VIRGINIA CASON

MAY 27

Life's Annoyances

Casting all your care upon Him, for He cares for you. 1 Peter 5:7, NKJV.

It was a day I didn't particularly want to repeat. Everything seemed to be an annoyance. I had been coordinating a major conference, and I was two days late in making hotel reservations because not everyone had sent in their RSVPs. I had asked three times for an important paper that should have been faxed the day before. Staff members continually interrupted me with their own needs, and someone called on the phone to complain about our receptionist.

I thought it was time for a break, so I grabbed my purse and headed for the front door; but naturally, the phone rang, and it was for me. The voice on the other end was a friend asking if I could go to lunch. I had to decline, since I had a 12:30 speaking engagement, but the calm of her voice brought me back into focus.

"How important is all of this in the light of eternity?" I asked myself, rounding the corner of my desk.

A few moments later as I drove in my car toward my destination, I reflected on my own question. How *really* important is it? In a few days or weeks it will all be of little significance. Life's annoyances began to slip away as I pictured the tranquillity of the new earth. There activities and responsibilities will be numerous, I'm sure, but I will be the one who is changed. No longer will I be so hurried and annoyed.

"Lord, I think I'll start the change now," I mused, relaxing into my car seat. As a car rudely whipped in front of me, I heard myself whisper, "Great peace have they which love thy law: and nothing shall offend them" (Ps. 119:165).

JOAN BOVA

MAY 28

The Chemistry Lesson

For the Lord gives wisdom; from His mouth come knowledge and understanding. Prov. 2:6, NKJV.

It was perhaps the most challenging period of my life, or at least I thought it was. I was a full-time college student enrolled in an off-campus adult degree program while working full-time as an intensive care nurse. Now in my last semester, I faced organic chemistry, required for graduation.

I reserved each Sunday to study chemistry. For the first few Sundays, all went well. Then about the fifth Sunday difficulty arose. Even with careful rereading, I was unable to understand the first two paragraphs of the chapter I was working on. Looking over the rest of the chapter, I realized that unless I mastered the concept described in the opening paragraphs I would be unable to go on. So with renewed determination I went back and read them again.

After about the twelfth reading I went into the other room and knelt in prayer to my Father in heaven. I first asked the Lord if I should look for a tutor, then changed my prayer to ask the Lord if He would be my tutor. Returning to the chemistry book, I reread the troublesome paragraphs with complete understanding. As if scales had fallen from my eyes, I now had complete understanding and finished the assignment without undue difficulty. From that point on, chemistry became my delight, despite the fact that it took a lot of study and hard work.

I have marveled at the beauty and wonder of chemistry and wished I had taken all I could of it in previous schooling. I even speculate on what fun it would be to really study it in heaven, where I will meet the One who taught me so well here on earth.

In Proverbs 8:14-17, He says, "Counsel is mine, and sound wisdom; I am understanding. . . . And those who seek me diligently will find me" (NKJV). Thank You, Lord, for always being there for each of us, with counsel and wisdom for all our needs.   MARILYN KING

MAY 29

Hearing Voices

But just as he who called you is holy, so be holy in all you do.
1 Peter 1:15, NIV.

*A*s an adult I still hear voices of conscience that say "Pick it up, even if you didn't put it there" or "Many hands make the work lighter." Our family favorite was "Girls, you'll feel so much better if you wash your face and brush your teeth before you go to bed." Mother would say that after we'd just finished a long trip on the road. I am grateful for her quotable quotes, yet I suspect the voices I still hear didn't originate with her.

Growing up, I heard the usual voices that were directed toward women. They said, "Be nice girls." "Be young ladies." "Be dutiful wives." And "Be seen and not heard." In the early 1970s they said "Be seen *and* heard." Now, in the 1990s, they say "Be yourself, but above all, be politically correct."

With so many different voices, I am driven to listen to the right voices and to make good choices. I am committed to obeying the voices that will allow me to live an abundant life now and in the hereafter. Of course, that doesn't mean I'll make no mistakes. It just means I will follow "the voice" that helps me to decipher the garbled messages that fill our crowded days. I crave clarity of purpose.

It's finally sinking in, after all of these years, that God's still small voice is "the voice" that I have been resisting. I have been kicking, screaming, and fighting within. I have learned that I am to acquiesce and fulfill the purpose for which we were created: Be holy! In sickness, be holy. At work, or in traffic, be holy. In your leisure, be holy.

"Your mission, should you choose to accept My offer of life everlasting, is for you to prepare to meet a holy God." He says (and I am paraphrasing), "Your ticket into My kingdom is a righteous character that's been fashioned during your struggles here and now. You are to build character, and I will give you the specifications. As you listen, I will guide you in laying a foundation that will prepare you to dwell in My presence forever. Continue building," I can hear Him saying.

One writer says, "God is holy and . . . none but holy beings can ever dwell in His presence" (Ellen G. White, *Early Writings*, p. 71).

I want so desperately to tune in and listen to God's still small voice. Would you like to as well? The good news is we are free to and may begin today. Will you join me in choosing to listen to that still small voice that invites us to be holy? LYNN MARIE DAVIS

MAY 30

I Can Do Something

And whatsoever ye do, do it heartily, as to the Lord, and not unto men. Col. 3:23.

I never had aspirations toward greatness during my lifetime. Neither do I cherish any earthshaking ambitions to have my name embedded in some marble statue. But I would like to contribute something to the world, no matter how insignificant.

It's easy to become disheartened at times when comparing my life to that of others. It's their acts of accomplishment, something to pass on to the world, that sets them apart from common folk such as I. I'm a resigned coward, so I've never considered donating my body to science. I have a terrible fear of high places and enclosures, so being an astronaut is out of the question. Even though I have two brothers who are artists, I've inherited none of their talent. Stick men are my forte.

I've made four different attempts to learn to play a musical instrument, and I never did master rhythm. Even though I've written 50 songs (for my own enjoyment only), I finally settled for chording in the key of C on the organ. The only problem is my waltzes and polkas sound just like my hymns.

If I have occasion to speak before a group of people, regardless of how small the number, I am inclined toward stage fright, and there have been times when I wanted to flee from the room. So I've discounted public speaking as a vocation.

I do many things poorly. I lay claim to a few accomplishments, and I'm expert at none; so with a record such as mine, what in the world can I contribute to humanity?

Even in my sphere I've decided I can do something. If I can't be an engine, I can be a caboose. If I can't be a chief, then I can be a brave. If I can't sing a solo, I can blend my voice in a choir. If I can't preach a sermon, I can talk to one person about Christ. Not everyone can do everything, but everyone can do something. We can all smile.

You don't have to be a genius to contribute something to the world. Just give your life to Christ, and He'll turn it into something of major significance. CLAREEN COLCLESSER

MAY 31

More Ways Than One

The prayer of a righteous man is powerful and effective. James 5:16, NIV.

*I*t wasn't with clenched fists that friends, family, and coworkers prayed for my husband's recovery on a designated day in 1989. The invitation to pray without giving up encouraged us, even though Gene's type of brain tumor was growing viciously. Just how that request would be answered was not questioned, and certainly not understood at the time. Hundreds of prayers went up for him from righteous men and women on that day, and continued throughout the following year, and longer. Those prayers brought a feeling of peace and calm that is not usually present amid the turbulence of living.

After doing everything we could to aid in the healing process—diet and exercise, surgeries and radiation implants—we anxiously faced each 24 hours. There were good days and days of uncertainty. When the doctor said "You're a miracle man!" we were overjoyed. But the miracles did not continue, and the tumor came back with a vengeance.

Over and over the "why" questions were asked. Were all those prayers ignored? Would the faith of so many not be rewarded with physical, as well as spiritual, healing? Where was our God now?

After Gene passed away, I wrestled with those questions for two years. Little by little I have been able to look back on that time of trouble with a more peaceful heart, realizing there are more ways prayers may be answered than can be imagined. Physical healing is one way, but it was not an answer for Gene.

Having given himself entirely over to the will of God, Gene had peace. Answered prayer? Yes. An answer that many long to see in the lives of their loved ones. But there was another wonderful answer. Throughout the illness, Gene had no pain. None at all!

Do I recommend storming the gates of heaven in prayer? Certainly! Do I know what to ask for, what is best? Certainly not. I do know that prayer is powerful and that my good and gracious God hears and answers our supplications—in more ways than one.

HELEN STILES

JUNE 1

Hurricanes

Therefore you also must be ready; for the Son of man is coming at an hour you do not expect. Matt. 24:44, RSV.

June 1 is the beginning of our fifth season in Florida—hurricane season. Unlike other seasons, this one lasts six months, ending on November 30. Just as winter has its own weather words—windchill factor, blizzard, flurry—hurricane season has terminology that residents quickly become acquainted with. We hear about tropical depressions, storm surges, and hurricane categories. About this time of year we become inundated with educational information from the media on safety precautions and checklists, evacuation routes, and shelters.

When we first moved to Florida, we took each precaution to heart and played it safe. However, as the watches and warnings have come and gone without so much as an inch of rain, a lackadaisical attitude has set in. We've stopped paying as much attention to broadcasters crying wolf. We've quit trying to be prepared ahead of time. And we are not the only ones. We've noticed that many people wait until the last minute before taking steps to protect their homes and families. A deadly storm may be only a day away before grocery stores become jam-packed with frenzied shoppers, disappointed to find that the shelves of water, bread, and canned food are empty. Hardware stores swarm with people waiting for flashlights, batteries, wood, nails, and duct tape. Gas stations become crowded with vehicles needing gas, and with people standing in line for propane.

The analogy is obvious, of course, but profound. We have lived our entire lives with the biblical warnings about end-time ringing in our ears. We have heard sermon after sermon and discussion after discussion about the last days. We know the signs and have seen many of them fulfilled, yet we get caught up in our lives and treat these cautions with apathy and disinterest. We fulfill Revelation's description of us as being lukewarm. Occasionally an event will arouse our interest and cause us to perk up our ears, but then we gradually turn our attention back to the temporal affairs of life and feel no urgent need to prepare. We think we can slide in at the last minute and do all the preparing then.

Jesus predicted our procrastination, our arrogance, and our foolishness. He cautioned us against those sins through the parable of the virgins. His second coming is certain. It is not a storm watch or warning. It is positively inevitable, unquestionable, and definite. It is not a tempest that will hit only those in low-lying flood zones. His return will affect every one of us. We need to prepare urgently for it, because, unlike a storm, there is a positive aspect to His second coming. We don't have to lose our lives; we can gain them. We don't have to dread it; we can eagerly await it.

Take time today to read His warnings. Make preparation a priority. Don't allow yourself to get caught up in the here and now. Don't procrastinate so long that He says, "Truly, I say to you, I do not know you" (Matt. 25:12, RSV). Get ready to meet Jesus face-to-face. His coming is a promise and a guarantee.

LAURA PASCUAL DANCEK

JUNE 2

Angel in the Red Car

Those who love me, I will deliver; I will protect those who know my name. When they call to me, I will answer them; I will be with them in trouble. I will rescue them and honor them. Ps. 91:14, 15, NRSV.

A sudden rush of adrenaline surged through me as I turned to see two ferociously barking dogs rushing toward me, teeth bared. It was so unexpected. A fast-paced early-morning walk has been my habit for more than 20 years, and never before had a dog done more than bark.

It is difficult to predict how you will respond in an emergency. I responded by charging them with a menacing crouching position and a wild stamping of my feet. I also used an old trick my father taught me as a child—I acted as though I was picking up a rock to throw.

Right in the middle of all this commotion, a red car appeared out of nowhere, blasting its horn, and drove toward the dogs. A woman on her way to work had seen the dogs attacking and was quick-thinking enough to put her car between them and me. The dogs retreated. I returned home, frightened but safe.

The dogs were pit bulls. The woman in the red car? Until that day I was not aware that angels traveled in fire engine red cars, but you'll never convince me of anything else. My heavenly Father watched over me. He'll watch over you today also if you put yourself in His hands and ask for His protection.   NANCY VAN PELT

JUNE 3

Education—God's Way

I will instruct you and teach you in the way you should go; I will counsel you and watch over you. Ps. 32:8, NIV.

The 100-degree heat seemed to smother me as I hung clothes on the line. My two small children were playing happily in the shade, running back and forth through a fountain at the end of a water hose. We had moved to the country for the summer before my husband returned to college in the fall. For the past two years he had been a pastor/teacher in a rural area. Three teenage boys had lived with us so they could attend the one-room church school my husband taught.

Even though I was in my early 30s, I was inexperienced in dealing with children. I had been the youngest child in a neighborhood of mostly older people and had been active in church work, but I had never worked in any of the children's divisions. My lack of preparation was evident as I mothered my two babies and the teenage boys.

However, God sustained me day by day as I learned by trial and error how to deal with the multitude of problems that seemed to keep coming. There had been many answers to prayer during those two years, but I was also thinking over what I considered to be failures. How I wished I had more experience and wisdom. As discouragement seemed to close in on me, I paused at the clothesline and looked up into a cloudless sky.

"Why did You send me here, Lord?" I pleaded.

A voice seemed to answer, "To teach you things."

What a new perspective! During it all, God was preparing me for the years ahead, working with my family and with youth. God thought so much of me that He was educating me in His school.

As Moses spent 40 years in the wilderness, and Joseph spent time as a servant and in prison, they must have asked many times, "Why did You send me here, Lord?" The Lord used those years to prepare them for the work He had for them to do in the years ahead.

Those very situations that may seem hopeless to you now, God can work out so your influence can be a blessing to others, just as the ministries of Moses and Joseph were a blessing. So when you feel you are in a trying situation and trials and perplexities come your way, pause to look for the lessons God is teaching you. Graduation from His school will result in eternal life, where all learning will be joyous.

BETTY PHILLIPS

JUNE 4

Yes, I Would

Be joyful in hope, patient in affliction, faithful in prayer. Rom. 12:12, NIV.

I was selected by my boss to attend an all-day administration seminar. Little did I know that God could use this secular event to teach me a spiritual lesson.

One of the presentations, about coping with stress on the job, was entitled "Yes, You Wood," an intentional pun. The speaker gave each of us a rectangular slab of wood. He had his petite female assistant place her slab of wood over two bricks and, with her bare hands, break it in two. We each took a turn doing this.

I stood near the front of the line and watched those ahead of me successfully break their wood slab, symbolizing that yes, they could conquer their fears and achieve their goals. When my turn came, I stepped up on the stage and placed my wood on the bricks. I tried with all my might to break the wood, but could not. Eventually the speaker told me to stand aside and try again. I made several more unsuccessful attempts and watched as another woman was also unable to break her wood. She quickly gave up and sat down, but I persevered. After a few more attempts, the speaker told me to return to my seat and try again at the end.

Suddenly I felt like crying. It was not about breaking a piece of wood anymore. It was about watching others succeed right away, while I failed. Right then I determined that I was going to break that piece of wood.

When the group dispersed for lunch I returned to the front of the room and approached the assistant who had been coaching me. I challenged her to break my piece of wood. She did, then gave me another piece. On my first try I broke it in two pieces! The feeling was exhilarating! I had persevered and succeeded.

I had been feeling discouraged over several things that seemed to take a long time to accomplish while others did them in a flash. God said to me, "Do not give up. You can accomplish your dreams. Forget about others. Work at your own pace, and you will succeed. If one method does not work, try another, but persevere."

I decided then that I would succeed at the dreams and goals I had set for myself. The ones that I had become discouraged over and had dropped by the wayside I would pick up again. The ones that I was about to drop, I would keep. I would succeed! Yes, I would!

KAREN BIRKETT

JUNE 5

The Cocoon

"Do not be afraid, O worm Jacob, O little Israel, for I myself will help you," declares the Lord, your Redeemer, the Holy One of Israel. Isa. 41:14, NIV.

While in the basement doing laundry one February morning, I noticed a small furry ball. Looking closely, I discovered the caterpillar our three young children had brought in during the summer. The insect had lain on the basement floor, virtually forgotten until now. I took the caterpillar upstairs to see what it would do. After being in the warmth of the upstairs for a time, she spun her cocoon. Almost two weeks later a lovely brown moth emerged.

But my mind still thinks of that caterpillar when I read today's verse. She was every bit as helpless as a worm, yet had not the Creator lovingly sustained her life throughout this historically cold winter?

She could keep only so warm in the sometimes flooded, and always frigid, basement. Even Sunny, our dog, shivered down there. Still, she slept all winter long, and, though without food, her fat did not go away. She survived with the help of God, the Holy One of Israel, who says, "I Myself will help you."

I remember that severe winter of 1994. I wondered at times how our family would make it through. We needed coats, gloves, snow boots, hats, scarves, and extra blankets. Now the snow is gone; the trees are budding. Spring is here, and God has kept us through another winter. Yes, just as surely as He kept the caterpillar, so He kept us.

Even in the middle of the summer soon to come, I'm sure I'll have many "winters." But every time I think of the caterpillar I shall remember: "'I Myself will help you,' declares the Lord."

MYRA OMELER

JUNE 6

Weed Whipping

For our light and momentary troubles are achieving for us an eternal glory that far outweighs them all. 2 Cor. 4:17, NIV.

*W*hile weeding carrots this morning, I thought, *The world of a weeder is certainly small.* From a stooped position the view is about three feet high and is made up of garden plants, weeds, and dirt. Though the weeds disappeared quickly, I kept being distracted. The sky was in the wrong direction and had no weeds, but it was so gorgeously blue it had to be noticed. A goldfinch sitting on a raspberry cane tweeted shrilly for attention. Teenage cardinals flitted around bragging about their new flying licenses. *Why so many diversions, God?*

Probably God knows I need to change position once in a while or I'll get stiff and sore. Also, He may want me to remember that the world is more than three feet high. If we think of our troubles as weeds in the garden of life, the same things are true. When we concentrate on weeding out our troubles, we live in a small world with no look upward. God wants us to focus on Him—His character, His power and might, the evidence He gives us today that He loves us, and the memories of the ways He's helped us in the past. Then our minds won't get stiff and sore from looking down at our problems. And with God in the picture the universe becomes bigger and the weedy worries we face, though still troublesome, are seen in proper perspective. Each trouble weed is small enough for His mighty hand to pull. It may take time, but all things will work for our good with our focus on God.

ALBERTA HACK

Our Generous Heavenly Father

Open your mouth wide, and I will fill it. Ps. 81:10, NKJV.

*I*n 1976, while we were still serving as missionaries in Bangkok, Thailand, we were privileged to be allowed to study at a university in Michigan. Each graduate credit cost $48, as compared with $5 per credit at our local university. We talked and prayed about the difficulty of going to the United States, yet the more we prayed about it, the more we became convinced that we should go.

Our employing agency would allow us to go only if we could deposit $8,000 in our account at its treasury—a guarantee that we would be financially stable in the States. My husband assessed the value of the few belongings we had, then suggested we sell them. We concluded that the most we could profit from the proceeds of those sales would be $5,000, including the meager savings in our bank account. Where would we get the remaining $3,000?

One evening, without my knowledge, my husband went to the mission office to pray most earnestly. He felt that this situation was not impossible for God. After all, the Lord Himself said that He owned the cattle on a thousand hills and everything in this world (Ps. 50:10-12). So why could he not ask our heavenly Father to help us find the money to go to college?

Two weeks later my husband met me as I was coming home, waving a letter from California. "What's $300 compared to the $3,000 that we need?" I asked when I finished reading it, feeling discouraged. He insisted I read the note again. My eyes grew big with disbelief. "He's sending us $3,000? Did you ask him to?"

My husband shook his head, assuring me that he hadn't asked this man for any money, but that this man was indeed sending us the funds. The letter further stated that he needed instructions as to when and where the check should be sent.

The money arrived in two weeks. We later learned that this man had been impressed we needed this amount of money. With his donation and the $5,000 we raised, we were able to fulfill the financial requirements necessary to attend the university.

Truly, our generous heavenly Father knows how to give us our needs—and even many of our wants.   OFELIA A. PANGAN

Use It or Lose It!

Take the talent from him and give it to the one who has the ten talents. . . . And throw that worthless servant outside, into the darkness, where there will be weeping and gnashing of teeth. Matt. 25:28-30, NIV.

Our family is headed to Germany this summer for two glorious weeks of doing the "tourist thing." Glorious, except that not one of us knows German. Oh, I took German for two years in college, but what do I have to show for that achievement? Three sentences, that's what! Having failed through the years to speak the German I learned, I will have scant advantage over those in the group who have never studied the language. I haven't used it; therefore, I have lost it.

Use it or lose it—an arbitrary rule, or a law of nature? What could you do once that you no longer can? Why can't you? Age, of course, is a factor, but probably more often the real truth behind why you cannot run, type, swim, or do math problems as fast as you once did is that you haven't kept practicing.

Atrophy of the muscles—how quickly it sets in. A brief six weeks in a cast, and a leg needs physical therapy. A few months out of practice, and even professional baseball players must put in time at retraining the muscles at spring camp in Florida.

And atrophy of the mind—how depressing! Why can't I take shorthand dictation at 120 words per minute anymore? I even have a pin to prove that I once could. Neither can I play that rapid passage from "The Irish Washerwoman" up to tempo on my piccolo as I used to. Use it or lose it. The law is inflexible.

Can the soul, too, atrophy from lack of use? Jesus thought so. "Take the talent from him and give it to the one who has the ten talents." We atrophy our souls when we neglect opportunities to use the talent of giving. I remember the story of a woman who was always lending her books to other people. It wasn't until her house burned that she realized that the only books she had were those she had given away, stored safely in other people's homes.

We atrophy our souls when we neglect to use the talent of witnessing, or when we neglect to use all our talents, cloaking our nonparticipation in lame excuses. "Let the men do it." "Others sing better than I do." "I'm too busy." "I work outside the home."

The fact that I can no longer take dictation at 120 words per minute, or speak German fluently, or play a certain song on my piccolo, will have minimal, if any, consequences. But spiritual atrophy of the soul has eternal consequences. "And throw that worthless servant outside, into the darkness, where there will be weeping and gnashing of teeth." Yes, Jesus knows all about the law of "use it or lose it."

WILMA McCLARTY

JUNE 9

Walk Beneath the Waterfall

On that day a fountain will be opened to the house of David and the inhabitants of Jerusalem, to cleanse them from sin and impurity. Zech. 13:1, NIV.

I don't recall the specific circumstances. All I remember is the dreariness of day following day, the sense of hopelessness in ever catching up on my work, the physical tiredness that a night's sleep never seemed to ease. All joy had vanished. My family was tired of it—and so was I.

One Sunday our church planned an outing in the desert. "I don't want to go," I said. "I have work to do."

But my pastor husband persisted. "Please, come," he urged. "You know you don't feel like working today. The desert air will refresh you."

It's hard to resist a sweet husband who seems to desire your presence, even when you are less than lovely. I packed a lunch, and we followed the caravan across the desert highway to Borrego Springs and took the winding road out to the campground.

"Let's hike up to Palm Canyon before we unpack the lunches," one hiker suggested.

So I put one weary foot in front of the other and followed the crowd up the seemingly endless path that crisscrossed the hillside, up and up. Then the path turned abruptly toward a welcome oasis. Palm trees and huge rocks offered shade, while cupped in the center was a large pool of sparkling water, continually being refilled by a refreshing spray falling from the rocks and hillside above.

The children in our group shed shoes in no time at all and waded into the pool of water while the adults stood watching on the rocky edge. Oh, how I wanted to be a child that day instead of a middle-aged woman! I felt no kinship with the adults. I hadn't been talking to any of them for weeks.

As the children began to splash and play under the waterfall, shouting with the chill and the thrill of it, my inner child urged me on. Unnoticed, I removed my shoes and rolled up my pant legs and edged cautiously out into the water, nearer and still nearer the waterfall. Soon I was drenched in the cold spray of the falls, shrieking with the children, refreshed by the cleansing spray.

When the call to lunch was heard above the tumult of the falls, the children and I reluctantly climbed out of the pool.

"Now, don't you feel foolish?" scolded a prim and proper schoolteacher as I sat on a rock to dry my feet.

I grinned up at her sheepishly. "No," I responded honestly. "That water was just what I needed!"

My frolic in the waterfall did more than cool off my body. It cleansed me of the weary depression that had hounded me for weeks. Water—inside and outside—is God's way of cleansing, both physically and spiritually. Every day I ask God to cleanse me in the fountain of living water He has prepared for the healing of His chosen people—all who will take off their shoes and walk out into the waterfall.

CARROL JOHNSON SHEWMAKE

JUNE 10

Modeling

If you really knew me, you would know my Father as well. From now on, you do know him and have seen him. John 14:7, NIV.

*B*ut what good does this do?" quizzed one of the kids in the front row.

Being a very prepared teacher, I had a very complete reply: "What?"

"I mean, what good is it? What does all this stuff you're telling us have to do with now? How does it help us?" This child was very persistent!

I'm ashamed to say that the answer I gave then sounded a lot like "because I'm the grown-up and I say so, that's why!" But the question stuck. It nagged at the back of my brain for several weeks, and I was far from satisfied with my too-quick answer. Of course, there was a little ego involved here, too, a little pride. All week I'd studied the lesson, gathered the materials for the activity, and practiced it. The packet had been so complete, filled with helpful hints and suggestions as to how to catch the attention of restless preteens and teach them about God. I was prepared, enthusiastic, and ready for everything—except that question.

I committed myself to finding the answer. What help did these lessons give the kids on a weekly basis? Where did the rubber hit the road? Or did it? Was it just an exercise to keep the kids busy and corralled while the parents studied their lesson?

No, I didn't believe that. I'd gotten something out of all those lessons when I'd been sitting in their places. But what was it? To my horror, I realized that I could not recall a single specific lesson. I didn't remember the themes, the posters, the rewards for memorized texts, or the songs.

But I remembered my teachers. Every week they showed up. Sometimes they were boring; sometimes they weren't. Sometimes they were prepared; sometimes they weren't. But they were always there. I can still hear the voice of one of them when she prayed, so confident she was in addressing her very best Friend. It made me feel closer to God. Boundless energy and an upbeat outlook characterized another teacher. He was always looking for that next mountain to climb, sure that God would climb it with him. They all, with their various personalities and styles, impacted my life. Different names and different faces, but they all modeled before me a rich and living faith.

Maybe that was the answer. After all, Jesus walked this planet for 33 years; He didn't just show up at Calvary. He modeled before us for all time the perfect relationship with God. Maybe that's the good all this stuff I'm telling them does. Maybe that's how it helps them.

CHRISTINA ENNIS

On Looking Good

Do not store up for yourselves treasures on earth, . . . but store up for yourselves treasures in heaven. Matt. 6:19, NIV.

In preparation for this past weekend I trimmed the grass around the trees, weeded the flower beds, and vacuumed under the shrubs. My expected guest, unlike me, is an avid gardener. Her yard looks like a page from *Better Homes and Gardens*. As I clipped and cleaned and pondered my motivation, I just could not afford to let her see my yard in its natural state. What would she think of me?

My concern about what Anne thought about me led me to look at my motivation for doing other things. How much of my life is an attempt to *look good*? Does it make sense to do the right thing just to be seen? How do I go about changing my reasons for doing what I do? My ponderings led me to Scripture.

Trying to look good is nothing new. Jesus talked to the issue in the Sermon on the Mount. Acts of righteousness, merciful deeds, prayers, and fasting—all need to be done to God, for God. Jesus called those who do these things to be seen hypocrites and warned them that being seen would be their only reward. God could not take into consideration anything done merely to be seen. He could only accept an offering lovingly given by the right hand without the left hand's knowing about it. Read the whole passage in Matthew 6:1-18.

The punch line of Jesus' sermon on not doing things to look good comes in verses 19 through 21. The whole object of life is to live for God, to lay up treasure in heaven. Doing things to be seen is like putting treasure in a box where mildew and moths can attack it. Doing things as unto God puts our treasure—and our heart—in God's heavenly kingdom.

Paul gives some advice about looking good in Colossians 3:22-24. To slaves he writes, "Obey your earthly masters in everything; and do it, not only when their eye is on you and to win their favor, but with sincerity of heart and reverence for the Lord" (NIV). Agreed, I'm not a slave. But the principle is clear. What needs to be done deserves to be done well, and for the right reasons. "Whatever you do, work at it with all your heart, as working for the Lord, not for men," Paul concludes.

So I should trim my grass—fix that special dish, edit that article, or present that devotional—not for the approval of Anne or anyone else, but for the Lord. Easier said than done.

Given my natural human bent toward wanting to look good, how to do this? I must learn to evaluate my actions differently. I should not ask How well did I perform? Rather, I should ask Did my action benefit someone? And above all, I must ask Did my action honor my Lord and Saviour? I should not ask myself whether the editors will think well of me for what I have written; instead, I should pray that someone may benefit from it. And I must ask myself whether my writing will glorify my Jesus. After all, He's the one who deserves to look good.

Obviously, I've only begun to walk this new path. But I am committed to making Jesus, the wellspring of my joy, "first and last and best," offering to Him my love, adoration, and good deeds.

NANCY JEAN VYHMEISTER

JUNE 12

Stopping to Smell the Roses

My people will dwell in a peaceful habitation, in secure dwellings, and in quiet resting places. Isa. 32:18, NKJV.

I'm a very goal-oriented person. Give me a job to do, and I'll work at it and think about it until it's done. I'm like that when I'm hiking, too. Our family enjoys hiking at a place called Ricketts Glen in northern Pennsylvania. We go there because of the beautiful waterfalls along the trails. The last time we were hiking there with friends I realized I was so intent on the goal of getting to the top, and then getting back to the bottom, that I wasn't enjoying the beauty along the way. The waterfalls and beauty of springtime were going by unnoticed by me. We were supposed to be there to enjoy the scenery, not just to make it to the top and back to the bottom. If that was the only reason we were hiking, then we wouldn't have needed to drive so far.

I began thinking that maybe I'm like that in my spiritual walk, too. I'm so intent on my goals that I fail to notice the beauty along the way. I think God wants us to take time to rest, to enjoy our walk with Him each day. You can set a goal to spend a certain amount of time with God each morning, then be so focused on actually spending that much time that you don't enjoy it. Or you can become so involved in doing things for Him that you neglect spending time with Him. When we spend time, we may not feel as if we've accomplished anything. Yet we have. How else can you really get to know someone unless you spend time talking, listening, and finding out what he or she is like?

And so I'm in the process of change. I've committed myself to enjoying the beauty along the way more. I'm slowing my pace. I'm noticing the little things along the way. I'm letting the vacuuming go and going outside to play ball with the boys or plant flowers in my garden. I'm letting the computer rest so that I can follow my husband around in the evenings, talking with him about our day and our plans. I'm not trying to accomplish a million things for the Lord; I'm listening to Him. I'm waiting on Him. Resting in Him. I'm enjoying the beauty He created instead of rushing past it each day. I've realized that He made me to be a human being, not a human doing.

Funny thing is, I seem to have more time to get things done than before. I'm not rushing through everything and rushing everywhere. I feel more peaceful. More confident in Him. I guess that happens when we get to the place where we abide in the places He has created for us, instead of rushing past them.

How about you? Have you stopped to smell the roses today?

TAMI HORST

JUNE 13

Peace and Quiet

Mark the perfect man, and behold the upright: for the end of that man is peace. Ps. 37:37.

As soon as I sit down at the computer shrill screaming jars my ears. Our two little girls simultaneously cry "Mine!" as they squabble over a toy ball. The telephone rings. While on the phone I hear *kurplunk!* as the doll's stroller, stuffed with dirt and pebbles, hits the clean floor. I want to scream "Calgon, take me away!"

It is on one of those days when I can faintly hear Christ say to me, Julie, Julie, "you are worried and upset about many things, but only one thing is needed. Mary has chosen what is better, and it will not be taken away from her" (Luke 10:41, 42, NIV).

Oh, how I want to be more like Mary and choose what is better. I too want to sit at the feet of Jesus and receive peace and healing from the emotional and physical drain of life. I'm tired of my own worries and anxieties. I long to experience lasting peace.

We all have minor irritations that plague us every day. Perhaps it is dealing with rude drivers or impolite store clerks. Yet even in the midst of these, we can still realize the evidence of God's goodness through His created world. Hearing the rhythm of the crickets, playing peekaboo with a baby, and gazing at the stars on a crisp, cold night can cause minor irritations to fade.

Yes, we may find tranquillity on the mountaintop or in the beat of the ocean waves, but what about when the problem is not a lump in the pancake batter, but a lump in the breast? Peace is easy to find on a mossy mountaintop, but what about peace in the pediatric intensive care unit? What about peace at the funeral of a child, particularly when it is your own son? Can I be at peace no matter what my situation? These are the weightier issues when it comes to *peace* and *quiet* of the soul.

How can I have this lasting peace that transcends circumstances? Can I accomplish tasks of life as well as Martha, and still be like Mary by sitting at the feet of Jesus? My Lord says to me, "Peace I leave with you; my peace I give you. I do not give to you as the world gives. Do not let your hearts be troubled and do not be afraid" (John 14:27, NIV). Yes, I can have peace and quiet of soul even on a day of sorrow or disappointment. God will give me His peace in all of life's endeavors.

God has promised to give us this mind that was also in Christ Jesus, a new mind, along with a new type of peace. How liberating and freeing it is to learn how to leave all our plans and worries at the Saviour's feet and accept His peace and quiet for our lives.

JULIE REYNOLDS

JUNE 14

Silver

I will refine them like silver. Zech. 13:9, NIV.

*M*y friend Eric McKnight is a silversmith who deals mostly with the repair and cleaning of precious silver plate, ornaments, and jewelry. He is also frequently called upon to identify silver objects by their markings, which, to the expert eye, tell when and where an article was made and by whom. Equally astonishing is the way he can restore a battered old piece of silver into something shining and useful.

Silver is mentioned frequently in the Bible. Abraham owned a great deal of it and used some of it to pay for the plot of land on which he buried his wife Sarah (Gen. 23:16). King Solomon was probably the richest man who ever lived. The Bible tells us that during his reign silver in Jerusalem was as common as stones, so common he wouldn't use it in his palace, preferring gold instead (1 Kings 10:21).

And it was for 30 pieces of silver that Judas betrayed Jesus.

From the fifteenth to the nineteenth centuries most of the

world's silver came from Mexico. In 1859, however, the famous Comstock Lode was discovered in Nevada in the United States, the annual output of which amounted to around $11 million. Fourteen years later, in the same area, the Big Bonanza mine yielded even greater amounts of silver.

Nowadays, although silver is used extensively in dental and photographic procedures, few of us use it for eating or drinking, and even our coins are no longer made of it. Pure silver is too soft to withstand normal use, so it is generally alloyed with another metal, such as copper, to make it more durable, without altering its image in any way. It would be easy for an unscrupulous dealer to claim an article is made of pure silver when up to 50 percent of it could be of another base metal. Therefore, objects made of silver must undergo chemical testing, or "assaying," before they receive the mark "sterling," indicating the content is 925 parts per 1,000 pure silver.

Eric tells me the surest way to test for purity is by using nitric acid. One drop placed on silver will bubble and turn red. The purer the silver, the redder the acid becomes; more copper in the article, and the acid drip will turn green.

What if we could be "acid-tested"? Would we meet the standard of purity a true follower of Jesus should have? Do we appear to be of "sterling" quality when, in fact, we are mostly base metal? There is hope for us. By following Jesus closely and beholding His purity we can grow daily to be more like Him, the supreme pattern for His followers.

He is willing to change us into silver. Are we willing to let Him?

EDNA MAY OLSEN

JUNE 15

Realities Beyond

He will cover you with his feathers, and under his wings you will find refuge; his faithfulness will be your shield and rampart. Ps. 91:4, NIV.

*I*t was a rainy Saturday afternoon. While the adults met for Bible study the two friends played with dolls on the porch. Gathering their babies together, they set up house with the chairs and boxes that cluttered that small area. Busy at play, the girls never for a moment realized that inches away from their feet lay the strike of death.

We'll never know when it came, or why. Whatever the reason, the deadly black mamba now lay coiled away from sight beneath the metal job box that vivid childish imagination had transformed into an elegant dining table from which to serve afternoon tea.

If those of us who loved these little girls had known the danger they were in, our hearts would have stopped cold. But, unknowing, we talked and laughed, relaxed people who considered ourselves safe from the sudden strike of tragedy.

The tea party was winding to a close when a whining baby called a make-believe mother to the corner chair. She murmured soothing words as a gun-barrel-gray head slithered from under their table and caught her eye. Letting out a scream, two little girls scrambled onto the porch couch, yelling frantically to their big brothers inside. Bounding from the house and grabbing a shovel, the boys thrust at the protruding head, which immediately retreated, leaving a faint trail of blood. Weapons poised, they tensely moved the metal box and found the snake sufficiently beheaded to render it harmless. A couple more thrusts totally severed the head. Even so, as if possessed by a menacing spirit, the six-foot-long body continued to slither and coil for more than an hour, chilling us with its fatal potential, forcing us to feel a vulnerability unknown to us a few moments earlier.

There are times in life when illusions burn dim and ominous images lurking in the shadows threaten to emerge as reality. Having lived in Africa for several years without ever encountering a black mamba, we considered ourselves safe from their deadly threat. But in one startling incident that illusion shattered, and suddenly black mambas were an ominous reality that threatened our sense of security, even though, cornered and vulnerable, the snake did not strike.

While it is too simple to say that God's children are insulated from the glare of ominous realities, as Christians we become aware of realities beyond, realities that are rooted in the realm of faith and by which we live and rest. He promised He is with us always and His angels are camped round about, a reality so powerful that even the threatening shadows yield to the light. Though our illusions flicker and fade, we are not left to the shadows, but can live in the brightness of realities beyond. DEBORAH AHO

The Three Fathers

God has sent forth the Spirit of His Son into your hearts, crying out, "Abba, Father!" Gal. 4:6, NKJV.

*Y*esterday, I was your little girl . . .
chasing lightning bugs,
running bases,
learning to drive.
And you were there,
putting holes in mayonnaise jars,
taking us to Wrigley Field,
keeping air in the tires.
And though you weren't always there
to pick me up when I fell,
you probably were the one
who paid for the Band-Aid.
Where have the years gone?
My father, my daddy, my friend.

Today, we have a daughter . . .
As you lie on the floor with Zoe,
bumping heads, laughing,
I'm remembering always
when you first held her,
counting her fingers (there were 10!),
studying her, memorizing her.
Sometimes
when you're sleeping I'm seeing
the two of you bumping heads
in the future,
as only girls and daddies will,
But I know you'll be there for her,
patiently
teaching her the lessons of life;
firmly
correcting her;
gently
guiding her into womanhood.
We're walking the road of parenting together.

My husband, my lover, my friend.

Always, I've been Your child . . .
You smiled when I was conceived,
then nestled me in my mother's womb and
    whispered,
"That's good."
And just as I know You
gently caused my eyes, heart, bones, and lungs
to develop in the right way, at the right time,
I also now know
that events in my life that I consider
coincidental or catastrophic
are all part of a plan designed for me
alone,
unfolding in Your perfect time.
You're the only One who loves me the same,
Yesterday . . . today . . .
Unconditionally.
Eternally.
My Saviour, my Abba, my Friend.

EMILIE K. WINSTON CARTWRIGHT

JUNE 17

Perfect Peace

May the God of peace provide you with every good thing you
need in order to do his will, and may he, through Jesus Christ, do
in us what pleases him. And to Christ be the glory forever and
ever! Heb. 13:20, 21, TEV.

I could hear the words screaming around in my head as I lay
in bed, dreading the day ahead. Having three of my husband's
relatives stay with us for six weeks was getting to me. "It's all right
for him," I fumed. "He's off to work at 7:30 in the morning and
doesn't have to put up with them all day. He's got no idea what it's
like. They just want to laze around all day smoking and drinking
while I do all the cooking and cleaning. Lord, I need space. I need
time for myself. I can't take much more of this. I need *peace!*"

I picked up my morning devotional book. I hadn't looked at it for a while. I'd been too busy catering to the needs of our visitors. As I focused on the words in front of me God spoke to my heart. "May the God of peace provide you with every good thing you need in order to do his will, and . . . do in us what pleases him."

Then it hit me. I wasn't doing anything pleasing in God's sight. I wasn't reflecting Christ. My attitude toward our relatives exposed something that had slowly crept into my life—inconsistent communion with the Lord. How had I allowed that to happen? I, who was always spouting off about the necessity for daily communion with God.

My reaction to the stress of having people in my home whose lifestyle was totally inconsistent with mine had been to resort to self-pity and withdrawal rather than seeking help in dealing with the problem. Instead of praying more, reading the Word more, and seeking God's strength and guidance throughout this time, I fretted and fumed until the situation overwhelmed me. Praise the Lord for His patience! He managed to get through to me. I was allowing pressure and stress to crowd Him out. Rather than needing peace, I needed the *God* of peace.

Our visitors soon tired of sitting around doing nothing. They decided to see more of our beautiful country. Off they went for days at a time on bus tours, train trips, picnics; sometimes including me, and sometimes leaving me at home in peace. The six weeks flew past.

Problems become so much easier to deal with when we allow the Lord to be our partner in handling them. I thank God that our visitors left with happy memories and an image of Him untarnished by a grumpy Christian.   MURIEL L. MOULTRIE

JUNE 18

I Told Jesus He Could Change My Name

But now, thus says the Lord, who created you, O Jacob, and He who formed you, O Israel: "Fear not, for I have redeemed you; I have called you by your name; you are mine. Isa. 43:1, NKJV.

*O*ur names are important to us, perhaps because we feel they embody our personality, or because they have a special meaning. Sometimes names reflect a family history. I have friends whose names are distinctive because they are a legacy from a significant other—mother, grandmother, aunt, teacher, doctor—or a significant place. On the other hand, my cousin loves her name because no one else seems to have had it before she did. It makes her unique and is an excellent icebreaker.

It's fun to read the Bible, paying particular attention to the meaning—implicit or explicit—of the names. I enjoy reading those passages that record moments when angels appear to expectant mothers and name their children, giving them special significance. In my mind's eye I see mothers nurturing the genius of those special children, instilling in their young children the spirit to accomplish the task for which they were called. Samuel, "my gift from God." Barnabas, "son of encouragement."

Even more precious to me, though, are the passages that document a renaming for people who had a change of heart. Their new names broadcast to all the world that pristine focus. From Jacob to Israel, "father of the nations"; from Saul, the "vengeance-wreaking zealot," to Paul, "dynamic evangelist."

I like my name because my mother once told me how she selected it and what she hoped it would mean for me: "a person growing up under the shadow of God's love, brilliant, resilient, and sensitive." I often wonder what name I would choose for myself should I have need to change. Krystyan, perhaps?

Names, no matter how beautiful, are never as important as the persons who are called by them and the expectations they fulfill in the heart of God.

Thank You, Redeemer God, for a new name and a new heart. I am honored by the legacy inherent in my name. Give me the grace and courage to fulfill the expectations embedded in it. Thank You for giving us all a name that means chosen and loved by God.

GLENDA-MAE GREENE

JUNE 19

A Word About Weeds

The owner's servants came to him and said, "Sir, didn't you sow good seed in your field? Where then did the weeds come from?" "An enemy did this," he replied. Matt. 13:27, 28, NIV.

*E*arly in the summer there appeared in my flower border a crop of newcomers, seedlings I'd never noticed before and certainly hadn't planted. What could they be? Consulting a gardening manual, I came to a conclusion: "I've got about a dozen self-sown zucchini plants," I reported confidently to a gardening friend.

"Very unlikely," she said.

Some folk are just distrustful by nature, I decided, so I watered my new additions to the border, and they grew much bigger, almost overnight. After a week or so I thought I'd take one of them to my doubtful friend so she could share my crop. She inspected it closely, felt its leaves, then said in tones of one who has discovered something nasty, "Not zucchini. Borage. Pull them all up, or they'll overrun everything!"

Borage? What was borage doing in my garden? I'd never sown any. They really looked like zucchini to me, and zucchini was a favorite vegetable in our household. So I flew in the face of wisdom and kept watering. Soon they were much taller, and clearly not what I had anticipated. But deep-blue flowers had begun to emerge. Very pretty. A shame to dig them up, so I thinned them. But by the time we returned from a short holiday, borage had taken over the border, and flowers that had once bloomed there had disappeared. Then I found a fellow victim.

Another gardening neighbor had had a very attractive bed of pansies back in the spring. One day when we were talking flowers I asked her how they were doing.

"Come and see," she said.

There was not a pansy in sight. Just a jungle of borage. So she'd been fooled too!

This wasn't a case of sowing bad seed, but neglecting to recognize weeds and root them out. You can see what happened. We thought they were something else. We were fooled by the flowers, and when we decided to act, it was too late.

In our lives the enemy aims to sow weeds. Let's make sure we don't cultivate them.

PEGGY MASON

JUNE 20

Making Memories With God

The voice of my beloved! Behold, he comes, . . . bounding over the hills. . . . "Arise, my love, my fair one, and come away. . . . The flowers appear on the earth, the time of singing has come. . . . Arise, my love, my fair one, and come away." S. of Sol. 2:8-13, RSV.

I am my beloved's, and his desire is for me. S. of Sol. 7:10, RSV.

*D*o you remember times during your dating days when you just sat silently with your boyfriend? Words weren't so important; you just savored being close. Or maybe as a parent your little child is playing, stops for a moment to crawl into your lap, snuggles close, and then is off again.

I've discovered that I need this same closeness with God. So I've started getting up 30 minutes earlier each morning to enjoy solitude with Him. Not primarily to pray to God or to praise Him, but just to relish His presence.

The house is still when I awaken. After a refreshing shower, I settle into my comfortable chair for this special time with God. Closing my eyes and clearing my mind of all distractions, I focus on sensing His presence. In my mind I envision us meeting—it's usually a different place every morning. Sometimes we walk hand in hand through a flowering meadow, or chase after flitting butterflies. Sometimes we settle in on a mountaintop overlooking majestic peaks and lush, green valleys. Sometimes we enjoy the still solitude of a cave. Sometimes a beach.

This morning we met at a playground. Now, a playground is not my typical place to spend time—with people or with God. My usual devotional experience for the past two decades has been in the form of reading. It's been important, and I've learned a lot. Yet it has fed my head more than my heart. I want to make memories with God now. Vivid, warm, special memories. I want to sense His presence, feel His love.

The playground. We have the place to ourselves. Arm in arm we walk around the lily-pad-covered pond. Ducks quack for our attention, so we stop to feed them. Their feathers are so soft to my touch. We wander over to the swing sets, where God offers to push me. I haven't been in a swing for years. Higher and higher I swing, almost reaching the tree branches, where shafts of light shimmer on dancing leaves. It's a glorious morning for us, just God and me. He envelops me in His attention. I melt in His smile. Words are not important; I just savor being in His presence. There's time to walk and talk later, to petition, to discuss problems, to study. But for now I just want to bask in His love.   HEIDE FORD

Guilty as Charged

Who is my accuser? Let him confront me! It is the Sovereign Lord
who helps me. Isa. 50:8, 9, NIV.

*L*ast Friday afternoon my husband came in from washing the
car. "I don't know how in the world that scratch got onto the
door of the car!"

Immediately my stomach flipped and my heart pounded, and
any hope of looking innocent faded as color rushed to my face.
"Well, don't look at me. I didn't put it there! Honest!" I was innocent, but even to me, I sounded guilty. I hate it, the automatic guilt
I feel when something is wrong, even if there is no way I could have
caused the problem.

It happens whenever I visit the dentist. The dentist pokes
around at my teeth and hits a tender spot. I jump. "Ah, a little cav-
ity there. Have you been flossing regularly?"

"Yes, of course, every evening. At least I try to. I mean, sometimes I am in a situation where I . . . [gulp]."

Another familiar scenario: I am in the office when one of the re-
ceptionists yells "Who took my pen?"

Instantly, I feel everyone's eyes on me. Flushed with embarrassment, I shake my head and hold up my hands to prove I don't have
the missing pen. At times I've even been known to reply "I'm sorry"
when someone remarks "It's raining."

My elder daughter, Rhonda, calls this my desire to "play God"—
that somehow or another I feel the need to keep the world operat-
ing smoothly, and that if I try hard enough I can make everything
right. She may be partly correct. However, I would rather call the
tendency to shoulder the world's guilt a "motherhood complex." It
surfaces with the first labor pain, I think, and grows with each
grunt, groan, and whimper the newborn makes.

Beyond my "God or motherhood complex," why do I feel guilty?
Because at times I am guilty. "For all have sinned, and come short
of the glory of God" (Rom. 3:23). Sometimes my guilt tells me that
I need to get right with my Father. Other times, however, this guilt
is not from God, but comes directly from Satan. He and his little
imps love to dump sludge into the stream of love flowing through
my life. They delight in making mud pies of my peace and splatter
filth and muck on all my joy. But good news, they're losing! Less

and less of their swill is sticking. It's as if the Holy Spirit is coating me with a healthy Scotchguard.

Day by day God is teaching me to see the difference between my sins against Him and my mistakes as a human being. He's helping me to discern the things I can correct and trust Him to deal with the things beyond my scope. Day by day He's teaching me to claim His grace and His love that washes away my guilt and makes me white as snow. And when I'm tempted to take on guilt that isn't rightfully mine, I can claim Isaiah's word, "Who is my accuser? Let him confront me! It is the Sovereign Lord who helps me."   KAY D. RIZZO

JUNE 22

Miracle on the Mountain

"Where is your faith?" he asked his disciples. In fear and amazement they asked one another, "Who is this? He commands even the winds and the water, and they obey him." Luke 8:25, NIV.

I was enjoying the summer as camp ranger on Casper Mountain in Wyoming. Fire danger was extremely high, and our group was desperate for rain when the clouds began to roll in. We praised the Lord with each rumble of rolling thunder, telling us that rain was on the way. However, when the storm blew over and the rain didn't come, we were all very discouraged.

That evening we were paid a surprise visit from Ben, our friend from the county parks department. We invited him in, wondering what brought him out so late. "Lightning has struck and a fire is burning out of control," he announced. "It's headed up the mountain toward your camp." He left, saying he would keep in touch in case we needed to evacuate.

At midnight the phone rang. "A breeze is blowing toward you," Ben warned, "and the fire is crowning in the treetops and still climbing up the mountainside."

Would the fire come into Mills Spring Camp? Would camp meeting, just a week away, have to be canceled? We prayed, imploring the Lord to send rain and save His camp from destruction.

We decided to hike out to the cliffs about a half mile from camp to observe the impending fire. As we walked across the thirsty meadow and into the darkness of the trees, dead pinecones and needles crunched beneath our feet. We again asked the Lord to save His camp. From our vantage point we stared awestruck at the sight of the blazing fire. It was still about a mile away, but the gentle wind was blowing the raging inferno toward us.

My husband raised his hands to heaven and prayed as the fire and smoke billowed upward. "Lord, this is *Your* camp. Your people will be gathering here next week. You control the wind and the rain. Please, send rain and save Your camp!"

We didn't expect what happened next. The wind started to blow furiously! We had to sit down on the rocks to keep from being blown off the cliff. We expected rain, but we were getting wind. Then we understood. The wind was blowing into the fire, forcing it back. We were elated as we witnessed a miracle! As we praised the Lord for the wind, we noticed that we were getting wet. While the Lord pushed the fire back with the wind, He dampened the ground with rain.

About an hour later we returned to our cabin. The wind continued to blow throughout the night, and by noon the next day the fire was out. Mills Spring Camp was saved! We thanked the Lord for allowing us to witness the miracle on the mountain.

CAROL GILLHAM

JUNE 23

Our Little Bundle of Love

In my distress I called to the Lord; I cried to my God for help. From his temple he heard my voice; my cry came before him, into his ears. Ps. 18:6, NIV.

Kathia grew bigger, fatter, and prettier every day. When she was 3 months old she started smiling. At 6 months she had teeth. But she was a little bit too slow in turning around in her crib. When the time came for her to start speaking, the words wouldn't come out as we expected. After her first year she could say only "Mommy" and "Daddy." She started crawling at 11 months and walked with difficulty at 2 years. She started having panic crises that shook her little body and set my heart to pounding very painfully.

I decided she needed help. But money was short, so I took her to a free institution two or three times a week for treatment. But it didn't work, although I persisted for two years. Then I thought, *Let Kathia be Kathia.*

Eventually many neurologists and a psychiatrist determined what caused the convulsions when she was very afraid. Now she takes medicine to control the electricity of her brain. Learning has become less difficult. A psychologist, an occupational therapist, a music therapist, and a teacher are working with her to help her reach her capacity.

She goes to school with normal children, and her little friends take turns helping her with her schoolwork. Kathia is happy, loved, and cherished by her friends and family.

Why am I telling you our story? Because only God knows how many mothers around the world are just like me, lost in the unknown world of an exceptional child. And, like me, asking God why, how, when, or where.

To you, mothers of these little (or maybe big) bundles of love, I say, "The Lord watches over you. . . . The Lord will watch over your coming and going both now and forevermore" (Ps. 121:5-8, NIV).

When you're not able to discern between to-do's and don'ts, fall on your knees and pray, "Show me the way I should go, for to you I lift up my soul" (Ps. 143:8, NIV). Do what your heart asks you to do. Try to live one day at a time. "Let the morning bring me word of your unfailing love, for I have put my trust in you" (verse 8, NIV).

Tears may fall, anger may arise, along with doubt, guilt, rebellion, and loneliness, but God knows that you are only a human being. He's patient and waits until you have digested the reality. The time will come when our children will run about healthy, happy, and perfect. That time is very near. CHARLOTTE FERMUM HESSA

JUNE 24

My Perfect Way

He maketh my way perfect. 2 Sam. 22:33.

You have to admit that you can't do much better than perfect! When I first read this text about the Lord making my way perfect, I must confess that I was pretty skeptical. You see, I came from a less than perfect home. My parents fought all the time, and when my mom began to fear for our lives, they finally divorced. My mother later remarried, and my stepfather liked me until he married Mom; then I became the "chore girl."

When I was 13 Mom had to send me away because I couldn't

live in their home anymore. I was left in a town I had never seen before, with people I had never met, living a life I didn't know much about. Thankfully, I had the ability to make friends and be happy anywhere, and by the time I graduated from eighth grade I decided to stay in the school dorm for the next four years until I finished high school. I worked my way through boarding school doing all sorts of jobs, but somehow it was fun, and I made many new friends. The staff were wonderful to me, and I met Jesus and accepted Him into my life. I also met my husband of 41 years there.

Yes, there have been troublesome times in our lives—my serious car accident, losing our home and its contents to fire, and, worst of all, losing our son. But I can still say with all confidence that God has made my way perfect.

Before you think I've lost it, let me explain. God doesn't define "perfect" just the way we humans do. I believe His definition is "whatever it takes to bring me through to the kingdom and to help others along the way." You see, if I never had any trials, I could not be so understanding of others. Through all the trials He has been there with me, and I have become ever closer to Him. I know He is preparing an eternal home for me right now.

Can my way be made much more perfect than that? When things don't seem perfect by your definition of the word, think again. You might be pleasantly surprised.

ANNA MAY RADKE WATERS

JUNE 25

God's Sparrows

Are not two sparrows sold for a farthing? and one of them shall not fall on the ground without your Father.... Fear ye not therefore, ye are of more value than many sparrows. Matt. 10:29-31.

J stopped dead in my tracks as my eyes caught sight of it lying on the grass beside the sidewalk. My 9-year-old heart was moved with compassion as I knelt down to examine the small bird. It was still and cold. Picking up its lifeless form, I gently laid it in my lunch pail and carefully carried it home.

Funeral arrangements were quickly made, with a shoe box coffin and a shallow grave in the empty lot next door. Calling a few friends together, I held a solemn service and with all due respects laid the tiny sparrow to rest.

The Bible tells us that not even one sparrow falls to the ground without God's noticing it (Matt. 10:29). He is a personal God who cares for each of the creatures He has made. But the love He has for you and me is far more intense than for any of His other creatures. We are immensely more valuable than many sparrows.

God notices when you are happy, cheerful, and bubbly. He also notices when you are hurting, lonely, and depressed. He knows everything there is to know about you, as if you were the only one on this earth. And He loves you with an everlasting love that is far above human understanding. So if He can use a little child to care for a lifeless sparrow, He has a thousand more ways to care for you, one who was made in His own image and redeemed by the blood of His only Son.

When you are tempted to worry because of circumstances in your life, read the following favorite quotation:

"Worry is blind, and cannot discern the future; but Jesus sees the end from the beginning. In every difficulty He has His way prepared to bring relief. Our heavenly Father has a *thousand ways to provide for us,* of which we know nothing. Those who accept the one principle of making the service and honor of God supreme will find perplexities vanish, and a plain path before their feet" (*The Desire of Ages,* p. 330; italics supplied).   NANCY CACHERO VASQUEZ

JUNE 26

Of Raincoats and Trials

The hand of our God is upon all those for good who seek Him. Ezra 8:22, NKJV.

It was pouring rain. Again. My husband, brother, and I had spent days paddling across raindrop-rippled lakes, portaging slick trails through rain-drenched foliage, and coaxing cooking fires from rain-soaked wood. Our long-anticipated canoe trip seemed overshadowed with rain clouds.

On previous trips to the canoe country of northern Minnesota and neighboring Ontario we'd averaged about one rainy day a week. We had waterproof packs, rain flies for the tents, and plastic tarps, just in case. This year both men had purchased brand-new rain suits—waterproof hooded jackets and pants that protected them head to ankle.

I, on the other hand, had decided to be frugal. The calf-length, ill-fitting, heavy, rubberized yellow slicker I already had would do for three or four drizzly days. My frugality would have proved foolish and resulted in a miserable trip if it had succeeded. A few days before our departure, though, I dropped by a resale shop in a neighboring town. When I turned to leave I noticed—a rain suit! Looking it over, I discovered the used outfit was in good condition and cost only $5. The jacket and pants fit perfectly, and I left the store pleased with my bargain find.

By the end of our canoe trip that unusually wet, cool summer, I knew how providential that find was. Our 21-day trip included only four days *without* rain. My Father had known I would need full, comfortable protection. And He provided it for an affordable price.

Isn't that just like Him? He foresees trials that lie in our paths ahead. No, He doesn't always prepare a detour around them. We may be subjected to a downpour of trouble. But He's already helped us equip ourselves for hardship and offered the protection of His presence.

More than that, He brings a special blessing from each trial. On our rainy journey He displayed a splendorous array of rainbows plentiful enough to fill a photo album.

KATHLEEN STEARMAN PFLUGRAD

JUNE 27

Why This Waste?

He went away sad, because he had great wealth. Mark 10:22, NIV.

Then Mary took about a pint of pure nard, an expensive perfume; she poured it on Jesus' feet and wiped his feet with her hair. And the house was filled with the fragrance of the perfume. John. 12:3, NIV.

What a contrast! Christ gave the rich young ruler the ultimate test: "'Go, sell everything you have and give to the poor, and you will have treasure in heaven. Then come, follow me.' . . . He went away sad, because he had great wealth" (Mark 10:21, 22, NIV).

Then there's Mary. She broke an alabaster jar of pure nard and poured the entire contents on Jesus' feet.

Prudence versus extravagance. Forethought versus madness. Or is there another view?

When the ruler saw Jesus blessing the children he was impressed. He had never seen so much attention lavished on children. Perhaps Jesus could bless him, too. He felt somewhat defective. Perhaps Jesus could make up for what he lacked. He sincerely believed that he kept all of God's commandments, but something was missing.

Jesus loved him. He valued him. He wanted more than anything to give him eternal wealth. He would reveal the man's weakness. "Go, sell everything you have and give to the poor," He said (verse 21, NIV).

It was too much. His wealth. His position in the Sanhedrin. Give it up? Live a life of uncertainty? Poor, powerless, despised as Christ's follower? He went away sad. He had great wealth. Great wealth indeed! While wise, he was a fool.

In contrast, imagine a party. All the town leaders sit huddled around the table in muted conversation. Here comes Mary, uninvited, hunched over, not daring to look at the dignitaries. She weeps at Jesus' feet. She slides a milky-white vase of pure nard from under her robe. Then she does the unthinkable—she breaks it. The fragrance fills the room and on a wisp of the wind, is gone forever. Or is it?

Before she broke the vase, Mary, like the ruler, had something of great wealth. But in Christ she saw the eternal wealth. She had received from Him love and forgiveness, and her gift was nothing by comparison. She held nothing back. She gave all. She risked all. In the presence of critical Pharisees she broke her vase and let its fragrance fly. She wept unabashedly, kissing His feet and wiping them with her hair.

Then a murmur. "Why this waste?" *Why this waste?* Jesus could not believe His ears.

Mary looked hopefully into Jesus' eyes. He understood. He accepted her gift, not only the nard, but her heart. "She has done a beautiful thing to me," He said. "I tell you the truth, wherever this gospel is preached . . . what she has done will also be told, in memory of her" (Matt. 26:10, 13, NIV).

Reckless extravagance? Mary was no fool. She gave everything to gain the eternal wealth. The young ruler? He kept everything, only to lose it all. KAREN LINDENSMITH

JUNE 28

No Fear

There is no fear in love; but perfect love casteth out fear: because fear hath torment. He that feareth is not made perfect in love. 1 John 4:18.

The gray fingers of dawn slowly drew back the curtain of the night, and a reluctant sun bade the day to begin. This was my signal to unwrap the mummy-like coverings from my head and rejoin the world of the living.

Afraid of the darkness of the night, I had lain terror-struck, certain that the sounds and sights that menaced the darkness bode me ill. I wrapped myself so tightly in the bedclothes that my family feared I would suffocate.

This is not the story of *one* night, but of nearly *every* night of my childhood and adolescence. My parents tried in vain to solve my situation, even allowing me to sleep with one, or both, of them. A night-light wasn't the answer, because I found the darkness outside my room and window to be menacing. Even into my adulthood, when my husband had to be away at night, I literally froze at the horror of being alone in the darkness. Self-talk and prayer didn't seem to make a difference.

In reading Scripture I was struck by how often the Holy Spirit admonished "be not afraid" or "fear not."

One day while reading my Bible I encountered Revelation 21:8. "But the *fearful*, and unbelieving, and the abominable, and murderers, and whoremongers, and sorcerers, and idolaters, and all liars, shall have their part in the lake which burneth with fire and brimstone: which is the second death."

Wow! Like a lightning bolt out of the blue that text brought me to attention in a hurry! Was this text saying that I, with my fearfulness, was sinning as seriously as those who were lying, murdering, and whoring?

When God commands us to fear not, He also tells us to be strong and of good courage. The request for courage and trust in God now became the focus of my prayer. What a difference this specific request made!

A few years ago I would never have believed that I would have the strength and courage to live alone, not only in the daylight, but in the deepest midnight. I praise God daily for giving me the courage to trust Him.

I live alone and I love it. Fear no longer haunts me. It is so wonderful that God has accomplished this miracle in my life.

JAYNE DOSWELL DARBY

JUNE 29

My Father

Rise up and help us; redeem us because of your unfailing love.
Ps. 44:26, NIV.

*L*ife with two active little guys, 22 months apart, was a hectic whirlwind! Oh, how much fun were these little blond cherubs who could get their heads together and come up with the craziest ideas for mischief to explore! Along with all the fun came many bumps and scrapes—elbows, knees, and hands were always getting "hurts" that Mommy would kiss away. Within a few minutes they would be on their merry way again, forgetting the tears and pain.

One evening as I was preparing dinner, my oldest, then about 4, came running into the kitchen. All out of breath and full of laughter and fun, he came up to me and wrapped his little arms around my legs and squeezed me with all his might. Looking down into that precious face ringed with blond curls, my heart melted within me.

"Oh, Mommy, I *love* you!" he panted.

I wonder how God must feel as He looks down upon me, His precious daughter. Does He shake His head in amazement at the craziest situations in which I find myself involved? Does He wonder just what will be the next predicament I get myself into? Does His heart ache over my losing sight of His will for me and going my own way?

Most important, when I realize my inability to live without Him to guide me, and I become all bruised and battered from the messes I've created, I come to Him in prayer. Wrapping my arms around His legs, I call up to Him, "Oh, my Father, I love You! Hear my prayer and grant me Your forgiveness." I'm so thankful His heart melts within Him and He extends His loving arms to me to pick me up, dust me off, and set me back on the right track.

Lord, by Your grace, help me leave a legacy of faith and trust in You.

CAROL BRACKETT

Peace Despite a Storm

You will keep him in perfect peace, whose mind is stayed on You, because he trusts in You. Isa. 26:3, NKJV.

*A*fter six months as volunteer missionaries, my husband and I left Sri Lanka for Bangkok, Thailand. While waiting in the airport for our connecting flight, I said to him, "I think I'll write in my diary these 30 minutes before the flight."

Suddenly I couldn't write. I tried again. No better. I looked up. Everything seemed blurry. A strange, numb feeling crawled from my right foot up my leg and into my arm. Dizziness and nausea overwhelmed me. With great effort I formed the words.

"Something's wrong with me." I held up my right hand and felt hundreds of "pins and needles" stabbing it. Slowly I described how I felt.

"Maybe we should go to the Bangkok Adventist Hospital, but it's about 40 miles away. If this is a stroke, it could be followed by another one," Jay said.

I stood up and tried to walk, but lost my balance and fell to one side. He caught me. My right leg felt 20 pounds heavier, but I could move it with great effort.

"Let's pray for wisdom and guidance." Jay had just finished his prayer when they called the plane. "What shall we do?" he asked.

"I want to go home! We'd be almost to Tokyo before we could get a taxi to Bangkok Hospital. Please, let's go home! Jesus will help us."

We let everyone else board, then Jay took all the carry-on luggage. Using an umbrella in my left hand to steady me, I held on to him with my right arm. Walking like a drunk, I stumbled through the jetway. I almost fell lifting my foot into the plane, but God helped me stagger to our three seats by the window. After we took off, I laid my head in Jay's lap.

The steward provided a wheelchair when we changed planes in Tokyo. Because the passenger load to San Francisco was light, I stretched out on five seats for the entire flight. Except for vomiting, I lay quietly. I couldn't sleep because of the strange, creepy feelings on my right side, but every time I opened my eyes I imagined Jesus holding me close in His arms. As I talked with Him I felt the comfort of His presence. All those long hours as we soared over that vast ocean I rested in His promises.

"Fear not; I promised you perfect peace. Trust Me, and don't be concerned about your life. I'll give you whatever you need. I am with you. I'll strengthen and help you, and hold you with My right hand."

He filled me with joy and peace so that I felt no worry or fear. Totally dependent on God and others, I felt content to let Jesus manage my future. He has blessed me in a marvelous way through the months of recovery, continuing that perfect peace He promised.

EILEEN E. LANTRY

JULY 1

Influence

The tongue that brings healing is a tree of life. Prov. 15:4, NIV.

I recently attended a family reunion. What a joy it was for family members to reconnect after lengthy separations! To touch hands, see a familiar smile, and hear laughter that stirred distant memories.

It was such an inspiration to see 70- and 80-year-old great-aunts and uncles singing and bearing testimony of God's faith, fullness, and love. Hearing these matriarchs and patriarchs testify of their determination to remain true to God strengthened my own determination to fight the good fight and renewed my courage. What these dear ones spoke and how they spoke had a tremendous effect on me.

This experience made me want to stop and consider the type of influence my life has on those around me. Do my words inspire hope and courage in others? Or are people cringing as I stomp my way through their lives? Is my influence one that God can bless? Or is it a breath of death to an already discouraged soul?

I was thrilled to receive a few of my great-grandfather's inspirational books. That they were published in 1904 only adds to their special charm. When I got them home and opened them I discovered that Great-grandfather Brown had written his name in them and had underlined numerous paragraphs and phrases throughout the volumes. That means that I can know my great-grandfather a bit by reading those things that held special significance for him.

A book we all have is the Bible. It is our heavenly Father's book. His name is written on every line, and He means it to be a letter of love to each one of us. In it He reminds us that He made us. He tells us that He died for us, intercedes for us, and will be coming to take us home, where we belong. The Lord wants us to know that He has made His power available to us. He will empower His children to be and to do in fulfillment of our divine destiny.

Dramatic things can happen while doing the seemingly insignificant. A captain's wife called for her little maid one day, as she had many times before, and found healing for her husband. Pharaoh's daughter went to have her bath in the river and found Israel's deliverer.

By God's grace our lives can be used to accomplish great good. We may never draw a baby from the Nile, but if we are willing, God will use us as channels of blessing to the women around us.

Today, whether or not we consciously choose to influence others, we will.   JOELLA BROWN DAVIS

JULY 2

If I Had Been God

For God so loved the world that He gave His only begotten Son, that whoever believes in Him should not perish but have everlasting life. John 3:16, NKJV.

I'm not sure if it's pneumonia," the doctor told me. "I want you to take him to the hospital for an X-ray."

I gathered my 9-month-old baby into my arms and pressed him against my chest to still the pounding in my heart. Pneumonia? Wasn't that really bad for little babies? He just didn't look that sick. He wasn't eating well and threw up a lot when he coughed. It sounded like radio static when he breathed, but he was still playing and laughing.

We waited in the lonely hallway at the hospital for more than 45 minutes. Josh had missed his morning nap and his breakfast, but he wasn't fussy. He watched nurses and orderlies hustle past us while I held him and worried.

I had expected that they would let me stay near my son, but I had to wait behind a partition while they set up to take the X-ray. They strapped him into a plastic sleeve with his little arms over his head and turned him to face a wall. Agonizing moments passed like entire lifetimes. Not knowing what they were doing to him and afraid because he couldn't see me, Josh started to cry, and I joined him. To keep myself from rushing out there and snatching him out of that contraption, I stood behind the partition and hugged my arms around myself so hard it made them hurt.

Finally it was over, and they unstrapped the plastic sleeve to free him. When I pulled him into my arms, he buried his face into my shoulder as I cried and shook.

"It's OK," the technician said. "It didn't hurt him."

"I know, I know," I told her. But it had hurt me.

They left to process the X-rays, and as I held my son, my only son, I felt a rush of love wash over me as I have never known before. "O, Lord, what have You done to me?" I breathed. "How can I love someone so much?"

I realized in that instant that if I had been God, I wouldn't have sent my only Son into a cruel place like earth to be beaten, mistreated, misunderstood, and killed. If I had been God, humans would have been on their own, left to figure their own way out of the predicament they had gotten themselves into. If I had been God, nothing could have convinced me otherwise.

I'm glad I was not God. CELESTE PERRINO WALKER

JULY 3

Nature's Surprises

For since the creation of the world God's invisible qualities—his eternal power and divine nature—have been clearly seen, being understood from what has been made, so that men [and women] are without excuse. Rom. 1:20, NIV.

More and more I have come to see that God reveals Himself in nature if we but view with spiritual, as well as physical, eyes. What delightful surprises God has prepared for us in nature!

One summer I went camping in the mountains with my daughter and two granddaughters, ages 4 and 6. We started out the first morning to explore the terrain around the camp, walking slowly, savoring the mountain air and the beauty around us. As we crested a small hill, I looked ahead and gasped. The ground before us was carpeted in purple, a vast expanse of small violets pressed together.

Four-year-old Kimi squealed in delight. Dropping my hand, she ran up the path. As the rest of us quickly followed, we saw small Kimi drop to her knees among the flowers.

"Our dear heavenly Father," Kimi prayed aloud, "thank You for giving us these beautiful little flowers!"

A patch of purple flowers, the eager response of a child—two of nature's delightful surprises—started off a camping trip that fulfilled our every expectation. Actually, I think every trip into nature should be taken with a child! Only a child views life with the proper eager expectancy.

Look today for God's surprises. Look through the eyes of an expectant child.　　　　　　　　　　　　　CARROL JOHNSON SHEWMAKE

JULY 4

Happy Dependence Day!

Trust in the Lord with all thine heart; and lean not unto thine own understanding. In all thy ways acknowledge him, and he shall direct thy paths. Prov. 3:5, 6.

No, the title is not a typo. The word shouldn't be "independence."

It's true that today in the United States we are celebrating our country's independence. The desire for independence is not new. There's emphasis on independent thinking. We are encouraged to assert our independence, and many, if not all, long to be financially independent. This desire for independence can even carry over into our spiritual life.

Over and over I have struggled to do the right things, to live as I believed the Lord would want me to. After making my plans, I'd then ask the Lord for guidance. In reality, I guess, I was asking Him to bless what I had decided to do. Then I read today's text one recent morning and began to understand anew the total dependence I had to have on the Lord.

Trust in the Lord.

Contrary to the direction and dictates of the world, I can't depend on my own understanding and limited vision. Instead, I must trust in the Lord, acknowledging my dependence on Him, being assured that He will direct me.

So today, and every day, I am celebrating my dependence day— for I depend on Him. You can do the same. Happy Dependence Day!
　　　　　　　　　　　　　　　　　　　　MAXINE WILLIAMS ALLEN

JULY 5

A Busy Woman

Many women do noble things, but you surpass them all. Prov. 31:29, NIV.

This career woman went to market . . .
This resourceful woman stayed home . . .
This balanced woman did both, *and* had children . . .
This fulfilled woman chose to have none . . .
And this undecided woman learned from the four and rejoiced all the way home.

We can gain so much by learning from other Christian women. Think about the women you know—each one unique, devoted to her trade, her home, her family, her Lord. We need to look at one another with multidimensional vision, because women are no longer expected to be one-dimensional—a mother, a working mother, a single career woman, a single working mother. Yes, we have these titles, and so much more. God is using us in all these capacities.

That a woman chooses a career outside the home *and* rears a Christian family, or chooses to forgo external career aspirations and stays home to raise godly children, is what lends to the experience of learning from and affirming one another.

Let's appreciate one another's circumstances, choices, and talents; let's encourage one another in Christ Jesus. No matter what we endeavor to accomplish, we'll do it for His honor and His purpose. We'll better understand and appreciate one another and be richer for it. ROSALYNDA "GINI" KOSINI

JULY 6

Hope for Happier Days

Happy is he that hath the God of Jacob for his help, whose hope is in the Lord his God. Ps. 146:5.

I really did not look forward to church. With three squirming, wiggly boys 3 years old and younger and a pastor/husband up front, I had what I considered to be an overwhelming job.

On this particular day we had to travel 30 miles south to a new company that was meeting in a very small church. Knowing the boys would need to unwind after the ride, I decided to carry the baby and walk the other two around the block. They still didn't seem ready to settle down, so I decided another trip around the block might make it easier for me to make it through the next hour.

When we entered the church, I fervently prayed that the back row would not be taken so the boys' antics would be less disturbing, but sadly I discovered the whole pew was filled. I had no choice but to sit in the next row up. The preliminaries were under way when we settled in, but it wasn't long until my worst fears were realized. The two older boys, even though sitting one on either side of me, were creating quite a stir. One was peeking over the back of the pew, making faces at the people behind, while the other one was down on the floor getting attention.

The books and soft toys I had brought held no interest for them, and there was no mother's room. So I took the only option open to me and left for another walk around the block. During that walk I poured out my heart to the Lord. I questioned why He had given me such an overwhelming handful of bubbling energy to cope with. I really didn't seem competent to handle the job. Stress was building up inside, and I wondered how I could go back and get anything out of the service.

With leaden steps I again entered the church and heard the opening song being announced. As I turned to the page and began to sing "O God, our help in ages past, our hope for years to come, our shelter from the stormy blast, and our eternal home!" my mind whirled. I realized that I was trying to keep those hyperactive boys in line by myself. I had planned everything I could think of to cut down on their misbehavior, but I really hadn't spent enough time leaning on the greatest Help available to me.

Instead of chafing under their boundless energy, I suddenly realized God could guide me in channeling this energy into useful avenues of service for Him. I wanted model children, but I realized God would help me to endure with serenity the sometimes impatient glaring of the "saints" when things were rough. I knew now that God would be not only my help through the rest of that church service, but also my "hope for [all the] years to come."

DONNA LEE SHARP

JULY 7

Just Like a Child

Let the little children come to me, and do not hinder them, for the kingdom of God belongs to such as these. Mark 10:14, NIV.

*S*leepily I brushed my teeth, wondering what I was doing awake on a holiday morning at 7:00. Then I remembered we were going to have an early game of badminton with the young people of our church. Suddenly I was jolted into life by the bathroom door swinging open.

There stood my two daughters. One was sniffling loudly while tears rolled down her cheeks. The other one stood with her hands on her hips, her face indignant, yet slightly worried. I knew she was the cause of my other daughter's distress, which was getting more and more dramatic as her oppressor stated her defense.

They had had an argument. I had been the cause of it, she said, by asking each of them to fill a bottle of water for the trip. They argued over who should fill which bottle! In anger the indignant one had stubbed the toe of the other one, who refused to give up the bottle that she considered rightfully hers.

I responded as most mothers do when they are in a rush. I yelled at them! The indignant one was told in a loud and assertive voice that violence never solves anything. The sniffling daughter, who by now was wearing a smile of satisfaction, was told in an equally loud voice that she was not to touch her sister's bottle. I told them to sort out their differences before the whole day was ruined, and firmly shut the bathroom door.

A few minutes later as I splashed cold water on my face, I was interrupted by another knock on the door. As I am not my best early in the morning, I opened the door muttering threats that if there was another problem with which to deal . . . There stood my daughters. This time they had their arms around each other and their faces were beaming. With pride they told me that they had apologized to each other and had shaken hands and hugged. As they scampered off I couldn't help feeling sad that adults are unable to behave like children when it comes to resolving conflicts.

I am sure it would warm God's heart if we could have the same attitude as a child when it comes to being friends with our supposed enemies. A child seems to be able to say "I'm sorry," "I was wrong," or "I made a mistake" much quicker than adults, who prefer pride to humility. Children seem eager to put away the cause of their differences, whereas adults view principle more important than relationships.

Children seem to possess short-term memories. Once a conflict is over, they will rarely refer to it again. As adults we tend to repeat our hurtful experiences to anyone who will listen. Maybe we need to pray for a childlike spirit toward those who cause us heartaches.

MARY BARRETT

I Wonder

And the Lord said unto Satan, Hast thou considered my servant Job, that there is none like him in the earth, a perfect and an upright man, one that feareth God, and escheweth evil? Job 1:8.

Of all the Bible characters, Job is perhaps talked about most—the patience of Job, the trials of Job, the friends of Job, the wife, the prayers, the riches, and yes, the final blessings of Job.

We see Job in full-blown misery and grief and marvel at his steadfastness. We understand his weariness, and even memorize his words to help us through our times of pain and agony. But I wonder how often, if ever, we take a close look at God's nature, His character that is revealed through all of this. God the Creator, the all-seeing, all-knowing God, God the omnipotent, the just, the wise, the powerful. And finally, happily, we see God as the rewarder of the faithful.

I see another side of God in this epic that causes me to marvel. I see the pride of God in His children. Just as a mother brags about her son, the doctor, or her daughter, the nurse, I see God bragging about one of His sons, the godly one. I can hear Him speaking to Satan, "Where have you been?"

Satan answers, "From going to and fro in the earth, and from walking up and down in it" (Job 1:7).

God asks proudly, "Have you seen My servant Job? A perfect man, who fears Me and eschews evil?"

I wonder as I read that portion of Job, *Would God be able to brag about me? Throughout the trials, tribulations, and temptations of life, am I building a character that God would be well pleased with, a firm faithfulness, no matter what? Would my heavenly Father ever be able to say of me, "Have you seen My servant Junell, one who loves God and avoids evil?"*

I wonder.

JUNELL VANCE

Make It Easier

Each of you should look not only to your own interests, but also to the interests of others. Phil. 2:4, NIV.

*M*elissa and I were eating dinner together, and it was her turn to give thanks. Halfway through grace she stopped, opened her eyes, and asked, "Why are some people disabled?"

I groaned inwardly. Not because grace had been aborted, but because I was simply too tired to come up with a rational answer for such a complex question. "Do you know someone who is disabled?" I asked, buying myself a little time.

"Yes, the new boy at school. He's in a wheelchair," she explained. "And some of the other students made fun of him yesterday when he couldn't reach over far enough to catch the ball. Why is he crippled?" she persisted.

"I don't know exactly what happened to him," I replied, then told her the essence of a sermon I once heard from the father of a son with a disability: "We are living in a battle zone. And in war some soldiers come through unscathed; some die; others are wounded; and some are disabled."

"But God *could* make every soldier come through unscathed," she challenged.

"True," I agreed, "but if God did that we might become very comfortable living in the war zone. Or stop planning to live in a better place. We might even neglect to think of ways in which to make this world a better place—while we are here."

Melissa was quiet for a long time while she pushed a few green peas around her plate. "I wish Tommy weren't disabled," she said at last.

We ate in silence for a few moments. Then, straightening up in her chair, she asked in her most grown-up voice, "What could be my role?"

I smiled. Melissa must have overheard a telephone conversation in which I defined my role at an upcoming retreat. She incorporates new words into her vocabulary as quickly as she hears them. "Perhaps you can just make it easier instead of more difficult for Tommy."

Before long we had come up with several ideas, practical ways in which Melissa could help to make life a little easier for Tommy at school. The last thing she said as she was getting into the car to ride home was "I'm going to have such fun in my role!"

Over time I have been amazed at how frequently ideas pop into my head as I try to incorporate that philosophy into my own life on a daily basis. Often doing something to make life a little easier for someone else takes very little effort, and it's such great fun. Why not try acting in this role today?   ARLENE TAYLOR

JULY 10

Preparing a Home

In my Father's house are many mansions. . . . I go to prepare a place for you. John 14:2.

As a pastor's wife I have moved often. One thing that I enjoy most about moving is the task of turning a new house into a home. After the flurry of unpacking boxes and arranging the furniture, the fun begins. Each room is carefully considered. How will it be used? Who will be using it? What special atmosphere do I want to create? The curtains are chosen—after much study of catalogs and browsing in stores. Knickknacks are unwrapped and given their own special places. Houseplants are purchased. Pictures are hung.

My husband's collection of pictures of Jesus takes the most thought. Each picture says something to me, and I want those words and feelings to fit the rooms where they are hung. I like to see a picture of Jesus laughing as I'm joining guests in the dining room, knowing how He loved to fellowship with people. Sallmon's portrait of Christ is one that reminds me of His lordship. It belongs over the piano in the living room as a focal point for all to see as they enter our home. *Jesus and the Children* fit so well in the boys' room, as I want them to grow up confident of His love for them. The Life of Christ series is hung as a gallery. I like to stop and reflect on each scene of His life and ask Him to change me and mold me into His character.

Jesus is doing the same thing up in heaven. He's preparing a home for His family, for me. Arranging furniture and decorations and pictures. Each room has to be just right for its occupants. Perhaps it is pictures of His children—you and me—that He is hanging.

I become totally absorbed in the project of turning a house into a home. Often I imagine the guests we'll have over and the special times we'll enjoy. And I think Jesus is doing the same. He's waiting for His children to come home, anticipating the times we'll share. He's longing for the reunion with those He loves.

I'm going to be there! What about you? "O, Father, please prepare our hearts to meet our Saviour." LILLY TRYON

JULY 11

In Quiet Solitude

In stillness and staying quiet, there lies your strength. Isa. 30:15, NEB.

*R*eading the book of Isaiah made me realize how true these words were to him. In the stillness and quiet he found his strength and inspiration to write some of the most powerful passages in the Old Testament.

After a hot and heavy day the evening light takes over from the sultry sun; the long shadows and the coolness descend on you. The children are playing cricket in the distance, and their laughter can be heard. A few people are walking their dogs. There's a soft mackerel sky dotted with fleecy gray-and-white clouds, with patches of blue above.

Just to sit and look around, not speaking, not doing, not worrying, is the gift of solitude, the art of quietness. A chance to say thank You, Lord, for a lovely summer's day, and now thank You for the peace of the evening.

Can you look back over the day and see what little pleasures you have enjoyed? Have you used your time wisely? Is this moment a pleasure, too? There's a time to talk and a time to be silent.

Many great things have been fashioned in silence. Some of the useful and modern equipment we use and take for granted, such as the radio and telephone, has been designed by our ancestors, quietly and patiently. Many hours of contemplation and research have inspired these great inventors, and we benefit from their dedication. We too can develop our talents through quietness and be surprised at the insight and guidance gained this way. There is so much noise and mental distraction these days in this stress-filled life that we need to find our own peace and serenity to dream and think of happy memories, to remember the good times and laughter.

Someone once said that happiness is like a butterfly. If you stay still long enough it may settle on you; it won't be afraid. Leave time for the little things, those "little things" that make all the difference, that give you new hope and enthusiasm. Frustrations disappear as you sit calmly and listen. Fill your mind with peaceful thoughts, with beauty of trees and hills, gentle valleys and lush green meadows. Wherever you are, you can visualize these soothing pictures of beauty and nature our heavenly Father has created for our pleasure. I can sit here and feel renewed and appreciate these special moments with another gift of life—solitude.   PHILIPPA MARSHALL

JULY 12

My Philosophy of Life

Do not be conformed to this world but be transformed by the renewal of your mind, that you may prove what is the will of God, what is good and acceptable and perfect. Rom. 12:2, RSV.

*M*y to-do list today included reorganizing the linen closet to create more storage space. For the past 10 years I had been ignoring the scrapbooks, dating back to grade school, that were stuffed in the bottom of the closet. Since it is a linen closet, I needed to remove the memorabilia to make room for the extra blankets and sheets we've accumulated. Sitting on the floor, cozily surrounded by the comforters and pillows waiting to be tucked away, I browsed through those yellowed, fragile pages, sentimentally thinking of friends whom I hadn't heard from in years.

An unanticipated revelation came when I read a paper that I wrote during my senior year of high school, assigned by our Bible teacher. He was an admired, devoted Christian counselor in our school who took many opportunities to help us apply our religion to our present and future lives. One of his self-analytical assignments was to write a paper entitled "My Philosophy of Life." As I read through my deepest thoughts as a 17-year-old I was intrigued to find how consistent my beliefs and views have been through the years. However, I was startled to see that my enthusiasm and outlook had changed so much, and I was grieved when I discovered goals and expectations that remained unfulfilled or completely abandoned. I considered what my paper would read like now, almost 20 years later. I painfully realized that although many components of my philosophy of life would be carbon copies, the revised sections would not necessarily be improvements. Too many paragraphs would be tinged with bitterness, hurt, and cynicism. At 17 my scale was tipped in favor of optimism, zeal, and an invincible spirit, but now the scale weighs heavily out of balance toward pessimism, weariness, and fear.

Sometimes we let life beat us down. We give others the right to trample on our feelings, our self-concept, and our dreams. We allow recurring disappointments to discourage us. In the face of failures we lose our faith. Our view of the world moves too rapidly from naïveté to skepticism, and our perceptions of ourselves, others, and God become jaded. Peter tells us that our "adversary the devil prowls around like a roaring lion, seeking some one to devour" (1 Peter 5:8, RSV). I used to contemplate that verse as if the devil would devour me in one big gulp, but as I look back on my life, I can see that he's been nibbling away bit by bit. He defeats us insidiously, piece by piece. We gradually start to lose sight of our dreams and aspirations, our beliefs, our purpose and goals. Soon we are only the sin-sick shell of the person we set out to become, and the devil has won.

What is your philosophy of life? Has sin marred your innocence or darkened your bright hopes? Have the temptations you've succumbed to robbed you of your mission? Have the repeated compromises you've made dulled your sense of values? The Bible contains an abundance of evidence to reassure us that it is never too late to improve our outlook. Paul tells us to "be renewed in the spirit of your minds" (Eph. 4:23, RSV). If you are dissatisfied with your attitude, if you don't find peace in your perspective, may David's prayer be yours today: "Create in me a clean heart, O God, and put a new and right spirit within me" (Ps. 51:10, RSV).

LAURA PASCUAL DANCEK

JULY 13

Mowing Through Life

Let the wise listen and add to their learning. Prov. 1:5, NIV.

The other day as I was mowing my mom's lawn with my dad's tractor, I was thinking about my dad, who had died recently. Tractors were a big thing to my dad. He loved to mow. Since it takes five or six hours to mow their yard, that gives one a lot of time to think.

I don't get that excited about mowing, but it needed to be done. This particular day things were going pretty well. The first section is full of pine trees to go around. I had just started clipping along pretty well when I had to slow down for a tree. Then I went in between two bushes. It looked as though I was going to make it through, but I didn't. All of a sudden the side of the tractor caught hold of the bush, and before I realized what was happening the side panel was off and bent up pretty badly. I quickly stopped and got off to access the damage. It was bad. I had wrecked Dad's tractor, his pride and joy. What would he have said? How mad would he have gotten? Close to tears, I called my husband at work to see if he thought it was safe for me to continue mowing. He thought I could finish. (I had barely started.) He also said that my dad wouldn't have been mad. He'd just be glad that I was OK.

I went back to the tractor and managed to push a lot of dents out of the panel and found a piece of wire and wired it back onto the tractor. Then I finished mowing, but a little more cautiously. While I mowed I thought about how much like life mowing is. Things are going pretty well, you're moving right along, when all of a sudden a pine tree is in your path and you have to slow down. Pine trees can be different things—problems, crises, struggles, discouragement—anything that causes you to slow down. One thing I noticed about mowing was that when I slowed down for an obstacle, I was more aware of how I was mowing, more careful. Obstacles in life can do that for us, too. Make us look at how we're doing. Evaluate the job we're doing. See areas we need to go back over.

I mowed the hills diagonally, instead of sideways as my brothers do, because I was a little afraid I might tip over. I realized that each of us approaches life in a different way, too. Some of us are a little more cautious than others. We each have our own style and way of doing things.

Once I had to stop and go for gas. We need to stop and refuel ourselves every day by spending time with the Lord in prayer and Bible study. Church is like a tune-up that recharges us and prepares us for a new week.

As I contemplated all of this and thought about how like our lives mowing is, I thought of my dad and smiled. I think he knew it all along. Maybe that's why he liked mowing so much. I think he'd be proud of my discovery, despite the dents in his tractor. Our heavenly Father is proud, too, as He watches us mow and learn the lessons He has for us.   TAMI HORST

Love Vignettes

And now abide faith, hope, love, these three; but the greatest of these is love. 1 Cor. 13:13, NKJV.

*T*he small, vivacious woman looked up at her bespectacled husband, her brown eyes dancing. A look of love passed between them, the same love that I had seen at their wedding three months earlier. They didn't even try to mask their feelings that shouted "I love you!" Their love was alive and well; I was reassured.

✧ ✧ ✧

His blond head bent down toward his week-old daughter, cradled in his arms. Sitting in a pew labeled "for parents with children," he was introducing his daughter to the church he loved. I saw his new-father's love as he looked down at his sleeping firstborn. As he reached down and kissed the soft cheek, his love for his daughter was unashamed.

I thought of God's limitless love for His children on earth and smiled, thankful for His unconditional love.

✧ ✧ ✧

My teenage daughter burst into the room, banging the door behind her. Her words "I'm home!" were really not needed. She raced to the refrigerator, took out a package of string cheese, and opened it with her teeth, pulling off small pieces as she talked.

"How was school?"

"Boring, as usual."

I smiled. I had heard that phrase before.

"I got a B on the science test. That's terrible. And ninth and tenth graders are dissecting a pig. I'll *never* do that."

"Good thing you are in eighth!"

"I'm not *ever* going to dissect anything."

I had learned long ago that arguing was futile. "I dissected an earthworm, a frog, and a pig in zoology."

"Double gross!" She raced outdoors to pet Sophie, her dog.

That evening after dinner, worship, homework, and TV she started to bed. "Good night, Mom. I love you." Her kiss felt good. It had been a long time. Her teenage, uncaring mask had slipped away for a moment. I, a teenager's parent, *was* loved. I smiled, grateful for evidence of her love.

God waits patiently for evidence that His love is returned. Let's shed our uncaring mask and tell Him that we love Him.

CONNIE WELLS NOWLAN

JULY 15

Zippy the Wonder Mouse

And do not lead us into temptation, but deliver us from the evil one. Matt. 6:13, NKJV.

*M*y husband and I had been married only a few months when an unwanted houseguest arrived. We discovered our visitor one morning when we opened the pantry. Gnawed cereal boxes and little dark droppings confirmed the fact that we had a mouse. And this was no ordinary mouse. We named it Zippy the Wonder Mouse for a very good reason—we could never catch it. Understand that I am not opposed to sharing the outdoors with God's little creatures, but I refuse to live with one.

The first night we set our trap, Dale had placed on it the most obvious mouse lure known to humankind—cheese. We turned our fan on so the awful smash of the trap wouldn't disturb our sleep. The next morning we discovered the trap had indeed gone off. The cheese was missing—and so was the mouse.

A neighbor suggested trying peanut butter because a mouse would have to try harder to get it off the trap, thus lingering in the perfect mouse-trapping position until the trap snapped. No success. Not only was there no peanut butter and no mouse, but our candy had been tampered with as well! Evidently Zippy was setting off the trap first with its tiny paw and quick reflexes, then devouring the goodies. This mouse had a brain, and it was too smart for us.

Zippy was also getting braver, even daring to venture out into our kitchen during waking hours. My husband almost had the mouse cornered during one of its escapades, but I distracted him from his task when I ran from the room in hysterics.

With renewed determination Dale coated that trap with layers of sticky candy so the mouse couldn't get away so quickly. It worked! We had found Zippy's weak spot. It had become comfortable with its surroundings and let its guard down. We were triumphant at last! But a strange feeling of sadness and admiration for the little critter overcame my husband as he laid Zippy to rest in the woods behind our home.

This story has a serious point. Satan works the same way we did. He tries every lure he can to ensnare us in his trap. Maybe he can't get you to steal or lie. Adultery may never even cross your mind. But be assured that he will keep at you until he finds something to distract you long enough to put his net over you, then relish in the victory of bringing another soul down with him.

Daily keep your guard up. Don't ever forget to pray to your heavenly Father to lead you not into temptation, but to deliver you from evil should you ever be led astray. Throughout today, and the rest of your life, remember the counsel of our brother James: "Therefore submit to God. Resist the devil and he will flee from you. Draw near to God and He will draw near to you" (James 4:7, 8, NKJV).

MERRI LONG

JULY 16

Except You Become as Little Children

Except ye be converted, and become as little children, ye shall not enter into the kingdom of heaven. Matt. 18:3.

Little children—how Christ loves them! They point the way to the kingdom of God, but how? What qualities do they possess that we grown-ups need to possess that will enhance our Christian life? Or to ask the question another way, what qualities that we once had as children have we lost in our fast-track adult life?

Many sermons are preached and many explanations given of those childlike qualities Christians need. My vacation this summer with two children, a boy, 4, and a girl, 8, gave me some real insights as I shared their lives for a few days. Three of the children's qualities stood out. I'd like to share them with you.

A sense of wonderment. They noticed and came alive at the world around them. They appreciated it. They loved their world of mountains, streams, trees, rocks, and animals. They took time to examine. A large sphinx moth flew into a glass jar that was sitting in the camp cooking area. I fished it out and showed it to Brea and Zach. They let the moth crawl on their fingers, their eyes taking in every detail of the lovely little creature, from its spotted wings to the white stripe on the side of its face.

Seeing beyond today. Adults call it faith. The children reminded me of a book entitled *I Never Saw Another Butterfly*. Its pages were filled with beautifully colored pictures of butterflies drawn by children in concentration camps. Behind barbed wire, housed within gray cement buildings, many of these children never saw another butterfly, nor got to roam the flowered fields of home. But in their minds they enjoyed the butterflies and drew them on paper.

A sense of trust. I suggested one evening that we walk to the Marriott hotel near our cabins, and two eager children took my hands. I hadn't walked that way before, and began to realize that walking along the narrow road with traffic becoming heavier could be dangerous. The hotel was farther than it had seemed while driving in the car, and there was little walking space for us on the curves. I decided to go back, and explained to the children that where we were walking wasn't safe. They trusted my judgment and didn't beg or whine in disappointment. And I thought of the times I trust God's judgment or Word when often I don't understand the situation either.

There are many other characteristics of children, but these in particular stood out as I vacationed and played with my friends. I want to nourish these childlike traits in my own life!

EDNA MAYE GALLINGTON

JULY 17

Marriage: A Three-legged Race

Love one another warmly as Christian brothers, and be eager to show respect for one another. Rom.12:10, TEV.

At some time or another you've probably been in a three-legged race. I remember a race my husband and I participated in at a church picnic one beautiful summer day. The sun was shining, and fluffy clouds drifted by lazily. Some people sat around on lounge chairs, chatting; some played table games or horseshoes; and those with more energy played softball or tug-of-war.

Then came the three-legged race! After the children had raced, it was announced that it was time for the married couples to race. Someone tied my left leg to my husband's right leg with a rope, and we put our arms around each other to steady ourselves. The starting gun went off, and we started toward the goal at the other end of the field. I laughed and squealed as we hurried as fast as we could to beat the other teams. There was no time to argue about who would lead, whose turn it was, or which way to go. We quickly agreed on our strategy to win, and neither of us tried running ahead of the other. If we hadn't worked together, we would have fallen, as some of the other couples did.

Marriage is a lot like that three-legged race, except that it takes a lot more to make it work! It takes a close, personal relationship with Jesus. It takes active communication—learning to really listen to what the other person is saying, and learning to express yourself in a nonthreatening way. It also takes cooperation, consideration, appreciation, determination, and a generous portion of laughter. We take vows to love, cherish, care for, and accept another person for better or for worse, yet it takes both partners, pulling together in the same direction, to win.

I thought I could change my husband once we were married, but that was unrealistic. I had to accept and love him in spite of his faults, just as he had to accept me. When we have had differences of opinion, I have learned to turn the matter over to God and pray, "Lord, one of us is right and the other one is wrong. If I'm wrong, change me. If he's wrong, change him, and give me the patience to wait for Your answer."

And you know what? It works! Try it and see!

CELIA MEJIA CRUZ

JULY 18

More Than I Asked For

He restoreth my soul. Ps. 23:3.

*I*t had been a difficult year at the school. *Teaching sure doesn't seem to get any easier,* I thought to myself. Now open house was coming up, and I was dreading having people ask lots of questions. Well, I would simply have to smile graciously and try to avoid inquiries and confrontations.

As I got into my car to drive to the school, I closed my eyes and prayed, "Lord, You're going to have to help me get through this!"

After some preliminary activities and a short program by the students, it was time for tours of the various classrooms. I had no sooner walked into mine, with parents and students streaming in around me, when a woman walked up to me and gave me a big hug. I gasped in delight. A surprise visit from a college classmate

I hadn't seen in 20 years was a welcome pleasure!

She had heard that I was in town and had been wanting to contact me. She had taken this opportunity to do so. We stood together talking, catching up on all the news of years gone by. As we talked, I acknowledged parents and students as they entered the classroom and suggested some projects the students could show their parents. My classmate stayed and engaged me in animated conversation until open house was over. When she left, I locked the door, walked out to my car, and sat quietly for a few moments before starting the engine. My heart was full of gratitude. I had hoped for stamina, and God had provided diversion as well. "Lord, You gave me an unspeakable gift! Thank You from the bottom of my heart," I prayed.

I continue to marvel at God's creativity, a Being full of surprises, interested in our daily struggles. We are encircled by a Presence who looks ahead, anticipates our needs, and smiles as plans are made to give us unique answers.

I drove home slowly, savoring the joys of the day. God had indeed restored my soul. — LORNA L. LAWRENCE

JULY 19

Hospitality

Do not forget to entertain strangers, for by so doing some people have entertained angels without knowing it. Heb. 13:2, NIV.

I'm sure my mother didn't have this text in mind when she invited people for dinner. It was obvious even to me, a child, that she didn't invite them in order to get an invitation back. Of course, we had friends over often, but many a day two old men whom I will always remember shared our meal.

These men smelled. That is the only way to say it. One was a bachelor who lived in a basement, cooked on a kerosene stove, and didn't wash often. But he was a faithful church member who came every week.

The other man was equally faithful. He was married and had a small farm. His wife so fiercely opposed his going to church that she hid—and even burned—his good clothes on several occasions. So he came to church in his work clothes, smelling of cows and manure. Our house needed a thorough airing out after they had gone, but they were a part of my childhood.

One day when I came home from school there was a baby in the house. My mother had met a woman who had to go in for surgery and didn't have anyone to leave her 4-month-old infant with. So my mother took him in. That was the way she was.

My mother died when I was 18. Some time after her death my father phoned to ask if he could bring a woman home for a bit of supper. She was an out-of-town woman, a new convert to our church. I said no. It didn't have to be anything fancy, my dad said, just a simple supper. Again I said no. I couldn't do it.

When my father came home he told me that this woman had been standing quite close when he called and had probably heard me. I felt terrible. For years afterward I got a knot in my stomach every time I met her.

This incident taught me a lesson I should have already learned from my mother: We may not have the time, energy, money, or desire to provide a three-course meal to those in need, but a simple dinner, served with Christian love and joyful hospitality, will do very nicely.

Our guests might not be angels, but they are the children of God and therefore our brothers and sisters, even though they may not be fellow church members. "Inasmuch as ye have done it unto one of the least of these my brethren, ye have done it unto me" (Matt. 25:40).

ANNA JOHANSEN

JULY 20

Waiting for the Lord

The Lord is not slack concerning His promise, as some count slackness, but is longsuffering toward us, not willing that any should perish but that all should come to repentance. 2 Peter 3:9, NKJV.

*I*t was July 20, 1993, when my husband and I started our journey from Bangalore to Jalandhar, in Punjab, to conduct evangelistic meetings. A few days later we were in Pune, attempting to board the train to Jalandhar. To our great dismay, we were told that all trains en route to Jalandhar were canceled because of the floods in Punjab, but we could try our luck in Bombay. After much thought and prayer we decided to trust that God would help us reach our destination.

Once in Delhi, we found there was only one train going to Jalandhar, and the tickets were issued only an hour before the train's arrival. I waited on the platform with our luggage for nearly five hours while my husband stood in the long line for the tickets. Waiting in a strange place, surrounded by strangers, without food and water was not easy. But I waited patiently, hoping and praying to see my husband coming with the tickets. Finally he came.

But the wait did not end there. For the Jalandhar train we had to walk to another platform, where we found hundreds of passengers waiting for the same train. More and more people were joining the massive crowd. The only place we could sit down was on our luggage.

It was announced that the train would be one hour late. All the passengers waited patiently. Another half-hour delay was expected. Again we were disappointed. My thoughts drifted to Christ's second coming. Waiting is difficult and unpleasant. It brings anxiety, tension, irritation, and disappointment. Jesus has promised "Behold, I come quickly." From our childhood we have heard our parents, teachers, and preachers say "Jesus is coming soon." Signs in nature echo the same thing. Often a question arises: "How soon?" Quite often the troubles, perplexities, sickness, natural calamities, and death become unbearable and we cry out "How long, Lord? How long?"

The train finally arrived nearly three hours later. The moment we heard it coming we were ready with our luggage in hand. We learned that the delay had been caused by flood damage to the railway track.

Friends, Jesus' coming is not delayed because of any damage between heaven and earth. He is waiting for you and me to repent and surrender completely to Him.

The meetings in Jalandhar were rewarding. We no longer thought of the hardships we had faced. Instead, we thanked God for the decision we had made. As we go on our heavenly journey, may we not become discouraged and go back. Instead, "let us run with patience the race that is set before us, looking unto Jesus the author and finisher of our faith" (Heb. 12:1, 2).   HEPZIBAH G. KORE

God's Garden

We [Paul and Apollos] are only God's coworkers. You are God's garden, not ours; you are God's building, not ours. 1 Cor. 3:9, TLB.

I bought my house because I fell in love with the backyard. It was truly love at first sight. I can sit every day and see it through my French doors, beautiful, large, green with splashes of color here and there, and most of all, peaceful. My real estate agent told me in all seriousness that it was a "low maintenance" yard. I am still laughing about that five years later. I have come to the conclusion that there isn't any such thing, but I love the place anyway.

I think that one day I would like to be a luscious purple pansy in a garden, then I think that I might like to be a dahlia, or perhaps a peony. After checking the definition of these flowers, I came to the conclusion that a peony would suit me best. It is a perennial, often double-flowered, with large pink, white, red, or yellow shiny flowers. Naturally, I would have to be a red peony.

The concept of being God's garden offers limitless parallels to our spiritual lives. I want the soil of my heart to be rich and fertile and open to the seeds of character and behavior God wishes to plant there. I know that God will give me some Miracle-Gro from time to time, and I want to grow stronger and more beautiful when I allow the Lord to remove the weeds around me. I thank God for the water of life and for His sunshine that I receive from daily communion with Him.

Each day I can grow more beautiful and my roots will sink more deeply as I talk with Him and listen to His leading. The knowledge that Jesus loves me and cares about me is the sunshine that completes the growth cycle, enabling me to become my flower of choice in God's garden.　　　　　　　　　　　　　SHIELA BIRKENSTOCK SANDERS

Unprofitable, Though Faithful

So likewise ye, when ye shall have done all those things which are commanded you, say, We are unprofitable servants: we have done that which was our duty to do. Luke 17:10.

*I*t was the annual girls' club program again. Excitement ran high and with it, of course, was hard work in preparing the program and the dinner. I was especially excited because, though I was small, I had been asked to play a part in the program. I was to sit on the stage with a big doll and rock it to sleep while a lullaby played. This was to be the closing item for the evening.

I sat through the program with great anticipation. As it came to an end my heart started to beat faster. I waited for the announcement, but I was not called. The program suddenly ended. The girls were thanked, and everyone dispersed. I said nothing to anyone, nor did I ask the dean why my item had been omitted. I was very disappointed, but I was not bitter. I continued to take part in other programs.

Years later I had a similar experience. I was asked to give a speech at a women's party. I accepted and prepared well for it. I sat there waiting for my turn to speak, but to my dismay, the program ended without my item. I was disappointed. However, I did not feel as bad as when I was a small girl. I took part in the refreshments and cleanup, and then I went home. In both cases I had wanted to do my faithful part, but felt I was considered "unprofitable" instead.

As a fugitive, David was homesick. He longed for a drink of water from the well at Bethlehem, his hometown. Three of his warriors broke through the host of Philistines in order to get to that well. They risked their lives and brought him that precious water. It must have been shocking for them to see David pour it on the ground instead of drinking it.

Abraham must have gone through a lot of stress when God asked him to sacrifice his son. Yet when he was willing and ready to do just that, God changed the order. No doubt Abraham was relieved, but what if I had been in his place? I could have been mad at God for putting me through all that stress for nothing!

In my disappointing experiences I am sure God wanted me to forget self and to be more forgiving. Probably my items were left out not intentionally, but by oversight. David's attitude toward the three officers was one of respect and regard for their lives. I am sure the three officers learned to love their leader all the more after that. They knew their service was appreciated.

Whenever we are disappointed, unappreciated, ignored, unwanted, or even exploited, we can still be willing to do our duty faithfully. It may be that there is something God is trying to teach us. Both our faithfulness in our duties and our right attitude in our disappointments can be a witness for Christ.   BIRDIE PODDAR

JULY 23

The Sunflowers

I am the good shepherd. John 10:11, NKJV.

Along the roads from Venice to Florence, Italy, are wide fields of sunflowers. In July the flowers are fully grown and wide open, their bright-yellow petals surrounding the seeds.

At 8:00 in the morning the flowers are drooping, but starting to straighten up. The big heads on the slim, necklike stems are still bowed at 10:00. They start to look up at 11:00, and by noon the flowers are fully up and facing the sun, their stems pointing straight into the sky.

All day long as the sun shines over the created beauty of the field those sunflowers continue to face the sun. About 4:00 travelers going east and sunflowers following the sun are now face-to-face, as though commanded by the sun king. Although occasionally there are a few out of the vast fields of flowers that behave contrarily and face the other way, most flowers "look" in the same westerly direction until the sun sets and the flowers bow in sleep.

While we were traveling in Europe, we followed our tour director's words very strictly, otherwise we would have been left behind or lost in the huge crowd of travelers. From early morning to late evening we found her instructions valuable. If she said that we were to have only 20 minutes here and only five minutes at the next stop, we knew to get back to the bus on time. Being late meant any one of the following: everybody in the group was affected, the bus had to move or else the bus driver got fined, or someone was left behind in a precarious place, unfamiliar and foreign.

However, much like the stubborn sunflowers in the field, there were always a few who chose to go their own way, in spite of the director's clear and repeated reminders. Our tour director was firm and straightforward. She always tried her best to guide us. Yet she was understanding, patient, and kind. When one of us was missing, she would blow the horn in all directions and call us by name. If she was unable to find the missing one, she stayed behind, waiting. If she had to leave, she put us in the hands of another capable guide.

Our Good Shepherd is like this tour guide, making sure all His sheep are safe and in the fold. John 10:11 tells us that the Good Shepherd is Jesus. "I lay down my life for the sheep. . . . My sheep listen to my voice; I know them, and they follow me. I give them eternal life" (verses 15-28, NIV).   ESPERANZA AQUINO MOPERA

Are We Plugged Into God?

With your help I can advance against a troop, with my God I can scale a wall. 2 Sam. 22:30, NIV.

The summer of 1977 three young men were in our neighborhood selling books and magazines to earn college scholarships. They slept in our church and ate at our house. Needing somewhere to wash their clothes, they asked if they could use my washer and dryer. I said sure and showed them the machines and demonstrated how they worked.

The next day when I got home from my church secretarial job, I saw a large pile of dirty clothes in the laundry room and wondered if the guys hadn't washed their clothes after all.

Just then they came in and said, "Oh, Mrs. Moyers, we're so sorry."

"Why?" I asked.

"We think we broke your washing machine. We put a load in and thought we did what you said, but the machine didn't come on."

"Let me look at it," I replied.

The boys went into the living room and sat down. As soon as they heard the washer start up, one of them asked, "What magic did you do? How did you get it to go?"

I grinned. "I plugged it in."

They looked at one another sheepishly, and then did their laundry.

I always unplugged the machine between washes, because when it was plugged in, the little red on/off light shone from the laundry room into the hall all the time and kept my children awake at night. Also, during the energy crunch several years earlier I had become sufficiently environmentally conscious that I made a habit of turning off unnecessary lights. But I had forgotten to tell my boarders.

Thinking about what had happened, I realized that this has the makings of a modern-day parable. As Christians, we are God's appliances. We are to do what we can to help clean up the mess that this old world is in and point people to Christ. To tap into our power source, we need to use the two prongs of prayer and church attendance. And we must also be sure we include a third prong, the study of God's Word, so that we will be spiritually well-grounded. Without God's power we're as useless as an unplugged appliance. We must make certain that we're plugged into God.

BONNIE MOYERS

JULY 25

Unburdening

Come unto me, all ye that labour and are heavy laden, and I will give you rest. Take my yoke upon you, and learn of me; for I am meek and lowly in heart: and ye shall find rest unto your souls. For my yoke is easy, and my burden is light. Matt. 11:28-30.

The story goes something like this.

Back in the horse-and-buggy days a woman trudged along the road with a heavy pack on her back, bent down under the load. She trudged on for a time, head bowed. Although she walked beneath a beautiful blue sky through a countryside filled with wildflowers, she saw nothing but the dust beneath her feet. She didn't turn to see the horse and buggy driving up behind her, but just stepped to the side of the road, waiting for it to pass. Instead, it stopped. The driver smiled and beckoned the burdened woman to climb into the buggy and ride. So the woman hefted herself and her burden onto the seat beside the kind stranger.

After some time had passed, during which the passenger still held her heavy burden on her lap, the driver asked, "Why don't you relieve yourself of your burden?"

"Oh, I couldn't do that!" the passenger objected. "You're already generous enough in giving me a ride. I couldn't ask you to carry my burden, too!"

We chuckle, but do we pay attention? Don't we do the same thing all the time? I must confess I do. I keep my burdens after I've asked God to help, and continue to fret. I keep my burdens if I ask for forgiveness again and again, as if I have to convince a vengeful God to forgive me. I keep my burdens if I fail to seek God's aid for small things, such as lost keys or a tricky recipe. I hold on to my burdens when, as a result of my own fiscal mismanagement, I get in a tight financial state and think I have no right to ask for God's help because I have been irresponsible.

Throughout my life I have been holding far too many burdens for just as many reasons. Like the woman in the buggy, I hesitate to ask for too much help because I feel that God has done enough for me as it is. I don't want to trouble Him further.

If, like me, you at times are determined to hold on to your burdens, God will not force you to relinquish them. You may be riding in God's buggy of salvation while still carrying your everyday burdens because you think *God has already done enough for me!* But Jesus tells us to lay our burdens on Him. It is only then that we will find rest for our weary, burdened souls. KATHLEEN TONN-OLIVER

JULY 26

Walk Safely

Whoso walketh uprightly shall be saved: but he that is perverse in his ways shall fall at once. Prov. 28:18.

It was a beautiful July day—wispy clouds weaving through the blue sky, not too hot, not too humid. I was only a half block from home. My morning walk had been exhilarating. Oh, how I enjoyed this quiet time of the day. The three miles or so of my route traversed our neighborhood park and brought me back down the quiet residential sidewalks. Even though I was striding confidently, I knew from previous walks that there was good reason to watch for unlevel spots in the cement.

I thought, *How lovely this summer day and place are. How can it be that in just a few more months it will be barren, icy, and cold?* I listened to the cardinals "talk" to each other. I greeted the familiar black kitty sitting lazily on its porch. I noted some new flowers—fragrant and colorful—in one yard. It was fun to watch the squirrels race about, scampering after each other, down a fence and up the next tree. A bunny quietly nibbled on some clover, hoping I wouldn't notice it. So many enjoyable sights, sounds, and I was keenly aware of all of them.

Then in an instant I was down on all fours, with searing pain in knees, hands, and wrists. Painfully I picked myself up. For just a few seconds I had forgotten to watch where I was going. An unlevel portion of the sidewalk had caught my toe. My mind had strayed; I was already home, mentally, planning my next activity. Too late! I was down. A neighbor and a motorist were suddenly there to see if I needed help. My pride and independence prodded me to limp home. Why did I forget I needed to continually be aware of where I was going, ascertaining any pitfalls ahead? After ice packs, X-rays, medical consultation, splints, and other minor treatment, I was grateful to learn there were no broken bones.

There are comparisons that can be made between my physical walk and my daily spiritual walk. All goes well when I faithfully watch where I am going. I enjoy the beauty surrounding me, but I must not forget to be on guard for pitfalls. We can get into trouble when we are distracted or forget to walk uprightly in the way of the Lord. Sometimes it takes just one misstep to make us realize that if we don't get back on track, we could be in serious trouble. Every day, whether walking physically or spiritually, we need to keep our eyes fixed upon Jesus, staying our course and maintaining the direction that will lead us to our heavenly home. ARLENE E. COMPTON

JULY 27

Of Cats and a Cat

God is love. Whoever lives in love lives in God, and God in him. In this way, love is made complete among us so that we will have confidence on the day of judgment. . . . Perfect love drives out fear. I John 4:16-18, NIV.

A skinny stray cat was wandering around our neighborhood. Everybody hoped she would just go away. But she didn't. We noticed that she often disappeared into the barn where stacks of hay were stored. One day my daughter decided to follow her and find out where she went. She discovered three baby kittens snuggled behind a hay bale. Suddenly the scraggly stray was transformed into a mother needing help. My daughter fed her because the cat was so malnourished that certainly she didn't have enough milk for her helpless babies. She became a bit friendly, knowing where her dishes of food were coming from.

But not so the little kittens. We would catch only glimpses of them occasionally, playing, wrestling, peering out from tiny cracks between the bales of hay. There is, of course, a magic about babies that stirs the heart and arouses sympathy, creates interest, and brings a smile to the face. But we could never get anywhere near them.

One evening we thought we had one kitten cornered for sure, but it disappeared down a dead-end corridor. We just knew we could catch it, and then we could give it to a home where someone wanted a kitten. Three of us sneaked up quietly, wearing gloves and long sleeves to protect us from scratches. We were armed with a blanket, towel, and basket to catch the little wild creature. When we tried to lay hands on the feisty kitten, it shot away between us like a bullet from a gun. There was no way we could stop the terrified creature.

One day my daughter's house cat was lonely for attention. She climbed up on the arm of the sofa where I was sitting. I reached over and petted her. She purred and climbed down into my lap and lay down, soaking up the attention. I couldn't help recalling our kitten-catching expedition a few days earlier. Our cat was begging me for attention and love; the wild kitten dashed away frantically, fearing for its life. What was the difference? Our own cat had once been a stray too, but love and care lavished upon her had taught her what love is, and she was no longer afraid. Perfect love had destroyed fear.

In a similar way, God's perfect love for us drives out our fear of God and the judgment. We love Him because He first loved us.

RUTH WATSON

JULY 28

Our Guardian Angels

For he shall give his angels charge over thee, to keep thee in all thy ways. They shall bear thee up in their hands, lest thou dash thy foot against a stone. Ps. 91:11, 12.

*M*ommy, Mommy, save me! Save me!" The screams of our 5-year-old son pierced the sounds of the rushing waters on Wheelbarrow Falls in Quetico Provincial Park that sunny day in Canada.

My husband and I, along with our four children and their two second cousins, were vacationing in this lovely place for 10 days in the late 1960s. Camping, canoeing, and hiking 150 miles with six

243

children, ages 3 to 16, may not be your idea of a vacation, but for us it was a wonderful change from milking cows and baling hay during the hot summer months. It had taken six weeks to plan and package meals and supplies for the eight of us. Everyone had a backpack to carry—even the "baby."

To save a long hike this fall day we were traveling upstream of the falls by walking alongside the water. We traversed the high rocks, pulling the canoes laden with our gear and children, by means of ropes tied to the canoes. Papa, with the four boys, guided the canoe in the rear; I guided the lead canoe with the two youngest children. Suddenly the rope on my canoe came loose and the canoe was caught in the rapidly flowing waters, swiftly carrying our small children on a wild ride downstream with no guidance from me. Our son's screams filled me with terror.

My husband leaped from the rock he was on, miraculously catching the canoe by its bow. The weight of his body provided sufficient balance to keep the canoe upright during its wild ride downstream. The episode had a safe and happy ending, thanks to his quick thinking, agile body, and the loving protection of one of those angels who have "charge over" us.

Many hundreds of years after this initial promise was given in the psalms, Satan used it as a billy club by quoting it to Jesus from the pinnacle of the Temple where he tempted Jesus to throw Himself off. He tried to put down the guidance of the protecting angelic beings and tempt Jesus to trust in a promise that, under normal circumstances, would bring hope, courage, and strength. Praise God that Satan was met on his own ground with the answer "Thou shalt not tempt the Lord thy God" (Matt. 4:7). Defeated for the third time that day, Satan left Jesus, and "angels came and ministered unto him" (verse 11).

What joy will be mine someday to meet these beautiful, strong, wonderful beings who have charge over us and to say thank you!

BETTY R. BURNETT

Forgiveness

Praise be to God, who has not rejected my prayer or withheld his love from me! Ps. 66:20, NIV.

Lord, children You have given me
 To parent and to love;
To train to walk the pathway of life
And to prepare for heaven above.

No skills I had for the job;
No manual came with their birth.
So I struggled along the pathway
 Of parenting on this earth.

But if I'd looked a little closer,
A manual I would have found.
But I thought it was only a book
To send me heaven-bound.

I now know if I had come to You,
My pathway You would have guided.
My stumbling ways of parenting
You would have cast aside.

But I didn't, Lord,
And now I see the mistakes of my hand.
So cover my mistakes with Your mercies
Wherever my children may stand.

As I pray for my children, it gives me great peace to know that God is always willing to accept my prayers. No matter how much I love them, He loves them more.

LORNA LANGLEY

JULY 30

Fear

For I am the Lord, your God, who takes hold of your right hand and says to you, Do not fear; I will help you. Isa. 41:13, NIV.

*F*ear is something I don't like. I feel two kinds, and both are bad. I hate being frightened. My heart stops. My stomach freezes. And right after I have gasped and sucked up all the air in the county, I stop breathing.

I also don't like being scared. The scared feeling comes on more slowly, but it lingers longer. My heart races, my ears can hear a feather drop, and my stomach climbs right up to my neck, where it dries out my throat and mouth. They get so dry that a cottonmouth could talk louder.

I didn't like fear when I was little, but I thought that I was the only one who felt that way. Now I know that you are like me. Now I know that it is part of the human package, even though we don't want it and some won't admit to it.

The Bible's first record of fear occurred in the Garden of Eden. Right there in a perfect place. There were only two people, but they clung to each other and hid—in fear. They had heard the sound of their Friend walking in the garden and His voice calling them. But they knew it was the Friend whom they had betrayed, the Friend who had advised them not to eat of the tree of the knowledge of good and evil or they would die. They had not listened to His advice. They had eaten, and the first result of what they did was that they saw themselves, their nakedness. Then they feared. That was the first acknowledged emotion after sin: fear. Fear of being seen for who and what they were: people who betrayed a trust.

Fear was right there in Paradise, when Paradise was lost. Fear came when the voice of God was put aside, when His counsel was disregarded. Fear came with sin, and we are born in sin. So we are born with fear. It grows and multiplies as sin is thrust upon us or as we volunteer to participate in it or watch it. The solution for our fear now is the same as it was then. We need to converse with God and let Him clothe our nakedness with His righteousness. It is only in relationship with God that we can let go of our fears.

It is also possible to live without fear if we *stay close* to our Friend ("Abide in me, and I in you. . . . Without me ye can do nothing" [John 15:4, 5]), *follow His advice* ("Whatsoever things are true,

... honest, ... just, ... pure, ... lovely, ... think on these things"
[Phil. 4:8]), and *remember His promises* ("Wait on the Lord: be of
good courage, and he shall strengthen thine heart" [Ps. 27:14]).

EVE GILKESON

Think of Something Good

Forgive whatever grievances you may have against one another.
Forgive as the Lord forgave you. Col. 3:13, NIV.

*D*eep within my heart I know there is nothing from the
unlovely aspects of my past that is out of the realm of
God's healing. There is no question in my mind that God loves me.
The question I ask is How can He love me so?

When I accepted Jesus Christ as my Lord and Saviour He showered me with His pardoning grace and mercy. My sins were forgiven. I became a new creature. Visible signs of former destructive
habits were gone. Cigarettes and alcohol no longer defiled my body
and mind. However, eliminating emotional bruises suffered in
childhood proved more difficult. A number of unresolved issues
surfaced time and again. Raw, emotional wounds refused to be denied. Unpleasant childhood episodes often pushed their way into
my mind. Stinging words directed at me as a child resounded in my
head. Fueled by low self-esteem, the emotional scars inflicted in my
youth vengefully carried over into my adult life.

Prayers for healing of past hurts and a forgiving spirit toward a
perpetrating family member were often on my lips. But again and
again I hindered God's answer by simply not accepting it. I wanted
proof. I wanted this "offender" to admit that she had hurt me and to
ask for my forgiveness.

One morning as I prepared to begin my day, a scene from my
childhood flooded my heart and mind. The family member who had
wounded my spirit had made one Christmas Eve very special for me
when I was about 5. I cried and cried as I relived that scene. The
Lord had broken through my unrelenting spirit.

"Think of something good" is what He penned inside me. I felt
impressed to stop dwelling on the negative. Hurt and ashamed, I immediately called her and through my tears thanked her for all she had
done for me, apologizing for all the pain I'd caused her in the past.

"I never meant to hurt you," she replied, her voice heavy with sorrow.

Jesus impressed the apostle Paul to write, "Fix your thoughts on what is true and good and right. Think about things that are pure and lovely, and dwell on the fine, good things in others. Think about all you can praise God for and be glad about" (Phil. 4:8, TLB).

The Lord can give us the love, the tenderness, and the forgiving spirit we need to function as whole human beings. When we forgive others, we cleanse ourselves of the ugliness of hurt.

God answered my question of how He can love me after all I've done with a question of His own: How can you not love others after all I've done for you?

IRMA R. LEE

AUGUST 1

Slugs

For where your treasure is, there your heart will be also. Luke 12:34, RSV.

On a bright, hot, summer day in Virginia my four boys were playing outside while I cleaned up the kitchen. My baby girl was entertaining herself in her little swing, watching the fish in the aquarium as I worked. Our three dogs lazily stretched out on the floor in the family room, soaking up the sun that shone through the sliding glass door. As I glanced out the window to make sure the boys were OK, I noticed the cat sunning itself on one of the railroad ties that separated the driveway from the yard, and our two geese following the boys.

A few moments later the boys came bounding through the door, perspiration on their foreheads and excitement in their eyes. They all began to speak at the same time as they excitedly asked for a jar. I collected plastic jars for them, since they always had some treasure they wanted to save. I gave them one, and they ran back out to play.

When I called them in for lunch, they came as if in a procession, the oldest one carrying the jar. From a distance I couldn't tell what was in it, but as they made their way through the door I could see that the jar was filled to the top with slugs! I gasped, then I told them the slugs had to stay outside. They protested, saying that the slugs were their fishing worms. After admiring their find, I was able to persuade them to leave the slugs outside in the shade while they washed their hands and ate their lunch. Then they rushed outside to play with the slugs again.

I sat at the kitchen table thinking about the boys and how reluctant they were to let their treasured slugs go free, and how much like them we adults are. We argue with God when He asks us to let go of our "treasures" that separate us from Him.

As you search your own heart today, listen to God's Holy Spirit as He pleads with you to let go of the "slugs" and take hold of the treasures He has to offer. CELIA MEJIA CRUZ

AUGUST 2

God Is Able

And God is able to make all grace abound to you, so that in all things at all times, having all that you need, you will abound in every good work. 2 Cor. 9:8, NIV.

The final chapter of World War II was coming to a close in Munich, Germany. My work was with children who were evacuated to the foothills of the Bavarian mountains. Each week I had a day off, and I planned to spend this one with my mother in Munich.

At 8:00 in the evening I boarded the train for the one-hour ride to Munich. All of a sudden the train stopped. Everyone left the train and fled into the woods. I was afraid that I would get lost in the night, so I stayed in the train. A very old man who was sitting across from me stayed too. We could hear the airplanes roaring overhead. Suddenly there was a terrible detonation, and I was hurled from my seat. After what must have been a very long time, I felt as though I was waking up from a lengthy nap.

My fellow passenger said, "I'm so glad you woke up. I was sure you were dead."

Many hours later part of the train continued the journey to Munich, arriving at a totally destroyed station at 4:00 a.m. The surrounding houses were also in shambles. It took me a long time to find my way home through all the destruction. By the grace of God, the apartment house my mother lived in was still standing, and my mother and brother were alive.

The next day my mother took me to the doctor to find out the cause of my prolonged unconscious state after the bombing. The doctor explained that the pressure of the detonation had injured my heart, and that I would need a lot of rest. He put me on unlimited sick leave, which was very extraordinary, because everyone had to work in this last total war effort.

Some weeks later the war was over, but now I was at home with my mother and brother. We did not know for many months if my father, my sister, and her baby were alive, because they had been evacuated to different places. God, in His goodness, made it possible for me to be safe with my mother and not alone in that little mountain village during that final war drama.

In times like these we need to remember the words in Psalm 91: "You will not fear the terror of night, nor the arrow that flies by day. . . . 'Because he loves me,' says the Lord, 'I will rescue him; I will protect him. . . . He will call upon me, and I will answer him; I will be with him in trouble'" (verses 5-15, NIV). Incidentally, thanks to God's tender care for me, I have never had the slightest trouble with my heart, and I am 70 years old!   SOPHIE KAISER

AUGUST 3

Pray for Your Children

Then Samuel said, "Speak, for your servant is listening." 1 Sam. 3:10, NIV.

*T*hat still small voice came so urgently: "Pray for your children." I'd heard that voice before and often prayed for my children during the day, but this time the message was more specific: "Pray out loud for your children."

For six months I had been part of a very special prayer group that met every Wednesday morning. For three hours we studied a Bible text and prayed for each other. It was a time of closeness with our Lord that I treasured. After our study I headed home on the freeway. It was about 12:30 p.m. when I was impressed to pray. Not knowing what to pray for, I began to pray for their health, their relationships, schooling—anything that came into my mind, and I prayed out loud.

A short time after I arrived home, the phone rang. It was Jason, our oldest son.

"Mom, there's been an accident."

My heart raced as I tried to remain calm.

"I'm OK, but my car isn't." Then he told me how he had been

driving down the winding, mountain road from camp. As he entered a curve, a large delivery truck suddenly appeared on his side of the road. On one side was a 30-foot drop-off, and on the other side was a dirt bank. Somehow—and he doesn't know how—he managed to go behind the truck and land in a ditch next to the dirt bank. He was uninjured, but his car was the recipient of a very flat tire. He was shaken but praising God for his close encounter. It was then I realized that the accident had occurred at the moment I had been impressed to pray for my children.

I have no answers for why some accidents happen and some accidents are prevented. All I know is that when God calls, I want to be like Samuel and say, "Speak, for your servant is listening," and then to listen to His instructions, even when I don't know what I am praying for. JANIS VANCE

AUGUST 4

Green Ice

He that endureth to the end shall be saved. Matt. 10:22.

The pictures and descriptions in rose catalogs entice you to order three times as many roses as you need. I had shades of red, pink, yellow, and many blends in-between. The catalog I was looking at even sold a green one. What would it look like? I decided to order Green Ice.

I gave Green Ice a home in a hanging basket, since it was a miniature. It did not grow fast and didn't send out long branches and produce many buds as the others did. In fact, it was very slow in producing anything at all. I thought perhaps it was one of those that had better be discarded at the end of the season. When it finally did produce three wee roses, they were white, not green. *Another example of misleading advertising,* I thought.

Every day I watered, sprayed, and cut off the faded roses in my deck garden. I began to notice something about Green Ice. Those three little white flowers did not fade. They slowly turned into a delicate light green, which deepened with the passing of time. They never seemed to fade. After they had been blooming for weeks, they finally dried up a bit, and I reluctantly cut them off. They were absolutely amazing in their endurance and perseverance, as well as their unusual color.

Then for a few weeks I was busy and neglected my careful attention to my roses. Some became badly infested with black spot, which kills the leaves and eventually the bush. Some bushes practically quit blooming, seeming to be barely surviving their cruel neglect and their exposure to the extremely hot and dry summer.

As I began working diligently to revive my emaciated plants, I noticed one that seemed to be thriving in spite of the intense heat and neglect. Green Ice had vigorous, healthy leaves and many blooms. No black spot or insect pests seemed to bother it. That modest little plant seemed to have an inner ability to conquer difficulties and come out stronger and more beautiful than ever. After many weeks of 100°F temperatures—and hotter—it responded with more blooms than ever. Toward the end of the season it was handsomely decorated with 20 blooms at one time. No other rose, even the hardy Simplicity, had more than four or five blooms during this trying time.

Maybe I can't be a dazzling splash like Fragrant Cloud or Sunsprite or some of the other famous and truly great in the rose world, but my prayer is that I will endure to the end with grace, dignity, and God's inner strength that thrives under the most adverse conditions. Just like Green Ice.   RUTH WATSON

AUGUST 5

Are You Homesick?

And if I go and prepare a place for you, I will come again, and receive you unto myself; that where I am, there ye may be also. John 14:3.

It was the day after my young daughter had returned home from summer camp, and she and I were sitting on her bed while she related her experiences. She described the horse she had gotten to ride, the pool in which she had cooled off, and the counselor she had come to love. But then, somewhat reluctantly, she admitted that she had felt homesick more than once during that week.

"So what did you do when you were homesick?" I asked, leaning across the bed to scratch her back.

"Well," she began, "I thought about Jesus, and that helped me. I figured that He probably got homesick when He was here on earth, too. Do you think He was homesick sometimes, Mama?"

I had to admit that I had never thought about it quite that way. But during the next few days I came to realize the truth that Jesus had every reason to feel homesick. He was light-years from His home, after all. I also remembered all the times I had asserted that I was homesick for heaven, almost without thinking about what it meant. I had never been there. In fact, I've been told that I can't even begin to imagine it. So how can I miss a place I've never seen?

The truth is, I am not homesick for the place. I am homesick for my Father. He's the one I miss. Heaven I have never seen, but not so my Father. I have seen Him a thousand times in my mind's eye. I have heard Him speak; we have walked together, and we've worked side by side. He is the one who will make heaven home to me. And because that is where He is, I can truthfully say that I'm homesick for heaven.

RETTA MICHAELIS

AUGUST 6

Through a Tomato Plant

Your Father knows what you need before you ask him. Matt. 6:8, NIV.

One time when things weren't going too well and I wondered why God wasn't answering my prayers the way I felt He should, God spoke to me in a most unusual way. Into my deaf ears He repeatedly said, "Child, stop and listen. I'm trying to tell you that I am still tenderly watching over you in a much better way than you understand. I am tending to every matter in your life, so calm your anxiety and lean upon your Father." He finally got through to me through a tomato plant.

We had just purchased a retirement home that we planned to move into after my husband's retirement in three years. It was in the beautiful area of Hagerstown, Maryland. The home had just been built, and the land had been leveled and graded. You might call it "virgin land," as far as gardens were concerned. My son, who worked nearby, was to be caretaker until the time of our retirement.

Each weekend we traveled the 70 miles to practice living in our retirement dream home. Our son had promised to plant us a tomato garden there, but with the trials and activity of his busy life he just never got around to it. Disappointed, I would tell myself that whether or not we had a tomato garden would not be earth-shattering. Reluctantly I put my wishes on the back burner.

Spring passed, and we were into summer when I noticed a tiny little tomato plant, growing, as if planted, beside my deck. It grew by leaps and bounds until the plant was sprawled over the ground. Because it had come up on its own, I never thought it would amount to anything, so I didn't even stake it. By the end of the summer we had harvested about 100 large, plump, delicious tomatoes, and when the frost finally took the plant, it had many more little green ones still coming.

You may say that it was just a coincidence. I say this was a special message from my Father in heaven telling me, "I will care for you down to your smallest needs and dreams. So don't fret over life; I have you in the palm of My hand."

So when life gets tough and things don't seem to be going your way, remember that He knew you while you were yet in your mother's womb; He loved you then and loves you now. He is touched even by your longing for something as simple as a tomato garden.

EDNA LEE JONES

AUGUST 7

Decide for Jesus

And Elijah came unto all the people, and said, How long halt ye between two opinions? If the Lord be God, follow him. 1 Kings 18:21.

*E*lijah spoke these words before thousands of people on Mount Carmel. The prophet decided to eliminate any doubt about who is the true God. Israel knew that the Lord was the true God, Creator of heaven and earth, and not Baal. In the words of this verse Elijah is inviting the people to make a choice.

Decisions both great and small are often made by small, everyday choices. We decide what kind of friends we'll have, the books we'll read, the music we'll listen to, the television programs we'll watch. All these choices are important and demonstrate our personal commitment to God.

In 1992 my husband and I were coming home from a trip. When we entered São Paulo state we came to a fork in the highway. It was raining heavily, and 93 miles later we discovered we had taken the wrong fork. We pulled over, hoping to get information from a passerby, but it was raining so hard no one would stop. Several miles down the road we finally found a gas station and got help.

All along it had been our sincere intention to travel in the right direction, but we never would have arrived home continuing the way we were going. In fact, we had to turn around and go in the opposite direction to find the route that led to our home. The Bible gives us guidance and shows us clearly which way we must go to get "home." If we choose to follow Jesus, we will reach our heavenly goal. If, by ignorance, we have gone the wrong way, the Bible can help us to correct our course.

You may be headed in the wrong direction, just as we were, but if you ask, Jesus will point you in the direction that will lead you home.

MEIBEL MELLO GUEDES

AUGUST 8

Thank God for Little Things

The heavens are telling the glory of God; they are a marvelous display of his craftsmanship. Day and night they keep on telling about God. Ps. 19:1, 2, TLB.

I walked to my garden, as I had done almost every day for several weeks, to deadhead the lilies. My mind and eyes were focused on removing every wilted and spent flower on each stalk to allow the plants to direct their energy into new blossoms. The task completed, I turned my steps back down the wooded path toward the house. Suddenly I realized that for several days I had seen only the wasted, shriveled blooms, ugly things to be discarded. The delicate beauty of my garden surroundings had completely escaped me as I focused on the dead remnants. I had missed so much.

Quickly retracing my steps, I feasted my eyes on the beautiful soft pinks and rich mauves, the brilliant oranges, lemony yellows, the deep reds, and shimmering whites of the enormous flowers. They were exquisite, breathtaking. As I looked closer I discovered, much to my delight, pinkish gray frogs, no larger than my thumbnail, nestled like tiny royal princes in the deep cups of several lily "palaces." Their bright, shiny eyes blinked out at me with as much interest as I gazed down at them.

How much like our lives. Too often our time is spent in deadheading. We focus on only the ugly, shriveled happenings of the day: the hurtful words spoken by a friend, the unfair judgment of a coworker, the unreasonable mandate handed down by an administrator, or the willful, naughty behavior of a child.

How many of life's pleasures we miss by not turning our attention instead to the beauty and delightful surprises God so much wants to give us—the friend who offered encouragement and a warm smile, the words of appreciation from that troubled soul with whom you shared a special thought, the beautiful day filled with sunshine and refreshing breezes, that special hug from a loved one, or the delight of seeing the bright reds, yellows, grays, and blues of the birds who visit the feeder. All are lovely vignettes of flowers our heavenly Father has scattered along our daily paths.

My prayer is that today we will remember to dwell upon the beautiful, to enjoy the flowers of life, and leave the deadheading to the care of the Master Gardener.　　　Barbara Horst Reinholtz

August 9

Changes

Before the mountains were brought forth, or ever thou hadst formed the earth and the world, even from everlasting to everlasting, thou art God. Ps. 90:2.

*C*hange. The only thing we seem to be sure of these days is that things will change. I sat numbly in the back seat of the car as my husband, new baby, and I headed for the biggest change I had ever experienced. But moving to another state wasn't the only change occurring at that time. I was a new mother of two weeks and had just begun an extended leave from my job to be with the baby. There were hormonal changes as my body continued the natural healing process after birth, and I was finally facing some painful truths as I reexamined my personal relationships. And so the breathtaking beauty of the sun sinking below the horizon was all lost to my tear-filled eyes, for it seemed to me that the sun had set in my life as well.

"Where are You, Lord? I can't feel You near," I prayed to the darkening sky. "Help me to cope with these changes." I heard no response. I felt no warm comforting feeling, as I had in the past. Where was my faith of so many years? I chided myself, but still I felt alone. Had the Lord changed too? Where was He?

It would be many days before that familiar tender voice would be heard. During that time all I could do was to cling to the verses I learned while growing up and pray continuously. It was when I began to recount the ways God had led me in the past that I first felt Him pulling me through the dense fog that had settled around me. Finally the Spirit began to help me to let go of the anxiety that had so filled my mind that He could find no way to speak.

"Yes, there are changes," He reminded me. "And there will be many more before we meet face-to-face, but be confident, for the sunset of one day brings with it the promise of the dawn—for I am the Lord; I change not."

Even though I had loosened my hold on Him and wrapped myself in a blanket of anxiety, He had been there all the time. He hadn't changed.   MAXINE WILLIAMS ALLEN

AUGUST 10

Anxious Thoughts

When my anxious thoughts multiply within me, Thy consolations delight my soul. . . . The Lord has been my stronghold, and my God the rock of my refuge. Ps. 94:19-22, NASB.

*O*ur family decided to take one last short vacation before school started. We planned a week of camping and boating with my parents at a mountain lake about 30 minutes from our home. We had four lovely days of fellowship, sleeping under the stars, and singing to the guitar accompaniment provided by my husband and son. My mother wrote poems, I caught up on some reading, the children perfected their waterskiing, and everything seemed idyllic.

Then my husband had a waterskiing accident. We rushed down the mountain to the doctor. X-rays revealed two fractured ribs. All sorts of thoughts were reeling through my mind. Here we were, suddenly torn away from our children during our family vacation. My husband was in a lot of pain, and life was no longer wonderful.

While I was waiting at the hospital, unable to concentrate on the television or the well-worn magazine in my hands, troubled thoughts tumbled through my mind. Why? How will I deal with things now? Then God sent me a text from my memory: "When my anxious thoughts multiply within me, Thy consolations delight my soul." What a comfort this was! My thoughts were certainly anxious ones!

During that first sleepless night spent away from our children I wondered, *Lord, what are Your consolations in this situation? Did we do something wrong?* Finally my prayer became *Please show me Your will in this situation.*

In all my wondering and questioning, doubting and fear, God consoled my soul. I read more of Psalm 94: "The Lord has been my stronghold, and my God the rock of my refuge." I was able to go to sleep with the thought that God has never failed our family in the past. He would work out this situation as well.

Five days later my thoughts aren't quite as troubled while I sit at the computer this early-morning hour. We are all back home together, and our camping gear has been stored away. Today is filled to overflowing. My 7-year-old is sick with the flu. Mountains of laundry await me. A writing deadline is fast approaching. This was to have been our official first day of home school. And now I have a temporarily disabled husband recovering upstairs.

Yet even with this busy day ahead I am remembering that God has proved to be my stronghold in the past. Each thing that happens to me shows me that I must continue to trust God. For today, and for the rest of my life.   JUDY MUSGRAVE SHEWMAKE

AUGUST 11

No Night There

And there shall be no night there; . . . and they shall reign for ever and ever. Rev. 22:5.

I had mixed feelings as I fastened my seat belt on that Delta Air Lines jumbo jet. I was in the company of 24 other teachers on a transcontinental flight from New York City to Moscow on a special mission to teach English to Russian people.

We had been flying more than two hours. Everyone who had access to a window was admiring the beautiful sunset, a most magnificent view. I decided to just focus on this sunset until I fell asleep. When I looked at my watch again, this breathtaking scene had not changed its position. I glanced at the monitor displaying time zones and noticed that we had already passed into the next zone. We were flying northeast toward the North Pole, and I realized that it would not be getting dark. We were entering the land of the midnight sun, where there is no night. I had captured a scene that I wanted to stay with all night, but I knew my body needed to rejuvenate itself, and only sleep could do it. I had lost myself completely in the beauty of the moment, and I didn't want to come back and become a part again of the 200 or so passengers on this aircraft.

One day Jesus will actually come and take us up, up and away from this dark and dismal Planet Earth. We will take a heavenly flight with Him, unlike any flight we have ever had before. We'll travel to a place where God is, and *there will be no night there.* Oh, what a glorious day that will be!   ZEOLA GERMANY ALLSTON

AUGUST 12

Keeping in Touch

Greater love has no one than this, that one lay down his life for his friends. You are my friends if you do what I command. I no longer call you servants, because a servant does not know his master's business. Instead, I have called you friends, for everything that I learned from my Father I have made known to you. John 15:13-15, NIV.

*T*he week had been full. Errands, calls, and to-do lists had kept me racing through each day. As I hurried through my Friday cleaning, the basket of letters caught my attention. *Her letters don't come as often as they used to,* I thought. I paused to think about my friend and the many letters I had received through the years as she shared what was on her heart and what was happening in her life. I cherished each one, rereading them often, and wrote notes to myself about how I wanted to respond to various things that she had written. They were all saved in this special basket. Her friendship is such a blessing to me. But no letters had been added to the basket for a while. There wasn't any rift between us—just extremely busy schedules for us both. Still, I missed the contact, the closeness.

As I turned to dust another room, I thought of another Friend. I imagined Him speaking softly to Himself. "She doesn't talk with Me as often as she used to . . ." I sensed the sadness He must feel when I allow busyness to envelop me and keep me from praying. He misses the closeness.

What a God! The Creator of the universe longing for my companionship! His desire is for me to know Him as a friend, to share intimately with Him the things that are on my heart. He treasures the time we spend together and misses me when I'm preoccupied with life.

Lord, put that same desire in my heart—to know You as a friend. Help me to cherish Your Word even more than letters from a human friend. And when life gets hectic, remind me gently to keep in touch with You.

LILLY TRYON

Change Me, Lord

Delight yourself in the Lord and he will give you the desires of your heart. Ps. 37:4, NIV.

I slammed my foot on the brake and screamed, "I can't do it!" Frustrated at attempting a three-point turn, I became even more flustered because I was being watched by several onlookers. "You can take over," I cried out to my husband. "I will never be a driver!"

Learning to drive is not an experience I would like to repeat. In fact, if Jonathan hadn't encouraged me as much as he did, I would have been quite happy to travel around on two legs rather than four wheels. Jonathan, however, felt it was his duty to make a driver out of me.

It was not easy. And after I failed two driving tests, even Jonathan began to have doubts. I frequently forgot which was my left and right side. I was always confused when reversing, and if there was no place large enough to park my car, I'd just keep driving.

I finally passed my third driving test. Shocked, I asked the examiner, "Are you sure? Would you like time to reconsider your decision?" He assured me he was sure. Excited at seeing my much-coveted driving license, Jonathan smiled broadly and wrapped his arms around me. My smile quickly evaporated. Until now, my husband had always sat with me as I learned to drive. Now I would have to do it on my own. My misery had not ended; it had only taken on a new facet!

That was several years ago. Recently Jonathan told me that I now drive "like a real expert." Even though I hadn't noticed it, my driving has changed. I still hesitate to drive to new places on my own, but with God's help I have made progress.

In our lives we hunger for change. We yearn not to lose our

tempers. We want to be gracious. We ache to face temptation with a resolute no! but instead give in with a feeble "just this once." We strive to face conflict with implicit trust in God, instead of falling to pieces. We desire to be different, positive, joyful—everything that God promises us we can be. And when God fails to improve us or put a new spirit within us as quickly as we think He should, we become weary of Him.

We forget that change is a by-product of loving and delighting in God. We take the promise in Psalm 37:4 and jumble it up. We figure that when God gives us the desires of our heart, then we will delight in Him. Taking pleasure in the companionship of God is the key to change. I gained courage when driving my car as I focused on the God in whom no fear, agitation, or nervousness reside. Delighting in His fearlessness, I asked God for a snippet of His courage. Over time it was deposited in my life.

Do not worry about being changed. Simply soak up God's love. Marvel in His unique character. Be vulnerable to His influence. Then as your desires intertwine with His, you will become like your Father.

MARY BARRETT

AUGUST 14

Sitting at the Feet of Jesus

And Jesus answered and said to her, "Martha, Martha, you are worried and troubled about many things. But one thing is needed, and Mary has chosen that good part, which will not be taken away from her." Luke 10:41, 42, NKJV.

I worked as a nurse's aide for 10 years in a nursing home and then had the opportunity to work as the recreational director. It required going back to school. With three of my five children still home it was a busy household, filled with many duties. I also worked at church with Vacation Bible School, did blood pressure screening, and was a part-time salesperson. To say I was under too much stress would be an understatement.

Unfortunately, this hectic lifestyle continued until September 14, 1992, when I underwent surgery for breast cancer. I was devastated! But God saw me through, as He promised in Hebrews 13:5: "I will never leave you nor forsake you." I am doing fine now, and I realize it could have been much worse. But I can't help wondering if all the stress didn't cause the cancer in the first place. I have learned to slow down and say no and spend more time in prayer and reading God's Word.

What really impressed me was this story of Jesus visiting at the house of Martha and Mary. Martha was busy cooking and serving, while Mary sat at the feet of Jesus. Martha complained to Jesus that Mary was not helping. I'm sure most women could sympathize with Martha. After all, wasn't she working hard? Wasn't she concerned with having the table set and the meal just so? Are not her efforts commendable? Wasn't Mary being lazy?

Let us remember Jesus' advice to Martha and follow Mary's example by being temperate in all things, making more time for prayer, meditation, reflection, and contemplating God's Holy Word. Let us all take more time to sit at Jesus' feet. Then we can claim the promise that "those who wait on the Lord shall renew their strength; they shall mount up with wings like eagles, they shall run and not be weary, they shall walk, and not faint" (Isa. 40:31, NKJV).

LENA CRESSOTTI

AUGUST 15

V-P Day

They will enter Zion with singing; everlasting joy will crown their heads. Gladness and joy will overtake them, and sorrow and sighing will flee away. Isa. 35:10, NIV.

On August 15, 1995, people all over Australia celebrated V-P Day in memory of the day the war ended in the Pacific, more than 50 years ago. Television extensively covered the original victory day of rejoicing, with its ticker tape parades and dancing in the streets, reliving the utter euphoria and relief the country's citizens felt after six years of fear and heartbreak.

There were reenactments of the parades of 50 years ago as old servicemen and servicewomen rode in state down city streets while others marched, watched floats, danced, shouted, cried, laughed, listened to speeches, laid wreaths, and observed two minutes of silence to remember the war dead and the sacrifice of lives given so that we may enjoy freedom.

Young people lined the streets and shouted their thank-you's to the veterans of World War II—today's youth thanking the youth of another generation for their courage and their gift to the nation.

The whole experience brought memories and emotions to the surface as all Australians, justly proud, heard again the words "Lest we forget" and gazed at the eternal flame in cenotaphs across the land.

It makes me ache for S-C Day, Second Coming Day, when Jesus will come and forever put an end to fear, misery, and death on this earth. What a day of rejoicing that will be! I long to join in the singing of victory songs and praise to our wonderful Redeemer, who sacrificed His life that we may have freedom from sin and guilt. That will be something we will never forget!   URSULA M. HEDGES

AUGUST 16

Trusting God in Trials

The God of my rock; in him will I trust: he is my shield, and the horn of my salvation, my high tower, and my refuge, my saviour. 2 Sam. 22:3.

My only child, Tony, was born in 1967, suffering from damage to both kidneys. Tissue had grown over the opening of his bladder, and urine had backed up in his kidneys. Surgery at 3 weeks of age revealed the problem, but the prognosis was totally negative. We were told soon after his surgery that he would not live. After several weeks the physicians explained that they had inserted a tube in each kidney so that Tony would be able to urinate, but he would soon have to begin dialysis treatment. Initially I saw this as a devastating experience for all of our family members, but especially for Tony.

The Lord reassured me through the comforting words of my husband. Harold said we must be strong in faith and accept with patience and spiritual wisdom the circumstances under which God had given us this beautiful child. After six or eight months the tubes were removed, and Tony did very well, with no sign of any problem. With gratitude and a thirst for knowledge to know how to rear and care properly for this child, we dedicated him to the Lord. At 8 years of age he was baptized.

Tony is now 29 years old and an active church member. He has completed a B.S. degree in math and is planning to begin work toward a master's degree this fall. He has been on dialysis for three and a half years, during which time he completed the last year of his college work and was employed as an engineering technician. He's wary of having a kidney transplant because of the side effects of the antirejection medicine he would have to take.

While we would not have chosen to have this illness befall our son, the experience has been a blessing in multiple ways. It has kept us humble and at the foot of the cross. Tony has had multiple surgeries, each of which has kept us totally dependent upon God and His mercy. I sincerely desire healing for my son, but more than anything else I desire that he be saved, and that he have rich, personal experiences with the Saviour I have come to know and to love. If I could, I would give these to my son. However, this experience comes through spiritual encounters with God amid life's difficulties and trials.

The road has been a long and difficult one, but not without peace, gratitude, and the revelation of God's goodness in allowing us the privilege to know Him better through these experiences.

Whatever trials you may face today, hang on to Jesus. He will give you the strength and courage you need to endure.

NELL RICE ANTHONY

AUGUST 17

Our Heavenly Father Cares

I sought the Lord, and he heard me, and delivered me from all my fears. Ps. 34:4.

*W*here shall we go this week?" Auntie inquired as we laid plans for an interesting holiday in Sri Lanka.

We eventually agreed to go to Ratnapura, the City of Gems, to watch the people sift out the gems from the sand. We set out for the city with Auntie at the wheel. Soon we came to a turn in the road leading to a mine. As Auntie turned the car, I noticed that we were on a very steep decline.

"Oh, Auntie!" I exclaimed, not knowing what panic it would drive her to. "Look at that road!"

One look, and Auntie swerved the car to the side, not realizing there was a ditch directly in front of her. We went into the ditch and hit a tree. The car was now badly damaged. A crowd began to gather around us. My forehead was bleeding profusely, and it was evident that I would need stitches.

A taxi driver offered to take me for treatment. Soon I found myself on a doctor's examination table, feeling alone and helpless, and very nervous about the sight of blood, not to mention the *thought* of stitches.

"O, Lord," I prayed, "I am in a strange place with no one whom I know. I have only You to help me. I feel faint and frightened, and now they are going to stitch up my forehead. Please help me to bear this without any difficulty." I closed my eyes tightly to shut away the pain the stitches would cause me.

"It's all done, lady," the doctor said in a few minutes.

It couldn't be! I asked the doctor if he had given me any anesthesia.

"No, I didn't," he answered. "I didn't have any to give you. But you did so well!"

Even as I walked out of the doctor's office to meet the rest of the family, I knew the Lord had heard my prayer and helped me—nervous, fear-stricken me—to go through it all without the slightest feeling of pain. I realized He had fulfilled for me that wonderful promise: "He shall call upon me, and I will answer him: I will be with him in trouble; I will deliver him, and honor him" (Ps. 91:15). Our God is an everlasting strength, and I knew I could always lean on Him.

INDRANI J. ARIYARATNAM

AUGUST 18

Mistakes, Mishaps, and Miseries

Teach us to number our days aright, that we may gain a heart of wisdom. Ps. 90:12, NIV.

I had it all planned. I would leave home at 8:35 a.m., fill up with gas, drive seven miles to the town of Newmarket, and arrive precisely at 9:00 for my appointment with the optician.

I encountered the first snag in my well-devised plan as I waited for my car to be filled with gas. Usually service is immediate, but then I waited behind two cars as the attendant chatted casually with his customers. *Not to worry,* I told myself, *I'll drive a little faster and still reach my destination on time.* There usually was not too much traffic on the road that I planned to use.

But that day was different. I was forced to follow what seemed like the slowest truck in Britain along a series of bends. To attempt to overtake it would have meant my next appointment might have been with the undertaker, not the optician. I began to fume. I didn't have time for delays. Finally the truck left the road, and my foot pressed down hard on the accelerator. My little red car strained and spluttered as it zoomed down the by then-deserted road. If I could just maintain this speed, I knew I would be OK. Then an ambulance suddenly appeared from nowhere.

Once again my car chugged behind what was definitely the slowest vehicle in Britain. After a while it turned down a side road. My path was once again clear. Ever the eternal optimist, I pressed my foot down on the accelerator once more.

Entering Newmarket, I was brought to a halt. Several thorough-bred horses proudly trotted across the road. Usually I admired the various shades of their shining coats, but my fingers impatiently tapped on the steering wheel, my foot poised to resume its attack on the accelerator.

When I had to stop at each of the three traffic lights on the last part of my journey, I finally resigned myself to being late. Rounding the corner that took me to my parking lot, I was slowed down again, this time by a car with two bicycles on its roof rack. The driver was so slow that he could have almost done better riding the bikes!

Running into the optician's office, flustered, out of breath, and full of apologies, I was told, "Don't worry, the optician has been delayed. Just sit in the waiting room until she arrives." I couldn't help wondering if she was taking the same route I had just taken.

As women, our lives are always chock-full of dreams and plain everyday living with its myriad responsibilities. We could alleviate many of the mistakes, mishaps, and miseries that interrupt our lives if we would be kind to ourselves. We allow our lives to become overfull, overburdened, and overcommitted to the extent that we experience more stress than peace. God gives us time for everything—why don't we do the same?   MARY BARRETT

Hand in Hand

If the Lord delights in a man's way, he makes his steps firm; though he stumble, he will not fall, for the Lord upholds him with his hand. Ps. 37:23, 24, NIV.

We walked along, my daughter and I, panting because of the steep climb but enjoying it nonetheless. We were conquering this mountain together. Through the treetops we glimpsed a sky of deep blue as a chorus of birds serenaded our ascent. From time to time we joined them, singing on our way. At other times we fell silent, content in the familiarity of each other's company, enjoying the cool morning air.

The path was long and steep. But that was not the worst of it. Rocks were strewn all along the mountain trail, making sure footing essential. Some rocks were large and foreboding; others were small and sharp. Because the loose rocks made our way somewhat treacherous, my small daughter kept her hand firmly in mine. There were many times when she nearly fell, but because her hand remained in mine I was able to steady her faltering steps and prevent disaster.

That morning hike has served to remind me on many occasions of another trip I am taking, a trip far more dangerous and with more lasting consequences. On this climb I am the small child. I walk with my Father. And the only way that I will keep from falling is to keep my hand firmly and continuously in His.

❖ ❖ ❖

Too often, though, I skip ahead or lag behind and suffer unnecessary hurt. Oh, He is willing to pick me up and brush me off. He doesn't point out my stupidity, and He never embarrasses me. He just offers His hand to me again. The interesting thing is that the longer I walk with Him, the less I want to be free of His grasp. In His hand is the only place I find complete safety and complete rest. I can rest as I climb because it is He who does the work of finding sure footing. I am free to enjoy the walk and relish the peace that comes from knowing that with my hand in His I cannot fall.

RETTA MICHAELIS

His Strange Ways

For the eyes of the Lord are on the righteous and his ears are attentive to their prayer. 1 Peter 3:12, NIV.

*T*he other night I was talking to my prayer partner about how disappointed I was about a particular situation. She listened, but offered no advice. I didn't mind; I just wanted a sounding board. I went to bed a bit relieved, but when I awoke, the feelings had resurfaced. The whole issue seemed senseless. I wanted to forget about the whole thing, but it just didn't seem to go away. I cried out to God: "Why do I have to do this? I am tired of it. Why, God, why?"

When I got to work at 8:00, I took the first 15 minutes to reflect quietly on the situation. I opened my Bible and started reading the book of James. I decided that I would claim the promise in James 1:5: "If any of you lacks wisdom, let him ask of God, who gives to all liberally and without reproach, and it will be given to him" (NKJV). I kept all avenues to my soul open for an answer to prayer.

During my lunch break I went to visit one of my coworkers in her office. As I was about to leave she said, "Wait, Andrea, I've got something to show you. It's a book one of my girlfriends gave to me."

I looked at the title on the cover—*When, God, When?* "This is pretty interesting," I remarked. "It was only this morning that I was questioning God."

As I read the book, it seemed as though the author had tailored his thoughts to my situation. On my way home I reflected on the experience. It confirmed my belief in the statement I read from one of my favorite authors: "If we take counsel with our doubts and fears, or try to solve everything that we cannot see clearly, before we have faith, perplexities will only increase and deepen. But if we come to God, feeling helpless and dependent, as we really are, and in humble, trusting faith make known our wants to Him whose knowledge is infinite, who sees everything in creation, and who governs everything by His will and word, He can and will attend to our cry, and will let light shine into our hearts" (Ellen G. White, *Steps to Christ,* pp. 96, 97).

God did not allow my prayer partner, who was familiar with the situation, to give me advice because He knew her admonition easily could have fallen on deaf ears. (She had told me before to trust God's timing.) Instead He provided an answer through an absolute stranger who knew nothing of the situation. What an omniscient God we serve! He can do the same for you. You need only ask.

ANDREA A. BUSSUE

Spiders' Surprises

Such is the destiny of all who forget God; so perishes the hope of the godless. What he trusts in is fragile; what he relies on is a spider's web. Job 8:13, 14, NIV.

Spiders! Some small, some large. There are more than 2,000 varieties on one continent alone, and lots of them spin webs. Usually the mention of spiders sends a shiver down one's spine. Destroy their webs today, and tomorrow there are brand-new ones in their places.

As I walk among our fruit trees to gather ripe fruit, I am constantly running into webs, barely visible, yet ready to snare their victims. Spiders, in spite of their size, are tenacious and achieving. Their slender webs, almost transparent, can cause the death of a moth or butterfly, and most winged insects.

As I made the rounds of our house, clearing away the spiders' webs, my mind turned to Satan and the webs he uses to entrap unwary children of God. He spins webs of deceit, spreading out temptations that appeal to the eyes and ears. You can hardly see the threads, but suddenly you are entwined and feel all mixed up and frustrated.

Someone has said that the web of a spider does not appear to be an instrument of death, yet it is admirably adapted to entrap its prey. So it is with Satan's sophistries. Let's watch and pray, lest we be caught in one of his deadly webs.

ALMA ATCHESON

The Raspberry Bush

Call to me and I will answer you and tell you great and unsearchable things you do not know. Jer. 33:3, NIV.

It was another sultry summer day. My two preschool boys were tired of playing outside, and it was too hot to stay in the house for long. They were getting cranky, and I was getting desperate. Although technically I was a stay-at-home mom, I worked several jobs to help make ends meet. I had just finished paying the bills, and the terms "balancing the budget" and "juggling payments" were too much a part of my monthly experience to be funny.

"God," I sighed, "sometimes it seems so futile. Am I going to have to go back to work full-time?" It wasn't really a prayer for help—I had prayed that prayer regularly, often tearfully, as I struggled with the bills. Our expenses weren't that high—they were just more than we had coming in. "I wish . . ." I wasn't even sure what I wished for. Maybe it was just a hug from someone I loved who did not have jelly on his hands.

With a lump in my throat that threatened to choke into a sob, I walked out into the backyard and filled the boys' little wading pool with fresh water. Maybe hearing their laughter would make me feel better. I wandered across the shady yard, with no particular destination in mind. Suddenly I stopped and stared. Standing in the middle of the path that led to the garden plot was a small raspberry bush, probably not more than 18 inches high. I couldn't believe my eyes. It hadn't been there earlier in the week, and although the boys ran through there all the time, the plant hadn't been trampled down.

I knelt beside the bush, almost in awe. Three raspberries, fully ripe and ready to pick, hung on the stems. Raspberries, my favorite fruit, and far too expensive to buy. My tears began to flow. "God, it was You, wasn't it?" Slowly, I picked each raspberry and savored its sweet-tartness. My heart leaped for joy. "Thank You, Lord," I said in awe. "You knew exactly what I needed."

I decided to move the raspberry bush to a safer location, but an afternoon thunderstorm threatened to delay my plans. The next day I would transplant my little hug from God to a safe spot. But the next morning when I walked to the garden path, the raspberry bush was gone. There wasn't even a dried-up stalk. In fact, there was no sign that anything had grown there.

I would have loved to keep that raspberry bush and tell my family about God's special hug each time it provided fruit for us, but instead God was telling me to keep it in my heart, sharing it only with those who needed encouragement that God really does care for us and know our needs.

Raspberries are still very expensive. I seldom buy them. Somehow they never seem to match the taste of those three berries on that bush in the garden path.　　　　　　CHARLOTTE ISHKANIAN

AUGUST 23

Empty Nest

For this very reason, make every effort to add to your faith goodness; and to goodness, knowledge; and to knowledge, self-control; and to self-control, perseverance; and to perseverance, godliness; and to godliness, brotherly kindness; and to brotherly kindness, love. For if you possess these qualities in increasing measure, they will keep you from being ineffective and unproductive in your knowledge of our Lord Jesus Christ. 2 Peter 1:5-8, NIV.

I felt an empty sadness after taking my husband to the airport and seeing him off on a long trip. It was, of course, the loss of a person and the fear of what might be in the future that overwhelmed me. I recall years ago standing at my dorm room window at boarding academy, with my shoes in the closet drawer and my dresses and skirts newly hung, watching my parents drive away.

This all comes to mind because the time has come for our twin sons to pack up for college. They have no other siblings. Their dad and I will now have the house, our time, newspapers, TV, and the lawn to ourselves. My husband was assured that mowing the lawn was really an excellent gift to him to improve his health. We will miss our sons, their friends, and their lively schedule of activities. When we come back home to an empty house, I anticipate that after the appropriate tears I will need to apply my four-point strategy that has worked before.

1. Get a couple good nights of sleep. Most things are much more manageable when I'm rested.

2. Reaffirm my purpose in life and set some new goals. "I chose you and appointed you to go and bear fruit—fruit that will last" (John 15:16, NIV).

3. Clean house. Putting things physically in order is tremendously restorative.

4. Plan some loving-kindnesses.

I will mail care packages to my sons. Find a gift for a friend's birthday. Perhaps invite some new people home for dinner. I might surprise my husband with a picnic supper to be eaten by the lake.

In the quiet of the night as I lie in bed, I give thanks again to God, who is my helper. He will help me choose my goals and refocus my life. Praise Him, for He is able to keep me from falling (see Jude 24). He has wonderful plans to prosper me and to give me a future and a hope (see Jer. 29:11). Yes, that's what I must do—follow His plans when it seems mine have come to an end. I am reminded that His plans continue through to eternity!

EVANGELINE LUNDSTROM

August 24

All Things Work Together for Good

If God is for us, who can be against us? Rom. 8:31, NKJV.

It was the night before I was to leave for college to room with the same roommate I had had two years before. Tired after a long day of packing, I was still very excited over this news when the phone rang. Beverly announced that she might not be able to return to school, even though it was her last year, because her stepfather wouldn't pay her expenses. We cried bitterly over the phone, refusing to believe this was possible after all we had gone through to be together again. We prayed about the situation, and as we hung up the phones a peace came over me. I just *knew* God would answer our prayers.

The next morning my mother and sister drove me to the campus. My mother was most concerned about my optimism. She counseled me not to be too disappointed if Beverly was unable to come. But I knew that God knew that I needed her to be there, so I knew He would answer our prayers for the best.

We arrived in back of the girls' dorm, and I ran inside, meeting the dean as she came downstairs.

"Where's Beverly?" I asked.

"She's down in the laundry room," she answered.

Oh, what shouting there was as we hugged! "I knew you would be here!" I exclaimed.

"How did you know? I found out I could come only a few hours ago!"

We thanked God right there for answering our prayers and caring so much that two best friends could be together.

I thought right away of the text "All things work together for good to those who love God" (Rom. 8:28, NKJV). It is so wonderful to have a Saviour who is interested in every aspect of our lives. Nothing is too small for Him to care about. So today, tell Him all your little problems. He cares about and loves you!

ANNE ELAINE NELSON

AUGUST 25

Not Mine to Give

And forgive us our debts, as we forgive our debtors. Matt. 6:12, NKJV.

The organist for the local church arose early each Sunday in order to practice on the church organ before the service began. On her way to the church she habitually stopped at a small neighborhood café for a cup of coffee and a sweet roll.

One particular Sunday morning she finished eating and decided to use the restroom facilities before heading for the church. As she stood in front of the sink washing her hands, a drug-crazed, ratty-looking young man burst into the restroom, brandishing a knife and demanding her money. He locked the door behind him and threw her to the floor, beating her face and breaking her arm.

The woman screamed, "Help, someone! Oh, dear Jesus, help me. Help me, dear Jesus!"

In the man's drug-soaked brain the word "Jesus" registered. And as he viciously pummeled his victim, he mumbled over and over, like a little child, "I love Jesus, I love Jesus."

The café patrons heard the woman's cries and came to her rescue. The police and the ambulance were called. The young man went to jail, and she went to the hospital.

Months later, after being found guilty and being sentenced to prison, the man, now sober and remorseful, asked the judge if he could speak with his victim. In the judge's chambers the man begged her forgiveness.

"I was a Christian once, you know. I attended Sunday school

with my grandmother. I got messed up with drugs, and, well, you know the rest. I've got to know—can you forgive me?"

She studied his face for several moments, fighting back the revulsion she felt inside. "Forgive you?" she asked. "No, of myself I couldn't begin to forgive you. Forgiveness is not mine to give." The woman massaged the ragged scar on her arm. "Only Jesus Christ can give me the grace to forgive you. In time, when He grants me the grace to forgive, He is the one to thank."

This is the proverbial "rubber meets the road" for the Christian. No other faith in the world demands forgiveness of one's enemies. I don't know about you, but sometimes I try too hard to forgive another for hurting me and wonder why, in the dark of the night, the pain from that hurt comes back to haunt me. Perhaps I need to learn what this woman discovered through her ordeal—that a true, cleansing forgiveness is possible only through the grace of Jesus Christ. He is there not only to heal physical pain, but also to erase the emotional scars.

Thank You, dear Jesus, for granting us the grace that forgives and heals.

KAY D. RIZZO

AUGUST 26

Kindness

Be kind and compassionate to one another, forgiving each other, just as in Christ God forgave you. Eph. 4:32, NIV.

Susan, a sweet little girl who was rather tall for her 7 years, was paying a visit to the new schoolroom with her mother. They saw someone they had not seen for some time. The woman remarked, "She's only 7? She's really tall!"

Susan drew back as if someone had struck her. This was not the first time a remark like that had been made in her presence, but she scarcely expected it from this refined person whom she liked and admired. Her mother tried to ease the situation, but the thoughtless words had made their mark, blighting a child's tender spirit.

Many of us may be guilty of acts like this. Repeated too often, they darken lives, and timid souls shrink within themselves, endeavoring to form a protective shell against such barbs. May God help us to be kind not only in acts but also in words. Kindness is essentially forethought—putting ourselves in the other person's place before we speak, asking ourselves, "How would this make me feel?"

How many more would be drawn to the Master if we manifested a little more human kindness and thoughtfulness in our lives? How often we could heal a broken spirit, soothe a troubled heart, or lift a despairing soul from defeat to victory if we were but kind!

So let's all be "kind and compassionate to one another," remembering the words of Jesus: "I tell you the truth, whatever you did for one of the least of these brothers of mine, you did for me" (Matt. 25:40).   MAE E. WALLENKAMPF

AUGUST 27

God Sent a Rainbow

I have set my rainbow in the clouds, and it will be the sign of the covenant between me and the earth. Gen. 9:13, NIV.

I was nervous as I got into my car to go to work that morning. Even after several years of teaching, the first day of a new school year always found me a little jittery. But that morning was different. I wasn't just jittery—I was scared!

In two hours I would face a brand-new class. I would be teaching a grade I had never taught before—kindergarten, in a multigrade setting. I was also piloting two new programs. Materials, methods—almost everything was going to be new and different. Although I had spent much of the summer going over the new material, and I was excited about the prospect of team teaching, I was still nervous.

As I pulled out of the driveway I tried to pray, as I usually do on my way to school, but that morning my mind seemed numb. All I could say was "Help! What did I get myself into?"

I flipped on the radio and headed for the highway. A few minutes later, as I rounded a bend in the road, I saw the rainbow. Seeming to touch the ground on both sides of the highway, it spanned upward to form a bright arch overhead. Spectacular! The brightest, most perfectly formed rainbow I had ever seen.

My mind went back to the story of the first rainbow. Noah and his family were facing a tough situation—much worse than mine. The world they had known had disappeared. Nothing remained—no houses, no familiar landmarks, no people, nothing. I faced a new work environment, but they faced a whole new world! They had to start all over, with no instruction manual to guide them. They couldn't even return to the familiar surroundings of home at the end of the day. Talk about scary!

But in the midst of that impossible situation, God gave them a visible sign of His presence and control. That sign, the rainbow, wasn't just a onetime occurrence; and the promise wasn't just for Noah. It was for me, too. The God who helped Noah start all over again was with me, too.

Now whenever I see a rainbow I am reminded not only of God's promise never again to destroy the earth by flood, but also of His promise "I will never leave you nor forsake you" (Joshua 1:5). No matter how challenging or formidable something appears, I know I don't have to face it alone. And neither do you!   SUZANNE HAYFORD

AUGUST 28

Sandbar Reflections

Those who seek the Lord lack no good thing. Ps. 34:10, NIV.

How could a day be more perfect than this one? The sky was blue and the ocean was calm. I was with friends. The tide was out, and the conditions were just right for collecting shells. The four of us had gone by boat to an island near a very good shelling area. I should have been purring like a kitten in my satisfaction, but I wasn't.

The water was about knee-deep and the current was strong, making it very difficult to walk. My physical vulnerability became a curse to me again, as it had many times before. My knees are sick. I hate it, I fight it, but it's a fact of life that at times is hard for me to accept. Even after major surgery it is very difficult for me to climb stairs or walk distances.

I couldn't keep up with the others. One of my friends lingered to stay near me. Then I felt guilty, knowing I was keeping her from having a good time. I felt very sad. In fact, I felt like crying. Here God had given me this wonderful opportunity to be at the ocean, and my legs weren't strong enough to allow me to look for shells. Finding a sandbar that protruded from the water a bit, I sat down on it to rest and to pray.

I told God about how sad I felt, and He answered me immediately. He didn't speak out loud, but I heard His answer in my heart. It was as if He told me, "Look close by you. You don't have to go a long way to be satisfied." I looked up from my prayer and saw exactly the kind of beautiful shell I'd been seeking—the sunray venus. I stood up, walked a few feet, and picked it up. Then I saw more and more of them lying in the sand. To me, these delicate shells look like butterflies with bands of pink or violet radiating from the center like rays of sunshine. Often the interior is buttercup yellow. I love to stroke my cheek with this shell and feel the porcelain-like texture. The sunray venus is one of the many things in nature that causes me to approach my Creator with awe and reverence as I think about how He tends to such detail. What a delightful God we have!

I learned that day that I should be content with what is at hand, for often the best reward is right under my nose. It's not always necessary to stretch oneself to bigger and better challenges. I also learned that God cares about what I care about. Today, please remember that He cares about what you care about also!

Barbara Huff

August 29

Judgment Day

For God so loved the world that he gave his one and only Son, that whoever believes in him shall not perish but have eternal life. For God did not send his Son into the world to condemn the world, but to save the world through him. Whoever believes in him is not condemned, but whoever does not believe stands condemned already because he has not believed in the name of God's one and only Son. John 3:16-18, NIV.

How could we ever pass? I groaned, examining six pages of minutiae just received over the fax, little details on which our clinic would be judged the next week. Debbie, at one of our state insurance companies, had phoned that quality control would be over in a few days to inspect our office. I asked her for a list of criteria by which we would be judged. Now I examined the list she had faxed me. Some of the items I had never heard of. Some we never attempted to do, such as having a living will on file for each patient. I shuddered at the "legibility" requirement. Our doctors' handwritten notes often take patience, persistence, and good luck to translate.

I set to work in earnest to try to comply with all the regulations, working especially hard on the items that we were needing. Our employees were also concerned. I reassured them that the insurance company wanted our business. They found few doctors who were willing to accept the state insurance, so they could not be overly harsh. Nevertheless, I felt as though this was judgment day. Would we pass? I knew there was no possible way we could prepare well enough to meet all the criteria. Would these state auditors grant us grace and pass us?

Suddenly I remembered another audit. I was aghast at the minute criteria upon which I would be evaluated:

"Whosoever hateth his brother is a murderer" (1 John 3:15, NIV).

"Thou shalt have no other gods before me" (Ex. 20:3, NIV).

I groaned and trembled with foreboding; then I remembered that the Auditor wants me to pass. He died for that very purpose. My strenuous efforts to meet the criteria will never be good enough. His grace is the only way I can possibly meet the criteria for the judgment.

RUTH WATSON

AUGUST 30

"And the Door Was Shut"

And the door was shut. Matt. 25:10, NIV.

Carrying a basketful of diapers and baby clothes, I stepped outside onto the back porch. A strong gust of wind slammed the door behind me. I quickly pinned the clothes to the lines and turned to reenter the house. The door was locked, and my baby was asleep inside the house!

Fearing the worst, I prayed, "Lord, please let the front door be unlocked so I can get inside before my baby awakes." Hot tears stung my eyes as I ran around to the front of the house. Our three small children were enjoying their sandbox, but quickly climbed out and ran along behind me. The front door was locked!

"What if Orvie wakes up?" they asked me.

At that moment I could imagine how the five foolish virgins must have felt when they attempted to enter the wedding hall, but "the door was shut"!

None of our neighbors were home. My husband, a letter carrier, was at work. He couldn't be reached by telephone and wouldn't be home for eight hours. In desperation the three children and I huddled together on the front doorstep.

"Dear God," we prayed, "please help us get inside before the baby wakes up."

I worried that when she awoke she would try to climb out of her bed and fall.

We stood up, and the children crowded around, watching intently as I tried turning the knob, as I had done a number of times in the past hour. This time the door swung open! Praise the Lord! The children jumped up and down, joyously clapping their little hands. The Lord had answered our prayers.

When the five foolish virgins were shut out, the door did not re-open for them. What a contrast!

Lord, help me surrender to You daily so I won't be shut outside when You come.   MABEL ROLLINS NORMAN

AUGUST 31

A Stepping-stone

But he that glorieth, let him glory in the Lord. For not he that commendeth himself is approved, but whom the Lord commendeth. 2 Cor. 10:17, 18.

*P*lease bless these caring hands,
        which in friendship are outstretched;
            make them ever so gentle and compassionate.
And open these listening ears,
        so another's needs I will sincerely hear;
            then keep in trust what's been revealed and shared.
Let me remember,
        it's not for me to judge or speculate
            as to the reasons and the ways You choose.
Touch and guide these human lips;
        always keep this willing heart in tune,
            and please help me to know what to say and do
                when another through me reaches out for You.
What a wondrous and magnificent gift,
        but a solemn responsibility
            to realize the privilege of being trusted and used.
I pray a stumbling block I'll never be,
        but a faithful friend and steward
            in another's journey, on the pathway leading to

our heavenly home
      a stepping-stone, Lord, if You please.
Sonny's mommy.

DEBORAH SANDERS

God Is Still the Same

But my God shall supply all your need according to his riches in glory by Christ Jesus. Phil. 4:19.

*M*y two children needed special help with some of their school subjects. One needed help in math, and the younger one had difficulty learning to read. I decided to home-school them. But what about my part-time job? The little money I earned was essential. What would my husband say?

I began to pray for guidance. The answer came while I was visiting my sister in Florida. During the church service that weekend, the pastor reminded us of the many things God had done for the children of Israel. And yet whenever another problem arose, they complained. God had delivered them from slavery in Egypt, but they were afraid when the Egyptians came after them. God brought them safely across the Red Sea, but they worried when their food ran out. God fed them manna, protected them from their enemies, preserved their clothes as they crossed the desert, yet they were afraid of the "giants in the land of Caanan."

The pastor continued, "Whenever a problem arises, we need only remember how God has led us in the past. We know He'll be with us once more."

Tears came to my eyes many times as God spoke directly to me. Praise God! I would home-school my children and not worry about my job. God would help me speak to my husband and my boss. It was truly a high day for me. I returned home to plan a school program, not even knowing how things would turn out. I trusted that God would provide.

When I spoke with my boss he told me I could keep my job and work two hours a day. My husband never questioned my decision. And my children got the extra help that they needed.

That's not all! The new clothes I had purchased for my children when I had begun wörking the previous winter were not outgrown until I returned to work two years later.

God is just the same today, just the same!

JOY NORMAN CAVINS

Cleaning Out Cluttered "Brain Closets"

Be still, and know that I am God. Ps. 46:10, NIV.

*D*o you have a closet in your home that you are afraid to open because something might fall out and knock you down? Have you ever been looking for something really special and couldn't find it for all of the clutter?

Recently I was cleaning out a closet and found some forgotten treasures. There was so much clutter that needed to be sifted through that getting to them was not an easy job. I found that I could do without a lot of things I previously thought were necessary. When I was finished I actually had room to move around. Everything was much easier to get to and the important things were back in sight and easy to reach.

Our brains are full of "thought closets." Some closets are filled with thoughts of yesterdays, while others are bulging with plans for tomorrow. Very often I open up a closet of the day's chores at the end of the day, only to find it still disarrayed and spilling over into tomorrow's plans. In this stressful world it is so easy for our brain closet to become cluttered. When this happens we can lose the treasures that are vital to abundant life.

I look forward to a few moments in prayer and devotion each morning so I can clean out the clutter. It helps me keep my relationship with God in clear sight and reminds me that He is always within my reach. It also gives me a new perspective on what is really important and what I can let go of. It is so refreshing to the soul to make room for the treasure of God's presence. To *be still* and know the magnificence of my Lord. TAMMY V. VICE

Divine Protection

The angel of the Lord encampeth round about them that fear him, and delivereth them. Ps. 34:7.

As a teenager I lived in Johannesburg, South Africa, with my missionary parents. To get to the church my father pastored, we had to pass through a dangerous section of an African township. Father had warned me of the danger for a young woman walking alone in this area.

One Wednesday evening Father and I had walked together to the church for prayer meeting. At the end of the meeting, much to my dismay, my father called a church business meeting. That meant for two hours I would have to remain at the church with nothing to do. I wanted desperately to return home, so I begged my father to allow me to walk home by myself, since there was still some daylight. Reluctantly he consented, and I was on my way.

Prayerfully, and with a quickening step, I made my way across the township and was almost through when I was accosted by a large man. As I fought him with my waning strength my desperate cry to God for help formed an appeal to the ear that is never too heavy that it cannot hear.

Out of nowhere a well-dressed man appeared and stood staring intently at my assailant. When my attacker saw this man, he released his grasp on me and ran for his life. Greatly relieved, I turned to thank the stranger for his timely appearance, but I was alone—the man had already gone. I have no doubt that the God of heaven delivered me by angel power.

This world is controlled by Satan and filled with sin. I don't know why God sometimes intervenes when His children cry out to Him, and why sometimes He does not, but I know I can trust Him. He had to stand by and watch His only Son be tortured and killed on Calvary so that we could be saved. Whatever He allows me to go through, I know He will give the strength to endure, and that somehow, sometime, He will cause something good to come out of it.

CELIA M. CLEVELAND

The Path

I am the light of the world. Whoever follows me will never walk in darkness, but will have the light of life. John 8:12, NIV.

It had been a stressful week, and relaxing for a few days while camping among the tall pines in the mountains was just what I needed. My friends and I carefully checked out the camping spots for just the right place to pitch our tent. One of our trio was a city girl, and this was her first time to sleep in a tent, so we wanted everything to be just right. Finally we found the ideal place, nice and level, with no humps and bumps, and most important to me, close to the toilet facilities.

We enjoyed watching the squirrels as they scampered across the ground and up a nearby pine tree, chattering all the while as they seemed to be scolding us for invading their territory. As we looked about us, the marvels of nature could be seen on every side.

The restroom building was only about 50 feet from our campsite, straight ahead through the trees. During the daytime it seemed so easy to go back to our tent. After dark was a different story. Although I thought I was following the path straight toward our tent, I always managed to stumble over bushes and logs, ending up down the hill in the wrong area. After several mishaps I finally started carrying a flashlight with me.

My camping experience is so much like everyday life. We think we know the way and don't need any help. But soon we find ourselves wandering in darkness and confusion. Sometimes it takes several of these experiences before we realize that we've forgotten to take Jesus with us as our guide. As we remember to follow Him we need never walk in darkness, but will have the Light of life to help us reach our heavenly destination.   BETTY ADAMS

My Father Knows Best

The Lord will keep you from all harm—he will watch over your life; the Lord will watch over your coming and going both now and forevermore. Ps. 121:7, 8, NIV.

Three months on the Hawaiian island of Kauai! It was like a dream come true. I could already see the palm trees swaying in the breeze. I could hardly wait to get away from graduate school for the three months of summer vacation.

Alas, my hopes were quickly dashed when the traveling nurse agency called to inform me that the dates needed for this position did not coincide with my availability dates. However, the agency had another wonderful position in Orlando, Florida.

Well, I thought, *maybe I won't have the chance to enjoy Kauai's sun this time, but I probably could meet an alligator or two this summer!*

Again, the plan did not come through, for different reasons over which I had no control.

The same happened with the plan to go to San Antonio, Texas.

I was very discouraged. The agency workers convinced me that I could get to those places, but doors kept closing on me. In the meantime I had already arranged to move out of the house that I shared with my roommate. But where to?

I was depressed and angry that God did not want to cooperate with me and my plans that I had brought to Him. Why did He open the door slightly and then let it slam in my face? I called my parents for emotional support and was reminded that God has reasons we might not know about yet.

In the next couple days another window of opportunity opened for work at the home health agency in a city an hour away, along with an invitation to stay with my sister and her husband for the next three months, close to work.

As time went by, I got to see that this arrangement was the best for me. Being in the area, I could look for and secure an apartment for September when I needed to go back to school. As it turned out, that summer brought severe hurricanes to the island of Kauai and the state of Florida. Many lives were lost, and properties were damaged. I've wondered what would have happened to me if I had been in one of those places during that terrible time. It certainly would have been very frightening!

My heavenly Father knows what's best for me, and I thank Him for His steadfastness and loving protection. When things don't turn out the way you want after you've asked the Lord's guidance in the matter, don't despair. Believe that God has something better for you. The Lord is our protector; in Him we can trust.   HILDA LIMONGAN

The Small Brindle Cow

My brothers, as believers in our glorious Lord Jesus Christ, don't show favoritism. Suppose a man comes into your meeting wearing a gold ring and fine clothes, and a poor man in shabby clothes also comes in. If you show special attention to the man wearing fine clothes and say, "Here's a good seat for you," but say to the poor man, "You stand there" or "Sit on the floor by my feet," have you not discriminated among yourselves and become judges? James 2:1-4, NIV.

During a recent drive through the countryside I came upon an interesting dilemma. A mixed herd of cattle browsed beneath a large oak tree. A small brindle cow stood out in a clearing, quite alone, gazing in the direction of the group under the tree. As I watched her, she walked toward them. For some unknown reason, they suddenly scattered, leaving her all alone again. A rhythmic story grew in my mind, playing out similar situations I have witnessed in human life.

Was a breeze on the meadow, and a breeze crossed my brow
The first time I saw her: the small brindle cow.
So different she looked.

Just minding her manners, her nose in the clover,
Other cows stood nearby her, seldom cared to look over,
So different she seemed.

Her odd little coat with colors like marble,
Made me ask the next question, "What mix caused the marble?"
I tried not to stare.

Does it go all the way through? Does chocolate cream rise?
Or is it quite true beneath color or size
They're all just the same?

Reminds me of people, so different and such,
With colors and types, we're afraid: *do not touch.*
So different they seem.

But under the wrapper, beneath jackets and ties,
When hearts rule brave heads, a new thought to the wise:
We're mostly the same.

More alike than we're diffr'nt, although not quite like me.
Like the small brindle cow, even though I can't see,
Underneath we're the same.

More alike than we're diffr'nt: some in pain try to cope,
All seeking to find life, beauty, truth, hope;
God loves us the same.

JUDI WILD-BECKER

SEPTEMBER 7

Mr. Stone Face

Give ear and come to me; hear me, that your soul may live.
Isa. 55:3, NIV.

I scanned the faces of the audience as I moved toward the microphone. Mentally reviewing my opening remarks, I smiled inwardly. I loved doing these workshops. It seemed that no matter how many I had previously conducted, each one was a new thrill and a challenge. It was fun to watch the expressions on the faces of the participants as they asked questions and interacted with me.

I heard myself beginning to speak as I focused on the sea of faces before me. Then I saw him: Mr. Stone Face. He was sitting in the back row on the left side. His body language screamed at me. His arms were folded across his chest; his face expressionless. I understood the message: "I don't want to be here, and I'm not interested in what you have to say."

OK, Mr. Stone Face, I thought to myself, *let's see what we can do with you.*

My workshop was on disability awareness, and I was there to educate employees on how to interact comfortably with people who have disabilities. As the audience roared with laughter over one of my humorous illustrations, I glanced at Mr. Stone Face. He didn't move.

For the next hour and a half, our group explored common misconceptions about people with disabilities, attitudinal barriers, usage of correct terminology, and the practical how-to's of positive interaction. I marveled at their openness and enthusiasm, but I kept thinking about Mr. Stone Face. How out of place he was with this group! I noticed when he unfolded his arms and shifted in his chair. For a brief moment we made eye contact, and I wondered if he might be listening.

I'm giving you all I have, Mr. Stone Face. It's up to you now.

A few minutes later as the workshop was dismissed, I saw Mr. Stone Face walking toward me.

"I just wanted you to know I didn't want to come to this today," he said. "But my boss said I had to. Now I'm glad I did. I learned a lot. Thanks."

O, God, how many times am I a Mrs. Stone Face? You talk and give illustrations. You explain, use humor, and rephrase when I don't understand. You give all You have: energy, knowledge, time. And I sit with an expressionless face, arms folded across my chest. Thank You for persevering with me. Please keep talking until I listen.

JOAN BOVA

SEPTEMBER 8

God, Where Are You?

The Lord is in his holy Temple; let everyone on earth be silent in his presence. Hab. 2:20, TEV.

*S*ome years ago when our hospitality group was going through the Bible looking for hospitality verses, it became a challenge for me to find hospitality in those books of the Bible when others could not find any. After reading through the whole book of Habakkuk (which is a rather doom-and-gloom book), I found this one jewel of a hospitality verse. This confirmed my view that God's hospitality is spread through every book of the Bible.

About this same time my husband lost his job of 12 years and was out of work for two and a half years. Our lives seemed totally turned upside down. I found myself making decisions that I never dreamed I would have to be making. He was going through depression and extreme discouragement and was in no condition to see beyond his own predicament. But life goes on, so somebody had to keep things rolling, and that lot fell to me. All the things that had been secure in our lives up to that point were gone. We had one another, and that was about all.

We sold our house and stayed a few months with our son and daughter-in-law while waiting to get into another place. I found that I could still share hospitality with visitors to our church and didn't have to cook! Preparing simple meals that were tasty and filling but that could be warmed in the microwave and easily served became something that I do to this day.

Sharing what we have, finding peace in our lives when they are turned upside down, is what this verse says to me. God is still in His temple (whether in heaven or in my heart), and everyone is to be silent—no groaning, complaining, sorrowing; just at peace in silence. Though Satan throws our world into chaos and we lose things we once thought were important, God is there, and we can be silent, in peace.

With more and more troubles coming upon this earth just before Jesus comes, I find security in this verse when all other security has disappeared. I see friends, acquaintances, and other people all around me suffering with different kinds of losses. Some suffer the loss of a loved one, loss of health, loss of a business, loss of a job. There is no peace or safety or security in this world except in God. Thank God that He is always near to each one of us through all our trials, suffering, and times of hopelessness.   PEGGY HARRIS

SEPTEMBER 9

Saving for a Doll

If you . . . know how to give good gifts to your children, how much more will your Father in heaven give good gifts to those who ask him! Matt. 7:11, NIV.

*M*y mom was basically the stable one in the family as far as making ends meet, but unfortunately, it took a lot of effort most of the time. Extras such as toys just were not high on the list of important needs.

Like all little girls—and grown-up girls, as well—I loved to look in the stores. On one of my trips through town I decided to go looking at the toys in one of the department stores. What caught my eye was the most adorable doll. It looked just like a real baby, and even felt like one. It cost $4.95, which by today's standard is pretty reasonable, but for me with nothing but holes in my pockets it was a prohibitive amount of money.

One thing that I had in my favor was persistence. Purchasing that doll became my number one objective. I helped my brother collect newspapers for which a recycling company gave us a pittance. Little by little, my hoard of money began to grow. Sometimes I would hitchhike to school with my brother, and that way I could save my bus fare. (Mom never knew about that.) One of my uncles gave me $1.00 for my birthday.

Finally the day arrived when I had $4.95 in my purse. I could hardly wait for school to be over that day so I could go to the department store and make my purchase. All day long the anticipation was there, the excitement that soon I would have the baby in my arms and it would be my very own.

School was finally over. I headed for the store and found the baby and carried her to the cash register. When it was my turn I emptied my purse of its dollar bills and many pennies, nickels, dimes, and a few quarters. I did have $4.95. But when the clerk rang up the amount, it wasn't for $4.95; it was for $5.20. I thought for sure there had been a mistake. I was very polite and told her that the dolly was only $4.95. She agreed, but then told me about sales tax. That was more than I could comprehend. No one had told me that I would need more money for tax. I was heartbroken. Little girls of 6 don't quite understand about giving the government its share of their money.

I had been very patient about waiting to get this dolly by saving up the money all by myself. But with victory in sight my patience was over, and I did the most natural thing for a little girl to do—I cried. I wanted to take that dolly home with me now. I didn't want to wait longer while I tried to save more money.

Someone in the checkout must have felt the same way I did. He wanted me to have that dolly. Or perhaps he was in a hurry and just wanted to get me through the line so he could go on with his business. While I was trying to be a brave little girl, he handed the clerk the quarter I needed to complete my purchase.

Baby Nancy was part of my life for many, many years. My daughter even enjoyed her.

I have thought of that kind person many times. I have thought how I would like to be able to bring joy to someone just as he brought joy to me that day. It was just a small act on his part, but for me it was a magnificent gift.

Isn't that just like Jesus? He sees our need and is there with out-stretched hands waiting to help us. Sometimes we don't even see our need until it is too late, but He is there waiting to share with us all the blessings and benefits He has for each of us.

ANITA WAKEM JACOBS

A New Song

I will never desert you, nor will I ever forsake you. Heb. 13:5, NASV.

I had lost my mother. I had lost my job. My brother and sisters had been placed in an orphanage. Now I was a struggling student literature evangelist. I felt totally alone. I had lost the song in my heart. Desperate for a sense of God's presence and love, I rose early. I hoped no one would waken and wish to join me. This was a private journey. I entered the dark woods without any qualms. Having explored the area the day before, I knew where I was going. Somehow God seems nearer in the first rays of dawn, especially in the quiet beauty of nature. There one can pour out his or her troubles, hurts, and sorrows to a loving and interested Saviour. There jangled nerves are soothed while one talks to God, and hears Him answer.

With reverent steps I crossed the small clearing that was laden with pine needles. I sat on a large rock near the cliff's edge and shivered, more from anticipation than from the cool breeze that whispered God's secrets of the morning in my ears. The grasses heard too; they rustled the news to the flowers. In exultation, the flowers nodded and whispered it across the breezes to the pines. The pines swayed to and fro until their song became a mighty crescendo.

My heart responded. I stood and swayed gently in rhythm with the pines. I sang out praises to God. The winds picked them up, carrying them to the valley below.

"Hel-loo-ooo!"

I leaned forward to catch the sound rising from the valley.

Someone in the darkness had heard my praises on the wind and called out to me.

Embarrassed, I sat in silence. Then, as I watched the first peep of sunrise, I realized my praise had reached someone below. Perhaps it was a ray of light in his spiritual darkness; an encouragement. Perhaps, like me, he had some burden that needed lifting. As I contemplated that possibility, my own burden was lifted and forgotten, replaced by awe and reverence.

A new song! I came there to cry out my heartaches to God. He heard my cry before it was uttered, and sent me a blessing. My response to Him had glorified God and possibly lifted another's weary soul.

I was no longer alone. I felt angels near. I heard the rustle of their wings. Their voices played music in the sighing of the pines. All of nature whispered to my heart, "God is near."

EMILIE ROBERTSON

SEPTEMBER 11

Angel Chauffeur

Now I know without a doubt that the Lord sent his angel and rescued me. Acts 12:11, NIV.

*O*n a clear Sunday morning I got up early to make a journey I had often made from my home. I was driving about 40 miles to London to visit a friend, a professional hairdresser working at home. We would chat, have lunch together, and then she would perm my hair. I would leave feeling like a new woman, having enjoyed a pleasant outing and wearing a new hairstyle.

But well-planned days can sometimes spring surprises on us. Out of nowhere a speeding driver cut directly into my path on the almost-deserted highway. Swerving suddenly—and too sharply—to avoid slamming into the rear of the car, I spun my own car out of control and went careening back and forth across three lanes of roadway. I battled with the steering wheel as I watched the central barrier, then the concrete embankment, speeding toward me.

There was no time to formulate any prayer, but the thought *O, God! My poor motherless children!* flashed through my mind. A pair of hands, stronger and steadier than my own, took control of that steering wheel and brought the car to a standstill, right way up and facing the right direction, on the shoulder of the road.

I was still shaking like a leaf when a passing motorist pulled up to check on me. She expected to see me badly injured and shook her head in disbelief. "You are very lucky!"

But I know it was more than luck. It was the angel of the Lord sent to protect me and my family. Since that occasion I have had many experiences of God's presence and intervention in my life, though not always as dramatic and immediate, that were the result of prayer and trust in Him. True, there have been ups and downs and times when I am tempted to doubt Him, but thank God I have experiences such as these to look back on and gain courage from.

Let us continue to trust Him, to look to Him, and to encourage one another until He comes to take us to be with Him.

ANN CASTELLINO

SEPTEMBER 12

As Gold Is Tried

Yea, though I walk through the valley of the shadow of death, I will fear no evil: for thou art with me; thy rod and thy staff they comfort me. Ps. 23:4.

I had been working in the yard with my family that hot September day. I went inside exhausted. Everyone else decided to go to bed, but I wanted at least to wash my hands and face before going to sleep. After washing up I was feeling dizzy, so I sat down on the side of the tub. Suddenly the entire room burst into flames, igniting the clothing I was wearing. When I realized what was happening, I started to scream, waking the rest of the people in the house.

By this time the clothes on my body had burned off. So I grabbed a sheet off the couch and ran outside, screaming for help. Seconds after all of us got outside, the fire hit the main gas line, and our home exploded like an atomic bomb.

Many things have happened in the years since. During that time I have found that God always walks beside us, especially during trials. We all escaped. I was the only one who suffered physical injuries. During the time when I barely clung to life, God continuously showed His love, mercy, and miracle-working power. Thank You, Father, for sparing my life so many times. What a wonderful God we serve.

JANICE M. CARVER

Blessed Are the Unique in the Lord

My grace is sufficient for thee: for my strength is made perfect in weakness. 2 Cor. 12:9.

*D*o your looks, height, and weight affect the way you feel about yourself, about the way you act toward those you love, and even toward those you relate to in public? Can an individual who is radically different physically, in a world based upon norms, have an identity that is of value to herself and that is accepted by those around her? What is the true essence of character that makes us who we are?

For me, it is my identity as a daughter of the living God. You see, because of a rare bone condition and more than 500 fractures, I am a very tiny woman in a wheelchair. I sure don't fit into the standard norm for body symmetry. And when I look into the mirror I wonder with awe, as I contemplate God's goodness, how His "strength is made perfect in weakness."

Oh, how Job is a man of my own heart and soul! Twenty-two years ago when I started to read the Bible, Job helped me tremendously in getting a handle on my uniqueness. He writes, "Though he slay me, yet will I trust in him: but I will maintain mine own ways before him" (Job 13:15). The word "maintain" in the Hebrew language means "to argue, or prove." Do you ever argue with God? I do, daily, but through it all I recognize that eternal justice is at work, and no one gets away with anything. In time, all will be made clear.

So many things seem so unfair! I think again of a text by my friend Job. "Seeing his days are determined, the number of his months are with thee, thou hast appointed his bounds that he cannot pass" (Job 14:5). We all have so many days to prove that Jesus Christ will see us through whatever Satan may throw at us.

I have overcome the limitations of my micro-mini size (less than four feet tall) and 4-year-old physical strength. For Him I continue to make a statement before all I meet that His strength is "made perfect in weakness." I am a teacher and a reading specialist. I drive a van. I have flown in several airplanes, traveling Europe. I garden and camp and write. I know, and I am telling you, "Blessed are the unique in the Lord!"

"Eye hath not seen, nor ear heard, neither have entered into the heart of man, the things which God hath prepared for them that love him" (1 Cor. 2:9). Among His many other surprises, we will get new bodies. No more flab or extra curves; just the right form and design to suit us!

The ultimate gift will be to meet Jesus Christ and say thank You to Him for making the plan of salvation possible and giving us our blessed hope, even in the light of uniqueness.   CHRISTINE CURTIS

I'm Free!

So if the Son sets you free, you will be free indeed. John 8:36, NIV.

It is amazing how God sends us revelations when we least expect them. But they certainly enrich our lives and leave memories that linger on to encourage us.

Cheryl sat with Daddy and Todd in the fifth pew from the front, just as they did each week when they came to the small, country church. Because there was a paucity of musicians, Mommy played the organ week after week, and this week was just the same.

Then the chorister stood up, faced the congregation, and said, "Let us sing with joy the lovely chorus 'I'm Free!' In Christ we are all free, aren't we?"

For Cheryl, this was a real problem. Hadn't she had her third birthday party only a few weeks ago? What was that chorister saying? He just did not make sense! Before Daddy could take in his little daughter's action, let alone respond, Cheryl was out of her seat, trotting down the aisle, calling out to everyone she passed on her way to Mommy, "I'm free! You're not free! I'm free!"

Mommy, who had played only two chords, stopped the music, scooped Cheryl into her arms, and whispered loudly enough for most of the congregation to hear, "Of course, you're 3, sweetie! Everyone here is happy for you to be 3. Now everyone is going to sing about it, OK?"

It was OK. It was very OK as Cheryl stood beside her mommy at the organ and sang "I'm free!" with all her might, a huge smile and sparkling eyes enchanting the congregation.

In Christ I'm free, and so are you. What a reason to rejoice! We may all be free from the guilt of sin and free to grow in grace in the Lord Jesus Christ. We are free to take our burdens to the foot of the cross and nail them there. Ah! That's really being free!

URSULA M. HEDGES

A Beautiful Sight

Then I saw a new heaven and a new earth, for the first heaven and the first earth had passed away. Rev. 21:1, NIV.

*M*any years ago when I was a young worker with no vehicle of my own, I had a kind and caring boss who took me to and from work each day. Most days one or two others rode along. My boss lived outside one town, the rest of us lived in a second town, and we all worked at the courthouse in a third town. Between towns we drove through miles of country.

One afternoon on the way home, my boss was gazing out his window and chatting amiably as we rode along. "It's a beautiful sight," he mused, "if you look far enough."

Turning to see what he was referring to, I saw a span of dun-colored grass stretching from the edge of the road to the bank of the river in the distance. But beside the river a regiment of cottonwoods proudly displayed the delicate silver tracery of their leafless branches. And far beyond the trees the majestic Sangre de Cristo Mountains of the Rocky Mountain range glowed with various hues of purples, fuchsias, and magentas as they reflected the glory of the descending sun. Some of the peaks wore snowcaps at rakish angles. Indeed, it *was* a beautiful sight—if one looked far enough, if one looked beyond the monotonous dun of the dry grass to the silver trees and the glowing mountains.

Life is like that. If we look beyond the cares and distractions, the hardships and suffering and violence, and lift our eyes to heavenly realms and eternal realities, the view is breathtakingly beautiful. But we *must* look far enough. In doing so we will be inspired and strengthened to be faithful while we wait for our King to come and escort us to the kingdom whose glory we behold by faith.

MARIA A. BUTLER

Frosting on the Cake

So don't worry at all about having enough food and clothing. . . .
Your heavenly Father already knows perfectly well that you need
them, and he will give them to you if you give him first place in
your life and live as he wants you to. So don't be anxious about
tomorrow. God will take care of your tomorrow too. Live one day
at a time. Matt. 6:31-34, TLB.

It was a time of great financial stress. My husband's reassign-
ment as a principal meant leaving our condominium in the
Southwest for a move hundreds of miles to the north. That meant
not only continuing payments on the condo until it sold, but paying rent at our new location. In addition, our son was to enter the
nearby Christian boarding academy.

In the past I had always been able to find employment as a secretary. Our new hometown (population 5,000) published a weekly
newspaper. Each week I eagerly scanned the ads; and week after
week there was nothing for which I was remotely qualified.

At last an ad appeared for a secretary at a school. I knew I was
qualified for that position. Eagerly I clipped the ad; but when the
day arrived for the interview I could not find the tiny notice. We
tried to find the school anyway, and must have checked a dozen
school sites that evening. Each was dark and deserted. Tears of
anger and frustration overflowed. How could I have been so careless? Did I even dare to ask God for further help?

"Maybe God has something better in mind for you," my husband suggested gently.

I found little comfort in his words; still, we continued to pray
about the situation. It was becoming increasingly urgent that we secure additional income.

Weeks later another advertisement appeared: "Part-time clerical
help, temporary; $4.25 per hour." The address was a health clinic.
When I went for the interview I discovered that the interviewer, the
chief executive officer of the clinic, was a woman from my own church.

"I was hoping you would come," she smiled.

That dear woman made a special trip to our apartment after
hours that evening to tell me I had been selected to fill the position.
"By the way," she said, "we are really behind just now. Would you
be able to work full-time for a few weeks?" Those few weeks turned

into two and a half years of full-time employment under the direction of this wonderfully kind Christian employer.

Now when I am tempted to worry about the future, God brings this incident to my mind. Not only did He provide the bread and water we so sorely needed, He gave us cake—with frosting!

DOREEN KITTO CLARK

SEPTEMBER 17

Cookies

So overflowing is his kindness toward us that he took away all our sins through the blood of his Son, by whom we are saved; and he has showered down upon us the richness of his grace— for how well he understands us and knows what is best for us at all times. Eph. 1:7, 8, TLB.

I enjoy baking cookies. All types of cookies—chocolate chip, peanut butter, chocolate, sugar, oatmeal—the list goes on. Whenever my husband has a meeting at work at which he needs to provide that "special touch," homemade cookies are requested. There are even times when my husband's employer has called to ask for a basketful of cookies for a particularly important meeting.

My children call from school to say they are coming home for the weekend. Their parting words are "Please make us some cookies to take back." Of course, I can't stop at only two or three dozen cookies. I have to go all out, and end up baking 10 to 15 dozen of these tasty morsels.

Baking cookies for others is my way of giving them something of myself. I always hope they realize I care about them and what they are doing. Whether the group is a dozen power-wielding businesspeople or the fellows on the second floor of the dorm, I send them cookies as an extension of me.

God is like this. He doesn't send us cookies, but He does send us grace. Again and again we ask Him for that extra-special goodness that only He can conjure up. God's grace is His way of touching us. He gives it to us in many ways. That special touch on our shoulder from our husbands; our children calling from school just to say hi; the girlfriend who knows when to send us a note that says "I care"; the flowers that bloom outside our doors—so many different recipes for grace. God freely gives us an extension of Himself so we might enjoy His love.

Bake a dozen cookies for someone you care about!

SUSAN CLARK

Needs Supplied

His bread will be supplied, and water will not fail him. Isa. 33:16, NIV.

*T*he phone rang on a busy Friday afternoon. As the teacher of the local one-room church school, I was preparing to leave on Sunday for the teachers' convention. I lifted the receiver, and my stomach gave a frantic lurch as I heard the message.

"Hello, Mrs. Ellis? This is the First Interstate Bank calling. Your house has been sold, and the buyers would like possession as soon as possible. How soon can you move out?"

Move! How could we possibly do that with school about to start? Where could we find a house now? The call was not entirely unexpected. Having been unable to find anything else in our new district, we had rented a repossessed house, knowing that it would still be on the market. But we had lived in it for 10 months. A few people had come to look, but none seemed interested. We had begun to feel reasonably secure. Now this!

After hanging up, I prayed, "Lord, You know we have to have a place to live. You know there is a house for us out there. Please help us find it!"

A quick look at the newspaper showed only three houses for rent. One was in an undesirable location. No response on a call to the next. At the third house I left a message on the answering machine.

Sunday morning the phone rang. We made an appointment to see the house on Monday. In a daze I began to pack for teachers' convention.

Soon my husband suggested, "Let's drive out and at least look at it from the outside. Maybe we won't even want it."

We went. It was a two-story frame farmhouse, sitting far back from the road behind a large green lawn. It looked fairly good. We drove by, turned, and slowly started back when, to our surprise, a man coming down the long driveway from the house flagged us to stop. We hadn't expected anyone to be there.

"Are you the people who called about the house?" he asked.

Assured that we were, he went on: "Well, come on in and look at it. Some other people are here right now, and they want it, but just for a year. If you are going to stay longer than that you can have it, but you have to decide right now. I don't want to bother with it again!"

Almost in a state of shock, we made a quick tour of the house, looked at each other, and my husband said, "Write the check!" The living room carpet was even the right color! God had a house waiting for us, ready the *next day* after we needed it! I still faced starting school and moving at the same time, but somehow I knew God would see me through that, too. God had supplied our needs by giving us our own very personal miracle. SYLVIA ELLIS

SEPTEMBER 19

Choices—Choices

Choose for yourselves this day whom you will serve. Joshua 24:15, NKJV.

We crossed the threshold and entered the largest atrium in the world, a 35-story steel-and-Plexiglas tent containing enough activities to keep the average family busy for half a week. The Luxor, touted as a futuristic state-of-the-art hotel with its diagonal inclinators, services hundreds of rooms that cling to the interior pyramid walls like bats hanging from a cavern ceiling.

The down escalator led to a replica of King Tutankhamen's tomb, exactly as it was found in 1922 by a British archaeologist. The perception of afterlife, as represented by the myriad of symbolic artifacts preserved in the various rooms, stood in stark contrast to the values Jochebed and Amram must have taught Moses during his early years. I could just imagine Moses' shock as he made the transition from his Goshen home to Pharaoh's palace. If Tutankhamen's tomb—gold leaf, mirrored, lacquered, ornately carved, ebony and ivory inlay, and precious stones—was any indication, the palace must have been a mind-boggling experience for the young Moses.

A group of tourists stood near us in front of the tomb's anteroom. Their colorful costumes held secrets of a faraway culture. Murmured words floated by on the cooled air. "Moses could have been buried in a similar tomb."

The child looked up and whispered back to the woman, "But he made a different choice."

A different choice. What powerful words. Because of that choice Moses' name is conspicuously absent from the royal chronology. He did not buy into the Egyptian hierarchy and embrace the gold glitter of temporal advantage. That didn't keep him from making some agonizing mistakes. We all do. Nevertheless, when presented with choices of eternal significance, Moses chose the truly valuable.

Outside the pyramid, we waited with the others and watched as the stars came out and took their places, one by one. The sand under our feet was burning hot, the desert air still like a furnace. Nearby, a sphinx and an obelisk leaned against the desert sunset. And then it came. Ethereal, almost imperceptibly at first, the three top stories of the pyramid came alive with the most powerful beacon on earth. According to our guide, one could read the newspaper 10 miles up in space by its light. On a clear night it could be seen from the Los Angeles airport, more than 800 miles away.

What a difference between that underground tomb and the light streaming from the pyramid's apex. As my husband and I strolled toward our convention hotel my resolve stirred anew. I decided to make choices that model the light of God's love and result in behavior that emphasizes eternal values.

ARLENE TAYLOR

SEPTEMBER 20

It's Scary

As a mother comforts her child, so will I comfort you Isa. 66:13, NIV.

I was at the airport waiting for my husband to return from his business trip. Looking out the window, I was amazed at how sinister the sky appeared with heavy black veils of clouds, occasionally shot through by forked lightning accompanied by rolls of thunder. The silent crowd in the arrival area seemed anxious and restless, their gaze on the sky.

A boy, about 2 years old, asked, "Can I go to the window, Mommy?"

His mother smiled and nodded, so the little fellow trotted to the large glass doors. Obviously the view was not sufficient for his curiosity, so he pressed his nose to the glass. Immediately there was a tremendous clap of thunder with a simultaneous flash of lightning. The terrified child ran howling with fear to his mother, who lifted him into her arms, comforting him with hugs and loving words.

Because those waiting for the plane found their personal anxiety diluted by the child's distress, they began to talk to each other. They felt bound together not only by their fears for the safety of the plane's passengers, but by their immediate response to the child's fears.

After a time the little boy was happy enough to stand on the floor again, and as he did so his fascination for the view beyond the glass doors lured him again. Once more he asked his mother's permission to move forward for a better view, and again he ran happily to press his nose against the glass. Immediately there was a terrifying clap of thunder and brilliant lightning. In astonishment he turned, raced to his mother, and hid his face in her skirt before letting out an agonized yell. It was obvious that he thought he had again caused a catastrophe, for as soon as his nose touched the glass this terrible thing happened.

The onlookers were as astounded as the child, and though there was a touch of hysteria to their laughter, there were also teary eyes in response to the child's reactions. Of course the child's actions did not cause the thunder to roar or the lightning to flash, but to his limited understanding, that seemed to be the case.

It is a bit like you and me who try to make sense of the bad things that happen to us and unnecessarily lay guilt upon ourselves, cowering in fear, when if we knew what God knows we would be released and at peace. It is not His purpose that we be scared, for as our heavenly Father He calls us by name, and we can be safe in the comfort of His arms until we have the courage to go out and try life again.

URSULA M. HEDGES

SEPTEMBER 21

A Thousand Ways

My son, give me thine heart, and let thine eyes observe my ways.
Prov. 23:26.

Obtaining spending money while I was a boarding academy student was limited to side jobs I could get cleaning homes, ironing, and doing odd household chores for faculty members. My parents would help out some, but with three daughters in private schools their resources would stretch only so far. I tried to limit my requests for extra funds from them. On occasion my grandmother would write a letter, and usually would enclose a dollar bill. Back in those days that much would help to buy panty hose or other necessities.

On one particular occasion there was a special off-campus skating event coming up. I wanted desperately to go and added up my available resources. I was short one dollar and thought about what to do. I decided to pray and leave the matter to God. I was really testing Him in my heart to see if He would answer. I had decided not to ask for the money from my parents, nor would I borrow it from anyone else.

The weekend of the scheduled event came. On Saturday I left campus for the day with the band for a concert performance out of town. So far no money had come, and I had decided that my last hope would be the mail. Perhaps my grandmother would write and enclose her usual dollar. On Saturday night the mail was handed out, and a list of those receiving mail was taped to the receptionist's window. After returning from the band program, I rushed to the window and checked for my name. When it did not appear, I tried hard to be calm and accept the "No" that I assumed the Lord was giving. As the event was the following day, I saw no further options for an answer.

While I was standing at the window gathering my thoughts and nursing my disappointment, someone behind the window said, "Oh, Sheryl, someone left this for you today." She handed me a brown paper bag.

Inside were cookies and an envelope with a note from my grandparents. And a dollar bill! Fighting tears of joy, I read the note, which said they had come to spend the day with me, not realizing that I was away on a band trip. I could hardly believe my eyes! Instantly I knew that God had heard and answered my prayer. He had worked in ways I hadn't even thought of and cared for me enough to grant such a small request.

As if that weren't enough, a few minutes later a friend came up to me and handed me a dollar bill. She said she had just gotten money in the mail and was returning the dollar she had borrowed from me. My heart could hardly contain the joy. I was eager to share it with everyone. Double what I had asked for, and in ways I hadn't imagined.

That day etched a lasting impression on my teenage heart, and many times since, God has proven even to my adult heart that He can be trusted and will answer according to His will. He has a thousand ways if we'll only fully trust in Him. SHERYL A. CALHOUN

Tornado Warning!

A thousand shall fall at thy side, and ten thousand at thy right hand; but it shall not come nigh thee. Ps. 91:7.

*I*t was a beautiful afternoon, and all the teachers and preschool children were scurrying to prepare for the kindergarten graduation. The final practice was finished, and parents had taken their children home to prepare them for the closing school exercises. The stage was full of tiny chairs and beautifully colored balloons.

Parents, friends, children, and teachers soon filled the building. Suddenly the sirens shrieked loudly on the campus. Security guards rushed through the buildings shouting, "Tornado warning! Take cover!"

Everyone was warned that they had 30 minutes to leave the campus and find shelter. Those who wanted to remain on campus were told where to go for safety. Children with graduation robes and caps ran to their cars with their parents. All other individuals attending the graduation cleared the auditorium and left the campus.

My secretary and I took the refreshments from the auditorium and carried them to the foods laboratory. Fear gripped our hearts as we hastened our pace to unload the food and run to our cars. As we headed toward our homes the tornado, with winds of more than 50 miles per hour, was touching down and destroying many homes as if they were matchboxes. Television stations issued warnings and showed clips of extensive damage. Large trees were ripped from the ground, and several individuals were taken to the hospital with injuries.

In the midst of all this turmoil and destruction, God preserved our campus and all the individuals on it. It is wonderful to know that God is indeed our refuge and strength. Even though we live in a tornado belt, God protected our campus from destruction. Truly, we can say, as did the psalmist David in Psalm 91:2: "He is my refuge and my fortress: my God; in him will I trust."

You too can trust God when the storms of life rage about you. He is always there to deliver you from evil. All you have to do is trust Him for all your needs.   RUTH F. DAVIS

Scary Moments

The angel of the Lord encampeth round about them that fear him, and delivereth them. Ps. 34:7.

Late one night our small poodle awakened us with her feverish barking. It took us no time to discover the problem. Three men with bandannas on their heads stood below our bedroom window, talking together as if they were holding a committee meeting. We immediately called the police, fervently hoping they'd arrive before a break-in took place. Then we kept very quiet and prayed for the Lord's protection.

Before long the men knocked at the front door, then tried all the windows. A sudden crash announced they had broken down the basement door. Thankfully, we had a dead bolt on the door leading from the kitchen to the basement. We called the police again. The dispatcher kept me on the phone, assuring me that the police were approaching our home. The three must have heard us walking around on the level above them and realized that we had called the police. They immediately left the house, got in a car, and sped away.

The police did a thorough investigation, but never found the culprits. We wish they had been apprehended, but the important thing was that we were safe. Truly the angel of the Lord had been present.

Our faith was strengthened in knowing that the Lord can deliver us and take away our fear. The fact that we were protected doesn't mean the Lord will always save us from the evils in this world, but if we trust Him, He will not permit more to come to us than we can bear.

JUNE LOOR

Trust in God's Protecting Care

I am not alone, for my Father is with me. John 16:32, NIV.

After spending two years teaching in Pasay City, a suburb of Manila in the Philippine Islands, I was asked to transfer to Bandung, Indonesia.

I found Bandung to be a delightful place with beautiful scenery and a comfortable climate that I called "forever spring." However, I was soon informed that a single, foreign teacher had been murdered one night shortly before I arrived.

In the Philippines missionaries lived on a compound surrounded by a wall, and had guards on duty all day and all night. Not so here. My nearest missionary neighbors lived two or three blocks from me. I had no telephone and no iron bars on my windows, as some houses had. I became even more worried when one of the missionaries carried sharp, pointed barber scissors as a "weapon" when she walked to my house with me after the evening meal. I was frightened. I confiscated a baseball bat from the classroom to take to bed with me as a weapon. I also left lights on in my living room until late, sometimes even all night.

After more than a week of this I came to my senses. I told myself, "The Lord called you here, and He will protect you!" Back to the classroom went the bat, and the lights were turned off at bedtime, although I did eventually get a watchdog. No harm came to me during the two years I was there.

When we put our trust in the Lord, we do not have to fear what may happen to us.   MARIEDA BLEHM

The Washer and the Toilet

Having then gifts differing according to the grace that is given to us, let us use them. Rom. 12:6, NKJV.

A number of years ago I had the unique opportunity to study in Argentina. After a couple weeks I needed to wash clothes. So I headed to the basement of the dormitory in search of those large, white, openmouthed objects that were just waiting for my dirty clothes. I looked and looked, but the picture of the machine I had in my mind was nowhere to be found. I hastily left the basement to tell the dean that the machines were not there! She assured me that they were there and sent a dormmate with me to the basement.

We approached an object that I had seen during my earlier visit—a wooden barrel with straps and movable wooden parts. The young lady pointed to the barrel and said, "There it is!"

In amazement I watched as she loaded the clothes into the "machine" and secured the door with the straps. I was even more amazed when the whole machine began to rotate and water, coming from parts unknown, began the wash cycle. After a time the machine stopped, and with some trepidation I approached it and removed my clothes. They were all *clean!* This wooden barrel with straps really worked!

Years later I traveled in Europe, visiting seven countries. I saw the familiar sights that people often talked about; however, those sights were not the most impressive part of my trip—the toilets were! In each country the mechanism for flushing the toilet was different. My challenge was to figure out how each country's toilet worked. Once I located the chain, the button, the lever, the handle, the pedal—whatever—I noticed something incredible. All the toilets flushed! Each was different, but each worked!

God has made each of us different, be it by our race, gender, ethnicity, culture, or ability. Each one has different talents, but each functions. Each person works in his or her own way to accomplish goals. Diversity, as I came to believe from these two experiences, is accepting that although people are different, they are all valuable. And we must believe that each person has meaningful contributions he or she can make to our society.

LARITA J. ALFORD

God's Love

As a father has compassion on his children, so the Lord has compassion on those who fear him. Ps. 103:13, NIV.

As a father loves his child,
guides its faltering, baby steps,
when it falls, wipes tears away
and helps it try again,
even so does God love me!
Through my child His love I see.

As a mother gently trains,
helps her children to obey,
nourishes a love for truth
and inspires to kindly deeds,
even so does God help me!
Through my child His love I see.

As a father sadly yearns
over his rebelling child,
welcomes back with open arms,
gladly pardons all mistakes,
even so God pardons me!
Through my child His love I see.

As a mother stops to hear
childish confidences sweet,
listens to each plea for help,
and shares each happiness,
even so does God hear me!
Through my child His love I see.

CARROL GRADY

Servanthood

He that is called, being free, is Christ's servant. 1 Cor. 7:22.

*A*s new missionaries we received much advice about servants. Then Yun-ssi came to our home for six years.
From this little woman, who had never attended school, I learned
about servanthood.

Yun-ssi's failure to bear children had ended her marriage to a
man she loved. Legally, she could claim his subsequent children,
but she chose not to inflict this pain on their mother. Instead, she
poured her maternal instincts on our four children. Her patience
threatened to spoil them.

When I returned from the hospital with our third child, she
said, "I'd hoped you would have twins, one for you and one for me."
No thought of the extra diapers.

As soon as possible, she tied the babies on her back, *obo*-style,
while scrubbing dishes and floors. Bobby's first word was "obo."

Once my husband and I left the country for a month.
Missionary friends volunteered to keep the boys and the baby. Yun-
ssi looked so hurt that we left 2-year-old Beth with her. For even a
matter so minor as diaper rash, Yun-ssi summoned a driver and
took Beth to the missionary doctor.

Yun-ssi apologized for not knowing English. "That's better," we
told her. "You help us learn Korean." Thus, when a child requested
a drink, Yun-ssi repeated the Korean equivalent in a singsong, refusing to comply until asked in Korean. Outside, she made a game
of counting fence posts. She talked as the children helped her cook.
When we didn't understand, she rephrased until we did. She explained Korean culture and interceded for us when we goofed.

If dishes were broken, Yun-ssi simply told me. Never did she
take anything of ours, though our home must have seemed vastly
wealthy. Unpleasant and routine tasks became her ministry. When
the electricity failed, she did the laundry in the creek. She scrubbed
our vinyl floors daily to remove the soot. After days without running
water she cleaned out the toilet cheerfully.

Yun-ssi was always there, the work always done. If she wasn't
sure how something worked, she asked. She didn't put poultry sea-
soning in the apple pie or use a whole can of imported wax on the
floor at once, as some servants did.

Yun-ssi witnessed family flaws that would have made juicy gossip, but instead she showed us in a better light than we deserved.

Her faith was simple, personal, real. She pored over her Bible daily, to read "my Jesus' very words to me," though she'd had only a few childhood reading lessons from a venerable teacher. Her mother had said, "You must learn to read, even though you're a girl."

When our family dragged in late on Saturday nights from missionary socials, hot chocolate awaited us. When we left for furlough during monsoon season with a baby with dysentery, Yun-ssi ironed the diapers dry. When we returned, she couldn't leave her current employer; but every few weeks, after a full day's work, she'd come out by bus—and wash dishes and make cookies as we talked.

Shortly before we left Korea, Yun-ssi saw me and explained, "I won't come to the airport, because I'd cry." Even as she spoke, tears began—and evolved into racking sobs. As she pulled off a sock to stanch the flow, I handed her a wrinkled handkerchief and assured her I understood. But at the airport she tucked the laundered hankie into my hand and followed as far as permitted, tears mingling with hugs. None of us ever doubted that Yun-ssi would have gladly died for us. Hers was real love, real servanthood, real ministry.

Yun-ssi stood in good company. The New Testament alone lists Paul, Timothy, Titus, Moses, James, Peter, Jude, and John as servants of Christ—who Himself took "the form of a servant." Someday I hope to hear, with Yun-ssi, "Well done, My good and trusted servant." MADELINE S. JOHNSTON

SEPTEMBER 28

My Best Friend

I have called you friends. John 15:15, NIV.

As I watched my 9-year-old daughter run with glee into school I saw a reflection of me! I know it's not the reading, writing, and arithmetic she runs to. It's her friends!

I rushed into church with joy and laughter in my heart. But was it God I couldn't wait to reach? No. It was my friends! Oh, how I loved my friends! It was a large church; an orchestra made up of church members, and of course, I played the guitar every week and almost always led the music for any special women's event. And ever important to any mother, the child-care system was well organized and required my participation only once a year. Wonderful!

Then one day during a quiet study of my Bible a still small voice led me to greater truths than I had known. I realized I was worshiping in a church that didn't preach the whole Bible truth. I accepted an invitation to visit a small church with approximately 35 members. It was quiet and too peaceful for what I was accustomed to, but it lined up perfectly with the Bible in theology. I would go home and lie on my kitchen floor, facedown (dramatic, right?), and pray. Sometimes I cried, "Lord! There must be another way! Certainly there must be another church!"

But gently He would impress my mind, *This is the way; walk ye in it.*

I continued to attend both churches. God repeatedly impressed me to read the letter in James that spoke to the heart of the double-minded woman I was becoming. With great dread and reluctance, I chose the church that preached according to His Word. I was re-baptized, and my heart started anew with the hopes of an even closer walk with God.

I grew in the stillness of this tiny church, but I longed for a friend! So I prayed, "Please, God, send me a zealous friend." God sent me Brenda. I was so happy. She was such fun. Once we skipped, arm in arm, down the lane on one of our walks with our children running on tiny legs to keep up with us!

In truth, God has sent me many friends. Through the years, one by one, all my friends have moved away. And for the first time in my sanguine life I feel no need to cry out, "Lord, will You send me a friend?" No, I have no inclination to pray this prayer, because I know He already has. In the past I would rush to phone a friend when anything exciting or troubling occurred. Now I find it easier just to call on Jesus. He already knows all the tedious circumstances of every situation, and were I to call a friend, inevitably we would land on our knees in prayer anyway.

As I take my morning walks He talks with me and helps me to process painful thoughts. He's my counselor. Yes, I realize, I *have* the best Friend. And when I go to church it's not for the people I'll find there. With joy and laughter in my heart I'm so excited to walk into church, and the thought that forms in my mind as I pass through the portal of the open door is *I'm here to see Jesus. He's my Best Friend.*

"What a friend we have in Jesus, all our sins and griefs to bear;
What a privilege to carry everything to God in prayer!
O what peace we often forfeit, O what needless pain we bear,
All because we do not carry everything to God in prayer."

SALLY ETTARI

The Man in the Black Chevy

Pleasant words are a honeycomb, sweet to the soul and healing to the bones. Prov. 16:24, NIV.

One summer when I was a kid growing up in Dover, Delaware, my brother Tom and I started a fruit stand. We visited neighboring farms and picked the vegetables, fruit, and berries that, supplemented by Dad's gifts from our large garden, formed our stock.

Business was good as friends and neighbors, and even passing strangers, stopped to buy our wares. I remember that we made $40 in one week—when the peaches were at their best. Unfortunately, we lost interest in the whole idea after a few weeks—I think it was blackberry season that did us in.

One memory stands out from that summer—stands out from the hot, itchy days in the tomato patch and the sharp smell of Mercurochrome being applied to blackberry bramble scratches. One day a black Chevy pulled up in the dirt at the edge of our front yard, and a tall man wearing a gray felt hat got out. He bought peaches and cucumbers and a dozen ears of corn, chatting pleasantly while Tom and I packed his purchases in an old cardboard box from the grocery store. Then, just before he left, while Tom lifted the box into his trunk, he quietly said to me, "You know, I just can't see why a pretty girl like you would bite her fingernails." Then with a quick smile and a wave he drove away.

As the dust from the big black car billowed around my legs I looked down at my 11-year-old nail-bitten hands. And I never bit my nails again. It may be going a bit far to say that stranger changed my life. But with just a few words he changed something about me.

I often think of that incident—and about the power of words to affect people. I wonder about that man and those few chance words he said. He never knew the effect they had.

And I wonder about my own words and how they affect other people—for good or for bad. Knowing that I sometimes speak without thinking, and that I love to say something that's funny—often without stopping to consider whether it may be hurtful or not—I can only pray daily that the Lord will help me guard my tongue. And more than that, I pray that He will help me know when and how to say words that will be sweet and healing. Words that will influence someone else for good—just as He used the man in the black Chevy to help a young girl break a bad habit a long time ago.

SUSAN HARVEY

SEPTEMBER 30

Of Hats and Decisions

Then these men were bound in their coats, their hosen, and their hats, and their other garments, and were cast into the midst of the burning fiery furnace. Dan. 3:21.

*S*trolling along a beautiful waterfront path with family recently, we came across an old lady with a tanned, wrinkled face, wearing a bright-red hat. She was sitting on the footpath enjoying her soda. Beside her was a shopping cart containing her worldly goods: food, blankets, and clothing. As we passed her by, I thought she looked so lonely and uncared for. I decided that if she was still there when we returned I must chat with her. She was, so I said hello and remarked on the lovely day.

She just looked at me and said, "I like your hat."

I felt I wanted to help her, perhaps direct her to a women's shelter, or just have a friendly chat. No. All she wanted to do was talk about hats. Whether it was a diversionary tactic to keep me from asking questions or that her only interest in life was hats, I couldn't find out. She kept on moving, telling me as she went, that she had lots of hats. Such a fine-looking lady, obsessed with hats.

Can we become so obsessed with the mundane things of life that when someone reaches out to tell us of Jesus' love and the wonderful things He is preparing for us in heaven we choose not to listen, instead talking only about hats?

Daniel and his friends, when confronted with the fiery furnace, were well clothed, as today's text says, even to wearing their hats, but they had chosen to listen to God and were ready to die rather than dishonor Him by following popular trends. Are we as willing to listen, heed, and follow His example?

ALMA ATCHESON

Nester

My soul finds rest in God alone; my salvation comes from him.
He alone is my rock and my salvation; he is my fortress, I will
never be shaken. Ps. 62:1, 2, NIV.

*H*er name was Nester, and she had weathered beneath the
African sun for 52 years. The hot, dry winds that had
dusted her skin in infancy blew her from childhood to womanhood,
and in those relentless breezes she now stood, bent and wrinkled,
but strong as the acacias that clung to the mountains.

While Nester was young and heavy with child, the Christian
mission had been established near her village. A woman who
walked her paths alone, she might never have set foot within their
boundaries had it not been for the consuming scorch of childbirth.
In the throes of pain, the touch of their caring hands was like drops
of water to lips that are parched. Over the next few years she returned again and again to those hands, fighting her way through illness, death, and disaster. Although Nester never attended the
mission classes, with every encounter tidbits of love, peace, and joy
were tucked away for her heart to savor until she became a woman
whose soul was fattened by the crumbs that fell from the table.

With no education and little religious training, Nester touched
the lives of people whose language and ways placed them beyond
the reach of the mission. In quiet faith she lived her testimony, a
beacon of light among the shadows, a sermon to every traveler
whose dusty path brought them near. Though not every heart was
listening, she never stopped believing, never stopped preaching, her
simple testimony all the more eloquent for the power with which
she met her adversity.

It was a hot October wind that whipped the flames across the
grasslands, hurling them over every barrier that stood between
Nester's home and their fury. When the storm at last burned itself
out, Nester returned to the charred heap of rubble that had been her
home. Her granddaughter stood by her side, angry and defiant at
the hardships and injustices of life.

"Grandmother," she spat out, "how can you believe in God
when nothing has ever gone right for you, when everything is
wrong? I believe in what I see, and I don't see God."

Wrapping her sooty black arm around her granddaughter's

shoulders, Nester quietly murmured, "Child, I believe because when I face the future and shake in fear, He pours courage into my heart. When my grief is so strong that I know that I cannot ever smile again, He sends a song to my spirit. When I feel the very sweetness crushed from me so that I cannot arise and face a new day, He breathes life into my soul. You have seen me walk strong for all these years. You have seen the touch of God, and you will now see His hand again."

With those simple words, Nester began to build again.

DEBORAH AHO

Hot Line to God

The eyes of the Lord are on the righteous and his ears are attentive to their cry. Ps. 34:15, NIV.

A friend gave me a music tape of a group she sings with that included the "Operator—information, get Jesus on the line." Somehow I can play that song over and over and not get tired of it.

I worked for some years on a mental health unit and with a voluntary crisis help line. There were some who called us frequently, or were admitted and readmitted to our unit. We all need support and help in our troubles, and some people have no personal help to get through tough times. Many indeed do not have any kind of support. As a nurse, I have been hurt to see the trouble and sadness others have to bear with little help.

One teenage girl said, "I wish you were my mother."

How sad to have no mother at all, or to have one who doesn't have time for you or who rejects you altogether. There were others who called when they were worried or sad. One good friend called long distance when her dog died; another friend called when she discovered her husband was involved with another woman and was leaving her. Many of us have been part of informal support systems, but we don't always have enough time to help our friends who are hurting.

How reassuring to know we have a God who cares—always! We can call His hot line any hour, day or night, and ask for His help.

In Jeremiah 33:3 He says, "Call to me and I will answer" (NIV). We don't even need a telephone; we have a direct line—no operators or answering machines. He is waiting for our calls. He already has the answers ready. I'm so glad that Jesus is on the line!

JULIA PEARCE

Beached!

Thou art my hiding place and my shield; I wait for Thy word. Ps. 119:114, NASB.

*I*t was a much-needed family vacation. The drain of evangelistic meetings, the frenzied packing and unpacking of our move, and the busyness of camp meeting had left me tired, easily irritated, and spiritually empty. But even though we had been at the shore nearly a week, I still felt out of sorts.

I can't continue like this, I silently cried as I walked alone on the beach one morning.

The tide was out, leaving a band of shells and little clams scattered over the sand. Seagulls laughed coarsely as they gobbled down an easy breakfast. How like those clams I felt. Tossed and carried by the waves to where there is no water. So vulnerable to the hungry gulls. Then I noticed something. Many clams had dug deeply into the wet sand, where they would be safe until the tide returned. A few had their syphons sticking up, expecting the water to rush over them again and give them the nutrients and hydration they needed.

That is the way God wants me to handle this time of my life, I decided. So I'm beached. I've taken a few rough tosses by the waves of life and have become easy prey for Satan. But I don't have to stay vulnerable; I can dig deeply into His Word. And I can expectantly claim His promises of life—the living water that cleanses, refreshes, and causes me never to thirst again.

Father, help me to hide in You, where I'll be safe no matter what happens to me. During those times when I feel storm tossed and beached, teach me to trust in Your promises. Like David I'll be able to triumphantly declare, You are my "refuge and strength, a very present help in trouble" (Ps. 46:1, NASB).

LILLY TRYON

OCTOBER 4

God Loves Banquets!

I have eagerly desired to eat this Passover with you before I suffer. For I tell you, I will not eat it again until it finds fulfillment in the kingdom of God. Luke 22:14, NIV.

The town hall student body assembly was in an uproar. The subject on the floor was school banquets. Students sat in orderly rows in the gym, randomly interspersed with faculty members. The missing principal had sent a letter to the student body, via the student body president, the gist of which was that the students could have no more banquets.

As the Student Association president read the letter, I knew why the principal had written it, because the faculty had sat in serious discussion on this subject. Our academy students were used to elegant banquets, catered by nice restaurants, with expensive entertainment after the meals. Because student enrollment was down this year, there were no school finances to supplement money received from the tickets sold. It was the consensus of the faculty that a change was necessary. But I had never dreamed that the principal would choose this way of communicating our decision.

The rumble in the gym became louder as student after student voiced indignation. They resented the fact that the principal had written a letter while sitting in the safety of his office, rather than facing them in person. They decided that the faculty—and the *church,* and maybe even *God*—didn't want the students to have a good time.

Rarely did a teacher speak out in town hall meetings. It was a time primarily for student expression. As the school librarian, I had never even thought of speaking up in a town hall meeting. But I surely wished that *someone,* student or teacher, would add a word of sanity to the rising mob spirit. I felt that God, especially, was being misrepresented.

The next thing I knew, I found myself out in the aisle holding a microphone in my hand, although I had no memory of making a decision to speak, of rising, or of stepping out into the aisle. But there I stood, ready to speak.

"Students," I began, "God *loves* banquets. He has invited all of you to the most glorious banquet ever planned." And I went on to tell about the great banquet Jesus is planning for the redeemed.

The noise in the gym subsided. I took my seat, and the student body president went on to other business. The meeting adjourned quietly, and subdued students went back to classes. The interesting thing to me was that *no one*, either faculty or student, ever mentioned to me my uncharacteristic speech in town hall. It was as though it had never taken place. But the effect remained. I heard no more of the rebellion against the school's restaurant banquet ruling. Other plans were put into effect. Banquets were held in the nearby church fellowship hall, parents and faculty members cooked the meals, and volunteer entertainment was provided.

I have often marveled at the smoothness of the solution. Why did I speak out? Who put those words in my mouth? I usually avoid confrontation at all costs. I feel certain that I was an instrument used by the Holy Spirit that day. I spoke with Holy Spirit power.

My prayer today: Lord, may I be open today to speak for You. Put Your words in my mouth, words that will quiet tumult, end strife, and offer banquets. — CARROL JOHNSON SHEWMAKE

OCTOBER 5

Words in Letters

So also our beloved brother Paul wrote to you according to the wisdom given him, speaking of this as he does in all his letters. 2 Peter 3:15, 16, RSV.

*T*he old folks gathered slowly in the lobby of the retirement center, some leaning on walkers, others resting in chairs. As I watched the group gradually get larger, I couldn't help wondering what the occasion was. After all, what happens at 10:30 on a Tuesday morning at the entrance to a senior citizen home that draws so many people? Too early for lunch. Maybe a bus was coming to take them to the mall.

"Sir," I asked a friendly-looking gentleman, "what are all you folks doing here in this lobby now?"

"The attraction, young lady, is that." He pointed with his cane toward the bank of mailboxes in the wall. "The mail is distributed about 11:00 each day." Then he smiled. "We all want to make sure we don't miss out. I'm hoping for a letter from my daughter. She's about your age . . ."

The aged, the hospitalized, the bedridden, those with disabilities—how they long for letters. Letters to remind them of younger days, of better health, of fulfilling jobs, of family ties. But mostly they yearn for letters to remind them they are still loved. Certain characteristics of letters make them so desirable. More lasting than speech, they can be reread, mulled over, shared, physically handled, compared, preserved, reopened. Cervantes was right: "The pen is the tongue of the mind," giving emotion form, a stay against the impermanence of the world.

But because of these very characteristics, people are hesitant to write. It is, after all, risky business to expose oneself by recording emotion in the permanence of writing.

The apostle Paul knew the characteristics, and hence the value, of letters. Paul, the learned theologian, scholar, and speaker, wrote numerous letters, too—letters communicating divine counsel fraught with love that conveyed advice, hope, and concern.

Yes, life and death are in the biblical letters of Peter, Paul, and John. But then, one letter from you to a friend or relative might give that person the will to live, the desire to continue and struggle.

To show appreciation for the letters of the Bible, why not write a letter or two of hope and love yourself? Peter, Paul, and John would be pleased. So would Jesus.   WILMA McCLARTY

OCTOBER 6

Outward Appearances

And as the Spirit of the Lord works within us, we become more and more like him. 1 Cor. 3:18, TLB.

*E*very year I like to do canning and freezing. It's so fulfilling to open my freezer and see the result of all my hard efforts of gleaning the fields and going from one farm to another. I also feel as though I'm helping the budget.

Last year we had a problem finding corn. This year it was strawberries. Because of the hard blizzard of last winter the blackberries and peaches were almost extinct. When I got some tomatoes, they were big and beautiful on the outside, but once my knife penetrated beneath the skin they turned to water. The same happened, on occasion, with the pears.

I got to thinking about our text today. How often we look at someone and think how beautiful, or how ugly. But praise the Lord,

He alone knows what's on the inside. Neither a person's stature, nor countenance, nor appearance plays a part in His love for us.

JULIE M. LYLES

OCTOBER 7

The Understood Cross

Take up his cross, and follow me. Matt. 16:24.

Following Christ: what does it mean? Some Christians believe they must carry a literal cross to follow Christ, so we hear of people who on Easter Sunday carry large crosses through the streets of their hometowns. To their way of thinking, the ultimate example of following Christ is to participate in the ceremony of crucifixion, hanging on the cross for about 20 minutes.

Others believe that Christ calls them to self-persecution, so they beat themselves or walk many miles on their knees or fast until they faint. Still others bring persecution on themselves by being obnoxious or by creating people problems through poor communication. They perceive themselves as the only ones left who are serving the Lord.

If the cross is to be understood, we must look to Jesus, who bore the cross. Christ lived a life of self-denial and calls us to the same. What is required is something that recurs and is therefore "more difficult than a single heroic act: it is the endurance of ordinary, normal, everyday suffering, which is then most likely to prove excessive. The cross to be borne is therefore the cross of everyday life" (Hans Kung, *On Being a Christian*, p. 577).

Bearing the cares of life, that is the rub. If God wants us to be heroic or extraordinary, we are willing. But what God calls us to is the mundane, the ordinary. The demands of family and work. The promises unkept and dreams unfulfilled.

Christ fought suffering. Can you imagine going back to your hometown and, because you are there, all the sick become well? That happened to Jesus. Could it be that He would do such a work through us? Could we relieve the pain of guilt and anger? of bereavement and disappointment? of discouragement and want?

We must not let the suffering of others pass us by while we remain aloof and refuse to get involved. The example of the good Samaritan is a pattern for all to follow. In the judgment will we hear "Come, ye blessed of my Father" (Matt. 25:34), or will we hear "I never knew you" (Matt. 7:23)? What a shame it would be to have borne our cross on earth and forfeited His crown in heaven. Let us be faithful in that which is least. BARBARA J. HALES

OCTOBER 8

Mildred

And the King shall answer and say unto them, Verily I say unto you, Inasmuch as ye have done it unto one of the least of these my brethren, ye have done it unto me. Matt. 25:40.

*O*ne day my friend Pam was at the grocery store and noticed an elderly woman mumbling to herself as she struggled with her bags. "It is so hard to get my groceries home on the bus," she wearily told Pam.

My friend quickly offered to give her a ride to her house and cheerfully added, "Just call me, and I will be happy to help you with your groceries anytime."

A grateful smile broke across the woman's face. "That's so nice of you. My name is Mildred."

When they arrived at her home in the mobile court, Mildred insisted that Pam leave the groceries on the porch. Pam is not an easy person to dissuade, and managed to carry the bags into the kitchen. When the door was opened, she smelled an unpleasant odor. The next time she brought Mildred home with her groceries she peeked at the rest of the house and saw only clutter and a bare mattress. "Mildred, I am coming back to clean your house for you," she said firmly.

In a few days Pam returned with a bucket of cleaning solvents. She worked hard until the place was clean and tidy, then rushed straight home and into her shower, clothes and all. The job was done. Pam felt good for Mildred and for herself. She started doing Mildred's laundry, taking it home on Thursdays and returning it on Mondays, all folded and clean.

One afternoon Pam was sitting at her desk thinking about Mildred. She had this persistent feeling that she should go visit her, but then she would argue with herself. "I'll be going on Monday with the laundry." Thoughts of Mildred continued to prey on Pam's mind until she gave in and drove to Mildred's mobile home. When she knocked on the door, no one answered. The door was locked. As she stood there wondering what to do, she heard a faint cry. She broke in through the window and found Mildred in a heap on the floor, where she had fallen two days earlier. Pam called for help and arranged for hospitalization. She went home late that afternoon, carrying the cage with Lewis, the bird, in it.

The next day as she was visiting her friend in the hospital, Mildred spoke in a tiny voice and asked, "Pam, will you look after Lewis for me?"

Pam smiled as she replied, "I have already taken Lewis to my home, and he is comfortable and happy. Don't worry about him."

Mildred was in the hospital for some time and was later transferred to a nursing home.

"I think the Lord needs to hit me on the head again and send me another Mildred," Pam grins.

Are there Mildreds waiting for you and me? "Inasmuch as ye have done it unto one of the least of these my brethren, ye have done it unto me."   DESSA WEISZ HARDIN

OCTOBER 9

Squirrels

Wherefore, if God so clothe the grass of the field, which to day is, and to morrow is cast into the oven, shall he not much more clothe you, O ye of little faith? Matt. 6:30.

*D*id you hear that?" I whispered. "It sounds as if someone is in the house!" My husband mumbled something unintelligible. I whispered louder and nudged him. "Did you hear that?"

Startled, my husband sat up in bed, then lay back down and said, "Oh, those are squirrels in the attic."

We had tried everything. We nailed down a patch of loose shingles and covered the spot with wire, but the squirrels found another weak spot to get into the house. We put sticky stuff at the entrance to the hole and later found fur stuck all over the entrance. Then we tried banging on the ceiling. For a while it worked like a charm: the squirrels fled in horror from the attic. But soon they returned, and eventually, banging on the ceiling yielded only a halfhearted move from the squirrels and a lot of plaster on the head for us.

We called the humane society and asked for suggestions on getting rid of squirrels. They had some cages they could lend us to trap the squirrels. We rushed right over. They instructed us to release the squirrels at least 10 miles away from our home, or they would find their way back to our attic.

We set the trap and waited. The next day we found a frantic squirrel in the cage. He fought and rattled the cage all day. When we retrieved the cage, the squirrel's nose and tail were bleeding. He was so preoccupied with getting free that he didn't even notice when we opened the door to let him out. We actually had to empty him onto the ground.

We went home and reset the trap and quickly caught another squirrel. This squirrel fought, but not as frantically as the first squirrel. He injured only his nose. As we rode the 10 miles to the release point, I could hear the squirrel's intermittent efforts to free himself. He scurried off immediately when he was released.

Once again the trap was set. The next day we checked the trap and were surprised to find another squirrel. This one was smaller and calmer than the other two had been, and had no injuries. He lay still as we took the trap to the car. He stood up once to reposition himself in the cage and then lay down. When we released him, he calmly sauntered off.

While in the middle of a personal crisis I sometimes cause myself needless pain. So often the Lord has a door wide open for me to walk through, but I'm so busy fighting with the sides of the cage that I don't see the open door. Time and time again I've promised that the next time something happens, I'll calmly look for the answer and not worry about the situation. Just as many times, I've failed. I still fight with the cage, although these days I'm fighting a lot less!

LaKetia W. Carrell

October 10

The Noisy Dishwasher

But the fruit of the Spirit is . . . peace. Gal. 5:22, NIV.

$\mathcal{I}$ once had a portable dishwasher. It cleaned well and saved me a lot of work, so I was happy to use it. But by and by it started to make an ominous rumble. I thought something must be wrong with it, but I continued to use it until I ran out of dishwasher soap. I didn't have the money to repair or replace the dishwasher, so I stopped using it.

Things went fine at first. I really didn't mind washing dishes by hand. It was sort of relaxing, putting my hands in warm water at the end of a meal and washing dishes until they shone. Then canning season came. One of my summer rituals included canning about 100 jars each of cherries, apricots, peaches, pears, prunes, and applesauce. Canning means sterilizing the jars before filling them. I had become accustomed to putting them in the dishwasher, and I dreaded the thought of boiling all those jars before filling them.

So I decided to use my noisy dishwasher. Not until after I loaded it with jars did I remember I had no soap. Not wanting to run to the store while I was knee-deep in cherries, I decided to use what I had—regular liquid soap. I squirted an ample amount into my dishwasher and shut the door. I could hear water running into the machine. And then the wash cycle began. As the water swished around inside, suds began to bubble slowly from the cracks of its door, and foam oozed down its front. My kitchen was in a state of emergency! Billowing, foamy suds covered the floor. Gingerly I opened the door and stopped the wash cycle. A frothy foam of aerated soap greeted my eyes. Suds covered the jars and the racks. I had a major mess. How could I clean up this disaster?

In my bewilderment I seemed to hear my mother say, "Necessity is the mother of invention," and that endowed me with a fresh burst of creativity. What would cut the suds? Any kind of grease seemed to make the suds disappear when I washed dishes by hand. How about cooking oil? I got out my bottle and squeezed a generous amount into the foamy abyss. Then I closed the door and started the rinse cycle. After a few repetitions of this process the suds gradually subsided.

But the most surprising thing that happened is that my dishwasher no longer rumbled. As long as I kept that dishwasher, it never made that horrible noise again. When we sold it to friends, it never made that noise for them, either. That oil had so permeated the dishwasher and all its parts that it ran quietly.

When my spirit occasionally seems to rumble noisily and my life is just not working very well, I need the oil of the Holy Spirit to quell my rumblings and help me run smoothly again. But I can't just squirt that oil into my life. I have to take the time to listen to God, talk to Him, and invite the Holy Spirit to live in me and be in charge of my life. He does such a good job at getting into all the cracks of my life, permeating and lubricating them, that everything works much better, just like that no-longer-noisy dishwasher did.

RHONDA HUFFAKER BOLTON

God's Healing

The Lord will sustain him on his sickbed and restore him from his bed of illness. Ps. 41:3, NIV.

*W*e had traveled out of state for a weekend retreat. A friend of mine brought along her 2-year-old grandson, who had recently undergone abdominal surgery. During the first night at the hotel the little boy became ill. He manifested similar symptoms to those he had prior to surgery. He cried very hard from excruciating abdominal pains. He clutched his fists over his lower abdomen and stiffened his entire body while writhing and screaming in pain. During most of the night he slept for short periods, only to awaken with deafening screams.

At breakfast the next morning, a roommate with puffy eyes told of the nearly sleepless night for the grandmother and herself and the little lad's anguish. She took breakfast upstairs to the grandmother. The young boy pushed away all food, even his favorite snacks. He only took sips of tea in between episodes of severe crying.

When I visited the grandmother later that morning, she was planning to return to our hometown to take the boy to the specialist who had performed the surgery two weeks earlier. She feared that taking him to a nearby physician would risk improper diagnosis, treatment, and follow-up.

The grandmother was unable to leave the child even to get dressed. He clung to her side as she lay beside him in bed. She feared that her slightest movement in trying to get out of bed, even when he slipped into light episodes of sleep, would arouse an outburst of tears, stiffened abdomen, and deep anguish.

We decided to pray to God, our Great Physician. He had healed so many, including little children, while He walked the dusty roads of Galilee. We prayed in faith, believing that God heard and answered our prayer for healing. At the end of the prayer the roommate volunteered to hold the boy so my friend could get dressed, and I then left the room.

I returned to the lobby after spending a half hour in my room, and who do you think I saw running, laughing, and playing around a group of five women? The same little boy!

I was amazed—even aghast! I had prayed in faith, but I did not expect such swift and effective results. The boy has been well since that time. No pain, no tears, no agony.

To God be all praise! He still answers prayers!　SHEROLIN DALEY

Difficult Questions for God

For I know that my redeemer liveth, and that he shall stand at the latter day upon the earth: And though after my skin worms destroy this body, yet in my flesh shall I see God. Job 19:25, 26.

*O*ne of the most difficult challenges Christianity faces today is attempting to answer the problem of pain. At 18, as a volunteer missionary in Japan, I was approached by a student who asked a variation of this universal question.

"If your God is so loving," he queried, "why does He allow children to starve in the developing countries?"

I mumbled an inadequate answer and prayed that God would somehow fill in the gaps for me. Six years later that same question echoed in my heart as I struggled with a painful bout of an ongoing illness. I wondered where God was and how He could justify allowing His followers to encounter so much hardship. I was often bedbound, allowing ample time for contemplation. I was not accustomed to so much time to think, nor was I comfortable with letting others take care of me. I realized how long it had been since I had had an unhurried season of prayer or a time to meditate without interruption. Through working full-time and attending graduate school I had made it nearly impossible for God and me to be alone together.

I began to reflect on how I had been neglecting that vital relationship and how self-sufficient I had become. In the quiet I found again how much I needed Jesus' spirit in my life and how desolate living without Him had been. It dawned on me one day that perhaps allowing me to get sick was the only way God could get my attention! In the whirlwind of my daily routine He couldn't get a word in edgewise. I decided that if that's what it took to refocus me on the important things in life, then all the pain was worth it. I resolved that I would not make it so difficult for Him to reach me again.

I don't presume to answer a centuries-old question so simplistically. But from my experience I've learned to stop and trust God when pain and trials occur. I can trust the One who's in control and know that He has a worthy purpose, even if I don't know what it is. I know that from heaven's vantage point we will all know it was worth whatever it took to draw us closer to Jesus.

KATHRYN GORDON

OCTOBER 13

The Search

"Rejoice with me, for I have found my sheep which was lost!" Luke 15:6, NKJV.

*I*t was a beautiful fall morning as I hiked up the Shenandoah Mountain trails with my mother and two of my sisters. The view at the top was breathtaking. Vibrant autumn colors unrolled beneath me like a patchwork quilt. I insisted on peering over a dangerous precipice to capture more of the view. My mother refused to let me walk out onto the ledge, which dropped off several hundred feet. Being 13 and very defiant, I stomped off down the trail to wait in the car until we were ready to leave. That's what I intended to do, only I took the wrong trail down and went in the opposite direction of where I needed to go.

Being a child lost in the mountains is scary. You become disoriented. Nothing looks familiar. You realize the possibility that you may never again see your family and friends. You begin to fabricate all kinds of morbid scenarios as to how you will die. Perhaps you will meet a bear, die of exposure or starvation, or get bitten by a poisonous snake.

But being a parent of a child lost in the mountains is even more scary. I know that now that I have two children of my own. I can empathize with parents everywhere who have ever lost a child for any length of time. The anguish and worry you feel when a child is missing is overpowering. You are helpless to do anything but look.

And so my mother began her vigilant search for her strayed child until I was found. She did not say "You know, I have five other children. I really don't need six. Let's just go home." Even though she sometimes joked about trying to sell us at yard sales, we knew each one of her children was special to her.

Jesus, our heavenly parent, feels the same agony over His lost children. He never says, "I have 2,450,000 souls in the kingdom. I really don't need any more. Let's just bring these on home." No, for

Him it's not enough. He is "longsuffering toward us, not willing that any should perish but that all should come to repentance" (2 Peter 3:9). He diligently seeks to find each of His strayed sheep, wherever it has gone, and to bring it back into His waiting arms.

Just as there was joy in my family when I was found, "there is joy in the presence of the angels of God over one sinner who repents" (Luke 15:10). He will seek until He finds you. You are that precious to God.   MERRI LONG

OCTOBER 14

As a Woman in Travail

And ye now therefore have sorrow: but I will see you again, and
your heart shall rejoice, and your joy no man taketh from you.
John 16:22.

The birth of my first child was an event that made me feel not only privileged but also thankful to God for having experienced it. Certainly childbirth is not without risks, and also not without pain, but it does have a good helping of joy mixed in with it too.

I remember the excitement I felt as I discovered that I was going into labor. Then as the contractions grew stronger and the hours passed into a night without sleep, I began feeling helpless as to how I should cope. Finally I came to where I felt that I couldn't go on anymore. But it wasn't long before I was able to hold the baby in my arms and gaze at his beautiful face.

In retrospect, I cannot remember much about the intensity of the labor at all—only my surprise at hearing his first cry and realizing that all the work and pain was for something after all!

Our life on this planet in many ways is like a child's birth. The older we get, the more we struggle with problems and encounter new challenges. We know this will always be, so long as our adversary exists. But many times in my life when I have felt that I could not go on and have cried out to Christ to save me, the Lord has sent help and relief.

What joy will be ours when finally we are able to gaze upon the face of our Redeemer and realize with joy that all the work and pain was for something after all! We will spend eternity with Jesus!

Perhaps having a child is not something that everyone has experienced or even remembers with gladness, but I know that when

we see our Saviour every earthly trial will pale into insignificance.
CAROLINE ANDREW

OCTOBER 15

Monuments of Thankfulness

Then Samuel took a stone and set it up between Mizpah and Shen, and called its name Ebenezer, saying, "Thus far the Lord has helped us." 1 Sam. 7:12, NKJV.

Whenever my friends and relatives visit Washington, D.C., I always take them to see the many museums and monuments. Each time I visit, there are hundreds of people, tourists and residents, either listening to a tour guide or wandering around reading the words that are engraved on these stones. They are interested in knowing the history behind the monuments. The monuments tell a story—a story of great people and important events in the history of a people or nation. Some monuments are so significant that people make yearly pilgrimages to visit them.

The various accounts of God's people in His Word makes me aware that building a monument isn't a modern idea. We have adopted a number of ideas from our ancestors. Monuments were erected to remind the people of God's goodness toward them and to serve as a memorial to future generations.

Each of us has experienced God's intervention in our lives. We too must build monuments to remind us of His goodness toward us—lest we forget. You may say "I do not see any stones where I live, and I haven't the faintest idea how to erect a monument." Don't worry; we can do at least two things:

1. We can tell others of the things God has done for us. Make no mistake. He did not allow them to happen for us to keep to ourselves. He wanted us to share them.

2. We can record the events in a diary or journal so that others can read about them.

These monuments also increase and strengthen our faith in God when times are rough and it seems that we are having a Red Sea experience. The psalmist said we must "give thanks to the Lord, for He is good! For His mercy endures forever" (Ps. 106:1, NKJV). Build yourself a monument to God today.
ANDREA A. BUSSUE

The Maples and the Oaks

Wherefore take unto you the whole armour of God, that ye may be able to withstand in the evil day, and having done all, to stand. Eph. 6:13.

There is an ancient legend that goes like this:

And God said to the trees, "Behold, the time has come for you to put on the coat of Joseph, for there is need of color and beauty in the land."

The sassafras trees made coats of gold and orange, and they said, "This is pretty enough."

The dogwoods created their coats of purple and commented, "We like the color of royalty. It makes us feel special. Purple is good enough."

The oaks retorted, "Humph! Who needs color?" and they promptly devised garments of brown.

But the maples cried, "Yes! We will do it!" and set about creating coats of brilliant gold and warm orange, deep reds and bright yellow-greens. They proudly displayed their splendor for all to see.

God looked upon the maples with great pleasure and said, "Bless you, O maples, for you have obeyed My words. Henceforth, I will cause all people to be awed by your loveliness and to linger in the magnificence of your grandeur."

And thus it is that each year during autumn, people flock to see the glory of the maples.

God has instructed us to put on special garments as well, the "whole armour of God," that we may be a beacon of light in a world of darkness. Do we, like the sassafras, say, "Knowing the truth and hearing the gospel are good enough for me"? Or like the dogwoods, are we satisfied with wearing only the shield of faith? Do we, like the oaks, simply push back the helmet of salvation?

Oh, that we each would follow the leading of the glorious maples, and with wholehearted enthusiasm shout, "Yes, I'll do it!" while donning all of God's armor—the loincloth of truth, the breastplate of righteousness, the shoes of the gospel of peace, the shield of faith, the helmet of salvation, and the sword of the Spirit.

When our Maker sees our life and heart clothed in the manner He has instructed and we're using His armor in the way He has designed, we will hear the voice of our heavenly Father say to us,

"Well done! I am pleased with your obedience. Enter into My joy."

And thus it will be that we can enjoy the glories and splendor, the peace and happiness, of the Christian life, not just for a season, but for all eternity.   BARBARA HORST REINHOLTZ

Prayers Up, Prayers Down

I will cry unto God most high; unto God that performeth all things for me. Ps. 57:2.

Finishing my chores for the day, I drove to the mall to do some early Christmas shopping. On the way I sang a song:
"God answers prayer in the morning,
God answers prayer at noon,
God answers prayer in the evening,
To keep your heart in tune."

Entering the mall, I took the escalator down to the bottom floor to purchase my first gift. Then I made a stop on the main floor before taking the escalator to the second floor to buy gifts for my two grandchildren. Not until I stepped up to the cash register to pay for my purchases did I realize I didn't have my purse. Panic began to set in, but at that moment the song I had been singing popped into my head again.

I took the escalator down to the first floor, praying as I went, and inquired about a blue handbag. No one had seen it.

"Lord, You have answered my prayers before. Help me find my handbag," I prayed as I went back up to the top floor to look around again. Still no purse. Suddenly I had the impression to go back down to the main floor, where I had stopped briefly to look at a jacket. There was my purse—right by the racks where I had stood trying on a jacket. I know God hid my handbag from the eyes of many early Christmas shoppers who had passed by.

I thank God for the ups and downs He permits in my life. May all of us keep our hearts in tune with the One who answers prayers in the morning, at noon, and in the evening.   ANNIE B. BEST

On Time Plus Two Minutes

Whatsoever ye shall ask the Father in my name, he will give it you. Hitherto have ye asked nothing in my name; ask, and ye shall receive, that your joy may be full. John 16:23, 24.

*I*t was already 7:20. I should have been on the bus at 7:15 so that I could get to work by 8:30. My 75-minute trip to work includes four bus and subway changes. Attending to last-minute details for the children, I hadn't left home on time.

Walking out the door at 7:22, I could see my bus turning at the intersection ahead—I had just missed it! At the bus stop I tried to make a hurried phone call to work to inform them that I would be at least 15 minutes late, but the phone was out of order! After what seemed an eternity the bus pulled up at 7:30. As I sat down I prayed, "Lord, help me to be on time for work. You have said in Your Word, 'If you ask anything in prayer, believing, you shall receive it.' Lord, in Jesus' name, help me to be on time."

It was rush hour. I began to think, *I really shouldn't have prayed that prayer; I was asking for the impossible to get to work on time—I shouldn't have asked God for something that was obviously impossible.* But faith is believing that God will do what He has promised—even the impossible. Less than confident, but curious to try God, I held on to my prayer.

In 10 minutes I was at the subway, running down the stairs to the train. As I walked along the subway platform I said, "Lord, if You're helping me, I need a train to be coming along right now." Just as I stopped at my usual waiting spot I turned around, and there was a train pulling in. As the train pulled into my third stop I still had 10 minutes left. I hurried through the long tunnel toward the next platform. As I emerged, dashing up the escalator, there was the 117 waiting! I ran for it and sat down just as the door closed behind me.

Tears came to my eyes and an overwhelming feeling of joy filled my heart as I praised God for His personal interest in me and for answering my prayer. God was giving me a message that I so much needed—if He cared for me in little things, I could trust Him for the bigger things. My faith was renewed!

Eight-twenty-nine. I got off the bus and crossed the street. I walked to the reception desk, plugged in the switchboard, and pressed the time button—8:30. Praise the Lord! Thank You,

Jesus; I made it! Oh, that we would believe God is able to do the impossible!

LUAN CADOGAN

OCTOBER 19

Monarch Migration

The Lord will watch over your coming and going both now and forevermore. Ps. 121:8, NIV.

I have always enjoyed learning about nature. No matter where I turn, I find lessons that apply to practical life. Recently I found another one, involving migration.

While on vacation I was reading a magazine that listed places of special interest. One of those places was a habitat dedicated to providing a safe winter home for the monarch butterfly. We arrived at the Monarch Natural Preserve at Natural Bridge's State Beach in mid-October. The butterflies were just beginning to arrive, migrating from as far away as Canada. By Thanksgiving there would be hundreds of thousands of them gracefully fluttering about or clinging to the tall eucalyptus trees.

The ranger explained the life cycle of the monarch butterfly. It takes a mere three weeks for it to mature through its life cycle: egg, caterpillar, chrysalis, and full-grown adult. The butterflies we were now watching against the bright-blue northern California sky had never been here before. They were the great-grandchildren of the butterflies that had migrated to Canada the previous spring. Most of them had completed their life cycle somewhere along the migratory routes.

"How do they know to come to this spot when none of them have ever been here before?" I asked. "There is no butterfly to lead the way or even to pass along information about the route!"

There was no definitive answer to my question. I stood among the towering trees and watched the orange, velvet-winged beauties flitting through the sunlight. They seemed too fragile to have completed such a journey. Over thousands of miles, flying at altitudes as high as 10,000 feet, they had contended with the elements. And they had won! No matter what the obstacles, their overpowering urge had pushed them toward the preserve, a habitat they had never seen, but one that an inner sense told them was home.

I am on a migratory journey to my future home as well, sometimes passing through pleasant meadows, other times traversing dark and difficult canyons. Some days the weather is fine; other days bring chilling winds and driving rain. One of my tasks is to be willing to change into the person God has planned for me to be. Another task is to trust that although I have never seen the home God has prepared for me, its reality is certain.

I can rest assured that God is with me on my journey, today and every day. The Being who cares for the monarch butterfly will also lead me home. DEBBY GRAY WILMOT

OCTOBER 20

Fix Our Eyes on Jesus

Let us fix our eyes on Jesus. Heb. 12:2, NIV.

My husband and I took turns teaching our daughter to ride her new bicycle. There was one problem, however. She kept looking down at her feet, across at one of us, or back at the other who was holding the seat. Of course, she could not keep her balance this way, and her frustrations became our frustrations.

After several training sessions she became concerned that she would never manage the bicycle alone. We assured her that she would, but she must keep her eyes fixed on the road ahead at all times. She determined to follow our plan, and before long she had mastered her two-wheeler.

Her experience is similar to that of all Christians. We must keep gazing at Jesus for lessons in perfect living. When we fail to look at Him, we tend to look back at our mistakes of earlier years and relive the guilt. We look down on those who should know better, or those who are new believers, and become critical of their actions. We look across to other cultures and indulge in feelings of spiritual superiority. Or we look up to those who appear to be without blemish and writhe in our inferior slush when we feel unable to climb to their spiritual heights.

When we keep our eyes fixed on Jesus, we are guaranteed victory in our encounters with the enemy. And Jesus promised that those who overcome will be given the right to sit with Him on His throne (see Rev. 3:21). MARIA G. MCCLEAN

Hidden Beauty

We also rejoice in our sufferings, because we know that suffering produces perseverance; perseverance, character; and character, hope. Rom. 5:3, 4, NIV.

*M*aple leaves are large, beautiful leaves with an interesting shape. But what most people think of when they think of maple leaves is the brilliant colors they display in the fall. People who will scarcely look at a tree when it is wearing its summer green will drive for miles to look at a grove of maples wearing their fall finery.

People talk about the leaves changing color. What actually happens is that a disk of cells grows across the base of the leaf, blocking the pipelines to and from the source of water. Without water the leaf stops making food. Chlorophyll, which makes the green color in plants, begins breaking down and other beautiful colors that have been hidden in the leaf are revealed. No new color is formed—we just become able to see the beauty that was once hidden.

Sometimes this happens in our lives. Stressful circumstances, such as the death of a loved one, a move to another city, or the loss of a job, separate us from a source of emotional and/or spiritual nourishment. We often react to this by becoming dormant and ceasing to participate in a world that is suddenly strange to us. But these events, these trials, while depriving us of a beautiful element in our lives, often reveals an even greater beauty that has been hidden. This realization makes it possible for us to rejoice in our sufferings as the Bible has instructed us to do.   KATHLEEN L. STAUBACH

Untangling the Threads

Though I walk in the midst of trouble, thou wilt revive me: thou shalt stretch forth thine hand . . . and thy right hand shall save me. Ps. 138:7.

With tears streaming down his cheeks, our 7-year-old grandson's eyes met mine. Never mind that the sink was filled with breakfast dishes and a pile of soiled clothing lay on the laundry room floor. My sympathy for Anthony's plight took immediate priority.

Earlier that morning when Anthony came to my house, he was very excited and held out his hands to show me his green butterfly-shaped kite.

"How will you fly it?" I asked.

"I don't know," he shrugged.

We drove to the store for some kite string. After a few flying instructions I returned to my chores, while Anthony enjoyed flying his new kite. Suddenly the screen door slammed, and I went to see what it was all about. Anthony stood just inside the door with his head down, sobbing.

"What's wrong?" I asked.

"My kite got caught in the tree across the street!" he wailed.

From the front porch I saw the kite dangling from the big oak tree, swaying crazily in the morning breeze. We had to cut the string with scissors. I returned to my chores while Anthony rewound the cord. When he finished, he brought the knotted mess to me and we began the difficult task of untangling the kite string. We spent 45 minutes patiently unknotting, passing over, under, and through, and finally managed to untangle most of the cord.

Many times we, as God's adult children, disregard the rules of life and encounter problems and trials that become more complicated when we attempt to unravel them. In desperation we, like Anthony, seek help. It helps to remember that when problems overwhelm us, our all-wise God will stretch forth His hand of mercy. Skillfully and tactfully, He untangles the difficult knots. His plans for our lives are not always known to us, but if we patiently wait He will reveal them.   MABEL ROLLINS NORMAN

Signs of Promise

Therefore do not throw away your confidence, which has a great reward. For you have need of endurance, so that you may do the will of God and receive what is promised. Heb. 10:35, 36, RSV.

*F*or about a year my husband and I lived in both Florida and Minnesota. We traveled back and forth every few weeks, usually flying, but occasionally driving. Our first drive from Florida to Minneapolis seemed endless. I had never made the journey before and had no landmarks to gauge how much longer we had to go. I depended on the road signs to see how many more miles we had to travel to reach our destination. I had to trust what the signs said, even though I had no empirical proof of my own. Nashville, 45 miles; Chicago, 97 miles; Madison, 24 miles. And when I saw St. Paul, 120, I knew we were nearer our second home. I felt relieved, even though I didn't see how I could take another two hours in the car.

During that trip I began to draw some analogies between my life and the tediously long hours spent driving without feeling as though we were getting anywhere. Like the trip, my life seemed to be dragging on without much to celebrate. For many months I had been praying without noticing any positive answers from God. I read and claimed Bible promises, but didn't see results. I felt as if I were plodding through each day, trying to reach a destination that was becoming foggier the longer I lumbered on. Because of my impatience and lack of endurance, my faith in God and His promises wavered. I likened God's promises to the road signs and wondered why I believed the information on billboards and state signs more than I believed His Word. Even when fatigued and irritable, I didn't doubt the accuracy of those signs. However, in my growing hopelessness and despondence about my life I did have doubts about promises I had been claiming, because I wanted God to be on my map at my speed.

God helped me to see the senselessness in where I placed my faith. I decided that even though the fulfillment of His promises to me may be hidden behind the winding road of the days and months ahead, I could be sure that my Creator would keep His word. During the following months, when I frequently thought of the promises I read as road signs, my weariness was transformed into energy, and my impatience turned into peace.

We finally did reach Minneapolis, and now, many months later,

I have had many of my prayers answered. God answered them on His timetable so that He could exceed my requests and hopes and at the same time give me more practice and patience and endurance.

As you drive today, look for a sign with your destination on it and think of a promise you are waiting for God to fulfill. You can believe His Word with even more certainty than you can that sign. God is faithful. He will answer your prayers and keep His signs of promise.

LAURA PASCUAL DANCEK

OCTOBER 24

God's Spell Check

Those who live according to the sinful nature have their minds set on what that nature desires; but those who live in accordance with the Spirit have their minds set on what the Spirit desires. The mind of sinful man is death, but the mind controlled by the Spirit is life and peace. Rom. 8:5, NIV.

Spelling bees still attract me. Spelling rules fascinate me. Learning to spell new words challenges me. The history of spelling changes in the English language reminds me that time and usage can affect change. The fun of participating in spelling bees in my youth is recaptured when I visit my grandsons' school for their spelling bees. Very little has changed. Contest rules still appear inflexible.

My husband, on the other hand, doesn't have to concern himself with spelling rules. He has me! But more than that, he has spell check, a vital part of his computer world.

Recently I was writing to a friend in Japan. When I had finished the letter on my laptop, he was printing out the results of his research. "Don't turn the printer off, Lou," I requested. "I'd like to print this letter to Teruyo."

"I'll do it for you, honey. In fact, I'll run it through spell check," he offered.

"Spell check! I never use spell check!" I proudly announced.

"Why don't you just check up on yourself now and then? Maybe you'd surprise yourself."

"OK. Go for it." I'd show him I wasn't afraid to be challenged. I waited, certain that my letter needed no correcting. However, spell check emblazoned the screen with two errors: "tho" and "primative." I was aghast! I had intentionally taken a shortcut on "tho," but I wasn't so sure about "primative." Had I spelled it this way before? I knew it should be "primitive," but why did the other somehow look acceptable? Clearly I was confusing right with wrong.

How about my spiritual values? Could I be confusing God's way with my way? God has given me His model, but have I been so self-confident that my copy of the real model is not clearly seen? Have I done things my way so long that I can't recognize error?

It's the small things in my life that complete the total picture. If words are continuously misspelled the narrative is flawed and the picture of my lovely Jesus is shadowed. He does not deserve this kind of representation. If I have grown careless in using God's spell check, I must consult it with every printing. His Spirit will keep me in line.

LORABEL HERSCH

OCTOBER 25

Rescue

And the Lord direct your hearts into the love of God, and into the patient waiting for Christ. 2 Thess. 3:5.

When will Dad be home?" my 4-year-old son asked. Again. Dad worked one mile away and often walked to and from work, and Ryan enjoyed waiting at the edge of our yard for the first glimpse of his hero. He would hide behind the tall grass until Dad came around the last corner, then jump out and race to meet him, yelling and laughing.

Today was no different, except that it was late fall, cool and drizzly. "Wouldn't you like to wait inside and watch through the window?" I asked.

But no, he didn't think it would be the same. So I bundled him up and sent him out just before the phone rang. It was my husband telling me that he was just leaving work. I relayed this message to Ryan and asked if he wanted to come in and start eating, since Dad wouldn't be home for 20 minutes. Again Ryan said no, he wanted to stay out and wait for Dad. I tied his sweatshirt hood tighter and sent him out again, but I couldn't help looking out the window occasionally. I expected him to busy himself with the swings or the sandbox, but he didn't.

The cover of the tall grass was abandoned in favor of the short grass and its clearer view. I wished I could read his thoughts, a small lone figure in the misty rain, waiting for Dad. The whole 20 minutes he stood there, waiting. Oblivious to the cold, the gray skies, and his growling stomach, he waited. Tears came to my eyes as I watched him, wondering if I would be so faithful and patient. When Dad finally came around the corner, Ryan's quiet patience turned to wild, exuberant joy! He *knew* his daddy would come! Personal discomfort, delay, and disappointment could not sway his confidence. Why? He knew his daddy.

Jesus has told me He is coming. Am I waiting? Do I know Him so well that I can patiently wait through storms and delays and personal discomfort? When tempted to become absorbed with the cares of this life and the rewards that the world has to offer, I pray that I can say with my son, "No, thanks, I'm waiting for Jesus."

LINDA MCCABE

OCTOBER 26

I Am With You

When you pass through the waters, I will be with you; and through the rivers, they shall not overflow you. When you walk through the fire, you shall not be burned, nor shall the flame scorch you. . . . Fear not, for I am with you. Isa. 43:2-5, NKJV.

At first I thought they were big dogs running along the fence at the top of the hill next to the busy stretch of road I was traveling. But as I came closer I saw that they were actually two young deer, racing wildly along the fence. Every few seconds they would try to run right through that fence, the force of the impact snapping their necks backward and throwing them to the ground, where they immediately scrambled back to their feet, only to repeat their crazed actions. My heart ached for these poor terrified creatures, who undoubtedly were trying to escape the traffic at the bottom of the hill. They didn't know that they were safe at the top; and if they had slowed down and looked around they would have found an open gate and freedom just a few yards ahead of them.

I felt so helpless knowing there was nothing I could do to help. There was no place for me to pull over, and even if I found a place, I would run the risk of being seriously injured by the deer. How do you reason with wild animals? In their state of panic they could never understand that I was trying to help them, and since I don't speak deer language, I would be hard put to explain.

I understand the terror of those poor deer. Sometimes the circumstances of my life swirl ominously around me, threatening to do me great harm. Panic-stricken, I forget to listen for the gentle guidance of the Holy Spirit, and I go scrambling about trying to fix things all by myself, running straight into many "fences" in the process. I don't understand sometimes how God works because His wisdom is so far beyond any of my reasoning. Sometimes I forget that the Lord is with me and that He will show me the open gate if I'll just slow down and look around. Sometimes I forget how completely I can trust Him to work in all of the circumstances of my life. I can avoid many scrapes and bruises if I just remember to bring my fears to God.

No, I'm not so very different from those two frightened deer. But I thank the Lord that He knows how to speak my language, and He's always there to remind me that I'm not alone.

Father, when the troubles of this life threaten to sweep me away, please help me to remember that You are always with me and I need not fear. Take my weak hand in Your strong one, and lead me into Your safety. Amen. LYNDA MAE RICHARDSON

OCTOBER 27

Before They Call, I Will Answer

And it shall come to pass, that before they call, I will answer; and while they are yet speaking, I will hear. Isa. 65:24.

I had been out of the full-time labor market for three years while I, on faith and a shoestring budget, completed the academic requirements for the bachelor's and master's degrees. At the time of my distress I was underemployed, and no amount of financial maneuvering would result in stretching my salary to cover my expenses for that month, the next month, or the month after that. Knowing that in order to survive I simply had to have more income, I had submitted applications for additional part-time employment to several businesses in the area, but there had been no response to any of them.

As I sat near the window worrying, I could see lightning streaking across the sky, followed by loud peals of crashing thunder and torrential rain washing the earth. The weather outside perfectly matched the turmoil within me. Finally I slipped to my knees and sought relief from my desperation through prayer.

"My Father," I pleaded, "I am facing an unsolvable predicament unless You help me. Will You please help me to somehow increase my income?"

At that very moment the phone rang. It was the manager of a nearby department store saying that he was presently reviewing my application for part-time employment and asking me to report for work in their business office the next evening! My heart leaped with joy. The storm outside became even more intense, but as I returned to my knees, the pent-up emotion within me overflowed in tears of thanksgiving that my Father had seen my need and had already set in motion the circumstances to answer my desperate call when it came, even while I was yet speaking.   THELMA LEWIS ANDERSON

OCTOBER 28

Be Ready

Therefore keep watch, because you do not know on what day your Lord will come. But understand this: If the owner of the house had known at what time of night the thief was coming, he would have kept watch and would not have let his house be broken into. So you also must be ready, because the Son of Man will come at an hour when you do not expect him. Matt. 24:42-44, NIV.

Late one evening while traveling in Europe my husband and I boarded an overnight train bound for our next destination. One by one the six of us in our sleeping compartment dropped into our bunks. No one checked the lock on the door. Soon the gentle rocking of the train lulled all of us to sleep.

None of us heard the stranger enter. But about 3:00 in the morning we were awakened by a scuffle in our compartment. An obviously intoxicated man was lying on the floor between our bunks, snoring contentedly. The conductor was trying to drag him out.

This break-in reminds me of the parable Jesus told His disciples. As Jesus enumerated the signs of His coming He warned that some would be as unprepared for it as the victim of a burglary. "Be ready," He admonished.

Since childhood I have wanted to be ready. Did it mean telling my neighbors everything that is wrong with them (for their own good, of course)? Did it mean shaking in my boots and biting my fingernails, wondering if I was ready?

In Matthew 24:45, 46 Jesus gives a simple description of those who will be ready: "Who then is the faithful and wise servant, whom the master has put in charge of the servants in his household to give them their food at the proper time? It will be good for that servant whose master finds him doing so when he returns" (NIV).

It sounds so effortless. Jesus has given me a responsibility. He merely expects me to fulfill it in the proper way at the proper time. A mother with small children to raise is being ready as she lovingly feeds, nurtures, and trains her children. A secretary who works conscientiously for a boss, regardless of his or her difficult leadership style, is being ready. A manager who treats employees fairly and helps each reach his or her potential is being ready. Being ready inside the heart is revealed through outside actions. What do I do, then, when my outside actions deny a ready heart?

I thank God for His forgiveness, His grace, and His Holy Spirit. I must constantly invite the Holy Spirit to work within me. I will steadfastly listen to His prompting and obey. I will submit to progressive heart change. If I let Him, the Holy Spirit, available to me every day, will faithfully prepare me to be ready.   JOYCE NEERGAARD

OCTOBER 29

Accentuate the Positive

Whatsoever things are of good report, if there is any virtue and if there is anything praiseworthy—meditate on these things. Phil. 4:8, NKJV.

*F*rom the time I saw her, I just didn't like her, and I still don't like her." I have heard that remark repeatedly, and probably you have, too. I wonder—is it fair to the person being talked about? Would I want that comment to be made about me?

In my profession I read evaluation reports by psychologists, doctors, and speech therapists about potential students for our classroom. Very often we find that a child is diagnosed with not only multiple disabilities but spurts of violent behavior. The evaluations are necessary so that educators can be aware of the potential behavioral problems that may be encountered. One doesn't want to be caught unaware—a chair could be flying through the air toward you. However, the reports can instill a certain amount of fear in anticipation of the arrival of the new student.

I have developed my own theory in dealing with these reports:

1. "Forget" the evaluation reports and treat the child as though you are totally unaware of his or her history.

2. When the child arrives, try to understand what his or her unique characteristics are.

3. After discovering his or her strengths (and there are strengths), try to incorporate them into his or her daily activities.

4. Shower the child with praise for each task accomplished, however small it may be. This will help improve the child's self-esteem.

When I have put this theory into practice I have witnessed amazing results. For example, Carl can find any country on the world map in a split second, tell about its political situation, and describe its national flag. Martha can look at the picture of a 60-piece jigsaw puzzle and put the pieces together without constantly looking at the picture on the cover of the box. Andy, a very caring and mannerly child, always makes one feel welcome after a long absence. Shaun can recall information about any sport event, the teams and the scores. Yes, even though there are limitations, they seem to vanish in the light of things the students are capable of doing.

This theory can be applied to anyone with whom we may come in contact. Try to ignore prior comments you may have heard about the individual. There is some good in the worst of us. Accentuate the positive. As you go through the day, think about the things that are lovely, pure, and praiseworthy in the people that you meet. It will give you a brand-new outlook on life.   ANDREA A. BUSSUE

OCTOBER 30

The Desires of Your Heart

Delight yourself also in the Lord, and He shall give you the desires of your heart. Commit your way to the Lord, Trust also in Him, and He shall bring it to pass. Ps. 37:4, 5, NKJV.

*D*uring the 12 years our family lived in Alaska, we often spent the long summer days enjoying the magnificent scenery and wildlife of Denali National Park. On one of our earlier visits to the park, a ranger was answering our questions about a hike to Horseshoe Lake. There was a beaver dam on the far side of the lake, and yes, he said, some large beavers had recently been spotted in the lake.

Having never seen a beaver before, I was excited about the prospect of finally being able to observe one, especially in such a beautiful setting. But past experience had taught me that wildlife can be very elusive. So on the way down the steep trail to the scenic blue lake, I prayed fervently, "Please, Lord, let me see a beaver today, if it is Your will." God wants us to take delight in His creation, and I believed it *was* His will.

The boys and I made our way around the horseshoe-shaped lake that was surrounded with tall spruce trees. We came to the beaver dam and, using walking sticks, picked our way carefully over the logs and sticks the beavers had placed there.

My camera was ready for any picturesque sight. A short distance past the dam I stood at water's edge, reveling in the beauty all around. Suddenly I spotted something swimming toward me—could it really be? Yes, it was! A beaver! It made a beeline right toward me, as if angel-directed! "Thank You, Lord!" I breathed, snapping picture after picture.

Imagine my delight when the beaver stopped about 20 feet directly in front of me, then slapped its tail sharply and dived gracefully into the clear water. Surfacing, it repeated this performance two or three times. My heart was beating wildly. Not only was it exciting to watch this beaver perform at such close range, but it was even more thrilling to know that my God loved me enough to arrange this private beaver exhibition!

"Delight yourself also in the Lord, and He shall give you the desires of your heart." At Horseshoe Lake I experienced again the great love of God as He intervened to grant me one of the desires of my heart. He will do the same for you!   VIVIAN PREWITT

OCTOBER 31

I'm Tired of Being a Pumpkin!

For you created my inmost being; you knit me together in my mother's womb. I praise you because I am fearfully and wonderfully made; your works are wonderful, I know that full well. Ps. 139:13, 14, NIV.

*I*t was Halloween, and the children in my daughter's immediate neighborhood were looking forward to wearing costumes and visiting each other's homes to collect a sweet of some kind.

Because of traveling, I had missed three Halloweens. So I was looking forward to spending the evening with our three grandchildren. I finished work and hurried to their home where I had to take a second look to discover my grandchildren. Six-year-old Ryan was dressed in army fatigues and face paint. Heather, 4, had borrowed her mother's emergency nursing garb, and with a stethoscope bouncing along as she ran, she informed me that she was a "doctor."

And then there was Eric, 2½, who stole the show in his pumpkin suit—a round, puffy, orange costume with holes for arms and legs. To top it off, he wore a hat with petals and stem. He was ready to go in search of the treats with his plastic pumpkin in hand—except for one thing. He wanted transportation! He made a convincing appeal to Grandma that he needed to be carried in order to keep up with the older kids.

I felt as though I was the one who needed to be carried, but I succumbed to his pleading and swooped up my precious pumpkin. So we did some walking, and I did some carrying in our hopeless attempt to keep up with his two older siblings. And after about two blocks of this he came off the porch of one house, sized up the small stash in his plastic pumpkin, and announced, "Grammie, I'm tired of being a pumpkin!"

"So soon?" I asked.

"Yes, I want to go home."

So we went home.

I've thought about this simple little exchange between a toddler and his sanguine grandmother who enjoys making analogies out of experiences just like this one. How often we get "dressed up" for the day, full of anticipation, hoping that the day will bring good things—quiet time with God, gifts of friendship, time with loved ones, the chance to learn something new, a phone call from a friend or lover, a new dress or haircut, a new chance at life. But in spite of all the possible outcomes of a new day, there are times when, like Eric, we are tempted to say, "Lord, I want to go home. I'm tired of being a pumpkin." For the costumes we wear on earth are only borrowed. But the King of kings is fashioning a beautiful robe of righteousness in my size and yours. And since He "knit us in our mother's womb" in a variety of colors and sizes, each robe will be "one of a kind." An original in the finest sense of the word.

And I hope the finishing touches are being put on mine, because just like Eric, "I'm tired of being a pumpkin!"   ROSE OTIS

November

Search me, O God, and know my heart; test me and know my anxious thoughts. Ps. 139:23, NIV.

I like November. True, it is gray and the trees are bare. But now you can see through the woods. Now the graceful (or knotty) shapes of the trees' limbs are revealed, branches and trunks—gaunt, without any adornment of leaves to cover them. I think they are beautiful.

From my southern California window in former days, above the orange groves I could see snowcapped "old Grayback" mountain in November. In summertime it was hidden from my view by foliage.

This November in Maryland, I can see the most gorgeous sunsets across the park below our hill. In the "good ol' summertime" the leaves of flowering pear trees line our sidewalks and obstruct my kitchen window view.

Oh, I love "October's bright blue weather," January's soft white snow, and September's goldenrod and fringed gentians. And I can sing with the poet, "And what is so rare as a day in June? Then, if ever, come perfect days." But give me a quiet, gray November day with the trees showing their true form in a stark, serene beauty. It's like February—a waiting month—a time of meditation and preparation for the spring that will come in March. November waits for Thanksgiving and Christmas, when we can take a little time to be more thankful and to celebrate our Saviour's first advent.

Yes, November is a special time to do a little soul-searching and to think about the meaning of those bare trees and woods that we can now see through. Now is the Lord's November. He sees through me. It is almost year's end and almost time's end. A poet has said it well:

"My soul before the Lord is always bare;
I wonder if He finds some beauty there."

MAE WALLENKAMPHF

NOVEMBER 2

The Hurting Parent

But she came and knelt before him, saying, "Lord, help me." Matt. 15:25, RSV.

sat in my prayer chair. It was Saturday night, and my 17-year-old daughter was leaving the house, eager to be with her friends. "Lord, be with her. I know she skipped church today and it seems as if she doesn't care, but please keep the Holy Spirit working on her heart." What had happened to my sweet child? Where were her preschool friends who had been part of my family? Why did she faithfully pay tithe but never set foot inside the church? As the car door slammed shut I bowed my head and wept. I loved her so much, but she was shutting me out. "Lord, I need reassurance. Is there a Bible story for hurting parents?" Yes, there was! I remembered the Canaanite woman. The devil had a hold on her daughter. Jesus heard her pleas. Turning to Matthew 15, I was comforted by the following thoughts:

1. Christ came to the area specifically to help the Canaanite woman. No other miracles were performed. He came, helped her, and moved on. This tells me that Christ knows and cares about my needs and stands ready to hear my requests.

2. The woman never asked for her daughter to be healed. She begged the Lord to have mercy on her and told Him about her daughter. But she never asked for a specific resolution. Am I telling the Lord what to do for my child, or am I acknowledging Satan's stronghold in her life and praying for mercy and intercession?

3. "He did not answer her a word" (verse 23, RSV). Christ's silence must have been the most painful part of this experience. She had come to Him seeking help, but for a moment it appeared that He was going to ignore her pleas. How long have you been hurting? A month? A year? Five years? Twenty? Does it seem that Christ is ignoring your prayers?

4. "And his disciples came and begged him, saying, 'Send her away, for she is crying after us'" (verse 23, RSV). The Canaanite woman knew separation, rejection, and criticism from those who would become church leaders. Many hurting parents experience these same feelings when dealing with their child's teacher(s), pastor(s), church members, and other parents. They feel isolated and lonely when their child steps out of their church circle. Afraid of building higher walls between their child and others, embarrassed by their apparent failure, or sensing others' criticism, many parents withdraw. Even good friends may not relate to their grief.

5. "She came and knelt before him, saying, 'Lord, help me'" (verse 25, RSV). This was God's special message to me that night. When it seemed hopeless the Canaanite woman drew nearer to the Lord and asked for help for herself. What are your needs? Do you need to know how to love and accept your child for who she/he is? Do you need patience? tact? wisdom? endurance? Whatever your need, use this experience to help you draw near to Jesus, and let Him refine your character. He will help you.   JOY COLBURN

NOVEMBER 3

The Hand of God

When you lie down, you will not be afraid; when you lie down, your sleep will be sweet. Prov. 3:24, NIV.

I grew up in a time when few houses had locks, bolts, or bars. Children were left unsupervised while parents went as far as the city, several miles away, to shop. It was not unusual for small children to be left in bed at night while adults socialized on the streets.

One night I was put to bed with my younger sister, Annette, while our mother and older sibling visited with friends. Before they left they placed a lighted lamp on the night table. It did not take long for Annette to sink into a restful sleep. Not so with me.

At first all seemed quiet. Then the sounds of the night gradually grew louder and more frightening. Suddenly I heard a loud crash outside. I sat up in bed, speechless with fright. Just then I saw a shadow of a man's hand appear against the wall behind the lamp. I stared at that reflection until the fear subsided. I was aware of a Divine Presence in the room. I knew enough Bible stories by then to recognize this as a sign from God, for Satan would want to terrify—

not calm. It was not long before I was sleeping peacefully.

That experience will remain with me forever. How can I forget a night when God looked down and saw me, a frightened child, and in a gentle, reassuring way reminded me of His protection, His love, His care? The worlds were kept on course. The heavenly bodies continued to shine. Yet my Abba paused to comfort me. Such supreme love breaks my heart.

God's hand continues to guide me. Through the years I have developed a closeness with Him that has sustained me in every circumstance in life. I live with a constant awareness of His presence. Whenever I stray I feel His loving hand steering me back to Him. Each day my prayer is "Into your hands I commit my spirit" (Ps. 31:5, NIV).

MARIA G. MCCLEAN

NOVEMBER 4

God Is Keeping His Promises

For no matter how many promises God has made, they are "Yes" in Christ. 2 Cor. 1:20, NIV.

God called Abraham the "father of nations"
    when he still did not have a son.
After waiting for years, and no son appeared, he said:
    "God needs my help to get it done."
But Ishmael was not the son of the promise;
    Isaac came when human hope was gone
So Abraham would know that when God says it's so,
    in His own time the promise will come.

God promised Israel a land of their own
    when the wilderness was their home.
But His word they forgot when they heard the report of
      the spies
    who said, "It can't be done."
Still, Caleb and Joshua had faith to believe
    that the fight was not up to them.
And 40 years later they crossed Jordan's river;
    God's promise had come through again.

At times in my life I look at God's promise and wonder:

"How can it come true?"
Then I work and I scheme, I plan and I dream,
  but then my way falls through.
Still God is beside me; He gently reminds me
  that the promise is His to keep.
So I pick up the pieces and I give them to Jesus;
  saying "Lord, I choose to believe."

Faith is believing that God is keeping His promises to me;
  For He is faithful, and I am thankful that what He says
    is certainty.
The more I know about His love,
  the more I learn to trust Him
in little things and through eternity.
  And I'm believing that God is keeping His promises to me.

LINDA MCCABE

NOVEMBER 5

Fish Flakes in the Soup

Serve him with wholehearted devotion and a willing mind, for the Lord searches every heart and understands every motive behind the thoughts. 1 Chron. 28:9, NIV.

I was making soup again. Soup is one of the most helpful things known to a mother, especially if you can whiz it all smooth in a blender and disguise lots of otherwise offensive vegetables, like peas, carrots, spinach, and onions. It is also quick and simple, a meal in itself with a hunk of bread. It makes for very little dishwashing, and it uses up lots of leftovers.

My daughter, Bethany, was "helping" me. She was about 3, and she sat on the kitchen counter. I would put some salt or herbs in her hand and she would have fun throwing them into the pot. Then the doorbell rang and I went to answer it. I chatted a few minutes, then went back to the kitchen. Bethany was still sitting on the counter.

"Mommy, I've been helping! Look, I put some of this in the soup too!"

I did look, and my heart sank. In her hand she held a little round pot that looked exactly like a pot of herbs, except that it wasn't. It was food for our goldfish. Dried flakes of something that smelled very fishy indeed. I looked into the pot. Most of the flakes were still clinging to the surface, and I tried to skim them off with a spoon. I knew I couldn't be sure I had them all.

It might not have been so bad if all the guests were fish eaters—but they weren't. They were all vegetarians. There was no time to make more soup. So I prayed as I poured the soup into the blender with a few extra herbs to help mask any odd aromas.

Then I wondered about God. How many times had God let me "help" Him by scattering oregano while He had been doing the real work. So often I feel good about what I think I'm doing to help, when my greatest contribution has really been only adding the herbs to His ready-made soup. And I wonder how often I've inadvertently added the wrong ingredients in my eagerness to be helpful and made a complete mess of things, so that God had to spend time making it all right again.

I don't know. And I guess I won't, till heaven. But spooning fish flakes out of lentil soup made me stop and wonder, and suddenly feel very small in it all.

KAREN HOLFORD

The Hair Hassle

Stop judging by mere appearances, and make a right judgment. John 7:24, NIV.

*D*uring the late 1960s when the British singing group the Beatles was making an impact upon the youth of the world, the most important occupation of many adults was to see to it that teenage boys did not emulate the Beatles' hairstyle. At least it seemed that way to me, a mother of three teenage sons. And my sons were just as determined to resist regulation haircuts and to grow their hair as long as possible. My minister husband and I battled that issue every few weeks with our three boys. The hair hassle was destroying our relationship with our sons.

As summer began we decided to forget about hair for the few weeks of school vacation. No required haircuts all summer. Good news for our sons. Our family spent an exciting summer centering in on family relationships, picnics, and camping trips, never mentioning hair at all. The boys hardly complained when the time came to get a haircut just before school began.

The second summer of the uncut hair, our youngest son, Tom, age 15, decided this was also the time to grow a beard. I swallowed hard a couple times at that news but managed to keep my equilibrium and said not a word. The first weekend of summer vacation Tom was off camping with friends. As the second weekend approached I apprehensively eyed his hairy face. But I managed to keep quiet, no small feat for talkative me!

My downfall came on Friday. I was working at the sink and turned quickly, not realizing Tom was standing right beside me. Not an inch away from my eyes was a dark, hairy face. It was too much!

"Tom," I burst out, "are you really going to go to church looking like that?"

"Yes," Tom answered, "and I'm going over to my girlfriend's, too."

As I visibly shuddered, Tom added softly, "And I'm going to heaven, too."

I stopped abruptly and looked at my hairy son. He did love the Lord, and his last statement was not made in jest, but in sincerity. I could well imagine Isaiah, Moses, and any of the patriarchs, or even the apostles, greeting Tom with acceptance. The things that might keep him out of heaven (or me, for that matter), did not grow on the outside, but on the inside.

"Tom, I really do think you will be in heaven." Silently I added, *Father, help me to get rid of any prejudice or sin that might keep me out of heaven.* CARROL JOHNSON SHEWMAKE

NOVEMBER 7

Seasons of the Soul

To every thing there is a season, and a time to every purpose under the heaven. Eccl. 3:1.

Countless seasons have come and gone since the creation of the earth, each with its variety and unique purpose. The bright spring, with its miracle of new birth, fills our hearts with hope. It evolves into the warmth and contentment of summer, a time of growth and maturity. When fall comes, we become discontent with the weather and the changes it makes in our activities. Then winter arrives. Dark clouds overwhelm us, and we long for spring again.

In the spring of our spiritual life we are animated by the miracle of our new birth. Growth comes quickly, and we drink deeply of the promises of God's grace. It is easy to break forth in a celebration of praise for His resurrective powers. We begin to explore His peace and love and are constantly amazed at His goodness.

In close fellowship with Christ we joyfully enter into the summer of our spiritual life, a time of maturing and solidifying our relationship with Him. We feel the sunshine and warmth of His love and revel in its reality. We find deeper meaning in His promises and the wonderment of His grace. We rely fully upon Him for acceptance and forgiveness. Faith and trust become a part of us, and we are watered by His Holy Spirit.

From real or imagined slights, we let the fall of our discontent chill our hearts. The newness of spring has faded. The happiness of summer gives way to doubt and anxiety. Illness, sorrow, or trouble rains discouragement upon us. We feel alone. Storms rage, and spiritual winter settles around us with all its fears and forebodings. Our very souls become stark and bare. We long for the inner peace of spring and summer.

Then through our darkness, the Holy Spirit turns our thoughts to the Creator. Light breaks through the joyless branches of our life. Looking to Him, we find peace. Golden threads of God's love dispel doubts and despair. Once again we live in the sunshine of His love.

By daily study, faith, and prayer we can prepare for the storms of our spiritual winters, which will surely come. They attack us in all their satanic fury. Clothed in the warmth of His Spirit, we can look up and claim His promise: "Lo, I am with you alway" (Matt. 28:20).

Quickly the storms pass. Spring and summer again reign in our hearts and we are stronger for surviving the winter. Hallelujah! What a wonderful Creator! What a wonderful God!

ELVA E. SPRINGER

NOVEMBER 8

Reach Up for Life

Look unto me, and be ye saved, all the ends of the earth. Isa. 45:22.

We were 13 hours out of Los Angeles on a nonstop flight to Sydney, Australia. Flying at 35,000 feet in a Qantas 747 jet, we had only one and a half hours to go on an uneventful flight. At this predawn hour most of the passengers were drowsing in the dimly lit cabin. Suddenly the cabin was ablaze with light and 400 oxygen masks plummeted from the escape hatches in the ceiling.

An authoritative voice thundered this sobering message: "Ladies and gentlemen, this is an emergency! The plane must descend steeply, so please reach up for the oxygen mask near you and breathe normally through it until further instructions."

Now fully awake, every man, woman, and child immediately carried out the instructions. This was a life-and-death matter. It was expected that the plane would descend to 10,500 feet, where we could breathe without the aid of oxygen gear. A strange eeriness pervaded our cabin as each person reflected on his or her individual situation.

After a long silence we heard the captain's voice again. "Ladies and gentlemen, we apologize for a technical error that triggered a false alarm. There is no emergency. You are safe. We apologize."

I felt my pulse rate slowing and the adrenaline receding. Smiles and jokes reflected the changed mood, while cameras quickly appeared to record the "emergency" that hadn't materialized.

I must confess, though, that I spent some time contemplating what would have happened if it had been a genuine crisis. In the midst of these musings, I saw a startling parallel. We are all passengers on a planet spinning through space. What's more, we are all victims of history's greatest disaster—the entrance of sin and death! What hope have we in this dark hour just before the dawn? The plane's captain urged, "Reach up for the oxygen masks—for life!" Our heavenly Captain echoes that command for threatened humanity: "Reach up, look up and live!"

Our Captain has much more to say about life. "Whoever believes in the Son has eternal life" (John 3:36, NIV). And our preacher once told us that the moment we believe in the Son, that moment we have that promised eternal life. It didn't take us long to reach up for the oxygen mask when we understood the alternative. And it takes only that long to receive the greatest gift of eternal life.

"Keep breathing through the oxygen mask until the emergency is over," warned the captain. And I don't see any point when it would be safe for me to stop believing in the wonderful Son for my eternal life, not till the emergency is over.

Thank God for heaven's marvelous emergency measure. Reach up for life. EDNA HEISE

My Psalm

Give thanks to the Lord, for he is good; his love endures forever.
. . . The Lord is with me; I will not be afraid. What can man do
to me? The Lord is with me; he is my helper. . . . It is better to
take refuge in the Lord than to trust in man. Ps. 118:1-8, NIV.

God, You've protected me and taken care of me in spite of my-self. You *never* give up on me—*never*. You answer my prayers. You supply my needs, and even my wants. You have filled my life with beautiful things and beautiful people. Friends and family who love and support me; who believe in me. Thank You for knowing I needed them.

You have given me laughter, even when there is pain. I smile even in my misunderstanding of You, because I know it's then that You are carrying me.

You restore me and give me peace and joy. I can't always see Your will or guidance, but I know that with Your leading everything will be all right.

Thank You for believing in my dreams. You have opened up so many doors of opportunity for me, doors I never dreamed would be open. I believe in what my sister says, "With God the sky is not the limit!" Thank You for making impossibilities possibilities!

You are my Saviour and my Friend; I owe You my life. Show me how to truly love and serve You. Help me make You proud, proud to call me Your daughter. I want to make You smile and sing. You have done that for me so often, now it's my turn.

Thank You for being who You are. You're all I need. Forgive me for forgetting that. Thank You for the promise and hope of eternal life.

This is my psalm of praise and thanksgiving to You.

TERRIE RUFF

Unruffled Hearts

So they received nourishment, praising God with happy and un-ruffled hearts. Acts 2:46, 47, RBV.

*I*t was late at night, and I would be leaving for the airport at 6:00 a.m. I would be staying 12 days in three different locations, then three more days in a colder area. I was trying to decide what to pack, but that old nagging thought *I'm taking too much* kept creeping into my mind. I took out a few articles of clothing, then put back a few more into the suitcase, "just in case."

The next morning I climbed out of bed before 4:00 so I could type an article on the "new" computer I had just purchased. I needed to get this article in the mail before I left, but in my haste I pushed a wrong key and had no idea what the machine was trying to say, much less how to get rid of the question it was asking. On top of that, I kept losing track of the cursor and couldn't get the article printed.

By the time I arrived at the airport and collapsed in my seat, I was more than a little keyed up. I had been reading the book of Acts for my morning worship, so I took out my little green New Testament and decided to begin all over again in this different translation. It wasn't long until I found something especially for me. Tucked in verse 47 of Acts 2 were these words: "Praising God with happy and unruffled hearts." An *unruffled* heart was just what I needed.

I was surrounded by people, but as far as I was concerned at that moment it was just Jesus and me. He was speaking to my ruffled heart, and I asked Him to please give me an *unruffled* one as I relaxed and watched the snow-covered landscape below.

PEGGY TOMPKINS

NOVEMBER 11

Today

Be still before the Lord and wait patiently for him; do not fret.
Ps. 37:7, NIV.

*W*hy not just enjoy today?" the little voice of reason asked. It was so simple, yet so profound. In the back of my mind there has been this nagging worry. What next? I would ask God to help me get through the current problem, but when there was a calm, when the Lord had delivered me, I would still look around suspiciously at life. "OK, when, and from which direction will the next problem arise?"

For years I've gone around with this calm-before-the-storm mentality, never enjoying the present moments of sunshine that I am afforded for fear and in anticipation of what would come next! Yes, most times it was wasted energy. I worried about things that never materialized, thanks be to God. I'd later regret not using the time for something more productive.

Today is yesterday's tomorrow, and tomorrow's yesterday. Lord, help me to learn from the past, plan for the future, yet live for You today, for today is all I have to give.   MAXINE WILLIAMS ALLEN

NOVEMBER 12

On Course

Do not be quick with your mouth, do not be hasty in your heart.
Eccl. 5:2, NIV.

I sat looking at a woman as she ranted on and on with great agitation about how she had been wronged by a certain organization. She was vigorously enumerating several incidents that had occurred, incidents that she felt justified her indignation. Her feelings and her ego had been badly hurt. As her anger increased, her conversation took an unexpected turn. Suddenly she swerved and lashed out at me and pointed out something that I had done that added to her long list of perceived grievances. I tried to stop her with a question about her last statement, but she went on as though I had not spoken, as though my question did not merit a reply. Several times I tried to divert her attention, and each time she avoided my questions. Finally, I stopped the conversation and walked away. I had very ambivalent feelings about being harshly accused and not having been allowed to talk about the subject.

For several days I puzzled over the incident and searched for a *label* for her behavior, something that would help me identify it as her problem rather than mine. None of my *labels* seemed to fit, however.

Several days later I happened to pull into a parking lot behind a car with a very interesting bumper sticker. "I swerve and hit people at random," it declared. I chuckled out loud, realizing here was my label for that woman's behavior. She had swerved and hit me at random with her barbed words.

Random behavior, random strikes, impetuous and violent words. Oh, how they can hurt. How they can leave one puzzled and slightly off center. The devil's attacks can also come randomly. They can leave me off center and keep my focus away from the significant quest in life. They can take my energy and momentum. They can twist my life to go off in another direction.

We choose our long-term response to such attacks. We may not be responsible for what happens to us, but we are responsible for our response. Fortunately, God is my Pilot, a guide who can keep me on course when others lash out with destructive words. I choose to cooperate with my heavenly pilot. I choose to stay on course, to remain centered, regardless of the word storms around me.

LORNA L. LAWRENCE

NOVEMBER 13

Left Out—Again?

Yes, and I ask you, loyal yokefellow, help these women who have contended at my side in the cause of the gospel, along with Clement and the rest of my fellow workers, whose names are in the book of life. Phil. 4:3, NIV.

*D*o you want to visit the Jewish cemetery?" the young Polish guide asked.

None of our group had been to Prague before or knew what was special about this cemetery, but we said sure, it sounded interesting.

So off we walked, past beautiful old buildings, and through picturesque winding lanes, and finally to the ancient synagogue. After paying our entrance fee and walking down the old stone stairs and through the gate, we were suddenly in the midst of hundreds and hundreds of old tombstones. They were leaning and broken, jammed in together, covered with moss, and worn with time. Some had sunk into the ground until only inches of their tops remained above ground. There are supposed to be 100,000 tombstones in this one cemetery, the result of hundreds of years of natural deaths and pogroms in the large Jewish community. There was even a special section for children, and another for stillborns.

All the thousands of tombstones, except for one, were for men. Men only. Where were the women buried? I wanted to know. Our female guide smiled and explained that the women were buried there too; there were just no tombstones for the women. No mention of them or of their names.

"I can't believe this!" I objected out loud. And then I thought of all the biblical and historical stories in which women were not named or counted, and thus not even remembered.

I'm so glad salvation and my position with God do not depend on tradition, culture, or the way women have been counted or treated throughout history. In Romans 16 Paul, who is often accused of being against women, names 16 women by name as being fellow workers. And when writing to the Galatians he encouraged them by saying that in Christ there is no male or female, no slave or free, no Greek or Jew (see Gal. 3:28). In God all are counted, recorded, forgiven, and saved by name.

And it is up to me whether or not my name is recorded in the Lamb's book of life. I don't intend ever to be left out again! "If you conquer, you will be clothed like them in white robes, and I will not blot your name out of the book of life; I will confess your name before my Father and before his angels" (Rev. 3:5, NRSV). No tradition in control here. Today I want my name there, and I want to do everything possible to make sure every woman and every man has an opportunity to be remembered there as well, not on worn and disappearing tombstones, but as living stones through eternity.

ARDIS DICK STENBAKKEN

It Took a Miracle

Remember the Lord in everything you do. And he will give you success. Prov. 3:6, EB.

*I*n the early years of my marriage a very special event dramatically altered my life. As a teen I'd daydreamed of marrying and raising two children—one son, one daughter. Ideally, they'd arrive in that precise order.

According to plan our first child, a son, arrived just before our fifth wedding anniversary. This event was followed several years later by the birth of a beautiful daughter. Our family was now complete.

Within weeks of my daughter's birth, however, my precisely calculated, well-thought-out family planning completely exploded. With complete disbelief and total bewilderment I heard the doctor announce, "You're going to have another baby."

"That can't be! It's impossible! I've had a tubal ligation! I can't have any more children!" I protested. This was not according to script. Unmistakably, God had other designs for my life, and for the new life I now unexpectedly and miraculously carried.

Our "miracle baby" (another adorable little girl) not only beat statistical odds for conception, but survived major surgery during my first trimester. Today she's completing dental school at a renowned medical university, and God continues to work miracles in her life.

One night her long-distance call reached me at nearly midnight, and I immediately sensed her anguish in trying to prepare for a final exam the next morning.

"I feel so overwhelmed," she confided. "The material is not difficult, but we have volumes to cover. I just don't know what to study or where to begin."

As mothers are prone to do, I offered every word of encouragement I could muster, concluding with "And remember to have your devotions and pray for guidance before you begin to study. You'll make it."

The next day's call was punctuated with sheer exuberance. "Mom!" my daughter shouted. "You know that test I was so worried about? I aced it! I followed your advice, and after prayer I felt a very strong impression to focus on the textbook review questions after each chapter. Then at the final exam I was amazed to discover that all of the exam questions were taken verbatim from those exact chapter review questions."

Coincidence or providence? God is not indifferent to the simplest prayer. If you lack wisdom, then "trust the Lord with all your heart. Don't depend on your own understanding. Remember the Lord in everything you do. And he will give you success" (Prov. 3:5, 6, EB).

BARBARA J. WARREN

NOVEMBER 15

The Forgiveness of Friendship

Thou wilt cast all their sins into the depths of the sea. Micah 7:19.

They were inseparable, these little girls, knit together in heart and soul like David and Jonathan. So it wasn't surprising that they arranged to be together whenever they could—weekends, after school, overnight. They finagled to be together all the time they could.

One rainy afternoon they found themselves in Amy's room putting on a "gymnastic show." As I listened from my ringside seat at the sewing machine outside the bedroom door I heard a running commentary on the proceedings as they shared a dual emceeship.

"You did this . . ."

"He said that . . ."

"Pretend this happened . . ."

Suddenly there came from behind the door a *thud* much louder than their previous antics, and the usual commentary was not forthcoming. I decided I had better take a look. Then I heard a little giggle.

"That didn't happen," said Keri with a finality that would convince even a full audience.

After a few more giggles, the show went on.

My Friend, Jesus, and I stay as close together as I am able to discipline myself in sustaining this long-distance relationship forced upon us. Sometimes when I fall flat on my face, it takes me some time to gather my thoughts back to Him again. But when I do, I look into His face and can tell that He sees how badly I feel. His healing finger gently lifts my guilty heart and makes it light again. I can imagine I see Him smiling as He says "That didn't happen." He has taken my sin to the bottom of the sea and covered it so completely that it's as if it never happened. Except for one thing. Both of us know that now I am a little closer to where we want me to be. SUSAN SCOGGINS

It's an Emergency!

There is a way that seemeth right unto a man, but the end thereof are the ways of death. Prov. 16:25.

Many times during the four years I worked at the emergency room admitting desk, I witnessed a sick child being brought in by a young, concerned parent. Most of the cases involved nonemergency medical care for a cold, the flu, a runny nose, coughing, or fever. During the usually long wait, the child would invariably whine for a snack.

"Later" would be the parent's reply.

"Now!" the child would wail, producing big crocodile tears, a pout, or even a temper tantrum.

Mom or Dad would give in, snatch the child up in a fit of anger, and head for the snack bar. The child would return, munching on a large-sized candy bar and, quite often, sipping a carbonated soda with caffeine. In the majority of cases the happy child even forgot how ill he or she was for a while.

Then, cranky and tired of doing nothing, the child would resume whining, and Mom or Dad would pull out another candy bar.

Well, the kid won again, I'd say to myself. Unfortunately, the kids almost always won. A few whines or tears, a strong will, an embarrassed mom or dad too tired to fight with them, and the "sick" one got to eat lots of junk. Of course, the hospital snack bar had some nutritious snacks to choose from, but the kids got what they wanted—what they were used to having. (And the parents wondered why their kids were always sick.)

Sometimes we feed our spiritual lives on the wrong stuff when the right choices are within our grasp. Sin-sick, we settle for quick (and often junky) fixes for what really ails us. And yes, we also wonder why we can't shake what's wrong with us. If we would open our hearts, minds, and souls, we could be filled with the good stuff, with Jesus Christ, our Lord and Saviour. IRIS L. STOVALL

Lurking in the Darkness

But whoso hearkeneth unto me shall dwell safely, and shall be quiet from fear of evil. Prov. 1:33.

A rapist had been terrorizing our neighborhood. Every few days there was a new report of another victim. It was the talk and fear of the town. One evening a group of friends and I attended a band concert on the steps of the U.S. Capitol. It was a thrill to listen to one of the service bands while the Stars and Stripes waved above our heads in the breeze. But during the 30-minute drive home, our conversation turned from the music of the evening to the latest report on the rapist.

"Now he's dropping out of a tree as a woman walks by," one of the women said. Others in the group had tidbits of information to add.

After I'd delivered all the women to their homes, I walked under my red maple tree, with its branches hanging over the walk, and entered my empty house. Safely inside, I prepared for bed but could think of little else except our conversation in the car. Before turning out the bedroom light, I opened my Bible. Thoughts of the man jumping out of the tree beside an unsuspecting woman filled my mind. By the time I got to the bottom of the page, I realized I hadn't remembered one thing I'd read. I flipped over a few pages and opened to Proverbs 1. Imagine my joy and thanksgiving when I came to the very last verse: "But whoso hearkeneth unto me shall dwell safely, and shall be quiet from fear of evil" (verse 33).

I accepted that promise as a promise not only for protection, but also for freedom from fear of evil. Thanking the Lord many times for pointing that particular verse to me just when I needed that assurance, I snuggled down in bed and fell asleep.   VERNA WHITE

Lessons From the Cat

"How often I have longed to gather your children together, as a hen gathers her chicks under her wings." Luke 13:34, NIV.

We have a cat who adopted us last year and had kittens in our storage shed. She was quite wild, yet wanted to be near and to be tamed. She eventually came to be part of the family. Food is often a high priority, but most of all she wants to have your full attention. A mere "Hello there, cat" doesn't do it. She wants you to bend down, talk to her, touch her, and take some time with her.

She recently had another family of kittens, and in the weeks just prior to their arrival she wanted constant attention. She meowed and called and went looking all over the house for one of us. The evening after the kittens were born she was really torn between her motherly duties and wanting some attention for herself. She finally jumped into my lap and pressed her body and head against me. She *had* to be loved. Then she jumped down and went back to her babies.

Now the babies are four weeks old and getting to be a little independent. She continues to call them, feed them, clean them, and look after their welfare. She will protect them from people she doesn't know and from other animals.

As I have observed her, I am reminded of God's care and His desire for our attention, and not just because He's a source of help with necessities. Often I seem too busy to spend time with God, too busy to have a real conversation or to talk over the events of the day. But if God really cares for me in the way this mother cat cares for her kittens and seeks my attention frequently, I must realize that God not only continues to meet my physical needs, clean up my messes, and try to guide my life, but He also wants to be a companion and friend who really is close, pressing against me, holding me near. This physical presence is something I have been wanting but didn't know how to find.

Why do I live in a rush and in careless isolation, if all I have to do is stop, wait, and be open to that warm, loving presence? This cat is *near,* she is attentive, she is caring and warm and persistent. If God is so near and wants so much to be touching my life, can't I live a life of peace and joy in His presence because I *really* am in touch with Him?

JULIA PEARCE

New Day at Sunset?

And the evening and the morning were the first day. Gen. 1:5.

*I*n a long-ago romance my friend and I stood watching the summer sun slide softly down a peaches-and-cream sky to rest in a quilt of haze, far beyond our horizon. One of the many things on which we disagreed was our feeling about sunset and sunrise. He always felt sad in the evening, perhaps because opportunities for service were over, and he felt that night and sleep were like precursors of death. He preferred the morning light—the white dazzle of dawn, the prospect of the day ahead.

I still love the sunset best, with its warmer, richer tones, its message that work is (mostly!) over, and rest is on its way. While I appreciate the remote magic of a summer dawn, I hate having to wake up early to see it.

Strictly speaking, a day is the time from one midnight to the next. To most of us it is new when we get up in the morning and ends when we go to bed. Even Jeremiah thought this way, with his view of God's compassions "new every morning" in Lamentations 3:23.

To God, however, a day is from one dusk to the next—sunset to sunset. Thinking God's way about a new day gives me quite a buzz. His idea is to start the new day with rest from work, a pleasant evening meal, an evening's recreation, worship time, and the prospect of a good night's sleep.

Of course there are chores; there may be homework, and some of us work evenings or night shifts. But it's refreshing just thinking that here is a new day beginning—especially as we can use sunset time to empty our minds of all slights and mistakes of the daylight hours, using the time to kiss and make up, making the evening glow and night duties light up with stars of peace.

For most of us evening generally spells home and rest. I watched a hot cherry sun drop behind a field of blond rye this week and thought, *Lord, surely as the heavens are higher than the earth, so are Your thoughts than my thoughts* (see Isa. 55:9).   APRIL DUNNETT

A Friend Loves at All Times

A friend loves at all times, and a brother is born for adversity.
Prov. 17:17, NIV.

*H*ow precious are our friends, and what pleasure it gives us to remember them. One of mine, no matter how busy she is, always has time for me. In whatever frame of mind I come, she always seems tuned in to my need. There is an unhurried ease about her that is like an oasis. I always leave feeling refreshed.

Another friend concerns herself, not with putting people in their places, but with building them up. You don't need a tonic from the doctor with a friend like that.

The weekly Keep Fit session is blessed with several specialists in the art of making people feel comfortable. No matter if your first attendance finds you stiff and in poor shape, they will make you forget you can hardly touch your toes. In their company you're bound to loosen up, and maybe even see your Olympic possibilities!

Then there's Barnabas. (She'd laugh if she knew I called her that.) Barnabas means "son of encouragement," and she's an artist in this sphere. Sometimes you've got an idea and think it's got possibilities, and you mention it to someone who says "It's been tried before but didn't catch on." Another may say "I'd like to help, but don't have time" (and seem relieved). Not Barnabas. Barnabas will laugh outrageously at the part that seems too adventurous. She'll trim your ideas with her infectious good sense and then share your enthusiasm to get started.

The world cannot have too many of these gifted people. So maybe it's time for a little self-examination.

Have I made time for someone this week?

Do I make it my aim to put people at ease?

Have I thought beyond myself and shared another's worries or enthusiasms?

If so, someone somewhere is blessed to have a friend like you.

PEGGY MASON

NOVEMBER 21

The Least of These

"No," said Peter, "you shall never wash my feat." Jesus answered, "Unless I wash you, you have no part with me." "Then,
Lord," Simon Peter replied, "not just my feet but my hands and
my head as well!" John 13:8, 9, NIV.

It was Communion day at church. As I left the sanctuary to go
to the room prepared for the ordinance of humility, I saw
her, a young woman everybody felt sorry for but tended to avoid.
She had been abused as a child, pregnant as a teenager, on welfare,
and considered not very bright.

"Won't you come and take part in the foot washing with me?"
I asked.

"Oh, n-no, I, I couldn't," she stuttered. "I'm not ready."

I could see she was embarrassed that I had asked. "Well, that's
OK," I said. "I'll wait. What do you have to do to get ready?"

More embarrassed now, she replied, "No, I mean I am not ready."

I smiled. "You don't have to do anything to get ready. Come,
take part in the service with me."

She hesitated. "Well, I guess I could wash your feet, but you are
not going to wash mine!"

"OK," I agreed. Silently I thought, *Well, this is a start. Lord, please
help me as I reach out to this girl.*

After she washed my feet, I once again asked her, "May I wash
your feet?"

She had weakened some, but still she replied, "No, I'm not ready."

"Do you love Jesus?" I softly asked.

"Oh, yes," she beamed. "I love Jesus."

"Well," I replied, "all you have to do to be ready is to love Jesus."

Her eyes filled with tears. "OK," she said. "I guess you can wash
my feet, but they are so dirty."

"That's OK," I said. "Just think how dirty those disciples' feet
must have been after walking through the hot dusty streets the day
that Jesus washed their feet."

When we had finished, we held hands and I prayed, then gave
her a hug and said, "I love you. Have a happy day."

No longer able to contain my tears, I rushed from the room,
went aside, and wept. Jesus' words filled my heart and mind:
"Inasmuch as ye have done it unto one of the least of these my

brethren, ye have done it unto me" (Matt. 25:40). "By this all men will know that you are my disciples, if you love one another" (John 13:35, NIV).

"Thank You, Lord, for this special blessing I have just received," I prayed. "Thank You for this young woman—and for Jesus."

KATHY JO YERGEN

NOVEMBER 22

Abolishing Slavery

The words of a talebearer are as wounds, and they go down into the innermost parts of the belly. Prov. 18:8.

When she didn't show her usual exuberance at being called to lunch, I asked my 10-year-old what was the matter. She stared ahead blankly for a moment, and then told me she had been reading about slavery. The book she had been reading showed a picture that had broken her heart. When I saw it, I understood why.

There, on the top half of the page, was a painting of a little Black girl of 11 or 12. She was being whipped by a cruel slavemaster while clinging desperately to her father. For several minutes I soaked in the scene, feeling indescribable grief. When I finally found my voice, I pointed out to my daughter that I could not begin to understand how one human could ever treat another human in such a terrible way. She shook her head, indicating that she couldn't either. For several minutes we clung to each other, crying.

But as the moments passed and I peered over the head of my child at the haunting picture, the awful truth began to sink in. Whippings such as this one are not the only way that people are in-human to others. The sickening truth is that our words can cut into the souls of fellow humans in much the same way as a whip can cut into flesh. And that pain can be equally unbearable. I had to admit that often those words are delivered in the same way as the whip-ping in the picture—behind people's backs. But pain is not partial to position—no matter where the pain originates, it ends up em-bedded in the soul.

Sometimes I wish I could somehow erase the picture. But even after the book has been closed and put away, the image remains. Sometimes I am thankful for the picture. Not thankful that the whipping took place, but thankful for what knowing about it does to me. Sometimes I pray about the picture. About all those who suffer in this world at the hands of brothers and sisters. And about the slavemaster in me that needs to be abolished and changed into a servant. RETTA MICHAELIS

NOVEMBER 23

Know Your Position

I write these things to you who believe in the name of the Son of God so that you may know that you have eternal life. 1 John 5:13, NIV.

*T*oo many people make the mistake of measuring the certainty of their salvation by their feelings instead of the facts of God's Word. In Jesus Christ you have a new life. See what God's Word says about your new position on His team.

N I am a *new* creation in Christ (2 Cor. 5:17).
E I have *everything* I need for life and godliness (2 Peter 1:3).
W I am His *witness* and His *workmanship,* created for good works (Eph. 2:10).

L I am *loved* and accepted completely in Christ (Rom. 8:38, 39).
I I am *indwelt* by the Holy Spirit (1 Cor. 6:19, 20).
F I am *forgiven* and *free* from condemnation (1 John 1:9).
E I have *eternal* life in Christ (John 5:24).

Trust God. Put your faith in His Word, not in your feelings.
HELEN LILLIAN WALLS

When My Husband Is Away

For your Maker is your husband—the Lord Almighty is his name.
Isa. 54:5, NIV.

*M*y husband's work involves traveling to the various countries of the Middle East. Every time he leaves, it brings
about some kind of foreboding I don't have control of. Being raised
in a big family, I was never by myself. I didn't mind so much the
times he was away when the children were home. These days it's different. Every time he plans a trip, I wish I could go along with him,
but it is just not possible.

This time I had appointments to meet. Our small support group
had to be attended to. I'd promised the girls in our group that I
would take them to visit one of their friends. So on Sunday we
packed a picnic lunch, and I drove. We got to our destination, visited for a while, and then decided to go to the seafront to eat our
lunch. But the car wouldn't start. What should I do? I drive, but I
don't know anything more about cars. Fortunately, a couple men at
the restaurant where we parked came to our rescue. They pushed,
and the car roared to life. We had accidentally left the lights on,
which resulted in a weak battery.

At 4:00 we headed home. You guessed it—the car wouldn't
start. Another push by two helpful men, and we all piled into the
car. One of the men noticed that a rear tire needed some air. What
next? We stopped at several gasoline stations, with no luck. We
found air pumps but no hoses. Since businesses were closed on
Sunday, I suppose the proprietors didn't want to risk having their
air hoses stolen or destroyed. We pressed on. Four gasoline stations
later we found what we needed and all breathed a sigh of relief.

I am secure when my husband is with me because I am confident he knows what to do when troubles like these come. He eases
my bits of insecurity by just being there and letting me know he
really cares for me.

So it is in my relationship with Jesus. But He doesn't leave me. I
am the erring partner, and He is the ever-faithful Husband. One day
John's disciples and some Pharisees asked why Jesus' disciples were
not fasting as they were. Jesus answered, "Can the friends of the
bridegroom mourn as long as the bridegroom is with them?" (Matt.
9:15, NKJV). I like to put it this way: Can anything go wrong when

Jesus is with me? Jesus says, "I will never leave you nor forsake you" (Heb. 13:5, NKJV). What an infallible way to feel secure, especially when my husband's away. And what comfort to those daughters of the King who do not have a husband. The loving Father promises that He will be a husband to them.   MERCY M. FERRER

NOVEMBER 25

Transformed

My God lights up my darkness. Ps. 18:28, Jerusalem.

*T*hanksgiving was approaching, and since no family was coming home for the holidays, my husband and I decided to spend the day in the Smoky Mountains. The brilliant fall colors would be gone, we knew, but the call of the woods, the crunchy leaf-padded nature trails, and crisp mountain air beckoned us. It would be invigorating.

The small Old World town of Gatlinburg, wedged in a valley of Tennessee's Smoky Mountains, looked drab and uninviting. Stark winter trees covered the hills and a dull gray sky overshadowed the valley. Beauty was gone, we thought. We spent some time following a nature trail on a mountainside high above the town. As the night shadows gathered, we drove down toward the town. Suddenly it became transformed into a twinkling fairyland as myriads of Christmas lights were turned on. We were jolted back in time to winter's magic kingdom, the appearance of snowflakes falling in the street, quaint lighted shops loaded with Christmas wares, narrow streets filled with busy shoppers wearing colorful coats, scarves, and earmuffs, and small children in snowsuits. The town was alive and beautiful, vibrant with anticipation.

Our lives are like that valley. We live through the seasons in turn, and when the drabness of winter comes, as it surely will, it takes a miracle—a power source outside ourselves—to transform our winter experience into something beautiful again.

Perhaps it is a heartache, a bereavement, or a sore trial that strips your life of its color and vitality. You may feel that you can never truly have life again. Humanly speaking, this may be true. We need a superhuman power source. God has promised it in Psalm 18:28: "My God lightens my darkness." Reach for that power source and watch the miracle of His light glow in your soul today.

JOAN MINCHIN NEALL

Fear Not!

Fear not, for I am with you; be not dismayed, for I am your God.
Isa. 41:10, NKJV.

*T*was sitting in the waiting lounge at my designated gate before boarding my plane when I was suddenly inspired to visit the bookstore around the corner. As I approached the news rack my eyes caught the headline on a *Newsweek* cover: "How Safe Is Your Flight?"

I froze instantly. "I certainly won't be reading this now that I am going to board a flight. Who wants to know the probability of their flight crashing?" I muttered.

I walked passed the magazine rack and left the store. I decided the book I was reading at the moment, and the Bible that I was carrying, were sufficient reading material for the trip. I returned to my seat and waited for the boarding call. However, I could not help thinking about that caption.

Lord, please take us safely to Baltimore. We are flying at night, and if anything were to happen I would not be able to see my way through. Please watch over us.

Five minutes after takeoff the captain announced that due to turbulence and strong headwinds we would be arriving in Baltimore 45 minutes late. The seat belt sign would remain on during the flight. I guessed we were in for a ride. I again whispered a short prayer and claimed the promise in today's text. Then I lifted the armrests of the seat next to me, took my coat and pillows, and lay down to sleep. I believed God was going to protect me, so it didn't make sense to stay up and worry.

Trust is complete rest in Him. Today, take your problems, your fears, and your concerns to Him. He promised He will be with you, and He will.

ANDREA A. BUSSUE

You Are My Joy

You have shown me the path that leads to life. You have filled my life with the joy of your presence, and throughout eternity there will be joys untold. Ps. 16:11, Clear Word.

*I*t's me, Lord. I'm so glad we have this special time together. You are my friend, and I have learned that You are really interested in me. Thanks for being such a good listener. That makes it so much more comfortable to open my heart to You.

First, I am remembering how important You are in my life. In the moments throughout the day as I think about You, the essence of Your presence, like sweet perfume, pervades my life to strengthen and renew.

The wonder of who You are and what You can do is truly breathtaking. I saw Your work last night in the sunset. You were magnificent! Glorious! Sparkling rays of Your joy and peace sank deep into my heart, even as the sun slipped behind the bay.

Every day You give me a thousand reminders of Your goodness. I want to be more aware of those gifts, Lord. Heighten my sensitivity through the presence of Your Holy Spirit. It makes me truly *tingle* to think that right now, even as I speak, You already know my thoughts, and You are answering the deep needs of my soul in ways I cannot begin to imagine.

Yes, I'll admit You have really surprised me at times with Your innovative plans. But as I look back I can see Your hand of love guiding me all the way. And because You love me so much, I know I can trust You with those who are special in my life. So I will leave them in Your care. My greatest desire as I interact with them is to speak the words and live the life that will make You attractive in their eyes.

I could talk on a long time about what You mean to me, but if one word could sum up my feelings today, it would be joy. You have brought a happiness into my life that nothing can ever take away from me as long as we are friends.

> You're the joy of my life,
> My Saviour and King;
> With a heart full of praise
> My voice I will raise.

You're the reason I sing.
Whatever tomorrow brings
The promise is sure,
You're there every day,
Each step of the way;
You are my joy, joy, joy,
You're there every day,
Each step of the way,
You are my joy.

DEBBY GRAY WILMOT

NOVEMBER 28

In All Things, Give Thanks

Blessed be the Lord, who daily loadeth us with benefits. Ps. 68:19.

I think back to Thanksgivings past, and one particular one comes to mind. It was in 1963. I was a young woman living in Oklahoma. I had just given birth to my fourth child and had so many things to be grateful for, yet it was a most difficult year. My husband had been off work for several months with a serious back injury. He was now facing major surgery. With a young family to care for, I was unable to work outside the home, and our budget was restricted by his disability.

It had been traditional since my marriage for my parents and my husband's entire family to come to our home for Thanksgiving. I enjoyed cooking and having the families all there together, and the grandparents enjoyed time with their only grandchildren. But I was so tired and anxious about our family needs and problems that I truly did not have much holiday spirit that year. I longed for family support, but there was no way I could come home with a new baby and celebrate with company. Nothing was said about Thanksgiving plans. The day before the holiday I returned home from the hospital to my waiting children with our new baby girl.

The next morning I had a surprise. Our families had come from states away, bringing with them an entire Thanksgiving feast. They spent the rest of the holidays helping me get my household back together. I really had the opportunity to appreciate and be thankful for family that year.

Remembering, I praise God that we can thank Him for the good life He has given to us, just as I can praise and thank Him for the family members who give new joy and meaning to our lives.

BARBARA SMITH MORRIS

NOVEMBER 29

Heart Guard

Rejoice in the Lord always. I will say it again: Rejoice! Let your gentleness be evident to all. The Lord is near. Do not be anxious about anything, but in everything, by prayer and petition, with thanksgiving, present your requests to God. And the peace of God, which transcends all understanding, will guard your hearts and your minds in Christ Jesus. Phil. 4:4-7, NIV.

My pastor shared with me the challenge of praying in every situation. He used the story of Israel's victory over the Amalekites because Moses, with the help of Aaron and Hur, held up his hands in constant prayer (Ex. 17:8-13). I wondered if praying can always be significant today and began to search for texts that would tell me more.

One day I discovered Philippians 4. Here was a formula for peace: (a) in everything, pray; (b) pray with thanksgiving.

Product: The peace of God will guard your hearts and minds. "Guard" brought up a picture of a sentry on duty, watching that no enemy would break in to destroy or kill.

But was this formula possible to follow? I am not always in the mood to pray, and I certainly do not always feel a spirit of gratitude. But the instructions were there, as simple and direct as directions for making bread or a casserole. I began to look for concrete ideas for which I could be grateful. Amazingly, even during the worst difficulties I could find some bright spots. If a patient was mean-spirited, I could be thankful I had good ears and could hear. If a patient was demanding and angry, I could be thankful I had an opportunity to calm someone's hostility. If I was stuck in heavy traffic, I could be thankful for the sky above that displayed God's handiwork. Amazingly, this continual thankfulness to God did produce the product promised in Philippians 4. It became a guard of peace.

As long as my conscious life shall last, there will always be certain things I can be thankful for—a beating heart, air to breathe, and (certainly the best) the salvation given freely through Jesus Christ.

"Two men look out through the same bars: one sees the mud, and one the stars." Thanking God for the stars instead of looking at the mud does create a fence protecting peace of mind. The Philippian formula works.　　　　　　　　　　　RUTH WATSON

NOVEMBER 30

Lice-infested Beds

Give thanks in all circumstances; for this is the will of God in Christ Jesus for you. 1 Thess. 5:18, RSV.

*Y*ou and I sometimes go through periods in which we think, *Give thanks for what?* The apostle Paul is insistent—in *all* things give thanks. Once I heard a retired minister say, "Misfortunes are only the rinds of blessings." Each cloud hides a brilliant portion and each tragedy brings with it a hidden blessing for the one who is in Christ.

You may have heard the story of the little old man who made it his practice to thank God for everything that happened to him. One day he was at the harbor waiting for a ship that was to take him on a trip. While he waited, he slipped and fell, breaking his leg. Though he missed his trip, he surprised everybody when he thanked God for the fall. Later, he learned that the ship he was to board had sunk. The old man was right on in praising the Lord; he had reason to be thankful.

Corrie ten Boom and her sister, Betsie, were in a concentration camp during World War II. One day they were transferred to new quarters, where their beds were filled with lice. They could not understand how God would allow this to happen to them. As they read the Bible, they found today's text, "Give thanks in all circumstances." Were they to thank God for the lice? Well, soon they discovered that the lice were indeed a reason to thank God. Because of the lice, the guards refused to enter their quarters. That gave them the freedom to read the Bible and to witness. Had it not been for those pesky creatures, this would not have been possible.

We too always have grounds for gratitude. When something negative happens to us, we are still to thank God. Praising God helps us to find the brilliant portion behind the dark cloud.

DINALVA PESSOA DE CARVALHO

Cross-outs, Mark-overs, and Erasures

To be held in loving esteem is better than silver and gold. Prov. 22:1, TLB.

*I*t's that time of the year again. The one time of the year when you hear from friends. Time to write and mail the annual Christmas cards. For some, it is a very pleasant task, and for others it is a necessary chore, but what a joy for all to see the mail carrier come!

I start addressing cards and envelopes, but along the way I feel a tinge of sadness. Last year it was "Mr. and Mrs." This year it's only "Mrs." I have been sending them cards for many years. Now the circle is broken. What can I say to help ease the pain that holidays bring to such a household? He worked faithfully for the Lord. He may be gone, but his influence will live forever.

A little further down the list is "Mr." but no "Mrs." She was a humble woman, a devoted wife and loving neighbor. A real encouragement to me.

Sometimes a family moves to a new location and you lose track of them. You cross off their old address, wondering where they have gone and how they are doing.

Five years have passed since I started this address book. Five years of changes. Who will it be this time next year? It could even be me. Will people remember me as a positive influence for the God I represent?

But all is not sadness. I have corresponded with some of these friends for 50 years. The warmth such friendships give is hard to describe. The fiftieth wedding anniversaries are becoming more frequent. How good God has been all these years!

A Christmas list and address book. So full of memories, history, sadness, gladness, and warm friendships. It's a tie that binds our hearts together. Pray that the Lord will help us never complain about addressing Christmas cards. Let us take time to appreciate the privilege that Christian friendship brings. It's a ministry that can have a worldwide influence, starting from the desk in your own home.

FONDA CORDIS CHAFFEE

Thanks for Remembering Me

He who is kind to the poor lends to the Lord, and he will reward him for what he has done. Prov. 19:17, NIV.

I created my own Christmas cards last year, and with the money that I saved I was able to greatly expand my list. I gave cards to almost 200 people, even though most of them were not especially close to me. I had a lot of fun carrying that box full of cards into the church and filling mailboxes—and so did my son, who got to play mail carrier.

The following week I found a few cards in my own mailbox, and one of them was from a woman who had received one from me the week before. I didn't know this woman very well—I had to look up her picture in the church directory. All I knew about her was that she was one of our senior citizens. She came to church alone, usually sitting in the back, but she always greeted me with a smile. She made it a point to tell me how much she enjoyed my special music. She also had the knack for remembering *my* name, which made for some embarrassing moments on my part because I could never remember hers. The card she gave me was so pretty, soft pastel colors and glistening snowflakes swirling about the standard sentiments of Christmas that were printed inside. She signed her name at the bottom, and under her signature were four words: *Thanks for remembering me.*

Tears sprang to my eyes as the implication of her words pierced my heart. This precious woman never acted in any way that would lead anyone to believe that there was anything wrong or that she was sad or needy in any way, but that little phrase at the bottom of her card spoke volumes.

To be remembered—is this something we take for granted? Of course, our friends and family remember us. And we remember them, don't we? But what about those people who don't have any friends or family, for whatever reason? Their church may very well be the only family they have. They may come, week after week, even sitting in the pew next to us. We go through the usual superficial pleasantries and then rush out the door to get lunch. But where do they go? Home to an empty house? What kind of loneliness do they experience on a daily basis? Do they feel totally forgotten? Do we *really* care?

It's so simple to drop a little note in the mail. It's so simple to pick up the phone and call them to see how they're doing. It's so simple to buy a little gift for Christmas or for a birthday. It doesn't take that much to show we care. And if we remain faithful to these simple little acts of caring, someday we just might hear Jesus saying to us, "Thanks for remembering Me."   LYNDA MAE RICHARDSON

DECEMBER 3

Be Encouraged

Be strong and of a good courage, fear not, nor be afraid of them: for the Lord thy God, he it is that doth go with thee; he will not fail thee, nor forsake thee. Deut. 31:6.

*T*he past year had been a tough one for our family, but as I looked back, I could clearly see God's hands of love supporting me through the darkest hours. My husband was working across the country from our four boys and me, and we had medical emergencies—major and minor. Finances were up and down. There were the usual small and large daily problems—like the transmission going out on my car, the washing machine breaking down, motor problems with the lawn mower, and simple things like lost glasses. In addition, I am committed to Christian education and drive 32 miles four times a day to keep our boys in a school that provides the quality of education we need. Raising four boys alone for God is a full-time responsibility, and life is rarely dull.

I personally have dealt with depression, loneliness, and exhaustion. I am often overwhelmed by the continuing challenge of keeping our marriage alive and healthy when we're separated by 3,500 miles. It's difficult to capture a clear revelation of Jesus Christ's love and build a closer relationship with our heavenly Father, as well as each other. But this difficult year is nearly over, and soon we will be reunited as a family.

I have learned a great deal during this year. I have learned that my relationship with Jesus is primary and must be kept alive and vital; that He is the only one on whom I can really depend. I have learned to be more real and vulnerable with those around me. If I need help, I must not wait and hope that they will notice; I must ask. Many are willing to help when there is a need and they are asked. I've learned that people are benefited by feeling needed. It helps them feel important. It does their spirits good to reach out and be of help to others. This is true Christianity in action.

Yes, this last year has been difficult, but in retrospect it is encouraging and exciting to see the Lord's loving hands not only leading, but also gently holding me up day by day. I praise His name for His everlasting love and care. You too can be encouraged by looking to Jesus. Regardless of what you struggle with today, choose to allow Him to lead your life in a real way.   CARLENE WILL

DECEMBER 4

Crumpled Treasures

She did what she could. Mark 14:8, NIV.

The Christmas tree has come down from the attic. It stands, bare and skeletal, at the end of the living room, shivering in the slight breeze from the window. We're waiting for the children to come home from school to help with the decorations. I open the boxes of tinsel and white silk angels, silver stars, doves, and the tiniest little boxes wrapped in iridescent paper with silver bows. Another box is full of sparkly snowflakes. The twinkly white Christmas lights lie tangled in an old cookie tin. Somewhere else there are four different sets of nativity figures.

But there is also another box. This box has little card shapes, smothered with finger paint and glitter. An angel with a ping-pong ball head and wonky wings; a lantern made from a cardboard tube; a little fat snowman covered in cotton balls with black paper buttons. A bell made from a plastic cup covered in silver foil. These are the real treasures, put together by chubby fingers covered with glue and paint. It doesn't matter that these ornaments are bent and misshapen, or that they don't coordinate with the rest of the decorations. They are special because my children made them for me. Their love transforms the paper and glitter into satin and diamonds.

Yesterday Bernie and I gave a seminar together. We were both still recovering from a vicious flu virus that had left us with coughs and little energy. Today I have that "morning after" feeling, the time for analysis and retrospection. I wonder how I could have done better, and regret the misplaced word, or the clumsy explanation that didn't seem to be clear. I feel badly, because as we were finishing the seminar I realized that we had been videoed and I had coughed and spluttered my way through the whole session. I feel as if I ruined the special atmosphere of the weekend.

"Dear Father, I'm sorry. I really messed up. I wanted to do my best for Your glory, and I tried so hard to make it perfect, and we had bathed the whole project in prayer. I'm just not much of a speaker sometimes . . ."

I picked up the angel Bethany made in preschool. The head is coming loose; I'll have to stick it back on . . .

"Karen, it's all right. You did the best you could, and you did it because you love Me. You are My child, and whatever you do for Me is beautiful because it's a gift of love. Just as you treasure this little broken angel, I treasure whatever is done for Me in love. Thank you."

KAREN HOLFORD

DECEMBER 5

Gasping for Air

Lo, I have given thee a wise and an understanding heart. 1 Kings 3:12.

I lay back in my hospital bed, gasping for air. I had just been encouraged to stand beside my bed while nurses changed the linen for the second time that day. Drainage continued to leak from the hole in my side where the chest tubes had been. Those few minutes standing seemed like hours! Concerned nurses repacked the drainage site, hooked up the oxygen, and rushed off once again to call my physician.

It had been nearly a month since I entered the hospital for a relatively simple surgical procedure that should have had me home in three or four days. However, within 48 hours of the surgery I had developed severe streptococcal pneumonia in my left lung. Eight major procedures later, involving four specialists, many blood tests, and myriads of X-rays, here I was fighting for my very life. I was so sick—sick of hospital walls, weary at heart, defying mortality, longing to be well.

The doctors stood around my bed, then spoke in hushed tones out in the hall. What will they suggest next? I wondered. I gazed up at the ceiling, familiar with every line and crack. "I didn't ask for this, Lord, and I sure don't know why it's happening," I prayed. "Please remind me of Your care and concern. This is far more frightening than I would have ever believed."

I decided to count my blessings. For one, several close friends were going the second and third mile to call, visit, and bring unique gifts of encouragement and support. They had assured me that four or five prayer chains across the nation were interceding on my behalf. Many of my family members had telephoned, and some had sent cards and flowers. The nurses had almost gone overboard trying to make me comfortable. The chaplains had been to see me every day to offer spiritual support.

The chaplains . . . I stopped short and actually chuckled. "Lord, is that it?" I asked. "Are You using this experience to help prepare me for the next chapter in my life?"

I had recently enrolled in a chaplaincy program, and my practicum was scheduled to begin in just a few weeks. I had worked in a hospital as a nurse's aide, but I had never been a bedridden patient before. In those quiet moments of reflection I knew beyond a shadow of doubt that my perception of chaplaincy had been forever altered. In amazement, I realized that because of my personal experience with illness I would be aware of pain and suffering in a way that would never have been possible before.

Each of us has endured experiences that are somewhat unique. When viewed as learning scenarios these experiences enable us to share with others and to encourage them as they pass through their valley.

"Thank You, Lord," I breathed. "As long as this had to happen, help me to learn from it. May I minister to others with a truly understanding heart."

LORNA L. LAWRENCE

DECEMBER 6

Let's Keep Christmas All Year Long

Do this in remembrance of Me. Luke 22:19, NKJV.

We love to see Christmas come, with bright lights and good cheer.
It is the happiest and most blessed time of the year.
We celebrate with goodwill, with joy and mirth,
the coming of the Christ child to save the earth.
Does it really matter in which month He was born?
When exactly *was* that first Christmas morn?
Was it July or September? May or December?
What really matters is that we remember.

We enjoy all the sights and the sounds of the season,
but we should never forget the beautiful Reason.
He came to bring life to all women and men.
He came to tell us He would come back again.
He came to assure us our sins are forgiven,
So He can take us to live with Him in heaven.

Love, peace, and goodwill are not just for this little while.
All year long we should greet people with kind words and
   a smile.
Our lives should be full of loving praises and giving.
Kindness should become the best way of living.
He gives us loving hearts and joyful song,
So we can keep Christmas all year long.

Lillian Musgrave

DECEMBER 7

Love Thy Neighbor

Bear with each other and forgive whatever grievances you may
have against one another. Forgive as the Lord forgave you. And
over all these virtues put on love, which binds them all together
in perfect unity. Col. 3:13, 14, NIV.

*W*ith little time remaining to meet my 10:00 appointment,
I rushed down the driveway, only to find my way blocked
by a car parked on the narrow access road. It was not the first time
this had happened. The family who lived along this road seemed to
feel it belonged only to them. They didn't appear to care about those
living beyond them who had no other way to reach their homes. In
response to my honking, someone finally came out and grudgingly
moved the car so I could be on my way to the main street.

The annoying problem persisted, and there seemed to be no
easy solution. Even "please" and "thank you" seemed to have no effect on the residents of the duplex. Then Christmastime came, and
I made some loaves of fruit/nut bread to give to the neighbors living
on either side of us. Suddenly the Lord spoke to me.

"The folks living down the lane are your neighbors too."

So the next time I went out I had two loaves of bread in colorful Christmas wrappings on the seat next to me. No one was around

as I drove out, but when I came back in, one of the men was standing in the road talking to a friend. It was just the opportunity I'd been waiting for. Surprise and pleasure were mirrored on his face as I stopped the car and handed him the gift with a pleasant greeting. "Merry Christmas from your neighbors up the hill!"

And what a change it made in our relationship! Where before they had only scowled as we drove past, now there was always a smile and a friendly wave. If a car should be parked in the way when we needed to pass, someone always hurried out to move it with a cheery "Sorry!"

It was such a little thing—just a little sharing, showing a little love—and yet it made such a big difference in getting along with our neighbors. Take time this season to "forgive whatever grievances you may have against one another" and do something nice for them today. May God bind you together in perfect unity, now and evermore.

BETTY ADAMS

DECEMBER 8

What Is Time?

A time to be born and a time to die. Eccl. 3:2.

I stepped off the plane in Copenhagen, Denmark, into the bright sun and unusually hot wind feeling like a zombie living in a senseless dream. We should have arrived many, many hours earlier. But problems with the takeoff had forced us to take a much different route and to spend exhausting hours waiting at airports. Although I was the very same person who had gotten out of my very own warm and familiar bed some 24 hours before, by crossing time zones I now had gained another seven hours to live all over again.

What is time? Time never seems to make much sense to me. Have you ever noticed how long—or short—a minute can be? A minute seems to last forever if you're sitting in the dentist's chair, waiting in a waiting room, or waiting for a loved one to arrive. But how quickly time passes when you are racing to meet a deadline or talking with a loved one by long distance. How often I have wished for a time stretcher! How I wish that I could make every golden moment last—cherished like the last delicious bite of some scrumptious morsel of food. And how I wish I had a fast-forward on those minutes when time seems to last forever, when pain or grief has a grip on my soul and I long for the agony or anguish to pass.

Do you suppose we will encounter a time problem in heaven? Will we feel an urgency to be in a hurry mode? Will we have to meet deadlines in heaven? Will we be racing the clock? There must be some time frames in heaven, as we are told that from one new moon to another and from one Sabbath to another everyone will come to worship the Lord (Isa. 66:23). When I analyze it all, it seems time is the invisible, intangible force we cannot see, feel, or taste. But this invisible force is with us from birth to death and influences everything we say and do.

Do we always prioritize time to best advantage? If you are one of those who is used to taking time for granted, just run out of it, and suddenly it will take on a whole new perspective. Each of us may view time in a somewhat different manner, but one thing is certain—we each have been given life on this earth, each minute containing 60 seconds. And each segment of time needs to be cherished so that our lives glorify the great giver of time. How will you spend your season and purpose here to assure your reservation in heaven, the place of time everlasting?

PAT MADSEN

DECEMBER 9

At the Wedding

Jesus saith unto her, Woman, what have I to do with thee? mine hour is not yet come. His mother saith unto the servants, Whatsoever he saith unto you, do it. And there were set there six waterpots of stone, after the manner of the purifying of the Jews, containing two or three firkins apiece. John 2:4-6.

I am like the waterpots. All I can do is wait, wait to be filled to the brim. I know not what marvelous changes will happen within me.

I am like the servants. I have been clued in that miracles can happen. My excited eyes are fixed on Him. I am eager to have a part and willing to stand by.

I am like Mary, learning to relax my control of the situation. Even if I know exactly what could be done, and what *should* be done, I simply invite all around me to stand by for instructions.

Let me be like Jesus, awaiting my hour, waiting for the needs and the people to come to me. I am aware that You have filled me and changed me. Now let me be at peace with waiting, not compelled to go around searching out people so I can "fix" situations.

Let me also be like the bride, believing quietly in Your desire for my happiness, always expecting that You will be at my party, celebrating my joy, available when something goes wrong.

WILMA ZALABAK

DECEMBER 10

The Tumbleweed Christmas Tree
The fear of the Lord is His treasure. Isa. 33:6, NKJV.

One Christmas when our children were young I decided to use a tumbleweed rescued from the windswept plains of North Dakota for our Christmas tree. After it was sprayed white and hung with colored ornaments, lights, and tinsel I was quite satisfied with the result. But more important, the money saved on buying a real tree was used on gifts for the girls.

The following year I planned a repeat performance. But one morning as we were getting ready for school I heard our youngest, Marilee, still clad in her nightie, singing in her sweet voice "O tumbleweed, O tumbleweed" to the tune of "O Christmas Tree." I got the message—expense or no expense, we would have a real Christmas tree, falling needles and all! Marilee's penchant for the real thing has continued. She will save and wait and plan her budget until she can afford the genuine item.

Today's world is full of fakes. Imitations. Copies. And unfortunately, this can be true of Christians, too. To be real means we are all unique, special, and one-of-a-kind, not stamped out by a machine, put on a conveyor belt, packaged, and finally put on the shelf. God just doesn't operate like that. He values being genuine and unique so much that He has made each snowflake, each flower, and each blade of grass different from all others.

I must tell you that the one quality I admire most in people is the quality of being genuine. That reminds us of the old truism "A diamond is a chunk of coal that made good under pressure." Let's resolve not to let life grind us down, but rather to polish us with a beautiful character. That is what God wants to do in your life and mine, and when He does we will become more valuable than any painting, carving, or sculpture that this world has ever seen. We will become an original, one-of-a-kind genuine treasure for Jesus.   HAZEL MARIE GORDON

DECEMBER 11

Crystal Bowls and Mousetraps

Just as each of us has one body with many members, and these members do not all have the same function, so in Christ we who are many form one body, and each member belongs to all the others. We have different gifts, according to the grace given us. Rom. 12:4-6, NIV.

*M*any years ago when my two older children were small, we lost their daddy. We moved into a new area with no family close by. I viewed the approaching Christmas with determination to make it a good one. The children and I had learned to depend on one another. Right or wrong, I wanted them to lack nothing for their holiday, and they wanted to be sure that Mommy had a beautiful Christmas. Accordingly, I gave them a small sum of money and sent them off with a student of mine to buy my gift. They were happy as they wrapped not one gift, but two, and put them among the others to await Christmas morning.

"Hurry, Mommy, open this one—this one's best!" they chattered excitedly, chocolate-brown eyes sparkling with the fun of it.

I don't remember what the first, "best" gift was, but I shall never forget the small flat package next laid in my hands. I carefully unwrapped it to find a mousetrap. Anxious eyes awaited my reaction.

"Do you like it, Mommy? We knew you'd want something you could use, and you said you thought there was a mouse in the basement."

I drew my darlings close and assured them it was a very fine gift, and so clever of them to get me *two* presents. It was true, I had seen a mouse. But a mousetrap? It was a trifle hard to be genuinely grateful for such a "practical" gift.

Although I tend to be a bit squeamish, I did eventually use that mousetrap. I baited it, set it, and when it had done its work I disposed of the mouse. Although I can't remember, I wouldn't be surprised if I used it more than once. It was a very good gift; I needed it, and it could be used.

Sometimes we tend to view the spiritual gifts God has given us as mousetraps. They aren't glamorous; they bring no glory to us; perhaps they aren't even fun to use. But if God gave them to us, He *wants* them used. Perhaps we think we'd rather have received crystal bowls. We want to teach, to preach, to heal, to win others for Christ by dazzling means, when perhaps what we've been given is the gift of intercession (nobody even knows we're praying), or the gift of helping (we're backstage with dust on our noses while all the "talented" people are out front receiving applause).

Do you know what gifts God has given you? If not, ask your pastor or women's ministries leader to help you find out. And remember, it may be more exciting to unwrap a crystal bowl, but the bowl can never do the work of a mousetrap. LEA HARDY

DECEMBER 12

My Exploding Pot

Though your sins be as scarlet, they shall be as white as snow. Isa.1:18.

My mother-in-law had a pressure cooker and seemed to use it every day. Her cooking was absolutely the most delicious food I had ever eaten, and I was sure her pressure cooker was part of the reason. So naturally I thought having one would make me a better cook as well. My husband and I shopped around and compared prices, but I wanted a stainless-steel one, and they were much more expensive than the aluminum ones. So I soon stopped talking about the pressure cooker. But Christmas was coming, and I was secretly hoping to get it.

I was like an expectant child on Christmas morning as I opened my presents. I was delighted to find my new stainless-steel pot and decided to use it that day. I got out my mother-in-law's recipe for Cuban black beans and gathered my ingredients. Soon the beans were cooking, and the jiggling sound of the five-pound weight beat out a steady rhythm. One of the children called me to their room, and time slipped away from me as I sat enjoying their company.

Soon we heard a scream and my oldest son's voice booming loudly, "Mom, come quick! The pot exploded!"

I jumped to my feet and ran to the kitchen. What a sight! The five-pound weight was on the floor, and a steady stream of steam was still rising from the pot. As I gazed upward I saw the black bean juice dripping from the once-white ceiling and running down the fronts of my kitchen cabinets. I seized the pot and put it under cold running water in the sink to cool it.

After an hour of major cleaning, the cabinets, ceiling, and counters were sparkling clean once again, but in the process of making them that way I thought about how much of a mess we sometimes make of our lives. We explode in rebellion against God, refusing to follow His counsel. Or we rebel against our mate or our boss. What a mess we make! If only our messes were as easy to clean up as the black beans! But God, in great love and compassion, and remembering our weaknesses, cleans us up. He washes away our sins and our guilt and makes us sparkling clean again. What a wonderful God!

CELIA MEJIA CRUZ

DECEMBER 13

Gift Wrapping

But the Lord said to Samuel, "Do not consider his appearance or height, for I have rejected him. The Lord does not look at the things man looks at. Man looks at the outward appearance, but the Lord looks at the heart." 1 Sam. 16:7, NIV.

Two presents lay side by side under the tree one Christmas evening. Both were very creatively wrapped. One was a square box wrapped and trimmed with old newspapers. The other was a narrow rectangle wrapped with 14 dollar bills.

"I'm prettier than you," the dollar-clad package gushed.

And indeed she was. Three crisp dollar bills were arranged in a fan at the top of the box and sprinkled with glittering gold dust.

"It's what's inside that counts," Newsprint cracked from her perch by the popcorn ornaments.

"I bet I'm worth more," Dollar preened, counting the dollars on her coat.

"Value is as value lasts." Newsprint was given to adapting maxims.

The gifts lay quietly for a time until Dollar could stand it no longer. "What's inside you?" she asked, trying to get a better view.

"A tiny photograph of a clump of orchids my owner took on her honeymoon. She matted it with loving care and put it in an antique copper frame. What about you?" Newsprint asked above Dollar's snickering.

"I have a gorgeous silver-plated spaghetti service," Dollar sparkled. "It was delivered to the store only this morning. None of the old stuff for me and my owner!"

"Everyone has been young before, but not everyone has been old yet." That was all sage Newsprint would say.

In time the wrappings were admired and the presents were distributed and fawned over. A couple years later the silver-plated server, now tarnished and dented, was sold at a garage sale for a dime. But the beautiful photo still hangs on the bedroom wall of two special lovers.

Newsprint was right. The gift is not in the wrappings. It's what is inside that counts. Our physical blemishes often may frustrate us. They may even hinder our interaction with others. But they don't affect our relationship with God. Thank God, He looks at our hearts.

GLENDA-MAE GREENE

DECEMBER 14

The Heart of Christmas

Behold, a virgin shall be with child, and shall bring forth a son, and they shall call his name Emmanuel, which being interpreted is, God with us. Matt. 1:23.

*C*hristmas will soon be here again, and already the little biblical town of Berea is starting to take on a festive appearance as shops get out their decorations and local council workers hang their colorful Christmas lights along the streets.

Not being a member of the state church and, therefore, considered something of an oddity, I am often asked if I celebrate Christmas. Through the years I have given many different answers, but now I usually reply, "Well, it depends on what you mean by "celebrate." But let me ask *you* a question: What picture does the word "Christmas" bring to your mind?"

Answers vary, but they always include the thirteenth wage and all it will buy—new clothes and furnishings for the home; fancy, festive food and drink; and, of course, the round of parties and dances. Then, rather apologetically, they usually add, "Of course, we'll go to church, too."

Christ is Christmas. Without Him there is no Christmas. Isn't it time to put that great, sacrificing heart of love back into a celebration that bears His name but little else? Then, and only then, as we celebrate once more the most beautiful story ever told, can we hope to experience that peace on earth and goodwill toward all men that only Emmanuel, God with us, can give.

He sleeps, a peasant's newborn babe,
Amid the dusty, prickly straw.
His tiny face,
Birth-puckered, red,
Reflects the wonder in the eyes
Of motherhood
As Mary stoops to kiss her Son.

He sleeps, God's precious only Son,
Creator of the universe.
For at His word
A myriad of spheres
Exploded into life and filled
The silent void
Of space with tokens of His power.

He sleeps, Redeemer of all earth,
But all too soon this evil world
Will change the crown
Of straws to thorns;
Will nail His hands upon a cross
And break His heart
That we might live eternally.

He sleeps, the Victor over death;
No tomb can hold the Prince of life,
For He'll come forth
From death's embrace;
And one day soon He'll come again
For you and me,
And then we'll share eternity.

REVEL PAPAIOANNOU

The Gift of Love

"The wedding banquet is ready. . . . Go to the street corners and invite to the banquet anyone you find." Matt. 22:8, 9, NIV.

*D*ecember was already half past and Christmas was fast approaching. My husband and I were living in Nairobi, Kenya, far from our children and their families; in fact, too far to even consider flying back to the States. How wonderful it would be to have our family and grandchildren with us. I reminisced about the many Christmases we had spent with our children, bringing back happy memories.

We knew a number of Ethiopian students who had come to Kenya to attend the university. They too would love to be with their families, but for many it was an impossibility because of financial and political reasons.

Why not invite these young people for Christmas? Many questions came to our minds. How many would come? How did Ethiopians celebrate Christmas? And how could we plan a program that would be interesting to them? What menu should we plan for the dinner? We wanted this holiday to be the happiest holiday possible for these dear young people.

Time passed quickly, and soon Christmas morning arrived. What a beautiful day! The sun shone warmly, conducive to a Christmas spirit in that part of the world. Chairs and tables were set up in the backyard. Dinner was well on its way, the decorations were in place, games were all planned, Christmas carols were chosen. We knew this would be a wonderful day.

Soon our guests began arriving. Much to our pleasure, there were 17 young people. There was plenty of food for everyone. After dinner we gathered in our small apartment and sang all the Christmas carols we could think of. Then we played games appropriate for the season. All too soon the afternoon came to an end. As we handed each one a small gift, bidding them farewell, they thanked us graciously, as only Ethiopian young people can do in their own unique way.

I can't help thinking ahead to the day when our dear Saviour will have a beautiful banquet for all who have loved and obeyed Him throughout the ages. It matters not whether the guests are old or young, rich or poor, handsome or plain, possessing many talents or few. All are invited. He does not want to have one vacant spot at His table.

How disappointed we would have been if our guests had not responded to our invitations to the Christmas party. How much more disappointed our Saviour will be if you or I do not make the necessary preparations to join Him on that beautiful occasion. I want to be there. Don't you?   ELEANOR HEWES

Welcome Home, Child!

Behold, I am coming soon! My reward is with me, and I will give to everyone according to what he has done. Rev. 22:12, NIV.

My husband and I are busy building a getaway place on a lovely wooded lot overlooking a lake in northern Virginia. It will be a place our family can find quiet togetherness amid the smell of the woods, the changing seasons, and the glassy lake inviting an early-morning ski.

Just last week I took our 4-year-old granddaughter with me to check on the progress of this hideaway place. What joy she found in its discovery! To her it was magical. Just weeks earlier she had come often to this spot to swim and picnic. She had even taken her first try at waterskiing and loved it! And now, as if it had appeared at the wave of a magic wand, a house stood on our property. A house with walls and a roof and windows and doors, and so many places to investigate.

I took her on a little tour to familiarize her with the layout of the house. "Heather, we can celebrate Christmas here this year," I said. "Help me decide where we should put the Christmas tree."

Without a moment's hesitation she walked toward the front door and pointed to the floor. "Right here will be perfect!" she declared, pointing to the small foyer just inside the door. "Then everyone who comes will be able to see it."

Trying to keep a straight face, I could only imagine guests struggling to get past the tree and into the house if I were to take her suggestion to heart.

And then a delightful game began. "Grandma, I have a great idea!" she shouted from outside. "I'll come to the door and knock, and you pretend that you are surprised that I have come for Christmas, OK?"

"Sure," I responded, realizing that there are several possible entries into the house, including the basement, and being sure that she wouldn't miss a one.

Knock, knock! "Oh, Bud!" I would say excitedly, pretending that her grandpa was along and in on our game. "Someone is at the door." Hurriedly, I crisscrossed the rooms each time answering the appropriate door with a shriek of delight. "Grandpa!" I would call back into the unfinished house. "It's our Heather. She's come for Christmas! Come in, my darling, and give me a hug. Oh, it's so wonderful to see you!"

Then she would cross the room to where she had positioned the imaginary tree and begin to exclaim over its beauty. "Oh, Grammie, look at the beautiful golden angels! Aren't they beautiful? And look at all the presents!" she exclaimed, stretching her arms as wide as they'd reach.

Again and again I answered the various doors, each time stopping to sweep her into my arms and welcome her home. Dress rehearsals for the real thing! It was her first visit to Grandma and Grandpa's house, and her dancing eyes and playful heart had lit a fire in an unfinished house that will linger as long as my memory lasts. A loving child of ours had come home. What unspeakable joy!

My heavenly Father is preparing a mansion for me in the new earth! And now in my mind's eye, just like Heather, I run to that mansion door and knock and picture Him answering the door and finding me there. "It's me!" I say with Heather's exuberance and see the twinkle in His eye when He lifts His voice and calls, "Look, it's Rose! She's come—she's come home!"

Yes, Heather has taught me the overwhelming joy at the sight of finding a loved one at your door—any door! The anticipated response of being welcomed with open arms! Oh, come, Lord Jesus. Come!

ROSE OTIS

"I Miss You!"

He heals the brokenhearted and binds up their wounds.
Ps. 147:3, NIV.

*T*think that the loneliest three words in my vocabulary are "I miss you." My heart aches with emptiness when I say them because it means that someone important to me is gone. But there is another kind of loneliness that is not caused by someone leaving us, but rather by being too busy to spend time with us. This is the kind of loneliness the Lord must experience when we are too busy to spend time with Him.

It's easy to get so caught up in our busy, day-to-day affairs that we find ourselves running frantically back and forth, taking care of endless "to do" lists, until finally we collapse in exhaustion at the end of the day, falling asleep before the words "dear heavenly Father" escape our lips. One busy day extends into two, then three . . . five . . . Suddenly it's time for church again, and we realize that we haven't had any special time with Jesus since last week. And we wonder why we don't have any peace in our hearts.

I can picture Jesus standing invisibly nearby, calling my name as I run crazily through my hectic day. I oversleep in the morning, so I breathe a hasty "Thank You, Jesus, for this day" as I throw my clothes on and run out the door. Two thousand appointments later I hear a song that reminds me of Him and realize that I haven't spent time with Him today. But then the phone rings and I get distracted and forget. I plan to make time later in the day, but something suddenly comes up and my time is gone. My stress level increases as I remember something else I was supposed to do today, so I skip my evening meal and take care of it at the last minute. I stumble through the door at the end of the day, exhausted.

"Come to Me, My child, and I will give you rest," Jesus invites, but I am so tired and preoccupied that I don't hear Him. And as I fall fast asleep after neglecting my Best Friend, I wonder if His tears flow in loneliness for me.

There are other times—precious times—when I must reluctantly end our special, intimate time together in order to carry on my necessary business. I often find myself breathing a wistful prayer, "Oh, Father, I miss You!" And I purpose in my heart to snatch whatever seconds and minutes I can during the day to sing to Him or to thank Him for His love. Then I return to the quietness of my home and rush back into our special time, for He has been on my mind—and I on His—all day.

I yearn for that day when I will be able to physically run into the loving arms of my Best Friend—and I'll never have to say goodbye again.   HEARTSONG

Part of the Team

Fear not, Mary: for thou hast found favor with God. And, behold, thou shalt conceive in thy womb, and bring forth a son, and shalt call his name Jesus. Luke 1:30, 31.

For years Jewish priests had studied prophecies pointing to the Messiah, and they knew that the time had come for the Redeemer to be born. Gabriel had appeared to Elizabeth's husband in the Temple and told him that his past-childbearing-age wife would be mother of a son who would announce the coming of the promised Messiah.

Gabriel, who stood in the presence of God, was sent again, this time to talk to Mary. God ignored the Temple protocol that women were barred from actively participating in the Temple service, and spoke to a woman directly. After listening to Gabriel's words, Mary asked one logical question: "How can this be since I 'know not a man'?" Her basic sensitivity to God would make one presume that she also wondered how Joseph, her fiancé, would accept her pregnancy. She was well aware of the penalty for adultery: death by stoning.

Before leaving Mary, Gabriel added another bit of information. "Your cousin Elizabeth is expecting."

Feeling the need to talk to someone about the angel's visit, Mary made haste to visit Elizabeth. The two had much in common. Both were pregnant, and both pregnancies were humanly impossible, for Elizabeth was too old and Mary was a virgin.

When Mary arrived at Elizabeth's home, the two compared notes as to what was happening. God's Spirit came upon Elizabeth, who prophesied about the baby fathered by God's Spirit, now growing in Mary's womb, acknowledging the unborn child as her own Saviour.

When she returned home, Joseph, who by now had also been visited by an angel, accepted Mary's pregnancy, knowing that her condition was of the Holy Spirit. And despite the fact that Mary was "great with child," the couple made the most well-known journey in Christendom—the trip from Nazareth to Bethlehem, where Jesus was born.

When Jesus was taken to the Temple to be circumcised, God's Spirit revealed the child's identity to two devout Jews at the Temple, Simeon and Anna. Both recognized the 8-day-old Jesus as the promised Redeemer.

God spoke directly to six people mentioned by name when Jesus came to the earth as a baby—Zechariah, Mary, Elizabeth, Joseph, Simeon, and Anna. Three of the six were women. God recognized women's worth. These three women were spoken to directly by the angel or by the Holy Spirit. This gives positive reinforcement to the position that God believed then, and believes now, that women are important to His church. We *are* part of His team on earth.

CONNIE WELLS NOWLAN

DECEMBER 19

Our First Love

Nevertheless I have this against you, that you have left your first love. Rev. 2:4, NKJV.

My husband offered to buy me a bread machine for my anniversary present. How happy I was! Imagine! No more kneading, waiting for the bread to rise, or ruined loaves of bread. Just perfect loaves of hot, homemade bread by simply tossing a few ingredients together and pushing a button! I could barely contain my excitement as we shopped around for the machine with the most features at the lowest price.

I lay in bed at night dreaming about the different kinds of bread I would make—French, honey wheat, raisin . . . The list was endless, limited only by my imagination and the ingredients on hand. Finally the day came when we brought home our new toy, and we immediately tried our first loaf. Delicious! I was amazed at the convenience and ease of the appliance, and I solemnly vowed to my husband that we would have fresh bread every day for dinner.

That was more than two years ago. Now he's lucky to have fresh bread once a week. What happened? The novelty wore off, and I simply fell out of love with my new toy, much the way children do after Christmas.

If we are not careful, the same thing can happen in our Christian walk. Think back to the time you first gave your life to the Lord. Oh, there were hundreds of people you wanted to share Christ with! You could read the Bible or pray for at least an hour. Scriptures were easily and habitually memorized. Songs of praise were always on your lips. You were more loving toward others—even those who had not been particularly kind to you. There was nothing you would not do for Christ.

And now? Has some of the novelty worn off? Yes, you still read the Bible and pray, but it's more like a chore now than the joy it once was. If so, you may need a little inspiration. The initial excitement I had for my bread machine comes back when I read bread machine recipe books. There are always new combinations I hadn't thought of. I also get inspired when I talk with other bread machine users or future purchasers. I like to share my loaves with them and bask in their compliments (even though the machine did all the work). I enjoy discussing the prices and features of various bread machines, as well as recipes and helpful hints I've discovered during my experimentation. Then I'm inspired once again to use the machine.

The same thing can be done with our first love. Get inspired by browsing your Christian bookstore or a friend's library. Buy or borrow a new book to read on the life of Christ. Sing a hymn and really listen to, and meditate on, the words. Talk to a fellow Christian or a "future purchaser" about what Jesus has done in your life, something new you have learned about Him, or just listen as others share with you. You'll once again "remember therefore from where you have fallen" doing the "first works" that you did at the beginning of your Christian life (Rev. 2:5).   MERRI LONG

Our Worst and Best Christmas

Therefore, as we have opportunity, let us do good to all people, especially to those who belong to the family of believers. Gal. 6:10, NIV.

I sighed as I tucked the fuzzy blue blanket more tightly around the hot, whimpering child in my lap. The emergency room was freezing, and I tugged at my jacket sleeves to cover my hands. My stomach twisted and churned constantly. My husband, David, sat in the seat next to me with Scotty, age 6, cradled in his arms. I watched as Scotty turned his flushed face upward and whispered something into David's ear. Suddenly they jumped up and dashed into the men's room, Scotty's little hand held tightly over his mouth. I knew the feeling. For two weeks, we all had known the feeling.

The night before, our usual family gathering on Christmas Eve had been canceled because of our extreme illness. Later, on that same night, 5-year-old Adam began vomiting dark-brown splotches. Was it blood? Frightened, my husband and I bundled up our sleepy children and rushed them to the nearest emergency room. Here we sat . . . and sat . . . and sat . . . for four and a half hours!

The nurse explained that there was only one doctor on duty. All the other doctors were home spending Christmas with their families. "There have been several automobile accidents," she had said. "I'm sorry, but we have to take patients in the order of their severity."

I was tired of waiting! I was tired of being sick! I was tired of seeing my family suffering so much! I was so angry! *God, it's Christmas, and here we are suffering!* I ranted silently. *Where are You?* I had missed the warmth of spending the holidays with relatives, and there would be no happy laughter and scattering of wrapping paper in our home the next morning. I cried out, "This has got to be the worst Christmas we've ever had!"

I was wrong. As I look back I realize that I was looking on the dark side instead of the bright. There were little rays of sunshine that shone warmly into our home even during that trying time. Once, when I couldn't bear the thought of having to prepare another meal, my dear mother dropped by with some steaming, homemade vegetable soup. My thoughtful mother-in-law called often to take over-the-phone orders for groceries and medicine that she personally delivered. Relatives and church members called or sent cards, letting us know that we were in their prayers. Our pastor braved the disease and came by for a short visit. We found a check in our mailbox from our church family to "help out in rough times."

About a week after the hospital incident we began to feel better and were in for a big surprise. My parents drove up and began carrying in armloads of presents. Our shabby little tree suddenly twinkled to life as presents were stacked high beneath its branches. Two squealing boys danced about, clapping their hands with joy.

Truly, this must be the genuine meaning of Christmas, what Jesus must want it to mean. May the good Lord bless all of you who are able and willing to assist the suffering and those less fortunate than you this season.

FRANCES YOUNG

DECEMBER 21

"Hi! My Name Is Jesus"

You are to give him the name Jesus, because he will save his people from their sins. Matt. 1:21, NIV.

Just before Christmas my husband and I returned to California to care for our daughter, who was expecting her first baby. She and her husband had just moved into a new house. Boxes and packing cases were stacked everywhere. Fighting jet lag, we set to work to help bring order from chaos before she was ordered to immediate bed rest. Our granddaughter arrived four days later.

There was so much to keep us busy we didn't know whether we were standing on our heads or our feet. The dogs had to be exercised every day. The car, which had been in a minor accident the week before, needed repairs. Housework, washing, shopping, cooking, and looking after our daughter and her new baby occupied almost every minute of our time. In-laws would also be visiting later in the month.

I hurried down the grocery aisles one day, my mind awash with "things to do today," grabbing items left and right. As I rounded the corner I almost stumbled over an industrial vacuum cleaner, its long blue hose sprawled across the floor. As I impatiently bumped my well-laden cart over it, a young man with a gentle brown face appeared, apologizing for the presence of the vacuum cleaner, and rolled it down the aisle out of the way. But not before I caught a glimpse of his name tag: "Hi! My Name Is Jesus. I'm Here to Help You."

Although fully aware the name isn't unusual among Hispanic men, reading it on his name tag made me stop and think. I continued my shopping in a quieter frame of mind, realizing, to my shame, that ever since we'd been in California I had been assuming we'd have to carry the load by ourselves. All the time He'd been waiting patiently for us to ask Him to help, willing us to look at Him and read His offer: "Hi! My name is Jesus. I'm here to help you."

No mortal man is bequeathed with power just because he bears the name Jesus, but there is all power in that name. Jesus. It is balm for every weary soul who will come to Him in faith and ask for help.

Jesus knows all about harried housewives, the Marthas among us who are "distracted by all the preparations that [have] to be made," and "worried and upset about many things" (Luke 10:40, 41, NIV). Why don't we let Him help us instead of trying to do it all ourselves?

"Therefore I tell you, do not worry about your life. . . . Who of you by worrying can add a single hour to his life?" Since you cannot do this very little thing, why do you worry about the rest? (Luke 12:22-25).

Why indeed, when Jesus is so willing to help us?

EDNA MAY OLSEN

DECEMBER 22

"From Whence Cometh My Help"

I will lift up mine eyes unto the hills, from whence cometh my help. My help cometh from the Lord, which made heaven and earth. Ps. 121:1, 2.

When we built our Parkersburg, West Virginia, house about 30 years ago the ash tree towered above us—60 feet tall and more than 16 feet around. Some said it was already 200 years old. Our children played in its shade. One end of my clothesline was anchored to the trunk. Black snakes wintered in the tree. Birds nested there, and at one time it even sheltered bees. Our family loved the big tree.

One winter day I was concerned about the shrubbery, weighed down by snow and ice. In my early devotional time I asked for God's protection, as always, then started the day's work. Bundled up in my down coat and my father's four-buckle arctics, I picked up the broom and trudged through 18 inches of snow to clean off the bushes. Next I fed the birds. Then there was paper to burn in the brick-and-block outdoor grill we also used as an incinerator. Just as I was striking a match to the papers I heard a cracking sound. I knew instantly what it was—the big tree, loaded with snow and ice, was coming down!

I tried to run, but fell facedown, right in front of the incinerator. As I fell I felt a strange sensation, almost as if something warm were covering my back. Cracking and breaking sounds were all around me. Snow and ice flew.

Inside the house my husband, Earl, heard the crash and rushed to the door, calling, "Dolores! Dolores!"

Voice trembling, I answered, "Honey, I'm OK."

Slowly and carefully I got up and looked around. A huge fork of the tree, more than a foot thick, had fallen right over my head. The heavy end landed on the incinerator, just inches from my back. One more step and I might have been killed.

The big ash tree was no more. Its four big trunk sections had broken into four pieces at the rotted core, all falling at the same time. One section hit our roof, another hit a neighbor's house, and the remaining two forks lay broken in the yard. But I was safe! I knew instantly that my Maker's hand had protected me. I was still shaking as I made my way back to the house. Over and over Earl and I said, "Thank You, Lord!"

We later discovered a smaller limb about six inches thick buried in the ground near the incinerator. It had missed my back by mere inches. It was so firmly embedded in the ground that my husband had to pull it out with the truck.

Surely "my help cometh from the Lord." DOLORES CLEGG

DECEMBER 23

My Christmas Lily

I am the rose of Sharon, and the lily of the valleys. Like a lily among thorns, so is my love among the daughters. S. of Sol. 2:1, 2, NKJV.

Serendipity—a happy moment life gives us, a special moment in time to revitalize us, a pause that brings a special joy. Such was a Christmas morning when I discovered my gift from God. The California winter had browned my back lawn, taking away the summer flowers. The orange trees, no longer in bloom, bore half-green fruit, and the crepe myrtle trees that once sheltered in a multitude of raspberry blossoms now entertained only a few gray-brown leaves that shifted in the wind. A gray brick wall on one side and a faded redwood fence of the other rounded out my dull yard.

But it *was* Christmas morning—bright, clear, and crisp. I was baking and would soon finish packing to drive to my family's for the holiday. As I walked out the back door, I noticed a spot of bright pink hovering against the wooden fence. Curious, I walked over to discover one slender stem reaching above the grass caught in the fence. On top was a perfectly round cluster of little lilies pulled together like one giant pink popcorn ball. I felt a thrill as I knelt beside the plant. I had never seen one like it before. Inside each miniature lily was a small yellow stem, each with five petals. I sat on the grass admiring it—a symbol of beauty amid drab surroundings.

Christ said that "even Solomon in all his glory was not arrayed like one of these" (Matt. 6:29). *What a Christmas gift,* I thought. *Thank You, Lord, for creating something so beautiful for me to see this morning.*

EDNA MAYE GALLINGTON

DECEMBER 24

One Blessed Child

"Do not be afraid. I bring you good news of great joy that will be for all the people. Today in the town of David a Savior has been born to you; he is Christ the Lord." Luke 2:10, 11, NIV.

I've been thinking a lot about that one special Baby whose birth we celebrate this month. Though He may not have been born this time of year, it seems important to commemorate the day of His birth. When labor pains came it was not a quick jump into the car and a short trip to Bethlehem hospital. In fact, it was a very long prebirth trip that Mary's obstetrician would sternly advise against today, especially considering her mode of transportation.

Upon arrival in Bethlehem, she was not taken to a clean, sterile birthing room where she and her husband could enjoy the birth of their first child. Instead, she went to a hay-filled stable where the smell, and presence, of animals was quite obvious. Still, it was shelter and a place to rest their weary bones.

On this holy night the labor pains came quickly, and her husband was there by her side—a very unusual occurrence for that day.

When Jesus arrived there were no nurses to weigh and measure and bathe Him. Just the two very special people God had chosen for the awesome task of raising His only Son.

I suppose that Mary counted each one of His fingers and toes, as all mothers do. Those wondrous hands that had formed the earth, and those feet that tread in the garden so very long ago with Adam and Eve, now lay tenderly cupped in her own hands. His soft murmurings were a foretelling of His gentle ways, even in rebuking sin. His arms, so little now, would be held out to each of us in love—a love so strong He would eventually outstretch them on a tree on a hill called Calvary. A birth so marvelous we cannot comprehend it, because He came with the ultimate mission of dying for our sins.

Do celebrate His birth, for it was all God's plan from the beginning. But as you celebrate, reconsider just why He came to this world. To give us a new birth. To give us the bright hope of forgiveness. And the best gift of all—eternal life!

Happy Birthday, King of kings!

MOIRA BARTHLE

DECEMBER 25

Reflections From His Star

For unto us a child is born, unto us a son is given. Isa. 9:6.

Do you wish you could have seen the angel star that
Christmas morn?
And with the shepherds heard their "peace on earth"
when Christ was born?
Do you wish you could have gone with Wise Men to that
holy place
And gazed with wonder on the infant Jesus' precious
face?

Would you have knelt in Bethlehem beside His cradle
small
To feel His tiny fingers, watch His little teardrops fall?
Would you have given all you had to hold Him in your
arms,
And rock Him, hear His cooing, cherish all His baby
charms?

Would you have studied prophets' scrolls concerning
    Jesus' birth
Like Wise Men sought to learn, just when and where
    He'd visit earth?
Would you have shared the story as your one supreme
    ambition,
And thrilled the hearts of others as you told them of His
    mission?

Do you hope that it will happen in your lifetime once
    again,
When a hundred million angels will comprise His royal
    train?
And will you watch in ecstasy to catch His loving smile,
And recognize Him, just because you've known Him all
    the while?

And when He folds you in His arms and wipes your tears
    away,
Will you clasp tight those nail-pierced hands that turned
    your night to day?
Not as a babe this time, He'll come, but as our glorious
    King!
No more in swaddling clothes, but on a cloud of angels'
    wings.

So as this Christmas morning dawns, though friends are
    far apart,
May heaven's star of hope shine down upon your wait-
    ing heart
And give you peace, and happiness, and love, and so
    much more;
We're one year closer home than we have ever been before!

LORRAINE HUDGINS

December 26

As a Little Child

Whosoever therefore shall humble himself as this little child, the same is greatest in the kingdom of heaven. Matt. 18:4.

*T*ime for bed."

"I'm not tired."

"Sorry, but you still have to go to bed."

Sound familiar? This age-old discussion was going on between my 5-year-old son and me. The interesting thing was that the entire time he was objecting, I noticed that he was taking off his clothes, putting on his pajamas, and getting ready to go to sleep. The complaint continued right up until the time he climbed into bed and waited for his story. Was he obedient? Yes. Was he happy? Somewhere, deep inside, one hopes. Could I object? Well, I remember a time . . .

I woke to my husband's asthmatic choking. Startled, I asked if there was anything I could do. Yes, I could go to the store to buy more medicine—regardless of the fact that it was 5:30 a.m. and the day after Christmas. Grumblings rose up in me as I dressed and went to the car. "Where am I going to find a store open at this hour? Why can't God just heal him?"

By the time I found a convenience store 12 miles away, a beautiful day had dawned. Even more surprising, the store carried the medicine I needed. As I paid for the medicine, still not feeling anything close to being a willing servant of the Lord, I noticed a raggedly clad woman looking about in a lost and forlorn way. As I passed her, she asked if I would give her a ride.

"No," I said quickly. But echoing in my brain I heard, *Even as you have done it to the least of these* . . . As my hand touched the car door handle, I sighed. I went back into the store. "Come on," I said, hardly in a kind tone. It made no difference to her; she was thrilled.

Her thin sweater and cotton dress were completely inadequate against the 10-degree temperature. I dropped her off with a perfunctory "God bless you" and drove home. There my husband lay, sound asleep, having found more medicine after I left.

I could be angry right now, I thought. Except . . . My God thought enough of me to wake me early in the morning and trust me with an errand to help one of His lost sheep. Me! The grumbling, stumbling servant.

So can I be upset with my son? No, he's taking after his mother. As I have learned, so he will learn, and someday we will both take after our Father. CHERI SCHROEDER

DECEMBER 27

Angels Unawares

Feed the hungry! Help those in trouble! . . . And the Lord will guide you continually, and satisfy you with all good things. Isa. 58:10, 11, TLB.

*I*t had been a very hectic year, and I was enjoying a few days in the peace and quiet of the Irish countryside. I had spent a day in the secondhand bookshops of Belfast and planned to start on the reading I needed to do for the second year of my university course as soon as I got home.

On the phone that evening my husband said how much he was looking forward to seeing me the next day. Then, almost as an afterthought, he said, "Oh, by the way, we have five Russians arriving tomorrow. Where shall I put them?"

"I was planning to start on my studies," I groaned.

"They won't be any trouble, and it's only for a couple weeks," my husband assured me.

He doesn't realize how long it takes to prepare a meal for nine people—six of whom would be working on a building site—not to mention the shopping, cleaning, washing, and changing beds, I thought.

Six weeks and hundreds of pounds of potatoes later, I was helping our new friends obtain the visas to drive back to their homes in Moldova. The first day of the new school term was looming. Driving through the London rush hour, I kept assuring myself, "God will make it up to you, Audrey, He really will." Then the thought came, *But how is He going to help me read 10 books by Monday?*

Well, of course, He didn't, and I couldn't, but as always He provided the grace to get me through the next few weeks, and gradually I caught up. The blessing of having our friends in our home is one we wouldn't have missed for the world. Every mealtime was an experience and every outing an adventure. What fun we had trying to communicate through one interpreter. How fascinated we were by the stories they told of life in their country, under Communism and afterward. How impressed we were by their many courtesies and considerations, and how enriched we were by the example of their dedicated Christian lives.

Their joy in the things we take for granted made us realize how blessed we are to live in a free society. The fact of their presence in our home, however, was a reminder of how quickly events in the world can change. A few short years ago they would never have contemplated working in the West. In other countries the reverse has happened and people who once were free now live in war-torn lands, having lost their homes, possessions, and, in some cases, their families. It brings home to us the importance of not putting our trust in earthly things. Instead we must make sure our treasures are in heaven.

AUDREY BALDERSTONE

DECEMBER 28

For the Love of Angels

For he will command his angels concerning you to guard you in all your ways. Ps. 91:11, NIV.

*B*rownie is the nickname I chose for a special friend—indeed, my closest friend. I don't know his real name. I suppose it's something quite beautiful, like Angelo. I chose this name because through the years several friends with the surname of Brown have looked after me, becoming bosom friends.

These sentinels of mercy are our specially appointed guardian angels, yet they are too seldom acknowledged. The thread that weaves such an intimate tapestry with our guardian angels is the knowledge that they, as we, are created beings. "What is man that you are mindful of him, the son of man that you care for him? You made him a little lower than the heavenly beings and crowned him with glory and honor" (Ps. 8:4, 5, NIV). Isn't it awesome to know that our relationship is so close?

My husband converses with his angel, especially while driving alone. He shares with his friend his joys and sorrows, and he thanks him for his presence.

A friend who was injured in a car accident that left him a paraplegic tells of "feeling the movement" of an angel's wings near him. My son tells me that a dying friend observed an angel by her bedside.

Once my daughter brought to mind a thought I'd never considered. She mentioned how seldom she and her brother get to see each other because of distance, work, and family responsibilities. But what joy their angels must experience when they are united. After all, these angels were always together when she and her brother were growing up. How they must miss each other now!

From Genesis to Revelation we read the record of angels' activities, and the amazing thing is that their number cannot be tallied! Just imagine the magnificent sound that will reel the world when Jesus comes again!

Of all the ministries of the heavenly host we mortals attach special significance to our guardian angels because of the part they play in the power struggle between good and evil. Yes, our special protector is concerned with our physical safety, but even more so with our spiritual safety. This is the area where his guardianship is finely focused.

Oh, the wonder of angels! It will be most intriguing to learn the scope of their God-commissioned challenges when we study such things in heaven. How blessed we are because of their assignments!

BETTY KOSSICK

DECEMBER 29

Mary Bates's Love Letters

Because of the Lord's great love we are not consumed, for his compassions never fail. They are new every morning; great is your faithfulness. Lam. 3:22, 23, NIV.

*W*hen I was a little girl I used to ride with the mail carrier on his rounds during the school holidays. It got me out from under other people's feet and saved the mail carrier getting out of his van so often. And I enjoyed handing out the letters. Part of his round lay through winding country lanes to outlying farms, and this I particularly enjoyed. So did my mail carrier friend until one winter when the snow was a good three feet deep with considerable drifting. I'm sure he could have taken all this in his stride if it hadn't been for one other factor.

At one particular farm there lived a farmer, his wife, and their daughter, Mary Bates, who was in her 20s and not long married to a soldier in active service. Forsaken she may have been, but certainly not forgotten. I don't remember where her husband was posted, but he used to write to her every day, and since the heavy snow made it impossible to drive down to the farm, Mr. Stringer had to leave the van—and me—at the end of the lane and stagger and clamber through snowdrifts to deliver her daily letter. He would return looking more like a snowman than a mail carrier! It was still three weeks before the thaw came when vehicles could once more reach the farmyard.

I never read today's text without remembering Mary Bates's daily love letters. New every morning, no matter what. And if human love can produce that degree of constancy, how much more our heavenly Father, who is love itself and promises love sufficient for each day's needs—sufficient strength, sufficient wisdom, sufficient faith, optimism, humor, and patience. New every morning. You can rely on it.   PEGGY MASON

DECEMBER 30

Let's Celebrate

In the same way, I tell you, there is rejoicing in the presence of the angels of God over one sinner who repents. Luke 15:10, NIV.

Some holidays are known for family gatherings and some for presents, but New Year's Eve is known for parties. Each year people everywhere gather to celebrate the end of an old year and the coming of a new one. People who can barely drag themselves out of bed in the morning to go to work, and who live for weekends so they can get some extra sleep, will stay up all night to greet the new year. But on January 2 everything is exactly the same as it was on December 30, and life goes on.

The Bible says there is great rejoicing over one sinner who repents. I'm not sure if the angels blow noisemakers and wear funny hats, but I am sure their celebration far surpasses any New Year's Eve party we have ever seen. We, on the other hand, barely notice. We shake the hand of a new member and welcome them "into the faith." And we give a resounding amen when we hear a report of someone who has turned their back on their wayward path. This seems unworthy recognition for someone who has not merely turned a calendar page, but who has turned into a new creation and has "passed from death into life." Maybe at the next baptism we attend we should join the angels and break out the noisemakers!

KATHLEEN L. STAUBACH

Threshold

No, dear [sisters], I am still not all I should be but I am bringing all my energies to bear on this one thing: Forgetting the past and looking forward to what lies ahead, I strain to reach the end of the race and receive the prize for which God is calling us up to heaven because of what Christ Jesus did for us. Phil. 3:13, 14, TLB.

*T*oday is the last day of the year. December 31. I've always found this to be a day filled with mixed emotions. Sadly, it marks the end of the holiday season for most, a time of year that seems to bring out the best in everyone. Gone will be the wishes from strangers for a happy holiday, or "all the best to you and yours in the coming year." Soon all the decorations and special treats will be gone too. What then?

I can look back over this past year and be filled with gratitude at the blessings with which the Lord has blessed me. I can see some growth and changes. I can think of many things that seemed like a crisis at the time. But those too have passed. I've come to many a fork in the road, and at the time I was making the decisions I sat there numb and terrified. What should I do? What could or would be the result? Now I laugh at my own cowardice in some areas and wish with regret that I could undo others.

But alas, time cannot be undone, and now here it is once again. December 31. I think of all the promises I made on January 1—lose weight, exercise more, spend more time in personal devotion, keep up with old friends, witness more to my neighbors . . . But here I stand again—so many remained simply a promise, mere good intentions.

Yet I am excited, for December 31 also brings with it the prospects of a new year! We're that much closer to eternity. December 31. By God's grace, the threshold of a new year—and a new year means another chance. Have a happy, blessed new year!

MAXINE WILLIAMS ALLEN

❖ ❖ ❖

Continue your rewarding devotional experience with the 1998 women's devotional, *From the Heart*. Available at all ABC Christian bookstores and other Christian bookstores.

Scripture Index

414

19:29-31 . . June 25	10:11 . . . . . July 23	**1 Corinthians**
21:22 . . . . . Jan. 23	13:3 . . . . . June 27	3:9 . . . . July 21
22:8, 9 . . . Dec. 15	13:8, 9 . . . Nov. 21	3:18 . . . . . . Oct. 6
24:42. . . . . Oct. 28	13:34 . . . . Apr. 16	10:12 . . . . . Mar. 8
24:44 . . . . . June 1	13:35 . . . . Jan. 15	13:12 . . . . . Mar. 1
25:10 . . . . Aug. 30	14:1-3 . . . Mar. 19	7:22 . . . . Sept. 27
25:28-30. . . June 8	14:2 . . . . . . July 10	4:17 . . . . . . June 6
25:40 . . . . . Oct. 8	14:3 . . . . . Aug. 5	13:13 . . . . July 14
27:29, 30 . Mar. 30	14:6 . . . . . . May 4	
	14:7 . . . . . June 10	**2 Corinthians**
Mark	15:5 . . . . . Mar. 12	1:20 . . . . . . Nov. 4
5:19 . . . . . Feb. 27	15:13-15 . . Aug. 12	2:14 . . . . . Mar. 21
10:14. . . . . . July 7	15:15 . . . Sept. 28	5:17 . . . . . Mar. 20
10:27 . . . . . Feb. 6	15:16 . . . . Apr. 2	9:8 . . . . . . Aug. 2
12:43, 44. . May 16	16:22. . . . Oct. 14	9:15 . . . . . . Apr. 3
14:8 . . . . . . Dec. 4	16:23, 24. . Oct. 18	10:17, 18 . Aug. 31
	16:32 . . . . Sept. 24	12:9 . . . . . Sept. 13
Luke	17:15-18. . . Mar. 9	
1:30, 31 . . Dec. 18		**Galatians**
2:10, 11 . . Dec. 24	**Acts**	4:6 . . . . . . June 16
2:45 . . . . . . Apr. 4	2:46, 47 . . Nov. 10	5:13 . . . . . . Jan. 22
7:13 . . . . . . Jan. 24	12:11 . . . . Sept. 11	5:22 . . . . . Oct. 10
8:25 . . . . . June 22	20:35 . . . . . Jan. 10	6:2 . . . . . . Apr. 30
10:41, 42 . Aug. 14	26:28. . . . . May 15	6:10 . . . . . Dec. 20
10:42 . . . . . Mar. 5		
12:15. . . . . May 10	**Romans**	**Ephesians**
12:34 . . . . . Aug. 1	1:20 . . . . July 3	1:7, 8 . . . . Sept. 17
13:34 . . . . Nov. 18	5:3, 4 . . . . Oct. 21	3:20 . . . . . Feb. 18
15:6 . . . . . Oct. 13	6:12, 13. . . May 26	4:32 . . . . . Mar. 17
15:9 . . . . . Feb. 21	8:5 . . . . . . Oct. 24	Aug. 26
15:10 . . . . Dec. 30	8:28 . . . . . Feb. 17	5:14, 15 . . Apr. 29
15:20 . . . . . Apr. 8	8:31 . . . . . Aug. 24	6:13 . . . . . Oct. 16
17:10 . . . . July 22	8:38, 39. . . Feb. 28	6:19, 20 . . Mar. 25
22:14 . . . . . Oct. 4	12:2 . . . . . . July 12	
22:19 . . . . . Dec. 6	12:4-6 . . . . Dec. 11	**Philippians**
	12:6 . . . . . Sept. 25	1:3-6 . . . . . . Jan. 3
John	12:10 . . . . . July 17	1:6 . . . . . . May 23
2:4-6. . . . . . Dec. 9	12:12 . . . . . June 4	2:4 . . . . July 9
3:16. . . . . . . July 2	12:13 . . . . . Jan. 30	2:5 . . . . Mar. 3
3:16-18. . . Aug. 29	12:20 . . . . Jan. 14	2:13 . . . . . Mar. 11
5:39, 40 . . . Jan. 5	15:5 . . . . . Apr. 12	3:13, 14 . . Dec. 31
7:24 . . . . . . Nov. 6	15:13 . . . . Mar. 23	3:21 . . . . . Feb. 20
8:12 . . . . . . Sept. 4		4:3 . . . . . . Nov. 13
8:36 . . . . . Sept. 14		4:4 . . . . . . Mar. 27